Using
Excel® & Access®
FOR ACCOUNTING
2016

Glenn Owen
Allan Hancock College

Using
Excel® & Access®
FOR ACCOUNTING
2016

Glenn Owen
Allan Hancock College

CENGAGE
Learning·

Australia · Brazil · Japan · Korea · Mexico · Singapore · Spain · United Kingdom · United States

Using Microsoft Excel and Access 2016 for Accounting

Glenn Owen

Vice President, General Manager, Science, Math & Quantitative Business: Balraj Kalsi

Product Director: Mike Schenk

Product Manager: Jason Guyler

Content Developer: Ted Knight

Product Assistant: Trisha Makley

Marketing Director: Brian Joyner

Senior Marketing Coordinator: Eileen Corcoran

Art and Cover Direction, Production Management, and Composition: Cenveo Publisher Services

Intellectual Property

   Analyst: Brittani Morgan

Manufacturing Planner: Doug Wilke

Cover Image(s): Rawpixel.com/Shutterstock.com

For product information and technology assistance, contact us at **Cengage Learning Customer & Sales Support, 1-800-354-9706**

For permission to use material from this text or product, submit all requests online at **www.cengage.com/permissions**
Further permissions questions can be emailed to
permissionrequest@cengage.com

Library of Congress Control Number: 2016938830
ISBN: 978-1-337-10904-8

Cengage Learning
20 Channel Center Street
Boston, MA 02210
USA

Cengage Learning is a leading provider of customized learning solutions with employees residing in nearly 40 different countries and sales in more than 125 countries around the world. Find your local representative at **www.cengage.com**.

Cengage Learning products are represented in Canada by Nelson Education, Ltd.

To learn more about Cengage Learning Solutions, visit **www.cengage.com**

Purchase any of our products at your local college store or at our preferred online store **www.cengagebrain.com**

Printed in the United States of America
Print Number: 03   Print Year: 2017

Brief Contents

Contents

Preface

What if you could integrate two critical business software programs into your accounting classroom without using confusing and complicated manuals? What if your students could use these programs to reinforce basic accounting concepts in an interactive case setting? What if you could do both without spending a fortune and a vast amount of time preparing examples, cases, and illustrations? *Excel and Access for Accounting* is a textbook that fulfills and expands upon all three of these "what ifs."

Why Is This Textbook Needed?

Many accounting educators are looking for ways to incorporate more business software into their accounting curriculum without displacing basic accounting instruction. They have tried to accomplish this by creating a stand-alone computer-based course, a lab component course, or by adding business computer software to their regular accounting curriculum. Current texts in this field are very generic in nature, spending little if any time on accounting-specific issues. Those that do address accounting issues address only worksheet or database issues but not both. Some texts that have a worksheet focus deliver a wide array of financial and managerial topics but lack a natural case flow. Some with a database focus emphasize the creation of accounting systems but do not address how databases are used to support the accounting function.

Moreover, employers expect today's college student to be computer literate in commercial accounting, worksheet, and database software. The demand for this type of training is growing daily as more and more businesses employ business software to solve real-world problems.

Instructors often want to incorporate business software into the first course but are reluctant to invest the time and effort necessary to accomplish this goal. Existing materials are often "preparer" driven in that they focus on the creation of worksheets and databases without addressing the effective use of these tools. Students are often discouraged in their use of computers because of the complicated and confusing manuals that concentrate on using the software without any business or accounting context.

This text responds to all of those needs. It provides a self-paced, step-by-step environment in which the students use a worksheet (Excel®) and a database (Access®) to solve real accounting and business problems. The text is designed to reinforce the concepts students learn in their first accounting courses and to show how worksheets and databases can help users make better and more informed business decisions.

What Are the Goals of This Textbook?

This textbook takes a user perspective by illustrating how worksheets and databases are used and created. Both Excel and Access are user friendly, with extensive help features and helpful toolbars to aid in accessing commonly used functions. The textbook uses a proven and successful pedagogy to demonstrate the features of both software programs and to elicit student interaction.

The textbook's first goal is to help students apply the accounting concepts they've learned to real-world problems, aided by the use of a worksheet and/or database. The content complements the first course in accounting and therefore should be used either as a supplement to that course or as the primary textbook in a stand-alone course that follows the first course in accounting. Some instructors have found this textbook and the *QuickBooks for Accounting* textbook or the *Peachtree for Accounting* textbook ideal matches for a stand-alone "Computers in Accounting" course.

The second goal is to motivate students to become more familiar with and more at ease using a worksheet and/or database to solve accounting and business problems. Using this software application in an accounting context maintains student interest and provides additional incentive for pursuing an accounting degree or emphasis.

The third goal of this text is to reduce the administrative burdens of accounting faculty by providing a self-paced environment for their students to learn how important software applications are used in business. Accounting faculty must manage different learning styles of students as well as teach accounting concepts and practice techniques. The additional task of integrating computer applications into the classroom will be made simpler by using this text.

What's New in Excel 2016 and Access 2016?

Excel 2016

Visualizations are critical to effective data analysis as well as compelling storytelling. In Excel 2016, Microsoft added six new charts—with the same rich formatting options that you are familiar with—to help you create some of the most commonly used data visualizations of financial or hierarchal information or for revealing statistical properties in your data.

Before analysis can begin, you must be able to bring in the data relevant to the business question you are trying to answer. Excel 2016 now comes with built-in functionality that brings ease and speed to getting and transforming your data—allowing you to find and bring all the data you need into one place. These new capabilities, previously only available as a separate add-in called Power Query, can be found natively within Excel. Access them from the Get & Transform group on the Data tab.

In previous versions of Excel, only linear forecasting was available. In Excel 2016, the FORECAST function has been extended to allow forecasting based on Exponential Smoothing (such as, FORECAST.ETS() ...). This functionality is also available as a new one-click forecasting button. On the Data tab, click the Forecast Sheet button to quickly create a forecast visualization of your data series. From the wizard, you can also find options to adjust common forecast parameters, like seasonality, which is automatically detected by default and confidence intervals.

Excel is known for its flexible and powerful analysis experiences, through the familiar PivotTable authoring environment. With Excel 2010 and Excel 2013, this experience was significantly enhanced with the introduction of Power Pivot and the Data Model, bringing the ability to easily build sophisticated models across your data, augment them with measures and KPIs, and then calculate over millions of rows with high speed. Here are some of the enhancements Microsoft made in Excel 2016, so that you can focus less on managing your data and more on uncovering the insights that matter.

- Automatic relationship detection discovers and creates relationships among the tables used for your workbook's data model, so you don't have to. Excel 2016 knows when your analysis requires two or more tables to be linked together and notifies you. With one click, it does the work to build the relationships, so you can take advantage of them immediately.

- Creating, editing, and deleting custom measures can now be done directly from the PivotTable fields list, saving you a lot of time when you need to add additional calculations for your analysis.

- Automatic time grouping helps you to use your time-related fields (year, quarter, month) in your PivotTable more powerfully by auto-detecting and grouping them on your behalf. Once they are grouped together, simply drag the group to your PivotTable in one action and immediately begin your analysis across the different levels of time with drill-down capabilities.

- PivotChart drill-down buttons allow you to zoom in and out across groupings of time and other hierarchical structures within your data.

- Search in the PivotTable field list helps you get to the fields that are important to you across your entire data set.

- Smart rename gives you the ability to rename tables and columns in your workbook's data model. With each change, Excel 2016 automatically updates any related tables and calculations across your workbook, including all worksheets and DAX formulas.

Multiple usability improvements have also been made. For example, delayed updating allows you to perform multiple changes in Power Pivot without the need to wait until each is propagated across the workbook. The changes will be propagated at one time, once the Power Pivot window is closed.

Access 2016

The first thing you'll see when you open Access 2016 is that it has the familiar look of 2013 with a more colorful border.

You'll notice a text box on the ribbon in Access 2016 that says Tell me what you want to do. This is a text field where you can enter words and phrases related to what you want to do next and quickly get to features you want to use or actions you want to perform. You can also choose to get help related to what you're looking for.

Can't find a button? Click inside the Tell Me box (it's the box at the top, with the light bulb). Type a button or command, like "filter," and you'll see all of your filter-related options listed for you.

There are now two Office themes that you can apply to the Access program: Colorful and White. To access these themes, go to File > Options > General, and then click the drop-down menu next to Office Theme.

Have you ever wanted to get a nice list of all the linked data sources from your Access database application into Excel? If you are working on a complex Access application, for example, that includes links to many different data sources, it can be helpful to have a nice list of all the various data sources and their types. This exported list can be especially helpful if you are working on an Access application you did not originally design. Now with Access 2016, you'll find this task much easier using new functionality built into the Linked Table Manager dialog.

Open the Linked Table Manager dialog by clicking External Data > Linked Table Manager. Select the linked data sources you want to list and then click Export to Excel.

What's New in This Edition?

The fifth edition of *Using Excel and Access for Accounting* includes many modified and updated assignments and cases. Also, a major addition to Chapter 4 now addresses partial year depreciation.

In our previous edition, calculating depreciation was done using full-year depreciation, assuming companies purchased their long-term assets on January 1 of the year of acquisition. That, of course, is rarely the case. Usually assets are acquired throughout the year; thus depreciation schedules should factor in a provision to account for this fact.

One key piece of information already included in the depreciation schedule is the date of acquisition. From that you can calculate the number of days of depreciation to be calculated for the first year. An additional year needs to be added to the schedule to account for the depreciation not recorded in the initial year of acquisition.

This major addition to Chapter 4 addresses partial year depreciation for the straight-line, double-declining, and sum-of-the-year's digits methods.

What Are the Key Features of This Textbook?

- The chapters incorporate a continuing, interesting, realistic case—What SUP, Inc.—that helps students apply Excel and Access features.

- A tested, proven, step-by-step methodology keeps students on track. Students enter data, analyze information, and make decisions all within the context of the case. The text constantly guides students, letting them know where they are in the course of completing their accounting tasks.

- Numerous screenshots include callouts that direct students' attention to where they should look on the screen. On almost every page in the book, you will find examples of how steps, screenshots, and callouts work together.

- *Trouble?* paragraphs anticipate the mistakes that students are likely to make (or problems they are likely to encounter) and help them recover and continue with the chapter. This feature facilitates independent learning and frees the instructor to focus on accounting concepts rather than on computer skills.

- The end-of-chapter material begins with questions intended to test students' recall of what they learned in the chapter.

- Chapter Assignments follow the Questions and provide students additional hands-on practice with Excel and Access skills.

- Four continuing Case Problems—Kelly's Boutique (a bookstore). Wine Depot (a wine distributor), Snick's Board Shop (a skateboard shop), and Rosey's Roses (a retail rose plant store)—conclude each chapter. These cases have approximately the same scope as the What SUP chapter case.

- The Instructor's Package contains an Instructor's Manual that includes solutions to end-of-chapter materials, and a link to a companion Web site with completed files for instructor use only.

Using This Text Effectively

Before you begin, note that this textbook assumes you are familiar with the basics of the Windows operating system: how to control windows, how to choose menu commands, how to complete dialog boxes, and how to select directories, drives, and files. If you do not understand these concepts, please consult your instructor.

The best way to work through this textbook is to read the text carefully and complete the numbered steps, which appear on a shaded background, as you work at your computer. Read each step carefully and completely before you try it.

As you work, compare your screen with the figures in the chapter to verify your results. You can use Excel 2016 and Access 2016 with either Windows 10, Windows 8 or Windows 7. The screen shots you see in this book were captured in a Windows 7 environment. If you are using Windows 10 or 8 you might see some minor differences between your screen and the screens in this book. Any significant differences that result from using the different operating systems with Excel or Access will be explained.

Don't worry about making mistakes—that is part of the learning process. The *Trouble?* paragraphs identify common problems and explain how to correct them or get back on track. Follow the suggestions given *only* if you are having the specific problem described.

After you complete a chapter, you can answer the Questions, Assignments, and Case Problems found at the end of each chapter. They are carefully structured so that you will review what you have learned and then apply your knowledge to new situations. Feel free to page back through the text to clarify how each task should be accomplished.

Student Data Files

To complete the chapter and exercises in this book, you must first download the student data files from the text's companion site. They include practice files you need for the chapters, the Assignments, and the Case Problems. Your instructor or lab manager may provide you with a link to these files in their labs. See your instructor for specific details. In any case, this text will assume you have already downloaded these practice files.

Excel and Access Versions

The text and related data files created for this text were constructed using Excel 2016 16.0.6001.1034 and Access 2016 16.0.6001.1034. To check your version and release number, click the File tab, and then click **Account**. Under the Product Information section for your Office product find the version number and product ID number. All references to Excel and Access throughout the rest of this textbook are to Excel 2016 or Access 2016.

Excel and Access Options

Excel and Access have many options that can be altered by the user. In a lab environment, or in an environment where different people use the same computer, these options may have been altered from the default settings set when the software was first installed.

About the Author

Glenn Owen is a 21 year professor of accounting in Allan Hancock College's Business Department, where he teaches accounting and until recently served as the College's Academic Senate President. He recently retired as a lecturer at the University of California at Santa Barbara, where he taught accounting and information systems courses since 1980. His professional experience includes five years at Deloitte & Touche and seven years as vice-president of finance positions at Westpac Resources, Inc., and ExperTelligence, Inc. He has authored many accounting related texts including his latest QuickBooks Onine for Accounting. He is the author of the popular *QuickBooks for Accounting* and *Peachtree for Accounting* texts and teaches both on campus and online courses in financial and managerial accounting. He joined Dale Klooster and Warren Allen as an author of the popular *Integrated Accounting*, eighth edition, general ledger accounting software and text. His innovative teaching style emphasizes the decision maker's perspective and encourages students to think creatively. His graduate studies in educational psychology and 41 years of business experience combine to yield a balanced blend of theory and practice.

Dedication

I would like to thank my family for all of their support over the years. I'd also like to thank my Dad, who at 93, still does his best at beating me at cribbage. His problem-solving mind-set is what drove me to the accounting profession and what prompted me to ask "why not" more often than I probably should have. Thanks Dad.

Excel for Accounting

part

1

Excel Tour

In this chapter you will learn:

- Excel's capabilities and new features
- How to start, navigate, and work with Excel files
- How to use Excel help
- How Excel is used in accounting

Case: **What SUP, Inc.**

Nathan Peters and Meagan Lopez own What SUP, Inc., located in Seattle, Washington. They've been in business for five years and have developed a number of online customers. The fast-growing sport of stand up paddleboarding (SUP) is a fun, easy way for their customers to go play on the water. With a minimum of equipment, their customers can paddle anything from ocean surf to lakes and rivers—no waves required. They are eager to expand their customer base and their supplier pool. Their local C.P.A., Kyle Ski, has suggested hiring a local college student to help them computerize their operations. He suggests they use QuickBooks to keep their accounting records but also encourages them to use a worksheet software application to help them analyze their business situation and support their accounting operations. Nathan, excited to get started, places an ad in the local college paper.

As an accounting student at the local college, you've become fairly adept at using computers to complete homework assignments but you're eager to broaden your horizons. You'd like to combine your accounting and computer skills with some practical experience. Lucky for you, an ad in the college paper for part-time computer and accounting help falls on your desk one afternoon. After an intense interview and background check, you're hired!

Your initial meeting with Nathan, Meagan, and Kyle reveals some unfamiliarity with the software application Kyle has suggested you use. Kyle has agreed to coach you through the basic use of the worksheet program after Nathan and Meagan reluctantly agree to pay his fees. They're hoping, of course, that you can learn the worksheet application quickly and help them use it to further their business expansion.

First off, Kyle introduces you to Excel, a powerful worksheet application he has been using since the mid-eighties. Kyle explains that this most recent incarnation of Excel is far more than a simple calculation program.

Understanding Excel's Capabilities

You have often used paper worksheets in your accounting courses and ask Kyle if Excel is just an electronic version of that same worksheet. He explains that, in essence, you are correct. In your beginning accounting courses, a worksheet might have been used to adjust a trial balance for accrual accounting and to create financial statements like the income statement, balance sheet, and statement of cash flows. You added columns of numbers, subtotaled them in places, drew lines, created titles, and so forth.

Excel is, however, much more than an expensive calculator or place to put information. Built-in functions can help an accountant create financial statements, pivot table reports, analyses, depreciation schedules, loan amortization schedules, cash flow budgets, cost-volume-profit analyses with charts, and more. But first, you need to become familiar with the multitude of Excel commands and procedures.

Starting, Navigating, and Working with Excel Files

Video Demonstration

DEMO 1A Exploring the Excel window

To begin, Kyle asks you if you are familiar with starting programs in Windows 7. Since Nathan and Meagan admit to very little knowledge of computers, you offer to demonstrate. First you explain that some of the company's computers use the Windows 10, Windows 8, or XP operating system but that the one you are most familiar with uses the Windows 7 operating system. In either case, you explain that starting Excel is the same in either operating system. You then offer to demonstrate the process for starting Excel in Windows 7.

To start Excel:

1 Click the **Start** button.

2 Select **All Programs** and then locate Excel 2016 from your list of programs. Your window may look like Figure 1.1.

Figure 1.1

Starting Excel

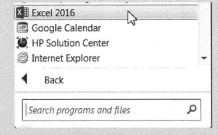

3 Click **Microsoft Office Excel 2016** to start the application.

Trouble? Your start menu may be completely different from that shown in Figure 1.1. See your instructor or lab personnel for instructions on starting Excel.

Kyle explains that Excel always opens a list of recent worksheets and thumb-nail pictures of built-in Excel templates. In this text, you'll be building your own worksheets or modify existing spreadsheets to solve accounting-related problems. To begin you'll often begin by double-clicking a blank worksheet. Your window should look like Figure 1.2. A worksheet is a grid of rows and columns into which you enter information. You can add additional sheets to a workbook if necessary.

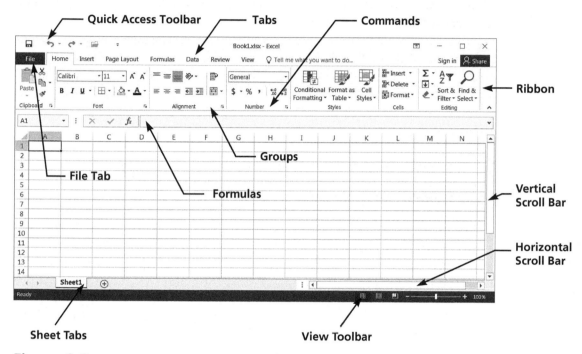

Figure 1.2

The Excel Window

Nathan has been replicating Kyle's actions on his own laptop, which has Excel installed as well. He notes that his screen does not exactly match Kyle's, whose Quick Access toolbar and Ribbon seem different than Nathan's. Kyle explains that screen size can change the appearance of the Ribbon and that both the Ribbon and Quick Access toolbar can be customized.

To illustrate, Kyle has captured his Excel window in Figure 1.2 and provided callouts and an explanation of the Excel window characteristics.

File – This is where you manage your files and the data about them — creating, saving, inspecting for hidden metadata or personal information, and setting options. In short, it is everything that you do to a file that you don't do in the file.

Quick Access Toolbar – At the top of the Excel window is the Quick Access Toolbar, which is designed to give you an easy way to execute the commands used most often. The default setting in Excel provides access to the Save, Undo, and Redo commands. The Quick Access toolbar can be modified to include the Print Preview, Open, Quick Print, and other commands as well. This is accom-plished by right-clicking the Quick Access Toolbar and selecting Customize

Quick Access Toolbar (or by right-clicking any command on the Ribbon and selecting Add to Quick Access Toolbar). Don't adjust your Quick Access Toolbar yet; we'll get to that shortly.

Ribbon – There are three basic components of the Ribbon, as follows.

1 *Tabs:* There are several of them across the top depending on whether you have added any add-ins to Excel. Each represents core tasks you do in Excel.

2 *Groups:* Each tab has groups that show related items together.

3 *Commands:* A command is a button, a box to enter information, or a menu. The principal commands in Excel are gathered on the first and second tabs, the File and Home tabs.

The commands on this tab are those that Microsoft has identified as the most commonly used when people do basic tasks with worksheets. For example, the Paste, Cut, and Copy commands are arranged first on the Home tab, in the Clipboard group. Font formatting commands are next, in the Font group. Commands to center text or align text to the left or right are in the Alignment group, and commands to insert and delete cells, rows, columns, and worksheets are in the Cells group. Groups pull together all the commands you're likely to need for a particular type of task, and throughout the task they remain on display and readily available instead of being hidden within menus. These vital commands are visible above your work space.

The commands on the Ribbon are the ones you use the most. Instead of showing every command all the time, Excel 2016 shows some commands in response to an action you take. When you see an arrow (called the Dialog Box Launcher) in the lower right corner of a group, there are more options available for the group. Click the arrow, and you'll see a dialog box or a task pane.

Other Excel Window Items – As with all Windows screens, scroll bars control your view of the worksheet (horizontal and vertical). Formulas contained in each cell are displayed in the Formula Bar. The View Toolbar gives you quick access to viewing your worksheet in Normal layout (shown in Figure 1.2), Page layout (shown in Figure 1.5), or Page Break preview layout.

To demonstrate some of Excel's features, Kyle suggests you follow along while he opens an old Excel file:

1 Open Excel, if you closed it previously.

2 Click on the right of the Quick Access Toolbar and then place a check next to the Open command. This will add the Open command to your Quick Access Toolbar if it is not already there.

3 Click your newly created Open icon in the Quick Access Toolbar to open a new file. (*Note:* if you are using Excel in a computer lab environment, your changes to the Quick Access Toolbar may not reappear the next time you start Excel.)

4 Navigate the Open window to the location of this text's student files. (The location would be wherever you downloaded the student data files from the text's companion web site as explained on page xi of the Preface to this text or from your computer lab's server.)

5 Double-click the file **ch1-01**, which should be located in a Ch 01 folder. The workbook shown in Figure 1.3 should appear.

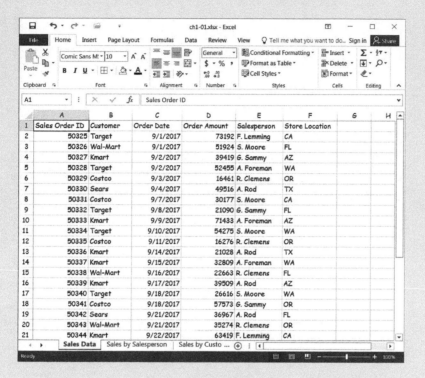

Figure 1.3

Sample Workbook

6 Click the **File** menu and then click **Save As**. (This is done to keep your original student file available in case you need it again and also to provide a unique name for your file.) Click **Computer** and then click **Browse** to navigate yourself to the location where you want to save your file.

7 Add your name to the file name using the underscore key as shown in Figure 1.4. In this example, the file will be saved as ch1-01_student_name (replace student_name with your name). To a removable flash drive called Removable Disk (L:) in a folder called Excel Files as seen in Figure 1.4. Your file location may be different but it is recommended that if you are working in a lab environment that you save your files to a removable disk or online location.

8 Click **Save**.

9 Click in cell **A1**. This is now the active cell.

10 Hold the Shift key down and then click in cell **F1**. This should then highlight cells A1:F1. Alternatively, you could click in cell A1 and, with the mouse button down, drag the cursor to cell F1.

Figure 1.4

Saving a Worksheet

11 Click the **Home** tab and then in the Font group, click the **B** icon to make the text in those cells bold.

12 In the Alignment group, click the **center text** icon to center the text in those cells.

13 Click in cell **D2** and then with the mouse button down, drag the cursor to cell **D31**.

14 In the Number group, click the **$** icon to format the text in those cells in currency format.

15 In the Number group, click the arrow next to the Number group name to launch the Dialog Box Launcher.

16 Type **0** in the decimal places text box, and then click **OK**.

17 Use the vertical scroll bar to move down the worksheet until you can see row 31.

18 Click in cell **D31**. Note the formula =SUM(D2:D29) which appears on the formula bar.

19 In the Font group, click the **Borders** icon and then select the **Top and Double Bottom Border** icon. Depending on the size of your Excel window, your screen should look like Figure 1.5.

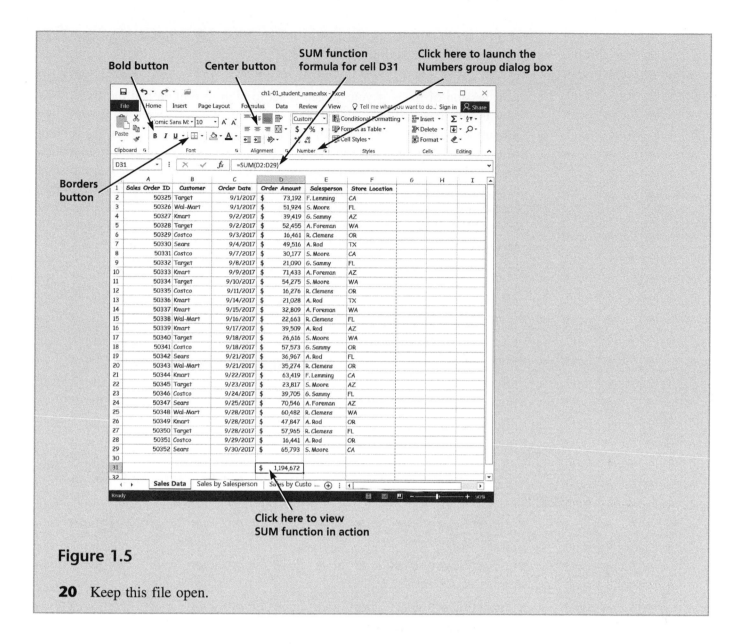

Figure 1.5

20 Keep this file open.

Kyle further discusses and then illustrates the changes in Excel's appearance when a different view is selected and when the screen resolution or size is changed.

Page Layout View – In Page Layout view, there are page margins at the top, sides, and bottom of the worksheet as well as a bit of blue space between worksheets. Rulers at the top and side help you adjust margins. You can turn the rulers on and off as you need them (click Ruler in the Show/Hide group on the View tab). With this new view, you don't need Print Preview to make adjustments to your worksheet before you print. It's easy to add headers and footers in Page Layout view; when you type in the new header and footer area at the top or bottom of a page, the Design tab opens with all the commands you need to create them. You can see each sheet in a workbook in the view that works best for that sheet. Just select, for each worksheet, a view on the View toolbar or in the Workbook Views group on the View tab. Normal view and Page Break preview are both there.

Screen Resolution and Window Size – The figures displayed so far should match your version of Excel if your screen is set to high resolution and the Excel window is maximized. If not, things look different. If your screen is set to a low resolution—for example, to 800 by 600 pixels—then a few groups on the Ribbon will display the group name only, not the commands in the group. You will need to click the arrow on the group button to display the commands. The groups that display only the group name in a smaller resolution are those with less frequently used commands. At any resolution, if you make the Excel window smaller, there is a size at which some groups will display only the group names and so you will need to click the arrow on the group button to display the commands.

To examine the affects of page layout view and screen size:

1 Scroll to the top of the worksheet so that row 1 is visible in your ch1-01 file.

2 Click the **View** tab and then select **Page Layout** from the Workbook Views group. Alternatively, you could have selected the Page Layout icon from the View Toolbar. Your screen should look like Figure 1.6.

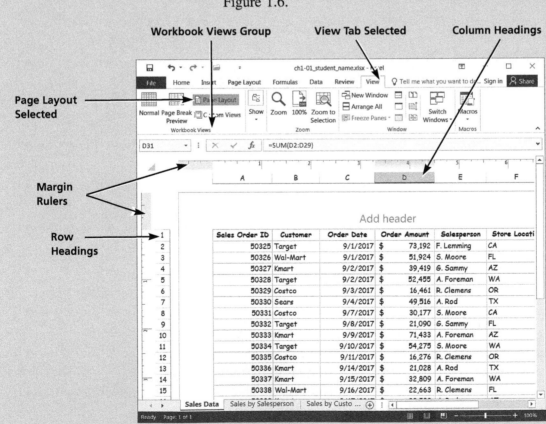

Figure 1.6

Page Layout View of the Excel Window

3 Click the **Show** group to see the expanded menu in Figure 1.7.

Figure 1.7

Show/Hide Group on the View Tab

4 Uncheck the Ruler, Formula Bar, Gridlines, and Headings checkboxes to modify the look of the worksheet.

5 Click the **Show** group and then check the Ruler, Formula Bar, Gridlines, and Headings checkboxes.

6 Click in the text **Add header** and then click in the left header box.

7 Type **September Sales** as the new header.

8 Select the **September Sales** text, click the **Home** tab, and click the **B** (Bold) button. Your screen should look like Figure 1.8.

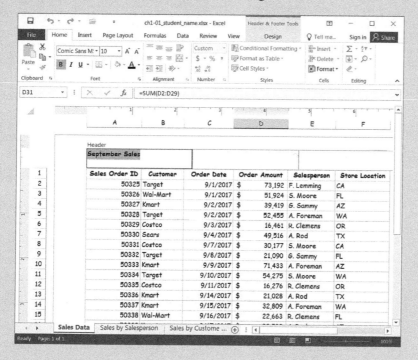

Figure 1.8

Modified View of the Sales Data Worksheet

9 With the text still selected, select **12** in the font size text box.

10 Click **A** (to select column A) and then click the center text button in the Alignment group twice.

11 Click **F** (to select column F) and then click the center text button in the Alignment group twice. Your modified screen should look like Figure 1.9.

Figure 1.9

Modified September Sales
Worksheet

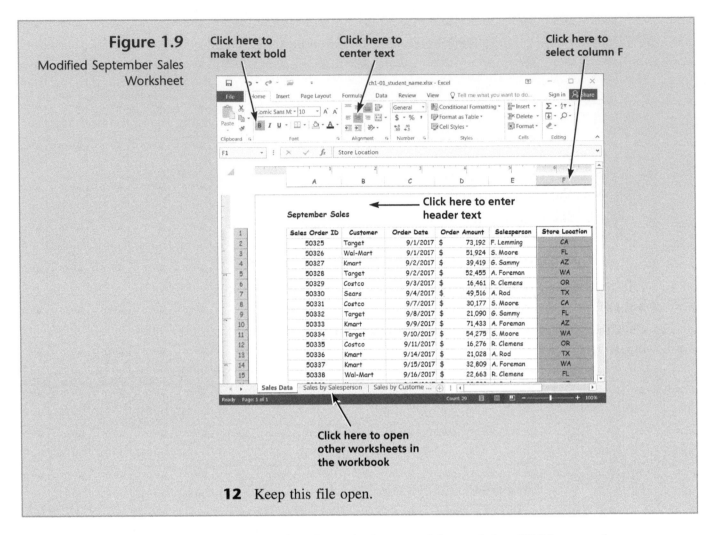

12 Keep this file open.

"What are the tabs at the bottom of the worksheet?" Meagan asks.

"Those are different worksheets contained in our workbook" Kyle explains. "I create those using Excel's Pivot Table feature, which I'll explain later. For now I'll have you look at them to see what they tell us."

Kyle then explains that the Pivot Table feature in Excel allows you to view data in multiple ways. In the Sales by Salesperson worksheet, he organized the sales data (located on the sales data worksheet) by salesperson, providing a total of the month's sales by individual salesperson. In the Sales by Customer worksheet, he reorganized the sales data by customer, providing a total of the month's sales by individual customer. In both cases, Kyle has used Excel's new conditional formatting feature to reflect graphically the values for salespersons and customers relative to each other. You can use conditional formatting to visually annotate your data for both analytical and presentation purposes. These tools will be demonstrated in later chapters.

To view additional worksheets in a workbook:

1 Click the **Sales by Salesperson** tab to reveal the worksheet shown in Figure 1.10.

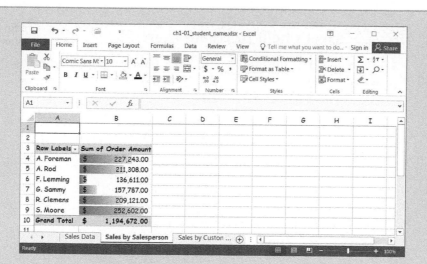

Figure 1.10

Sales by Salesperson Worksheet

2 Click in the down arrow next to the Row Labels text to view alternative ways of sorting or organizing this information.

3 Click the **Sales by Customer** tab to reveal the worksheet shown in Figure 1.11.

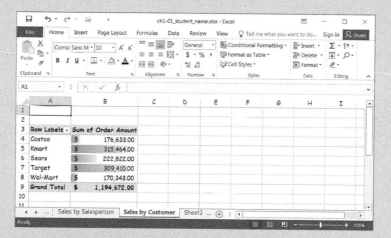

Figure 1.11

Sales by Customer Worksheet

4 Again, click in the down arrow next to the Row Labels text to view alternative ways of sorting or organizing this information.

5 Click on the **Sales Data** tab to re-open the Sales Data worksheet.

6 Keep this file open.

Now that you've had a brief view of how to start, navigate, and work with Excel files, it's time to become familiar with Excel's help features.

Getting Excel Help

Excel's help features are quite extensive. Anytime you are working with Excel and are not certain how to accomplish a task—for example, format a cell, write a formula, or create a chart—you can either press the [**F1**] function key or you can type word(s) into the **Tell me what you want to do** text box. To illustrate, Kyle decides to show you Excel's help feature when trying to create a new chart.

To view Excel's help to create charts:

1 Press the [**F1**] function key to open Excel's help window as shown in Figure 1.12.

Figure 1.12

Excel's Help Window

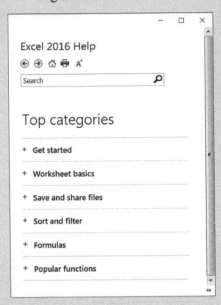

Trouble? Help is only available online. You must be connected to the Internet to access Excel 2016 Help.

2 Type **Chart** into the Search help text box and then press [**Enter**].

3 Click **Select data for a chart**.

4 Read the text as shown in Figure 1.13. Then close the Excel Help window.

Figure 1.13

Excel Help for Creating a Chart

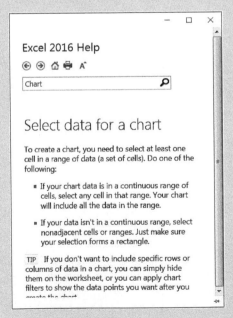

5 Alternatively, type **Chart** into the **Tell me what you want to do** text box.

6 Select **Create Chart** from the drop-down list to reveal the dialog box shown in Figure 1.14 and then click **OK**.

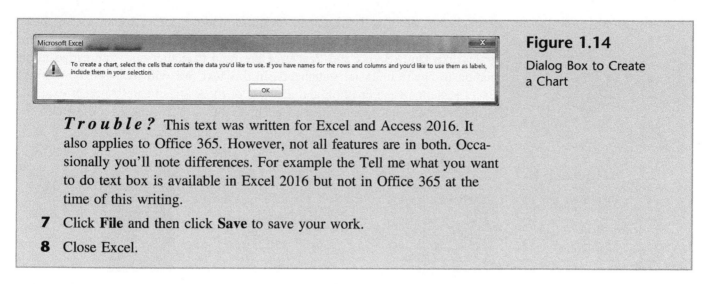

Figure 1.14

Dialog Box to Create a Chart

Trouble? This text was written for Excel and Access 2016. It also applies to Office 365. However, not all features are in both. Occasionally you'll note differences. For example the Tell me what you want to do text box is available in Excel 2016 but not in Office 365 at the time of this writing.

7 Click **File** and then click **Save** to save your work.

8 Close Excel.

Now that you're familiar with Excel's help feature, Kyle thinks it is a good idea to explore how Excel is used in the accounting field.

Examples of How Excel Is Used in Accounting

There are an unlimited number of ways Excel can be used in accounting. This text will focus on building worksheets by using formulas, functions, and features available in Excel to create and analyze inventory and financial statements, calculate depreciation and create depreciation schedules, create loan and bond amortization schedules, and create cash flow budgets.

You may have previously learned how to create financial statements from a trial balance. For example, the trial balance in Figure 1.15 contains data that,

Figure 1.15

Trial Balance

	A	B	C
1	Coast Jewelers, Inc.		
2	Trial Balance		
3	December 31, 2017		
4			
5	Account	Dr.	Cr.
6	Cash	$ 25,412.35	
7	Accounts receivable	84,245.25	
8	Inventory	125,351.45	
9	Prepaid expenses	15,625.26	
10	Supplies	10,245.15	
11	Land	120,000.00	
12	Building	300,000.00	
13	Accumulated depreciation: Building		$ 60,000.00
14	Equipment	65,000.00	
15	Accumulated depreciation: Equipment		8,000.00
16	Accounts payable		75,182.10
17	Long-term debt		400,000.00
18	Common stock		10,000.00
19	Retained earnings		15,000.00
20	Sales revenue		1,527,515.65
21	Cost of goods sold	993,900.30	
22	Advertising expense	54,215.45	
23	Depreciation expense	16,000.00	
24	Payroll expense	240,451.45	
25	Utilities	45,251.09	
26	Total	$2,095,697.75	$2,095,697.75

through the use of cell references, formulas, and other Excel features, might be used to create an income statement. However, in most cases, accounting programs like QuickBooks and Peachtree are used to gather and summarize information to create financial statements. In this text, we will focus on how to use Excel to support the creation and analysis of those statements. Another example is the creation and maintenance of an inventory list. Figure 1.16 illustrates the use of Excel to manage inventory items, which you'll do in Chapter 2.

Figure 1.16

Inventory Listing

	A	B	C	D	E	F
1	Rosey's Roses					
2	Inventory					
3						
4	Type	Description	Quantity	Cost/Unit	Cost	
5	Shrub	Abraham Darby #5	25	$39.99	$999.75	
6	Shrub	Be My Baby #5	30	$18.99	$569.70	
7	Shrub	Deja Blu #5	18	$25.99	$467.82	
8	Shrub	Koko Loko #7	17	$17.99	$305.83	
9	Shrub	Peach Drift #10	33	$12.99	$428.67	
10	Shrub	Red Drift #10	15	$6.99	$104.85	
11	Shrub	Sedona #5	3	$14.99	$44.97	
12	Shrub	Sweet Intoxication #5	17	$9.99	$169.83	
13	Shrub	Wing Ding #5	30	$11.99	$359.70	
14	Climber	Climbing Orange Crush #7	16	$32.99	$527.84	
15	Climber	Don Juan Climber #5	25	$37.99	$949.75	
16	Tree	Barbara Streisand 36in Tree	50	$52.99	$2,649.50	
17	Tree	Firefighter 36in Tree	14	$55.99	$783.86	
18	Tree	Trumpeter 36in Tree	4	$65.99	$263.96	
19						
20	Total				$8,626.03	

In Chapter 3, you'll learn how to perform a financial statements analysis. For example, income statements between 2014 and 2015 are compared via a horizontal analysis in Figure 1.17, which includes a "percent of change" column. An analysis of expenses for a given year is depicted in the pie graph of Figure 1.18.

Figure 1.17

Horizontal Income Statement

	A	B	C	D	E	F	G
1	Kelly's Boutique						
2	Income Statement						
3	For the Year Ended						
4							
5		31-Dec-14	31-Dec-15		% of Sales		% Change
6	Sales Revenue	$ 345,274.22	$420,755.88		100%		22%
7	Less: Cost of Goods Sold	164,217.74	225,154.87		54%		37%
8	Gross Margin	181,056.48	195,601.01		46%		8%
9	Expenses:						
10	Advertising	$ 25,871.45	$ 28,741.55		7%		11%
11	Depreciation	8,431.22	8,000.00		2%		-5%
12	Interest	15,574.15	19,412.51		5%		25%
13	Payroll	105,487.51	99,413.44		24%		-6%
14	Supplies expense	4,732.84	4,561.11		1%		-4%
15	Utilities	10,847.00	8,424.71		2%		-22%
16	Net income before taxes	10,112.31	27,047.69		6%		167%
17	Income taxes	3,784.44	10,847.55		3%		187%
18	Net income	$ 6,327.87	$ 16,200.14		4%		156%

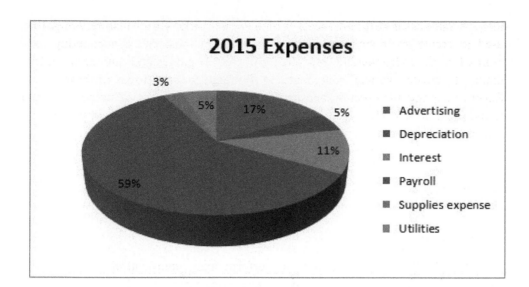

Figure 1.18

Expense Chart

In Chapter 4, you'll learn how to perform depreciation calculations and create a depreciation schedule. For example, you'll use Excel's SLN (Straight-line depreciation function) to calculate the depreciation expense for each year and related accumulated depreciation, as shown in Figure 1.19. You'll also use Excel's DDB (Declining balance depreciation function) to calculate depreciation expense for each year, as shown in Figure 1.20.

	A	B	C
1	**Coast Jewelers, Inc. Depreciation Schedule**		
2			
3	**Asset #**	1001	
4	**Asset**	Display Cases	
5	**Date acquired**	1/1/2017	
6	**Cost**	$ 15,000.00	
7	**Depreciation method**	S/L	
8	**Salvage value**	$ -	
9	**Estimated useful life**	5	
10			
11	**Year**	**Depreciation Expense**	**Accumulated Depreciation**
12	2017	$3,000.00	$3,000.00
13	2018	$3,000.00	$6,000.00
14	2019	$3,000.00	$9,000.00
15	2020	$3,000.00	$12,000.00
16	2021	$3,000.00	$15,000.00

Figure 1.19

Straight-line Depreciation

Figure 1.20

Double Declining Balance Depreciation

	A	B	C	D	E	F	G	H
1	Coast Jewelers, Inc. Depreciation Schedule							
2								
3	Asset #	1001						
4	Asset	Display Cases						
5	Date acquired	1/1/2017						
6	Cost	$ 15,000.00						
7	Depreciation method	DDB						
8	Salvage value	$ -						
9	Estimated useful life	5						
10								
11	Year	Depreciation Expense	Accumulated Depreciation		Straight-Line Test	Switch	Depreciation Expense	Accumulated Depreciation
12	2017	$6,000.00	$6,000.00		$3,000.00	-	$6,000.00	$6,000.00
13	2018	$3,600.00	$9,600.00		$2,250.00	-	$3,600.00	$9,600.00
14	2019	$2,160.00	$11,760.00		$1,800.00	-	$2,160.00	$11,760.00
15	2020	$1,296.00	$13,056.00		$1,620.00	X	$1,620.00	$13,380.00
16	2021	$777.60	$13,833.60		$1,944.00	X	$1,620.00	$15,000.00

In Chapter 5, you'll learn how to perform loan amortization schedules and calculate loan payments given an interest rate, term, and loan amount. For example, you'll use Excel's PMT (Payment function) and formulas to produce the loan amortization schedule shown in Figure 1.21.

Figure 1.21

Loan Amortization Schedule

	A	B	C	D	E
1	Coast Jewelers, Inc.				
2	Loan Amortization Schedule				
3					
4	Amount	$ 75,000.00			
5	Rate	10%			
6	Term	3			
7	Payment	$30,158.61			
8					
9					
10	Payment #	Payment	Interest	Principal	Balance
11					$ 75,000.00
12	1	$30,158.61	$ 7,500.00	$22,658.61	$ 52,341.39
13	2	$30,158.61	$ 5,234.14	$24,924.47	$ 27,416.92
14	3	$30,158.61	$ 2,741.69	$27,416.92	$ (0.00)

In Chapter 6, you will learn how to prepare cash receipts budgets based on a pattern of expected cash collections; see Figure 1.22 for an example.

Figure 1.22

Cash Receipts Budget

	A	B	C	D	E	F
1	Coast Jewelers	1st	2nd	3rd	4th	
2	Cash Budget	Quarter	Quarter	Quarter	Quarter	Year
3						
28	Cash from (to) operating activities	58,500	34,500	8,750	(5,750)	96,000
32	Cash from (to) investing activities	-	(300,000)	-	-	(300,000)
36	Cash from (to) financing activities	-	250,000	(20,000)	(20,000)	210,000
37	Change in cash	58,500	(15,500)	(11,250)	(25,750)	6,000
38	Beginning cash	25,000	83,500	68,000	56,750	25,000
39	Ending cash	83,500	68,000	56,750	31,000	31,000

Finally, in Chapter 7, you'll learn how to use Excel to prepare a present value analysis (Figure 1.23), predict future costs (Figure 1.24), and calculate an allowance for uncollectible accounts (Figure 1.25).

Figure 1.23

Present Value Analysis

	A	B	C	D	E	F	G
1	Coast Jewelers						
2							
3	Present Value Analysis						
4							
5				Year	Interest	Annuity	Investment
6	Future need:	$75,000.00		0			$0.00
7	Term (in years):	3		1	$0.00	$24,026.14	$24,026.14
8	Interest rate:	4%		2	$961.05	$24,026.14	$49,013.33
9	Annuity payment required:	($24,026.14)		3	$1,960.53	$24,026.14	$75,000.00
10							
11				Year	Interest	Investment	
12	Current investment:	($23,000.00)		0		$23,000.00	
13	Interest rate:	6%		1	$1,380.00	$24,380.00	
14	Term (in years):	3		2	$1,462.80	$25,842.80	
15	Investment value in future:	$27,393.37		3	$1,550.57	$27,393.37	
16							
17				Year	Interest	Annuity	Investment
18	Current annuity investment:	($13,500.00)		0			$ -
19	Interest rate:	5%		1	$0.00	$13,500.00	$13,500.00
20	Term (in years):	3		2	$675.00	$13,500.00	$27,675.00
21	Investment value in future:	$42,558.75		3	$1,383.75	$13,500.00	$42,558.75
22							
23				Year	Interest	Investment	
24	Future need:	$16,500.00		0		$13,468.91	
25	Interest rate:	7%		1	$942.82	$14,411.74	
26	Term (in years):	3		2	$1,008.82	$15,420.56	
27	Invest now:	($13,468.91)		3	$1,079.44	$16,500.00	
28							

Figure 1.24

Predicting Future Costs

	A	B	C	D	E
1	Coast Jewelers		Quarter	Hours Open	Expense
2			1st	480	15,000
3	Predicting Costs		2nd	500	18,000
4			3rd	410	14,500
5			4th	600	20,000
6					
7	High Expense			600	20,000
8	Low Expense			410	14,500
9	Difference			190	5,500
10					
11	Hi-Lo Method				
12	Variable cost/hour open		$ 28.95		
13	Fixed cost		$2,631.58		
14					
15	Prediction of expense if open	550	hours =	$ 18,553	
16					
17	Least Squares / Regression Method				
18	Variable cost/hour open		$ 30.51		
19	Fixed cost		$1,694.18		
20					
21	Prediction of expense if open	550	hours =	$ 18,477	

	A	B	C	D	E	F	G	H
					0 - 30 Days	31 - 60 Days	61 - 90 Days	> 90 Days
1				Current	Past Due	Past Due	Past Due	Past Due
2	Allowance for Uncollectible Accounts			58,000	18,000	3,000	2,500	1,000
3				1.00%	8.00%	20.00%	25.00%	50.00%
4								
5	Facts:			Past experience ratio		0.60%		
6	Accounts receivable balance (beg)	75,000						
7	Sales on account	850,000						
8	Collections on account	(837,500)						
9	Write-offs of accounts receivable	(5,000)						
10	Accounts receivable balance (end)	82,500						
11								
12	Percentage of Sales Method							
13	Allowance for Uncollectible accounts (beg)	3,000						
14	Write-offs of accounts receivable	(5,000)						
15	Uncollectible accounts expense	5,100						
16	Allowance for Uncollectible accounts (end)	3,100						
17								
18	Aging Method							
19	Allowance for Uncollectible accounts (beg)	4,500						
20	Write-offs of accounts receivable	(5,000)						
21	Uncollectible accounts expense	4,245						
22	Allowance for Uncollectible accounts (end)	3,745						

Figure 1.25

Calculating an Allowance for Uncollectible Accounts

End Note

The three of you are somewhat overwhelmed by your first exposure to Excel but are pleased with what you've accomplished. You've learned some of Excel's capabilities and new features; how to start, navigate, and work with Excel files; how to use Excel help; and how Excel is used in accounting.

In the next chapter, you will learn how to enter information, create formulas, use functions, and print in Excel.

Chapter 1 Questions

1 Refer to the front matter at the beginning of this text and then identify some new features in the 2016 version of Excel.

2 Why would you use conditional formatting?

3 Explain the difference between a worksheet and a workbook.

4 Describe the nature of the commands found on the File and Home tabs.

5 What and where is the Quick Access Toolbar?

6 Describe the three basic components of the Ribbon.

7 How do you modify the Quick Access Toolbar to add the Open command?

8 What is the Page Layout view?

9 What is the quickest way to get help while in Excel?

10 What are the key accounting topics addressed in this text that relate to your learning Excel?

2

Excel Basics

Case: **What SUP, Inc.**

After providing you a tour of Excel, Kyle suggests you all practice entering information into Excel using some formulas, functions, and features that are common to almost all accounting applications. He has created a preliminary trial balance for you to work on.

Entering Information

Video Demonstration

DEMO 2A Entering information into a work

To complete the trial balance it will be necessary to enter additional text and numbers. The basic data entry container for Excel is a cell. Each cell has an address determined by its location on the worksheet grid. The column number and row number determine the address.

Entering Data

Kyle explains that, before putting data into a cell, you must first select the cell by clicking on it. As you type, the data is also automatically entered into the formula bar. Text entries into cells are often referred to as *labels*, whereas numbers or formula entries are referred to as *values*.

To open the trial balance file and enter data into the worksheet:

1 Start Excel and then click **Open Other Workbooks**.

2 Click **Browse**. Navigate the Open window to the location of this text's student files. (The location would be wherever you downloaded the student files as explained on page xi of the Preface to this text or from your computer lab's server.)

3 Double-click the file **ch2-01**. The workbook shown in Figure 2.1 should appear. (You may have to click **Enable Editing** before you begin.)

Figure 2.1

Partially Completed Trial Balance

	A	B	C
1	What SUP, Inc.		
2	Trial Balance		
3	December 31, 2018		
4			
5	Account	Dr.	Cr.
6	Cash	25,412.35	
7	Accounts receivable		
8	Inventory		
9	Prepaid expenses		
10	Supplies		
11	Land	120,000.00	
12	Building	300,000.00	
13	Accumulated depreciation: Building		60,000.00
14	Equipment	65,000.00	
15	Accumulated depreciation: Equipment		8,000.00
16	Accounts payable		
17	Long-term debt		
18	Common stock		
19	Retained earnings		
20	Sales revenue		
21	Cost of goods sold		
22	Advertising expense		
23	Depreciation expense		
24	Payroll expense		
25	Utilities		

The formula bar shows cell B6 with value 25412.35.

4 Click cell **B7**, type **84245.25**, then press the [**Enter**] key. Note how the number is automatically formatted for you (more on this later). Note also that the active cell is now one row lower, at cell B8.

5 Type **125351.45** in cell B8, and then press the [**Enter**] key.

6 Click cell **C20**, type **1527515.65**, then press the [**Enter**] key. Note that the cell value may show several # signs. If this happens, you will need to resize the column width (more about this later).

7 Click cell **A26**, type the label **Total**, then press the [**Enter**] key. We'll format this cell later.

8 Continue to fill in the remaining empty cells so that your worksheet looks like that shown in Figure 2.2.

Figure 2.2

Almost Completed
Trial Balance

	A	B	C
	B26		
1	*What SUP, Inc.*		
2	*Trial Balance*		
3	*December 31, 2018*		
4			
5	Account	Dr.	Cr.
6	Cash	25,412.35	
7	Accounts receivable	84,245.25	
8	Inventory	125,351.45	
9	Prepaid expenses	15,625.26	
10	Supplies	10,245.15	
11	Land	120,000.00	
12	Building	300,000.00	
13	Accumulated depreciation: Building		60,000.00
14	Equipment	65,000.00	
15	Accumulated depreciation: Equipment		8,000.00
16	Accounts payable		75,182.10
17	Long-term debt		400,000.00
18	Common stock		10,000.00
19	Retained earnings		15,000.00
20	Sales revenue		######
21	Cost of goods sold	993,900.30	
22	Advertising expense	54,215.45	
23	Depreciation expense	16,000.00	
24	Payroll expense	240,451.45	
25	Utilities	45,251.09	
26	Total		

You have thus entered both values and labels into your worksheet. Now you can make changes to the data already entered.

Changing Column Width and Row Height

Perhaps now is a good time to fix that sales number on the trial balance as Kyle suggests. The problem occurred when a number entered in cell C20 was wider than the column permitted. The result was a cell filled with # signs. To fix it, Kyle explains, all you have to do is resize column C. However, for uniformity, you should resize not only column C but also column B.

To change the column width and row height of a worksheet:

1 Place the mouse pointer between column C and column D at the top of the columns so that the mouse pointer cursor changes into a line with two arrows pointing left and right.

2 Double-click the mouse. Then click and hold the mouse button down to reveal the new column width as being Width: 11.4 (121 pixels). Your width may be different.

3 To resize both column B and C point the mouse pointer to the B of column B and click once. (This selects the entire column B.)

4 Now click and drag from the B of column B to the C of column C. (This selects both columns B and C.)

5 With both columns selected, place the mouse pointer between column B and column C at the top of the columns so that the mouse pointer cursor changes into a line with two arrows pointing left and right.

6 Click and drag the column width to the right until the width is 14.00 (147 pixels). Both columns should now be the same width.

7 To resize the height of row 4, click between rows 4 and 5 at the far left of the worksheet until the mouse pointer cursor changes into a line with two arrows pointing up and down.

8 While still holding the mouse button down, drag the row height down until the height is 21.00 (25 pixels).

"If you are like me," Kyle admits, "you will find yourself making a few mistakes along the way."

Editing Data

Nathan agrees and wants to know about correcting errors. He claims he's not very good at typing and has made some mistakes when entering previous information. Kyle explains that you can always edit the information entered into a worksheet regardless of whether you've already pressed the Enter key or not.

Excel gives you two ways to edit data. You can either edit the formula bar or edit data directly in the cell. For instance, let's assume the utilities expense number you entered in cell B25 was 45251.09 when it should have been 45251.90. Also assume that the prepaid expenses entered in cell B9 was 15624.26 when it should have been 15625.45.

To edit data in the worksheet:

1 Click once in cell **B25**.

2 Double-click the value you entered into the cell. Note that this opens up the cell for editing.

3 Double-click the value again and the entire value is selected.

4 Type **45251.90** and the press the [**Enter**] key.

5 Click once in cell **B9**.

6 Double-click the value you entered into the cell. Note that this opens up the cell for editing.

7 Double-click the value again and the entire value is selected.

8 Type **15625.45** and the press the [**Enter**] key.

9 Since you actually did enter in the correct values you should undo your changes. Click the **Undo** button from the Quick Access Toolbar two times.

Meagan says she will probably have to use this procedure often because her keyboarding skills are rather weak. Fortunately, it is easy to use this process for correcting errors and making changes to a worksheet.

Controlling the Appearance of Data

You ask Kyle why the numbers on the trial balance are formatted with commas, since you didn't type commas when you entered the values. He explains that initially he formatted both columns B and C to be in the "comma" format. Formatting does not change the text or numbers in the cell itself; rather, it changes the way the text or numbers appear in the worksheet. To experiment, he suggests you modify the format of cells B6, C13, B26, and C26 to a "currency" format, since the top and bottom of a column of accounting numbers are usually formatted with the $. He further suggests that you replace the format with a "comma and cents" format using the format painter.

To apply the currency format to specific cells:

1 Click cell **B6**, then click the **Home** tab and then click **$** in the Number group in the Ribbon. Note how the number still has the comma and cents formatting from before but now contains the $.

2 With cell B6 still selected, click the **Format Painter** tool (it looks like a paintbrush) on the Clipboard group. Note that cell B6 now has ants dancing around the border of the cell and that the mouse pointer has an added paintbrush. Your screen should look like Figure 2.3.

Figure 2.3

Using the Format Painter Tool

B6	▾ ⋮ ✕ ✓ *fx*	25412.35	
	A	B	C
1	*What SUP, Inc.*		
2	*Trial Balance*		
3	*December 31, 2018*		
4			
5	<u>Account</u>	<u>Dr.</u>	<u>Cr.</u>
6	Cash	$ 25,412.35	
7	Accounts receivable	84,245.25	
8	Inventory	125,351.45	

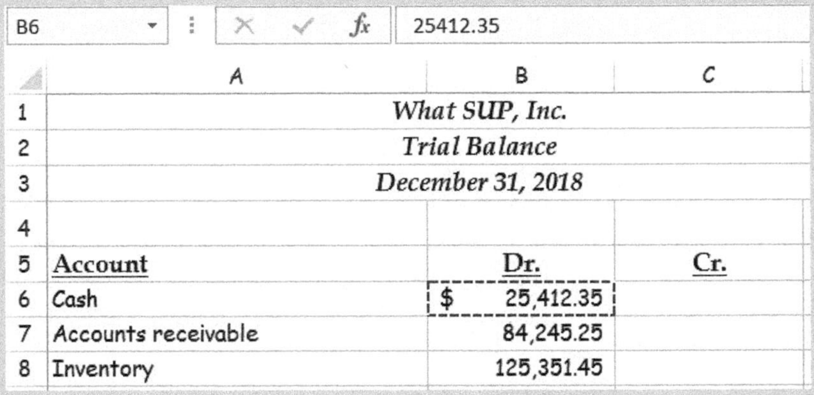

3 Click cell **C13**. You have now painted the Accounting Number Format to that cell.

4 While **C13** is still selected, click the **Format Painter** tool again.

5 Click in cell **B26** and, with the mouse button still down, drag it to the right to include cell C26; then release the mouse button. You have now painted the Accounting Number Format to cells B26 and C26, which will soon contain the total of each column.

Kyle also explains that it is common practice to total the debit and credit columns of a trial balance and include a double underline under such totals. Because you are in the midst of formatting cells, he suggests you format the two "total" cells before you create a formula adding a column of cells.

To format the "total" cells with a double underline:

1 Click and highlight cells **B26** and **C26** by clicking first in B26 and then dragging the mouse to C26 while holding down the mouse button. (This won't be necessary if you haven't moved the cursor from step 5 above.)

2 Place the mouse pointer over the Borders tool located on the Font group—specifically, over the small arrow located on the right of the Borders tool. Click the arrow to reveal several border options as shown in Figure 2.4

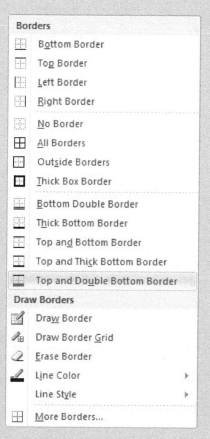

Figure 2.4

Selecting a Border

3 Click the **Top and Double Bottom Border** tool to format the cells.

To finish the trial balance, all you need now is a total for each column.

Entering Formulas and Using Functions

Formulas in Excel always begin with an equal sign (=). These formulas can use numbers; math symbols to add, subtract, multiply, or divide (+, −, *, /); cell references; and/or functions. Nathan asks if Excel has a calculator built in so one could add the column and then put the result in the total cell. Kyle explains that the disadvantage of such an approach is that, if your numbers later change, then you'd have to re-add the column. Meagan asks if the best way to add a column of numbers is therefore to add each *cell*. Kyle explains you could certainly do that by typing a formula like this: =B6+B7+B8 et cetera.

However, Kyle explains that Excel includes some functions that accomplish this task in a more efficient manner. The SUM function, for instance, will sum up specified series of cells.

"Hold on," you say. "Functions sound like programming and I'm just an accounting student who has no desire to learn computer programming."

"Don't panic!" Kyle advises. "Excel's functions are fairly simple. Each function reacts to certain arguments you provide. For instance, the SUM function is written as follows: =SUM(argument). The argument is a series of cell references you want summed. Let me show you how to add the sum function to your trial balance to add up the debit and credit columns."

To use the SUM function to add a column of numbers:

1 Click cell **B26**.

2 Type **=SUM(B6:B25)**, then press [**Enter**]. The result of that function should be the amount $2,095,697.75.

3 Click cell **C26**.

4 Dancing ants should now be marching around the cells C15 to C25, as shown in Figure 2.5.

5 Click the upper right handle and, with the mouse button down, drag the ants up until you reach cell C6.

6 Release the mouse button and press the [**Enter**] key.

Figure 2.5

Using AutoSum

| SUM | ▾ | ⋮ | ✕ | ✓ | *fx* | =SUM(C15:C25) |

	A	B	C
1		*What SUP, Inc.*	
2		*Trial Balance*	
3		*December 31, 2018*	
4			
5	Account	Dr.	Cr.
6	Cash	$ 25,412.35	
7	Accounts receivable	84,245.25	
8	Inventory	125,351.45	
9	Prepaid expenses	15,625.26	
10	Supplies	10,245.15	
11	Land	120,000.00	
12	Building	300,000.00	
13	Accumulated depreciation: Building		$ 60,000.00
14	Equipment	65,000.00	
15	Accumulated depreciation: Equipment		8,000.00
16	Accounts payable		75,182.10
17	Long-term debt		400,000.00
18	Common stock		10,000.00
19	Retained earnings		15,000.00
20	Sales revenue		1,527,515.65
21	Cost of goods sold	993,900.30	
22	Advertising expense	54,215.45	
23	Depreciation expense	16,000.00	
24	Payroll expense	240,451.45	
25	Utilities	45,251.09	
26	Total	$ 2,095,697.75	=SUM(C15:C25)

7   Alternatively, you can enter the argument by clicking and dragging the mouse pointer over the cells to be added. Click the **AutoSum** button in the Editing group of the Home tab. Your screen should look like Figure 2.5 just after you click the AutoSum button.

8   Click the **File** menu and then click **Save As**. (This is done to keep your original student file available in case you need it again and also to provide a unique name for your file.)

9   Add your name to the file name using the underscore key as you have done previously. In this example, the file will be saved as ch2-01_student_name (again, replace student_name with your name). Be sure to save your file to a location (e.g., a USB drive) from which you can later retrieve it.

10   Click **File** and then click **Close** to close this file.

Kyle explains that now you've used two different methods of entering a sum function to add up both the debit and credit columns. In both cases, the resulting formula is the same; you've simply used different methods to achieve the same goal. Moreover, if you enter different data in the cells B6 to B25 or C6 to C25, the SUM function will automatically add them up.

More Extensive Use of Formulas

Nathan comments that he envisions another use of this worksheet software. Weekly he prepares, by hand, a "Badfish SUPs sales" worksheet that identifies how many Badfish SUPs have been sold each week as well as their cost, markup, sales price, discount, and total sales. Kyle suggests that this might be a good opportunity to illustrate a more extensive use of formulas in Excel.

Entering and Editing Formulas

Formulas in Excel always begin with an equal sign (=). These formulas can use numbers; math symbols to add, subtract, multiply, or divide (+, −, *, /); cell references; and/or functions.

Kyle prepares a worksheet with titles and headings that are similar to Nathan's hand-prepared worksheet. In it he includes the names of the four types of Badfish SUPs sold that week, the cost or price What SUP paid for each SUP, the usual markup on cost used to determine the price, the discount offered that week on each SUP, and the quantity of each SUP sold. Kyle then recommends that you, Nathan, and Meagan use this form to prepare a weekly Badfish SUP Sales worksheet for the week of November 12, 2015.

The price for each SUP is based on the SUP cost and markup percentage. For example, if a SUP costs $100 and the markup is 50 percent, then What SUP sells the SUP for $150 (the $100 cost plus a markup of 50 percent × $100, or $50).

The total column is the product of the price less discount times the number of SUPs sold. For example, if the price (as previously determined) was $150 but that week it was discounted 10 percent, then the net price would be $135 (the selling price of $150 minus the $15 discount). If five SUPs were sold, the total would then be $675 (5 × $135).

Kyle offers to walk you through the creation of formulas, the use of references, and (later) manipulating the data.

To enter and edit formulas for the Weekly Badfish SUP Sales worksheet:

1 Open **ch2-02** to reveal a file that should look like Figure 2.6.

Figure 2.6

Badfish SUP Sales

	A	B	C	D	E	F	G
1	What SUP, Inc.						
2	Badfish SUP Sales						
3	Week of November 12, 2018						
4							
5	Product	Cost	Markup	Price	Discount	Quantity	Total
6	River Surfer 6'11"	450.00	100%		10%	7	
7	River Surfer 8'	520.00	100%		9%	3	
8	River Surfer 9'	600.00	100%		8%	8	
9	MCIT Inflatable 10'6"	700.00	80%		15%	15	
10	Total						

2 Click in cell **D6**, where you will place the formula to calculate price.

3 Remember, the formula for determining price is cost plus markup; hence you must enter a formula that computes the markup and then adds it to the cost. Type the formula **=B6+(B6*C6)** into cell D6 and then press [**Enter**]. Note that B6 is the location of the cost and C6 is the location of the markup percentage. Note also that the cell has been preformatted so that two decimal places are always shown.

4 Click in cell **G6**, where you will place the formula to calculate the total sales of the River Surfer 6'11".

5 Recall that the formula for determining total sales is price less discount times the number sold; hence, you need to enter a formula that computes the net price and then multiplies it by the number sold. Type the formula **=(D6–(D6*E6))*F6** into cell G6, then press [**Enter**]. Note that D6 is the location of the price, E6 is the location of the discount percentage, and F6 is the location of the number sold. Note also that the cell has been preformatted so that two decimal places are always shown. Figure 2.7 shows the worksheet just before you press [Enter].

Figure 2.7

Entering a Formula

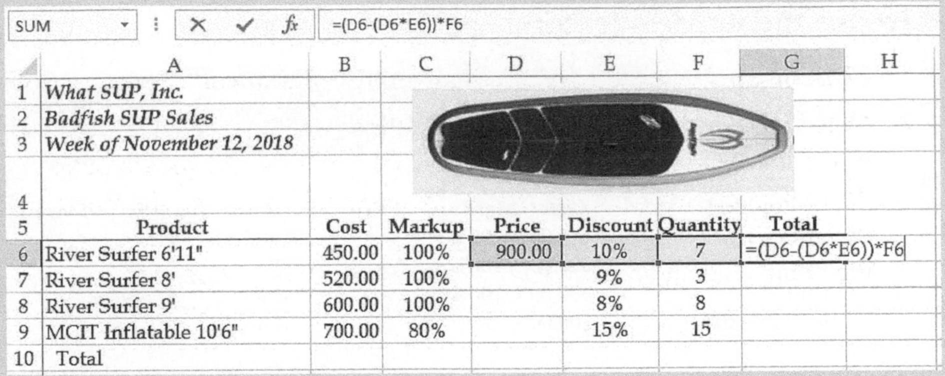

| SUM | ▾ | ⋮ | ✕ | ✓ | *fx* | =(D6-(D6*E6))*F6 |

	A	B	C	D	E	F	G	H
1	What SUP, Inc.							
2	Badfish SUP Sales							
3	Week of November 12, 2018							
4								
5	Product	Cost	Markup	Price	Discount	Quantity	Total	
6	River Surfer 6'11"	450.00	100%	900.00	10%	7	=(D6-(D6*E6))*F6	
7	River Surfer 8'	520.00	100%		9%	3		
8	River Surfer 9'	600.00	100%		8%	8		
9	MCIT Inflatable 10'6"	700.00	80%		15%	15		
10	Total							

6 Keep this file open.

"Hold on a minute," Meagan says. "All of those parentheses are confusing me."

Kyle explains that the formula required those parentheses to specify the order of calculation. The formula (D6–(D6*E6))*F6 requires the innermost (here, bold) set of parentheses to be calculated first. This is the calculation of the discount (the price times the discount percentage). The outermost set of parentheses in the formula (D6–(D6*E6))*F6 is acted on next. This is the calculation of the discounted price (price less discount). Finally, the formula multiplies the newly calculated discounted price by the number sold to yield the total.

"Do we now have to type additional formulas for the other Badfish SUP?" you ask.

"Thank goodness, no," Kyle replies. "Excel has an AutoFill feature that saves you the time and effort of reentering similar formulas."

Manipulating Data and Structuring Worksheets

The AutoFill feature is handy whenever you need formulas or data replicated down or across a worksheet. Kyle mentions that understanding this feature requires that you also understand the concept of relative and absolute references.

Using AutoFill

In the Weekly Badfish SUP Sales worksheet, you created formulas to calculate price and total sales for the River Surfer 6'11″ SUP. Now you want to use a similar formula to calculate the price and total sales for the other Badfish SUP. Kyle suggests you try the AutoFill feature yourself.

To use the AutoFill feature:

1 Click in cell **D6** on the Weekly Badfish SUP Sales worksheet.

2 Note that, when selected, the cell is outlined and a small square appears in the lower right corner of the cell. Click and hold the mouse button down so the mouse pointer is over that square. Then drag the frame down to cell **D9** and release the mouse button. Double-click between the D and E columns to resize column D. See Figure 2.8.

	A	B	C	D	E	F	G
1	What SUP, Inc.						
2	Badfish SUP Sales						
3	Week of November 12, 2018						
4							
5	Product	Cost	Markup	Price	Discount	Quantity	Total
6	River Surfer 6'11"	450.00	100%	900.00	10%	7	5,670.00
7	River Surfer 8'	520.00	100%	1,040.00	9%	3	
8	River Surfer 9'	600.00	100%	1,200.00	8%	8	
9	MCIT Inflatable 10'6"	700.00	80%	1,260.00	15%	15	
10	Total						

Figure 2.8

Filling a Formula Down a Column

3 Click in cell **G6**.

4 Click and hold the mouse button down so that the mouse pointer is over the square in the lower right corner of the cell. Drag the frame down to cell **G9** and then release the mouse button. Your revised worksheet should look like Figure 2.9.

	A	B	C	D	E	F	G
1	What SUP, Inc.						
2	Badfish SUP Sales						
3	Week of November 12, 2018						
4							
5	Product	Cost	Markup	Price	Discount	Quantity	Total
6	River Surfer 6'11"	450.00	100%	900.00	10%	7	5,670.00
7	River Surfer 8'	520.00	100%	1,040.00	9%	3	2,839.20
8	River Surfer 9'	600.00	100%	1,200.00	8%	8	8,832.00
9	MCIT Inflatable 10'6"	700.00	80%	1,260.00	15%	15	16,065.00
10	Total						

Figure 2.9

Watch Sales with Price and Total Values

5 Keep this file open.

"I see," you say. "By using the AutoFill feature we've copied the same formula down the worksheet."

"Not exactly," Kyle responds. "In fact, you've copied a similar formula down the worksheet, but it's not the same."

Kyle suggests that this is a good time to explain the worksheet concept of relative and absolute references.

Using Relative and Absolute References

The formula placed in cells D7, D8, and D9 after using the AutoFill feature is similar but not exactly like the formula you wrote in cell D6. If you look at the resulting formula created in cell D7 and compare it to the formula in cell D6, you will see relative referencing at work. Cell D6 contains the formula B6+(B6*C6). Cell D7 contains the formula B7+(B7*C7). In other words, using AutoFill changed the formula by increasing the row reference by 1, from row 6 to row 7. This will continue to occur as AutoFill moves down relative to the original formula. Once again, looking at cell D8, you see the formula B8+(B8*C8) and at cell D9 the formula B9+(B9*C9).

"Do you always want AutoFill to change the references?" Nathan asks.

"Not necessarily," Kyle answers.

Kyle points out that relative referencing works well in this particular worksheet. An alternative scenario that would *not* use relative referencing is one where the discount is some specific percentage for all sales. If you locate that percentage in one cell, then relative referencing would not create proper formulas. He suggests you create a cell that specifies a discount percentage for that week, clear the discount part of the worksheet, and rewrite the total formula.

To use absolute references in the worksheet:

1 Before making the following changes, click the **File** menu and button, then **Save As** to save the Excel file.

2 Name the file **ch2-02_student_name** (replacing student_name with your name as before), then click **Save**. You will now make changes to the file to illustrate absolute references.

3 Type **Discount %** in cell A13. This is a label for the value you will place in cell B13. Press [**Tab**] to move to the next cell.

4 Type **10%** in cell B13, then press [**Enter**].

5 Select cells E6 through E9 by clicking in cell **E6** and then, while holding down the Shift key, clicking cell **E9**. (This selects the four contiguous cells.) Alternatively, you could click in cell **E6** and, while holding the mouse button down, drag the mouse pointer down to cell E9.

6 Right-click the selected cells to reveal the Shortcut menu, then click **Clear Contents** as shown in Figure 2.10. This removes values and text previously shown at E6 through E9.

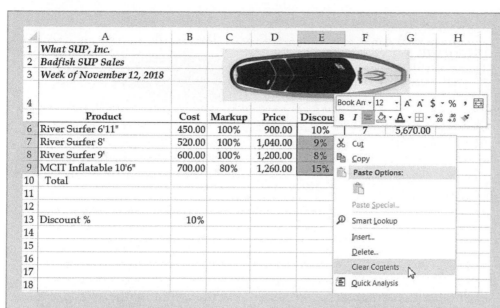

Figure 2.10

Right-Click Menu

	A	B	C	D	E	F	G	H
1	What SUP, Inc.							
2	Badfish SUP Sales							
3	Week of November 12, 2018							
4								
5	Product	Cost	Markup	Price	Discou			
6	River Surfer 6'11"	450.00	100%	900.00	10%	7	5,670.00	
7	River Surfer 8'	520.00	100%	1,040.00	9%			
8	River Surfer 9'	600.00	100%	1,200.00	8%			
9	MCIT Inflatable 10'6"	700.00	80%	1,260.00	15%			
10	Total							
11								
12								
13	Discount %		10%					
14								
15								
16								
17								
18								

7 Click cell **E6**.

8 Type a new formula **=B13** in cell E6 and then press [**Enter**]. The value now showing in E65 is 10%.

9 Using AutoFill, like you did before, replicate the formula in cell E6 down to E9. This, however, causes a problem due to relative referencing: the formula in E7 now contains a reference to B14 instead of the discount specified in B13. What we should have done is changed the B13 reference from a relative reference to an absolute reference.

10 Change the formula at E6 to **=$B$13** by placing a $ in front of the B and the 13. The addition of the $ freezes the reference to an absolute cell, regardless of where the cell may be copied to or automatically filled using AutoFill. Alternatively you could have selected the formula in cell E6 and then pressed the **F4** function. After you have edited the formula, press [**Enter**].

11 Using AutoFill, replicate the modified formula in cell E6 down through cell E9. Your worksheet should now look like Figure 2.11.

Figure 2.11

Using Absolute
Referencing

	A	B	C	D	E	F	G
1	What SUP, Inc.						
2	Badfish SUP Sales						
3	Week of November 12, 2018						
4							
5	Product	Cost	Markup	Price	Discount	Quantity	Total
6	River Surfer 6'11"	450.00	100%	900.00	10%	7	5,670.00
7	River Surfer 8'	520.00	100%	1,040.00	10%	3	2,808.00
8	River Surfer 9'	600.00	100%	1,200.00	10%	8	8,640.00
9	MCIT Inflatable 10'6"	700.00	80%	1,260.00	10%	15	17,010.00
10	Total						
11							
12							
13	Discount %	10%					

12 Keep this file open.

"So what happens if I change the discount from 10 percent to 13 percent?" Nathan asks. Kyle demonstrates that the new formula creates new totals as a different discount percentage is entered into cell B13. He suggests you try some alternative percentages to see the effects on the total column. When you are finished experimenting, return the discount to 10 percent.

Inserting and Deleting Columns and Rows

Nathan wants to know how to add a row if a different SUP is sold. He would also like to insert a new column, which would display the discounted price.

To insert columns and rows on a worksheet:

1 Click the **8** in row 8 to select the entire row.

2 Right-click the **8** in row 8 to reveal the Shortcut menu, then click **Insert** to add a new row. Figure 2.12 shows the window right before you click Insert.

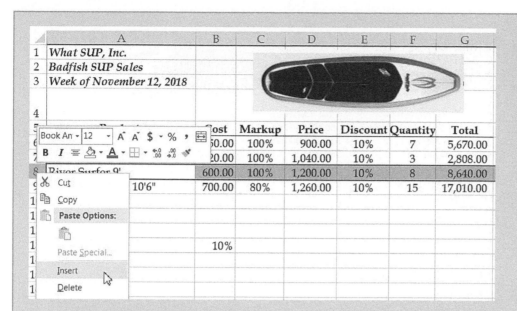

Figure 2.12

Inserting a Row

3   After you click Insert, add the following SUP sales information to the new row 8: product, **River Surfer 8′6″**; cost, **560**; markup, **100%**; quantity, **4**.

4   Use AutoFill to fill down the proper formulas for cells D8, E8, and G8.

5   Click the **F** in column F to select the entire column.

6   Right-click the **F** in column F to reveal the Shortcut menu, then click **Insert** to insert a new column.

   Trouble? Excel has an Undo command which you were instructed to use earlier in this chapter. Recall that this Undo command allows you to reverse any number of actions you have executed on a worksheet. If you accidentally delete the wrong column or too many columns, click the **Undo** button on the Quick Access toolbar.

7   Type **Net Price** in cell F5, then press [**Enter**].

8   Type **=D6−(D6*E6)** into cell F6, then press [**Enter**]

9   Format cell F6 in a comma style format.

10 Use AutoFill to fill down the formula in F6 through F10.

11 Click cell **H11** and then click the **AutoSum** tool from the Editing group, then press [**Enter**]. Note how Excel's AutoSum feature automatically selects cells adjacent to cell H11 that it thinks contain data you want to sum. This is a handy feature, but it doesn't always select the cell you want to sum. In this case it worked great!

12 To polish off your worksheet, click cell **H11** again and format it with a **Top and Double Bottom Border** by using the Borders tool from the Font group.

13 Click cell **A14**. Format the cell to make the label bold by clicking the **Bold** tool from the Font group. Your completed worksheet should look like Figure 2.13.

Figure 2.13

Final Badfish SUP
Sales Worksheet

	A	B	C	D	E	F	G	H
1	*What SUP, Inc.*							
2	*Badfish SUP Sales*							
3	*Week of November 12, 2018*							
4								
5	Product	Cost	Markup	Price	Discount	Net Price	Quantity	Total
6	River Surfer 6'11"	450.00	100%	900.00	10%	810.00	7	5,670.00
7	River Surfer 8'	520.00	100%	1,040.00	10%	936.00	3	2,808.00
8	River Surfer 8"6"	560.00	100%	1,120.00	10%	1,008.00	4	4,032.00
9	River Surfer 9'	600.00	100%	1,200.00	10%	1,080.00	8	8,640.00
10	MCIT Inflatable 10'6"	700.00	80%	1,260.00	10%	1,134.00	15	17,010.00
11	Total							38,160.00
12								
13								
14	Discount %	10%						

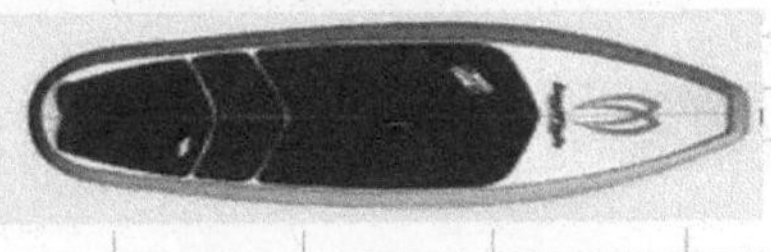

14 Click the **File** menu and then click **Save** to save your work.

15 Keep this file open.

Working with Multiple Worksheets

Meagan is pleased with the results of the completed Weekly Badfish SUP Sales worksheet, but now she would like the sales to be summarized in 4-week increments. Kyle replies that the best way to handle this would be to use multiple worksheets. You can create a worksheet for every week and a summary sheet for every 4-week period.

At the bottom of the worksheet in Figure 2.13, you can see the Sheet1 label. Kyle suggests you first re-label Sheet1 as November 12 indicating the start of the week. Then he suggests you copy the November 12 worksheet and create a November 5 worksheet, then again for November 19, and again for November 26.

To work with multiple worksheets:

1 Double-click the tab **Sheet1**, change the name of the worksheet to **November 12**, and then press the [**Enter**] key.

2 Right-click the newly labeled tab **November 12** to reveal the Shortcut menu, then click **Move or Copy**.

3 Check the **Create a copy** checkbox and then click **OK** in the Move or Copy window. A new worksheet labeled November 12 (2) appears in the workbook.

4 Double-click the tab **November 12 (2)**, change the name of the worksheet to **November 5**, and then press the [**Enter**] key. You now have two identical worksheets.

5 Repeat this process two more times to create a total of four worksheets, the last two labeled November 19 and November 26. Click and hold the tabs and then drag them left or right to place them in order. To see all the worksheets, you may have to shrink the scroll box on the bottom of the worksheet.

6 Place the mouse pointer just to the left of the arrow on the horizontal scroll box. Click and drag the mouse pointer to the right until all four weekly worksheet tabs are visible.

7 Change the title of each worksheet to reflect the new dates by editing cell A3. Click cell **A3** on the worksheet November 5 and change the date to read November 5. Continue the same process for the last two worksheets. Remember: to change active worksheets, click the title of each worksheet on the bottom tabs.

8 Change the number of Badfish SUP sold for the week of November 5 (located in cells G6 to G10) to **3,2,7,1,4** respectively. Also change the discount percentage of cell B14 to **0%**.

9 Change the number of Badfish SUP sold for the week of November 19 (located in cells G6 to G10) to **4,1,8,2,5** respectively. Also change the discount percentage of cell B14 to **5%**.

10 Change the number of Badfish SUP sold for the week of November 26 (located in cells G6 to G10) to **3,6,7,4,8** respectively. Also change the discount percentage of cell B14 to **15%**.

11 You now have four worksheets with different sales information for each period. The November 26 worksheet on your screen should look like Figure 2.14.

	A	B	C	D	E	F	G	H
1	What SUP, Inc.							
2	Badfish SUP Sales							
3	Week of November 26, 2018							
4								
5	Product	Cost	Markup	Price	Discount	Net Price	Quantity	Total
6	River Surfer 6'11"	450.00	100%	900.00	15%	765.00	3	2,295.00
7	River Surfer 8'	520.00	100%	1,040.00	15%	884.00	6	5,304.00
8	River Surfer 8"6"	560.00	100%	1,120.00	15%	952.00	7	6,664.00
9	River Surfer 9'	600.00	100%	1,200.00	15%	1,020.00	4	4,080.00
10	MCIT Inflatable 10'6"	700.00	80%	1,260.00	15%	1,071.00	8	8,568.00
11	Total							26,911.00
12								
13								
14	Discount %	15%						

Tabs: November 5 | November 12 | November 19 | **November 26**

Figure 2.14

Final Badfish SUP Sales Worksheet

12 Save the updated worksheet.

13 Keep this file open.

Finally, a Summary worksheet can be created that summarizes sales from each week. Kyle suggests you set up a new Summary worksheet using the copy and paste features of Excel.

To set up a summary worksheet:

1 Right-click the tab **November 5**, and then click **Insert**, and then double-click **Worksheet** and press [**Enter**].

2 Change the name of the new worksheet to Summary.

3 Click the **November 5** worksheet tab.

4 Select cells **A1** to **A3**, right-click the mouse to activate the Shortcut menu, and click **Copy** to copy the worksheet title.

5 Click the **Summary** worksheet tab, click in cell **A1**, right-click the mouse button, and click **Paste** to paste the worksheet title. If the picture is captured as well, click to select it and then press [**Delete**].

6 Click cell **A3** and type **Summary**.

7 Resize the height of row **4** to **46** pixels.

8 Click the **November 5** worksheet tab.

9 Select cells **A5** to **A11**, right-click the mouse to activate the Shortcut menu and click **Copy** to copy the product title and names.

10 Click the **Summary** worksheet tab, click in cell **A5**, right-click the mouse button, and click **Paste** to paste the product title and names.

11 Resize column A to fit the product title and names (250 pixels).

12 In cells B5 to F5 type the various weekly dates: **Nov 5**, **Nov 12**, **Nov 19**, **Nov 26**, and **Total** respectively.

13 Format cells B5 to F5 using the **Bold, Center,** and **Bottom Border** tools on the Format toolbar. The resulting worksheet should look like Figure 2.15.

	A	B	C	D	E	F
1	*What SUP, Inc.*					
2	*Badfish SUP Sales*					
3	*Summary*					
4						
5	Product	5-Nov	12-Nov	19-Nov	26-Nov	Total
6	River Surfer 6'11"					
7	River Surfer 8'					
8	River Surfer 8"6"					
9	River Surfer 9'					
10	MCIT Inflatable 10'6"					
11	Total					

Figure 2.15

Creating a Summary Worksheet

14 Keep this file open.

The Summary worksheet you've set up is now ready for weekly data. Rather than typing the totals from each product for each week, Excel enables you to link the Summary worksheet with the weekly worksheets.

To link the Summary worksheet to weekly worksheets:

1 Click in cell **B6** of the Summary worksheet.

2 Type = into cell B6.

3 Before pressing Enter, activate the November 5 worksheet and click in cell **H6**; then press [**Enter**]. This automatically enters the reference 'November 5'!H6 into the Summary worksheet cell B6.

4 Use AutoFill to replicate the formula now entered in the Summary worksheet cell B6 down the worksheet to cell B10.

5 Click in cell **C6** of the Summary worksheet.

6 Type = into cell C6.

7 Before pressing Enter, activate the November 12 worksheet and click in cell **H6**; then press [**Enter**]. This automatically enters the reference 'November 12'!H6 into the Summary worksheet cell C6.

8 Use AutoFill to replicate the formula now entered in the Summary worksheet cell C6 down the worksheet to cell C10.

9 Repeat this same process for November 19 and November 26.

10 Use the SUM function to total sales by product in cells F6 through F10 on the Summary worksheet.

11 Use the SUM function to total weekly sales in cells B11 through F11.

12 Format cells B11 to F11 with a Top and Double Bottom Border.

13 Increase the size of any column to remove the # signs found in cells.

14 Reduce the size of the horizontal scroll box to reveal all worksheet tabs in your Badfish SUP Sales workbook. The completed summary worksheet should look like Figure 2.16.

Figure 2.16

Completed Summary Worksheet

	A	B	C	D	E	F
1	What SUP, Inc.					
2	Badfish SUP Sales					
3	Summary					
4						
5	Product	5-Nov	12-Nov	19-Nov	26-Nov	Total
6	River Surfer 6'11"	2,700.00	5,670.00	3,420.00	2,295.00	14,085.00
7	River Surfer 8'	2,080.00	2,808.00	988.00	5,304.00	11,180.00
8	River Surfer 8"6"	7,840.00	4,032.00	8,512.00	6,664.00	27,048.00
9	River Surfer 9'	1,200.00	8,640.00	2,280.00	4,080.00	16,200.00
10	MCIT Inflatable 10'6"	5,040.00	17,010.00	5,985.00	8,568.00	36,603.00
11	Total	18,860.00	38,160.00	21,185.00	26,911.00	105,116.00

◄ ► | **Summary** | November 5 | November 12 | November 19 | November 26 | ⊕

15 Save your work.

16 Keep this file open.

Using Headers and Footers

Often you will create multiple versions of a worksheet and, when they are printed, you won't know which version is which. Thus, it's important to include a date and time stamp on each worksheet. Kyle indicates that Excel has a built-in function that will not only date and time-stamp your work but also indicate the file name on each worksheet when printed. Both of these functions can be placed in either the header or footer of a worksheet.

To use headers and footers in a worksheet:

1 Click the **View** tab on the Ribbon, then click **Page Layout** from the Workbook Views group. Scroll to the top of the page so that the Add header text appears.

2 Click the text **Add header**, and then type **&[Tab]** (this will insert the sheet name as the header when the worksheet is printed).

3 Press **[Tab]** to move to the right section of the header.

4 Type **&[Date]** into the right header text box. (This will print the system date in the upper right corner of each worksheet; the *system date* is the current date you are printing your worksheet.)

5 Press [**Tab**]. Your screen should look like Figure 2.17 except for the current date, which will instead be the system date at the time you complete this work.

	Summary					11/16/2015			
What SUP, Inc.									
Badfish SUP Sales									
Summary									
Product	5-Nov	12-Nov	19-Nov	26-Nov	Total				
River Surfer 6'11"	2,700.00	5,670.00	3,420.00	2,295.00	14,085.00				
River Surfer 8'	2,080.00	2,808.00	988.00	5,304.00	11,180.00				
River Surfer 8"6"	7,840.00	4,032.00	8,512.00	6,664.00	27,048.00				
River Surfer 9'	1,200.00	8,640.00	2,280.00	4,080.00	16,200.00				
MCIT Inflatable 10'6"	5,040.00	17,010.00	5,985.00	8,568.00	36,603.00				
Total	18,860.00	38,160.00	21,185.00	26,911.00	105,116.00				

Figure 2.17

Adding a Header to Your Worksheet

6 Scroll to the bottom of your worksheet.

7 Click the text **Add footer** located in the center footer text box, and then type **&[File]** into the footer. This will print the worksheet file name in the footer of each worksheet.

8 Press [**Tab**] and note the file name (ch2-02_student_name) in the Footer preview box with your name in place of student name.

9 Click outside the footer in any cell and then click **Normal** from the Workbook Views group on the View tab of the Ribbon.

10 Keep this file open.

Printing

Printing often requires three steps: previewing the print job, editing the page setup, and then finally printing the worksheet. Kyle suggests that, to save paper, these three steps should always be performed.

Using Print Preview and Page Setup

Previewing the print job will save you lots of paper and headaches, Kyle explains. A print preview is available from the File menu. In addition to previewing the print job, the Print window also gives you the option of zooming in on the print job, modifying margins, viewing page breaks, and printing the job.

Page Setup establishes the worksheet's page orientation and scaling, margin specifications, headers and footers (which we just addressed), and "sheet" provisions that include print area and print titles.

The Page section is the first tab, located on the far left of the Page Setup window. Here you can specify the page orientation (Portrait or Landscape). Kyle prefers the terms vertical and horizontal, which more accurately communicate the direction the worksheet will be printed on a standard 8½″ by 11″ piece of paper. If the worksheet is too big to print on just one sheet, the user can scale the printing by a percentage of its normal size or to fit on a specific number of pages.

The Margin section is the second tab. Here you can modify the header and footer depth as well as the top, bottom, right, and left margins. In addition, you can specify that the worksheet be centered on the page either horizontally, vertically, both, or neither.

The Sheet section allows you to restrict printing to a certain segment of the worksheet and to repeat titles at the top or left of the worksheet if your printing runs more than a single page. While editing worksheets, Kyle likes to print his work in process and take it on the road, where he doesn't have a computer. In this case, he prints the gridlines and row and column headings so he can write additional formulas by hand.

Kyle decides to modify the page setup for the Summary worksheet by specifying a portrait orientation, centering the worksheet horizontally, and with gridlines and row and column headings.

To preview a print job and edit the page setup of a worksheet:

1 Click the **File** menu and then click **Print**.

2 Select **Landscape** orientation option if it is not already selected (See Figure 2.18.).

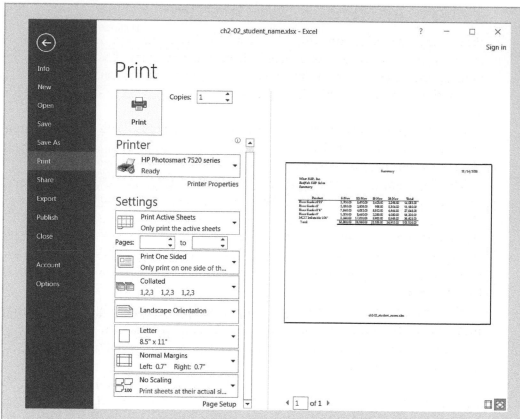

Figure 2.18

Print Options

3 Click **Page Setup** from the bottom of the screen and then click the **Margins** tab and then click the **Horizontally** checkbox on the Center on page section.

4 Click the **Sheet** tab and click the **Gridlines** and **Row and column headings** checkboxes.

5 Click the **Header/Footer** tab; note that your previous modifications to the header and footer (during the page layout) have been preserved here.

6 Click **OK**.

7 Click the **Zoom to Page** icon located in the lower right hand corner of the screen to magnify the pending print job, then use the scroll bars to move around your view of the print job. The preview portion of your window should look like Figure 2.19.

Figure 2.19

Print Preview with
Magnification

	A	B	C	D	E	F
			Summary			11/16/2015
1	What SUP, Inc.					
2	Badfish SUP Sales					
3	Summary					
4						
5	Product	5-Nov	12-Nov	19-Nov	26-Nov	Total
6	River Surfer 6'11"	2,700.00	5,670.00	3,420.00	2,295.00	14,085.00
7	River Surfer 8'	2,080.00	2,808.00	988.00	5,304.00	11,180.00
8	River Surfer 8"6"	7,840.00	4,032.00	8,512.00	6,664.00	27,048.00
9	River Surfer 9'	1,200.00	8,640.00	2,280.00	4,080.00	16,200.00
10	MCIT Inflatable 10'6"	5,040.00	17,010.00	5,985.00	8,568.00	36,603.00
11	Total	18,860.00	38,160.00	21,185.00	26,911.00	105,116.00

8 Keep this file open.

Printing a Worksheet

As already mentioned, you can print from the Print Preview window or print directly from the worksheet. Kyle once again suggests that you always preview your work before printing and thus that you get into the habit of printing from the Print Preview window.

The Print Preview window allows you to select a printer (assuming more than one printer is connected to your computer or network). In addition, you can specify the print range (which pages to print), what you wish to print (the entire workbook, the active sheet(s), or a specific selection you've already highlighted on the worksheet), and/or how many copies you want printed.

Meagan suggests you print one copy of the entire workbook with the gridlines and row and column headings specified previously as well as one copy of the summary worksheet without gridlines and row and column headings.

To print the workbook:

1 Click the Zoom to Page icon again to reduce the print preview window.

2 Select a printer from the Printer drop-down list and then select **Print Entire Workbook** from the Settings drop-down list.

3 Click **Print**. This should print five pages.

Trouble? You may have to modify which printer to print to in lab situations. Please see the lab consultant or your instructor for instructions.

4 Save your work.

Nathan notices that, when the workbook was printed in total, only the Summary worksheet had a header and footer. Kyle explains that this happened because you had set up the header and footer for the Summary worksheet only; thus, headers and footers for the remaining worksheets should not be expected.

Nathan also noticed that some worksheets printed in portrait view, and he suspects that this is due to not setting all worksheet to landscape as well.

Printing and Viewing Formulas

"Is there any way to look at a worksheet and see all the formulas in the worksheet without clicking on each cell?" Nathan asks.

"Yes," Kyle replies. "You can not only view the underlying formulas, but often you'll want to print them for later analysis."

Kyle offers to demonstrate this Excel feature and advises that, whenever you print a worksheet with formulas, you be sure to include gridlines and row and column headings for easy reference. He suggests you print the formulas found on the November 5 sheet.

To view and print formulas in a worksheet:

1 Click the return arrow (the arrow with a circle around it at the upper left-hand corner of the Print window) and then click the **November 5** worksheet.

2 While holding the **Ctrl** key down, press the [`] key (located just above the Tab key). This reveals all cells as formulas, a feature known as the Formula view. Observe that the columns become larger when you press these keys.

3 While holding the **Ctrl** key down, press the [`] key again and the worksheet reverts back to values (known as the Value view). Simultaneously, the columns return to their original, smaller size.

4 Switch to the Formula view once again. (While holding the **Ctrl** key down, press the [`] key.)

5 Resize each column so that all formulas are viewable. (This will require some columns to be widened and others to be narrowed.)

6 Click the **File** menu and then click **Print**. Note that printing this worksheet requires two pages, as indicated in the lower left corner of the Print Preview window.

7 Select **Landscape Orientation** if it is not already selected.

8 Select **Fit Sheet on One Page** from the last drop-down list, which should currently say No Scaling.

9 Click **Page Setup** and then click the **Sheet** tab and check the **Gridlines** and **Row and column headings** checkboxes (if they are not already selected) so that the worksheet, when printed, can help you decipher the formulas.

10 Click **OK** in the Page Setup window (note that printing now requires only one page, as specified in the lower part of the window). Your print Preview screen should look like Figure 2.20.

Figure 2.20

Print Preview of
Worksheet Formulas

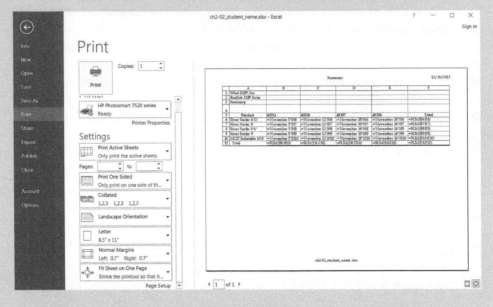

11 Click **Print** in the Print Preview window.

12 Click **OK** in the Print window.

13 While holding the **Ctrl** key down, press the [`] key and so return to Value view.

14 Resize all columns so that all values are shown.

15 Close the worksheet and save your changes.

Kyle explains that printing the Formula view is an effective way of examining your worksheet logic and correcting any errors. It also allows you to view the formula logic when a computer is not available.

"That's a lot to grasp in one sitting," you complain.

"Oh there's a lot more to come, but let's take a break and start again tomorrow," Kyle says.

End Note

The three of you are somewhat overwhelmed by the capabilities of Excel but are pleased with what you've accomplished. You've learned some basics about Excel's help system, how to work with files, and how to enter information into a worksheet, use formulas, manipulate data, structure a worksheet, and print worksheets in both Value and Formula views.

In the next chapter, you will learn how to use Excel to create financial statements.

Chapter 2 Questions

1 Explain how information is entered into an Excel worksheet.

2 Identify the difference between labels and values.

3 What does it mean when a cell or cells in a worksheet include a series of # signs?

4 Explain the process for changing column width or row height.

5 How do you control the appearance of data in a worksheet?

6 What does the Format Painter tool do?

7 How are formulas written in Excel?

8 Explain the arguments used in the SUM function.

9 Explain the importance of parentheses in formulas.

10 How does the AutoFill feature of Excel help the worksheet user?

11 Why would you want to use absolute references instead of relative references?

12 How do you change a relative reference to an absolute reference?

13 Describe the procedure used to insert a column or row into a worksheet.

14 How do you change the name of a sheet in a workbook?

15 What is the recommended procedure for printing a workbook or worksheet?

Chapter 2 Assignments

1 Create a trial balance for What SUP as of March 31, 2019

You are to create a trial balance in a format identical to that created in this chapter. Include a debit and credit column, totals for each column, and appropriate labels and formatting. Start with blank spreadsheet and once you have created the spreadsheet save the file as ch2-03_student_name (replacing student_name with your name). An alphabetical listing of account information as of March 31, 2019, follows.

Accounts payable	80,000.00
Accounts receivable	95,000.00
Accumulated depreciation: Building	60,000.00
Accumulated depreciation: Equipment	17,000.00
Advertising expense	15,000.00

Building	405,000.00
Cash	30,000.00
Common stock	1,000.00
Cost of goods sold	345,000.00
Depreciation expense	5,000.00
Equipment	98,000.00
Inventory	120,000.00
Land	115,000.00
Long-term debt	500,000.00
Other expense	4,000.00
Payroll expense	72,000.00
Prepaid expenses	14,000.00
Retained earnings	135,000.00
Sales revenue	550,000.00
Supplies	10,000.00
Utilities expense	15,000.00

a. Print the completed worksheet in Value view, with your name and date printed in the lower left footer and file name in the lower right footer.

b. Print the completed worksheet in Formula view, retaining gridlines and row and column headings, with your name and date printed in the lower left footer and file name in the lower right footer.

2 Modify What SUP Sales Worksheet

Using the student file Ch2-04.xlsx, add appropriate formulas to the existing Fanatic SUP Sales worksheet to calculate price, total sales for each SUP for the week, and total sales for all Fanatic SUP. Complete this worksheet in a manner consistent with the Weekly Badfish SUP Sales worksheet completed in this chapter.

a. Print the completed worksheet in Value view, with gridlines and row and column headings and with your name and date printed in the lower left footer and file name in the lower right footer.

b. Print the completed worksheet in Formula view, retaining gridlines and row and column headings, with your name and date printed in the lower left footer and file name in the lower right footer.

Chapter 2 Case Problem 1:
KELLY'S BOUTIQUE

Kelly's Boutique, located in Pewaukee, Wisconsin, sells a unique combination of books and women's shoes. Customers love to peruse her book inventory while trying on the latest in shoe fashions, often buying both books and shoes even though they came in to buy only one type of merchandise. Casey, Kelly's youngest son, a college student studying accounting, is home for the holidays and can't wait to help his mom come in from the dark ages and use computers in her business. Throughout this text Casey will make every attempt to bring his mom up to speed by teaching her the use of Excel and Access as they apply to her accounting and business needs.

To begin, Casey suggests that Kelly use a worksheet to make a list of her book inventory. She doesn't maintain a large inventory, but she does carry books that she thinks moms in the community might be interested in reading or buying as gifts for their children or friends.

Start with worksheet ch2-05. Format this worksheet using bold and italics formatting for the titles and bold and border formatting for the column names. Add formulas for column E to compute the sales price as list price less the discount specified. Add the following two books and related information to the list. (Be sure the list maintains its alphabetic organization by inserting rows in the correct place.)

Dept	Product	Author	List Price
Children	Make Way for Ducklings	McClosky	17.99
Adult	Snow Falling on Cedars	Guterson	21.95

Insert a new column D with the title "On Hand" in bold, centered, and center justified. Change the formatting of the column to no decimals. Add the following on hand values to column D.

Product	Author	On Hand
Angela's Ashes	McCourt	5
Betsy – Tacy	Lovelace	2
Blueberries for Sal	McCloskey	2
Caddie Woodlawn	Brink	1
Deep End of the Ocean	Mitchard	4
Divine Secrets of the YaYa Sisterhood	Wells	3
Green Eggs and Ham	Seuss	1
Harry Potter and the Chamber of Secrets	Rowling	4
Harry Potter and the Prisoner of Azkaban	Rowling	3
Harry Potter and the Sorcerer's Stone	Rowling	2
Hop on Pop	Seuss	1
Horse Whisperer	Evans	2
Lentil	McCloskey	2
Make Way for Ducklings	McCloskey	2
Memoirs of a Geisha	Golden	4
Message in a Bottle	Sparks	2
One Morning in Maine	McCloskey	1
Snow Falling on Cedars	Guterson	2
The Cat in the Hat	Seuss	1
The Notebook	Sparks	3

Add a "Total" label in cell B27 and a SUM function in cell D27 to add up the quantity of books on hand. Change the name of Sheet1 to "8% Discount." Create a copy of this worksheet and place it before Sheet2. Change the name of the newly created worksheet to "12% Discount." Change the discount in cell F1 of this worksheet to 12%. Save the file as ch2-05_student_name (replacing student_name with your name).

a.   Print the completed 8% Discount worksheet in Value view, with your name and date printed in the lower left footer and file name in the lower right footer.

b.   Print the completed 12% Discount worksheet in Value view, with your name and date printed in the lower left footer and file name in the lower right footer.

c.   Print the completed 8% Discount worksheet in Formula view, with gridlines and row and column headings, landscape orientation, scaling to fit to 1 page wide by 1 page tall, and with your name and date printed in the lower left footer and file name in the lower right footer.

d.   Print the completed 12% Discount worksheet in Formula view, with gridlines and row and column headings, landscape orientation, scaling to fit to 1 page wide by 1 page tall, and with your name and date printed in the lower left footer and file name in the lower right footer.

Chapter 2 Case Problem 2:
WINE DEPOT

The Wine Depot, located in Santa Barbara, California, imports and sells high-quality wine from around the world. Owner Barbara Fairfield is curious to see how Excel might help her manage the business and account for its inventory. Her husband, Bud, is the accountant in the family but hasn't had much experience with Excel. He's hired you to help him construct several worksheets to help the business better understand the financial and managerial aspects of the company.

To begin, you decide to create a worksheet of some of Barbara's wine inventory. Start with worksheet ch2-06. Format the company name and worksheet title bold and italics. Format the title of each column of data bold with a bottom border. Format all values for the column Price as Accounting Number Format. Add two column labels, Quantity and Value, to the right of the existing data and then insert quantity amounts as shown below [Note: SKU (Stock Keeping Unit) is a unique identifier for each of the distinct products and services that can be ordered from a supplier.]:

SKU	Quantity
17521	4
16716	10
16528	12
16739	5
15347	7
17539	3
11599	1
14539	5
17840	12
13883	12
15966	24
17454	24

SKU	Quantity
17024	10
16554	8
17425	7
17549	3
17578	2
17275	1

Insert a formula to calculate value as quantity times price in cell I9, then fill-down this formula for all cells in the table. Insert a text label "Total" in cell H28 and a formula to calculate the total value in cell I28. Insert two additional rows after row 26. Add two American Syrah wines in those two rows: Carhatt, $34 (750 ml, year 2014, SKU 16769), quantity 10; and Cafaro, $35 (750 ml, year 2014, SKU 16874), quantity 15. Delete the row containing the American Merlot from Wildhorse. Change the formatting of the Price and Value columns to include no decimals. After using Excel's Help function to learn how to sort items in a worksheet, sort the information on your worksheet by location, by type, and then by winery, in A to Z order. Change the name of Sheet1 to "Pricing." Create a copy of this worksheet and place it before Sheet2, then change the name of this sheet to "Cost." Add a label at cell C4 of the Cost sheet called "Cost %" in Bold, Italics. Type 60% as the cost percentage in cell D4 of the Cost sheet. (Make sure this cell is formatted as a percent.) Change the name of the column "Value" to "Cost." Create a new formula in cell I9 to calculate cost as Price times Cost % times Quantity. (Be sure to use absolute or relative references where appropriate.) Fill the formula in cell I9 down to all items. Save the file as ch2-06_student_name (replacing student_name with your name).

a. Print the completed Pricing worksheet in Value view, with landscape orientation, scaling to fit to 1 page wide by 1 page tall, and with your name and date printed in the lower left footer and file name in the lower right footer.

b. Print the completed Cost worksheet in Value view, with landscape orientation, scaling to fit to 1 page wide by 1 page tall, and with your name and date printed in the lower left footer and file name in the lower right footer.

c. Print the completed Pricing worksheet in Formula view, with gridlines and row and column headings, landscape orientation, scaling to fit to 1 page wide by 1 page tall, and with your name and date printed in the lower left footer and file name in the lower right footer.

d. Print the completed Cost worksheet in Formula view, with gridlines and row and column headings, landscape orientation, scaling to fit to 1 page wide by 1 page tall, and with your name and date printed in the lower left footer and file name in the lower right footer.

Chapter 2 Case Problem 3:
SNICK'S BOARD SHOP

Snick's Board Shop is located in La Jolla, California, and specializes in complete and longboard skateboards and equipment. Owner Casey "Snick" Miller is curious to see how Excel might help him manage the business and account for its inventory. His girlfriend Caitlin handles the financial aspects of the business but hasn't had much experience with Excel. They have hired you to help him construct several worksheets to help the business better understand the financial and managerial aspects of the company.

To begin, you decide to create a worksheet of Snick's inventory. Start with worksheet ch2-07 and make the following changes:

1 Format the company name and worksheet title bold and italics.

2 Format the title of each column (located in row 5) bold with a bottom border.

3 Format all values for the column Price as Accounting Number Format.

4 If necessary, resize all columns and rows so that data does not wrap.

5 Add one column (titled Quantity) to the right of column Product # and then type 10 as the quantity for all items. Add an additional column (titled Retail Value) to the right of column Quantity. Format both column titles as all other column titles.

6 Insert a formula to calculate the retail value as quantity times price in cell I6, then fill down this formula for all cells in the table.

7 Insert a text label "Total" in cell G19 and a formula to calculate the total retail value of all products in cell H19.

8 Format cell H19 with a top and bottom double border.

9 Insert two additional rows after row 9.

10 Add two products in rows 10 and 11 as follows.

Category	Ramp	Ramp
Manufacturer	Element	Mojo
Product Name	Element Launch Ramp	Mojo Wedge Ramp
Price	209.99	215.99
Style	Black/Red	Black/Blue
Product #	65-01837	65-00011
Quantity	5	8

11 Change the name of Sheet1 to "Retail Value."

12 Create a copy of this worksheet and place it before Sheet2, then change the name of this sheet to "Cost."

13 Add a label at cell E2 of the Cost sheet called "Cost %" in Bold, Italics.

14 Type **40%** as the cost percentage in cell F2 of the Cost sheet. Change the name of the column "Retail Value" to "Cost." Center the Cost title.

15 Create a new formula in cell H6 to calculate cost as Price times Cost % times Quantity. (Be sure to use absolute or relative references where appropriate.) Fill the formula in cell H6 down to all items.

16 Save the file as ch2-07_student_name (replacing student_name with your name).

   a. Print the completed Retail Value worksheet in Value view, with landscape orientation, scaling to fit to 1 page wide by 1 page tall, and with your name and date printed in the lower left footer and file name in the lower right footer.

   b. Print the completed Cost worksheet in Value view, with landscape orientation, scaling to fit to 1 page wide by 1 page tall, and with your name and date printed in the lower left footer and file name in the lower right footer.

   c. Print the completed Retail Value worksheet in Formula view, with gridlines and row and column headings, landscape orientation, scaling to fit to 1 page wide by 1 page tall, and with your name and date printed in the lower left footer and file name in the lower right footer. Resize column D to 330 pixels and all other cells so that formulas are viewable. Don't save these changes.

   d. Print the completed Cost worksheet in Formula view, with gridlines and row and column headings, landscape orientation, scaling to fit to 1 page wide by 1 page tall, and with your name and date printed in the lower left footer and file name in the lower right footer. Resize column D to 330 pixels and all other cells so that formulas are viewable. Don't save these changes.

Chapter 2 Case Problem 4:
ROSEY'S ROSES

Rosey's Roses is located in Savannah, Georgia, and specializes in the sale of roses. You, as the manager of the business, are curious to see how Excel might help you manage the business and account for its inventory. To that end, you have hired a local college student to construct several worksheets to help the business better understand the financial and managerial aspects of the company.

    To begin, the two of you decide to create a worksheet of Rosey's inventory. Start with worksheet ch2-08 and make the following changes:

1   Format the company name and worksheet title bold and italics.

2   Move the company name and worksheet title from column C to column A.

3   Format the title of each column (located in row 4) bold with a bottom border.

4   Add a column (titled Quantity) to the right of column Description.

5   Format the Quantity title aligned centered, bold with a bottom border.

6   Format the values under the Quantity title as comma style with no decimals.

7   Resize column C to 95 pixels.

8   Add an additional column (titled Cost/Unit) to the right of column Quantity.

9   Format the Cost/Unit title aligned centered, bold with a bottom border.

10   Format the values under the Cost/Unit title as currency.

11   Resize column D to 115 pixels.

12   Add an additional column (titled Cost) to the right of column Cost/Unit.

13   Format the Cost title aligned centered, bold with a bottom border.

14   Format the values under the Cost title as currency.

15   Resize column E to 115 pixels.

16   Enter the following values for Quantity and Cost/unit

Type	Description	Quantity	Cost/Unit
Shrub	Abraham Darby #5	25	$39.99
Shrub	Be My Baby #5	40	$18.99
Shrub	Deja Blu #5	18	$25.99
Shrub	Koko Loko #7	17	$17.99
Shrub	Peach Drift #10	33	$18.99
Shrub	Red Drift #10	15	$ 6.99
Shrub	Sedona #5	3	$14.99
Shrub	Sweet Intoxication #5	20	$ 9.99
Climber	Climbing Orange Crush #7	16	$32.99
Climber	Don Juan Climber #5	25	$37.99
Tree	Barbara Streisand 36in Tree	50	$52.99
Tree	Firefighter 36in Tree	14	$55.99
Tree	Trumpeter 36in Tree	4	$65.99

17   Insert a formula to calculate the cost as quantity times cost/unit in cell E5.

18   Format this cell aligned right.

19   Fill down this formula for all cells in the table.

20 Insert a row below the last shrub listed.

21 Add one additional item into your newly added row with a type "Shrub," description "Wing Ding #5," quantity "20," and cost/unit "13.99."

22 Type Total in cell A20.

23 Insert a formula to calculate the total cost of all roses into cell E20.

24 Format cell E20 to align right with a top and double bottom border.

25 Save the file as ch2-08_student_name (replacing student_name with your name).

    a.   Print the completed worksheet in Value view, with portrait orientation with your name and date printed in the lower left footer and file name in the lower right footer.

    b.   Print the completed worksheet in Formula view with gridlines and row and column headers, with portrait orientation, with your name and date printed in the lower left footer and the file name in the lower right footer.

3

Financial Statement Analysis

In this chapter you will learn:

- How to perform a vertical financial analysis
- How to create a pie chart of expenses
- How to perform a horizontal financial analysis
- How to create a column chart of expenses
- How to calculate financial ratios

Case: **What SUP, Inc.**

Nathan and Meagan are ready to evaluate the company's performance, examine trends and relationships, and assess liquidity and solvency. Kyle suggests three forms of analysis that can provide information to Nathan and Meagan for business decision making: vertical, horizontal, and ratio analysis.

You recall learning about these three methods of analysis while studying financial accounting. Kyle reminds you that Excel is a great tool for preparing these analyses and suggests that you take the lead in explaining the formulas used in creating these types of worksheets.

"Can Excel also help us prepare charts? We have to prepare some information for our bankers, and they seem to prefer both numbers and charts," Nathan asks. "Most definitely!" Kyle answers. "We'll use Excel to look at the financial information we recently created, and then we'll compute vertical, horizontal, and ratio analyses as well as prepare charts to describe important relationships and trends."

Vertical Analysis

Video Demonstration

DEMO 3A Vertical analysis with a pie chart

Vertical analysis, often referred to as *component* analysis, is used to express each item on a particular financial statement as a percentage of a single base amount. In an income statement, the base is sales revenue. Each expense is expressed as a percentage of sales revenue. Meagan seems very interested in comparing what percentages of revenues are spent on various expenses and how that compares from one period to the next.

To create a vertical analysis on an income statement:

1 Click **File** and then click **Open**.

---

2 Navigate the Open window to the location of this text's student files. (The location would be wherever you saved the downloaded student files from Cengage or from your computer lab's server.)

3 Double-click the file **ch3-01**, which should be located in a Ch 03 folder. (You may have to click **Enable Editing** before you begin.)

4 Click the **Income Statement** tab if it is not already active.

5 Right-click column **C** and click **Insert** to insert a new column.

6 Click cell **C4** and type **%** as a label to the new column.

7 Click cell **C5** and type the formula **=B5/$B$5**; then press [**Enter**]. (*Note:* use an absolute reference in the denominator so you can fill down the formula later.)

8 Click cell **C5** again and reformat the cell by clicking the **%** tool in the Number group of the Home tab.

9 Resize column C to reveal the value in cell C5.

10 Fill down the formula in C5 to C16 by dragging the handle in the lower right corner of cell C5 to C16. (*Note:* this will also copy down the formatting from cell C5, removing border formats that you can fix later.)

11 Eliminate the formula from cell C8 by clicking the cell and pressing [**Delete**], then [**Enter**].

12 Add appropriate border formats to cells C6, C13, and C16.

13 Repeat Steps 6 to 11 in column E, substituting E for C in all column references. Substitute D for B in the formulas. Your worksheet should look like Figure 3.1.

	A	B	C	D	E
1		What SUP, Inc.			
2		Income Statement			
3		For the Year Ended			
4		12/31/18	%	12/31/19	%
5	Sales Revenue	$ 850,511.65	100%	$ 925,614.50	100%
6	Less: Cost of Goods Sold	442,619.87	52%	489,547.25	53%
7	Gross Margin	407,891.78	48%	436,067.25	47%
8	Expenses:				
9	Advertising	20,654.21	2%	25,124.88	3%
10	Depreciation	22,000.00	3%	23,000.00	2%
11	Interest	40,846.24	5%	38,412.11	4%
12	Other	5,421.55	1%	3,200.74	0%
13	Payroll	115,365.11	14%	126,141.84	14%
14	Utilities	23,541.25	3%	24,788.14	3%
15	Net income before taxes	180,063.42	21%	195,399.54	21%
16	Income taxes	65,218.98	8%	69,451.14	8%
17	Net income	$ 114,844.44	14%	$ 125,948.40	14%

Figure 3.1

Income Statement Vertical Analysis

14 Click **File** again and then click **Save As**. (This preserves your original student and provides a unique name for your file.)

15 Change the file name to reflect the vertical analysis just performed and your name by using the underscore key as before. In this example, the file will be saved as ch3-01_Vertical_Analysis_student_name (replace student_name with your name). Save your file to a location (e.g., a USB drive) from which you can retrieve it later.

16 Switch to a Page Layout view. Place your name in the left section of the footer. Note that the file name is already in the right section of the footer.

17 Switch back to a Normal view.

18 Click **File** and then click **Print** to make sure the worksheet will print the way you want.

19 Click **Print** to print your analysis.

20 Save your file once again but do not close it.

Meagan is pleased that Excel can produce these amounts so quickly. She notes that the firm's gross profit percentage is down from the previous year and that the cost of goods sold as a percentage of sales is higher. This helps explain the reduction in net income as a percentage of sales.

"Is the balance sheet used for vertical analysis as well?" Nathan asks. "Yes," you respond.

In a balance sheet the base is total assets. Each asset, liability, and equity component is expressed as a percentage of total assets.

To create a vertical analysis on a balance sheet:

1 Click the **Home** tab and then click the **Balance Sheet** worksheet tab.

2 Right-click column **C** and click **Insert** to insert a new column.

3 Click cell **C5** and type **%** as a label to the new column.

4 Click cell **C7** and type the formula **=B7/$B$17**, then press [**Enter**]. (*Note:* Once again, use an absolute reference in the denominator so you can fill down the formula later.)

5 Click cell **C7** again and reformat the cell by clicking the **%** tool in the Number group of the Home tab.

6 Resize column C to 61 pixels.

7 Fill down the formula in C7 to C17 by dragging the handle in the lower right corner of cell C7 to C17. (*Note:* This will also copy down the formatting from cell C7, removing border formats that you can fix later.)

8 Eliminate the formula from cell C12 by clicking the cell and pressing [**Delete**], then [**Enter**].

9 Add appropriate border formats to cell C17.

10 Repeat Steps 3 to 9 in column E, substituting E for C in all column references. The asset part of your worksheet should look like Figure 3.2.

	A	B	C	D	E
1	*What SUP, Inc.*				
2	*Balance Sheet*				
3	*as of*				
4					
5	**Assets**	**12/31/18**	**%**	**12/31/19**	**%**
6	Current Assets:				
7	Cash	$ 25,412.35	4%	$ 20,182.15	3%
8	Accounts Receivable	66,365.79	10%	102,544.24	14%
9	Inventory	125,351.45	18%	152,154.21	20%
10	Prepaid Expenses	15,625.26	2%	15,241.75	2%
11	Supplies	10,245.15	1%	9,877.65	1%
12	Property, Plant, and Equipment:				
13	Land	120,000.00	17%	120,000.00	16%
14	Building	300,000.00	43%	315,000.00	42%
15	Equipment	95,000.00	14%	105,000.00	14%
16	Less: Accumulated Depreciation	(68,000.00)	–10%	(90,000.00)	–12%
17	Total	$ 690,000.00	100%	$ 750,000.00	100%

Figure 3.2

Balance Sheet Assets
Vertical Analysis

11 Save your work.

12 Click cell **C22** and type the formula **=B22/$B$28**; then press [**Enter**]. (*Note:* Again, use an absolute reference in the denominator.)

13 Click cell **C22** again and reformat the cell by clicking the **%** tool in the Number group of the Home tab.

14 Fill down the formula in C22 to C28 by dragging the handle in the lower right corner of cell C22 to C28. (*Note:* This will also copy down the formatting from cell C22, removing border formats that you can fix later.)

15 Eliminate the formula from cell C25 by clicking the cell and pressing [**Delete**], then [**Enter**].

16 Add appropriate border formats to cell C29.

17 Repeat Steps 12 to 16 in column E, substituting E for C in all column references. The liability and equity part of your worksheet should look like Figure 3.3.

18 Switch to a Page Layout view. Place your name in the left section of the footer. Note that the file name is already in the right section of the footer.

19 Switch back to a Normal view.

20 Click **File** and then click **Print** to make sure the worksheet will print the way you want.

Figure 3.3

Balance Sheet Liabilities and Equities Vertical Analysis

	A	B	C	D	E
19	**Liabilities and Stockholders' Equity**				
20	Liabilities				
21	Current Liabilities:				
22	Accounts Payable	$ 75,182.10	11%	$ 66,095.32	9%
23	Payroll Liabilities	5,013.87	1%	8,152.25	1%
24	Long-Term Debt	400,000.00	58%	320,000.00	43%
25	Stockholders' Equity				
26	Common Stock	110,000.00	16%	130,000.00	17%
27	Retained Earnings	99,804.03	14%	225,752.43	30%
28	Total	$ 690,000.00	100%	$ 750,000.00	100%

◄ ►   Income Statement   **Balance Sheet**   ⊕   ┇ ◄

21 Click **Print** to print your analysis.

22 Save your file but do not close it.

Once again Meagan notes some interesting facts from the vertical analysis of the balance sheet. A larger percentage of total assets are invested in accounts receivable and inventory than in the prior year. Yet long-term debt is down, offset by an increase in retained earnings as a percentage of total assets.

To complete the vertical analysis, you offer to demonstrate Excel's charting capability by creating a pie chart of expenses for the year ended December 31, 2019.

Pie Charts

"Excel's chart wizard makes creating a chart from a worksheet a breeze," you remark. "This will give you a graphical picture of the firm's expenses as a percentage of revenues."

To create a pie chart of expenses:

1 Click on **Income Statement** worksheet tab and select cells **D9** through **D14**.

2 Click the **Insert** tab on the Ribbon and then click the **Pie Chart** tool on the Charts group.

3 Select **3-D Pie** as shown in Figure 3.4. **Trouble?** If your window is too small you may not see Pie as an option in the Charts group and instead will only see the text Charts. Widen the window to reveal the chart options available or click the Charts group and select Pie.

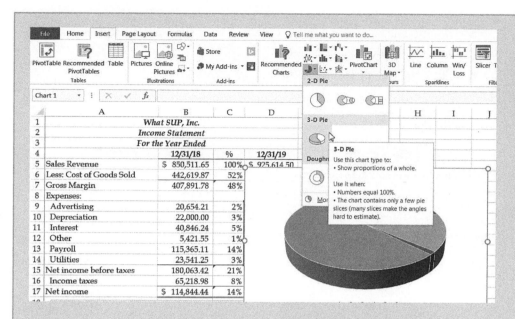

Figure 3.4

Creating a New Pie Chart

4 In the Chart Layouts group select **Style 6**. See Figure 3.5. Your window may look different if it is sized larger. If so just select Layout 6 from the Chart Layouts group.

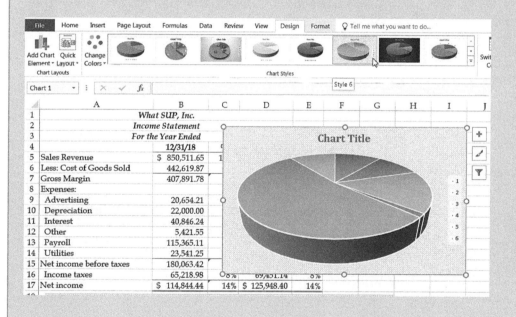

Figure 3.5

Modifying a Chart Layout

5 Double-click the text **Chart Title** and then type **2019 Expenses** as the new chart title.

6 Click the **Select Data** tool in the Data group.

7 Click **Edit** under the text Horizontal (Category) Axis Labels as shown in Figure 3.6.

Figure 3.6

Editing the Pie Chart Axis Labels

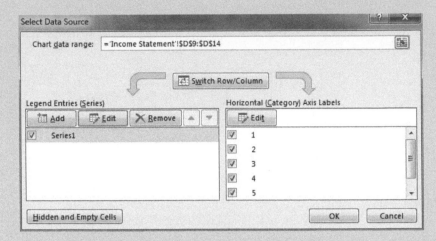

8 Type **='Income Statement'!$A$9:$A$14** as the Axis label range and then click **OK**. (Alternatively, you could click the button on the right-hand side of the window and then select the range A9:A14 instead of typing the cell location.)

9 Click **OK** to close the Select Data Source window.

10 Click anywhere in the chart and, holding the mouse button down, drag the new chart so that it appears below the data.

11 Click in the lower right-hand corner of the chart and, holding the mouse button down, resize the chart so that it fits in the window; see Figure 3.7.

12 With the chart still selected, click **File** and then click **Print** to make sure the chart will print the way you want.

13 Click **Print** to then print the chart.

14 Save your work and then close the file.

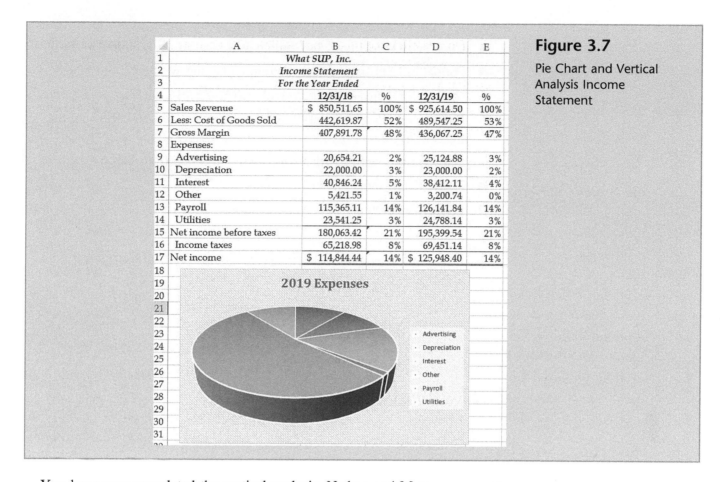

	A	B	C	D	E
1	What SUP, Inc.				
2	Income Statement				
3	For the Year Ended				
4		12/31/18	%	12/31/19	%
5	Sales Revenue	$ 850,511.65	100%	$ 925,614.50	100%
6	Less: Cost of Goods Sold	442,619.87	52%	489,547.25	53%
7	Gross Margin	407,891.78	48%	436,067.25	47%
8	Expenses:				
9	Advertising	20,654.21	2%	25,124.88	3%
10	Depreciation	22,000.00	3%	23,000.00	2%
11	Interest	40,846.24	5%	38,412.11	4%
12	Other	5,421.55	1%	3,200.74	0%
13	Payroll	115,365.11	14%	126,141.84	14%
14	Utilities	23,541.25	3%	24,788.14	3%
15	Net income before taxes	180,063.42	21%	195,399.54	21%
16	Income taxes	65,218.98	8%	69,451.14	8%
17	Net income	$ 114,844.44	14%	$ 125,948.40	14%
18					
19	**2019 Expenses**				
20					
21					

Figure 3.7

Pie Chart and Vertical Analysis Income Statement

You have now completed the vertical analysis. Nathan and Meagan are eager to examine the percentages and the chart more carefully, but not until they see how horizontal and ratio analyses can be created in Excel.

Horizontal Analysis

Horizontal analysis examines trends over time. This can include comparisons of months, quarters, or years for both the income statement and the balance sheet. Income statements and balance sheets for two or more periods are compared side by side, and a percentage increase or decrease is computed between periods.

"Isn't that what we just did in vertical analysis?" Meagan asks. Kyle replies: "The percentages computed in vertical analysis are usually done for just one period, although they are often compared period to period. Remember, vertical analysis compares each statement element with a single base amount, such as sales or total assets, whereas horizontal analysis compares elements side by side with other periods."

To create a horizontal analysis on an income statement:

1 Open ch3-01 (This is the same file you opened for vertical analysis. It should still look the same, because the changes you made were saved under another file name.)

2 Click the **Home** tab on the Ribbon and then click the **Income Statement** worksheet tab if it is not already active.

3 Click cell **D4** and type **% Change** as a label to the column.

4 Format cell D4 bold, center, bottom align, and with a bottom border.

5 Click cell **D5** and type the formula **=(C5–B5)/B5**; then press [**Enter**].

6 Format cell D5 as Percent Style by clicking cell **D5** and selecting the **Percent Style** tool on the Number group on the Home tab.

7 Use the fill-down procedure to copy the formula from D5 to D17.

8 Delete the formula in cell D8.

9 Format cells D6 and D14 with a bottom border.

10 Format cell D17 with a top and double bottom border.

11 Resize column D to 96 pixels. Your completed income statement with horizontal analysis should look like Figure 3.8.

Figure 3.8

Income Statement
Horizontal Analysis

	A	B	C	D
1	What SUP, Inc.			
2	Income Statement			
3	For the Year Ended			
4		12/31/18	12/31/19	% Change
5	Sales Revenue	$ 850,511.65	$ 925,614.50	9%
6	Less: Cost of Goods Sold	442,619.87	489,547.25	11%
7	Gross Margin	407,891.78	436,067.25	7%
8	Expenses:			
9	Advertising	20,654.21	25,124.88	22%
10	Depreciation	22,000.00	23,000.00	5%
11	Interest	40,846.24	38,412.11	-6%
12	Other	5,421.55	3,200.74	-41%
13	Payroll	115,365.11	126,141.84	9%
14	Utilities	23,541.25	24,788.14	5%
15	Net income before taxes	180,063.42	195,399.54	9%
16	Income taxes	65,218.98	69,451.14	6%
17	Net income	$ 114,844.44	$ 125,948.40	10%

12 Click **File** and then click **Save As**. (Again, this preserves the original file by giving a unique name to your file.)

13 Change the file name to include a reference to your horizontal analysis, and then add your name to the file name using the underscore key as before. In this example, the file will be saved as ch3-01_Horizontal_Analysis_student_name (replace student_name with your name). Save your file to a location from which it can be retrieved later.

14 Switch to a Page Layout view. Place your name in the left section of the footer. Note that the file name is already in the right section of the footer.

15 Switch back to a Normal view.

16 Click **File** and then **Print** to make sure the worksheet will print the way you want.

17 Click **Print** to print your analysis.

18 Save your file but do not close it.

"The trends shown here are good and bad," Nathan says. "The analysis reveals an increase in sales of 9 percent but a 11 percent increase in the costs of goods sold."

Kyle explains that the income statement analysis reveals operational and profitability performance and trends while the balance sheet reflects financial stability and solvency trends. The horizontal analysis on the balance sheet compares current balances for each asset, liability, and equity element with the same element in the prior period.

To create a horizontal analysis on a balance sheet:

1 Click the **Home** tab on the Ribbon and then click the **Balance Sheet** worksheet tab.

2 Click in cell D5 and type **% Change** as a label to the column.

3 Format cell D5 bold, center, bottom align, and with a bottom border.

4 Click in cell D7 and type the formula **=(C7–B7)/B7**; then press **[Enter]**.

5 Format cell D7 as Percent Style.

6 Use the fill-down procedure to copy the formula from D7 to D28.

7 Delete the formula in cells D12, D18–D21, and D25.

8 Format cells D17 and D29 with a top and double bottom border.

9 Resize column D to 93 pixels. Your completed balance sheet horizontal analysis should look like Figure 3.9.

10 Switch to a Page Layout view. Place your name in the left section of the footer. Note that the file name is already in the right section of the footer.

11 Switch back to a Normal view.

12 Click **File** and then **Print** to make sure the worksheet will print the way you want.

13 Click **Print** to print your analysis.

14 Save your file once again.

Figure 3.9

Balance Sheet
Horizontal Analysis

	A	B	C	D
1	What SUP, Inc.			
2	Balance Sheet			
3	as of			
4				
5	Assets	12/31/18	12/31/19	% Change
6	Current Assets:			
7	Cash	$ 25,412.35	$ 20,182.15	-21%
8	Accounts Receivable	66,365.79	102,544.24	55%
9	Inventory	125,351.45	152,154.21	21%
10	Prepaid Expenses	15,625.26	15,241.75	-2%
11	Supplies	10,245.15	9,877.65	-4%
12	Property, Plant, and Equipment:			
13	Land	120,000.00	120,000.00	0%
14	Building	300,000.00	315,000.00	5%
15	Equipment	95,000.00	105,000.00	11%
16	Less: Accumulated Depreciation	(68,000.00)	(90,000.00)	32%
17	Total	$ 690,000.00	$ 750,000.00	9%
18				
19	Liabilities and Stockholders' Equity			
20	Liabilities			
21	Current Liabilities:			
22	Accounts Payable	$ 75,182.10	$ 66,095.32	-12%
23	Payroll Liabilities	5,013.87	8,152.25	63%
24	Long-Term Debt	400,000.00	320,000.00	-20%
25	Stockholders' Equity			
26	Common Stock	110,000.00	130,000.00	18%
27	Retained Earnings	99,804.03	225,752.43	126%
28	Total	$ 690,000.00	$ 750,000.00	9%
29				

"I'm a little concerned about the 55 percent growth in accounts receivable, the 21 percent growth in inventory, and the 21 percent decrease in cash," Meagan says. Kyle reminds her that, when those events occurred, long-term debt decreased 20 percent and retained earnings increased 126 percent. "Excel can also provide some graphical evidence of these trends by creating column charts using the chart wizard," Kyle says.

Column Charts

Previously you created a pie chart of expenses using Excel's Chart Wizard. Now it is time to create a column chart comparing expenses from one period to the next. This column chart will illustrate expenses side by side for the two years ended December 31, 2018, and December, 31, 2019.

To create a column chart comparing expenses:

1 Click the **Income Statement** worksheet tab.

2 Select cells **A9** through **C14** (expenses for both periods).

3 Click the **Insert** tab on the Ribbon and then click the **Column** chart tool from the Charts group.

4 Select **3-D Column** as the chart type as shown in Figure 3.10.

Figure 3.10

Creating a Column Chart

5 Click and hold down the mouse on the top border of the chart created; then move the chart to a location below the data.

6 Scroll down the worksheet so that row 8 is at the top of your screen and the chart is fully visible, as shown in Figure 3.11.

Figure 3.11

Modifying a Column Chart

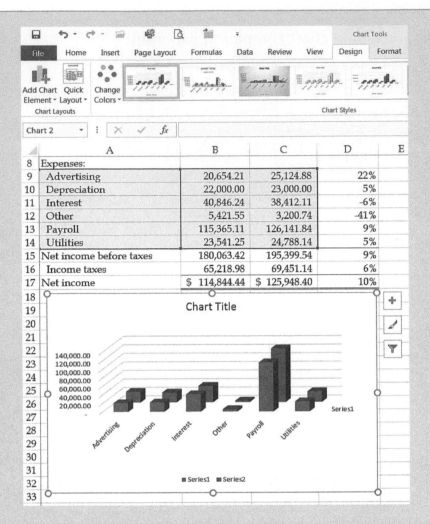

7 Note that the Design tab is now selected and Chart Tools are visible in the Ribbon.

8 Click **Select Data** from the Data group.

9 Click **Series1** from the Legend Entries (Series) section (see Figure 3.12).

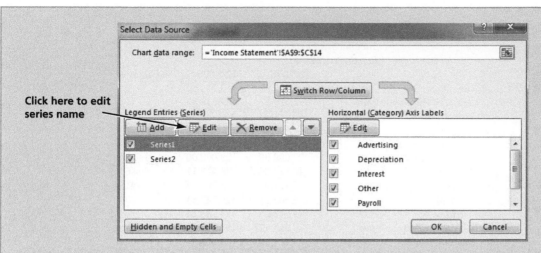

Figure 3.12

Editing a Data Source

10 Click **Edit**.

11 Click inside the **Series name** text box and the click in cell **B4**. This should enter the formula ="Income Statement"!$B$4 the Series name text box. Click **OK**.

12 Click **Series2** from the Legend Entries (Series) section.

13 Click **Edit**.

14 Click inside the **Series name** text box and the click in cell **C4**. This should enter the formula ="Income Statement"!$C$4 into the Series name text box. Click **OK**.

15 Click **OK** again in the Select Data Source window.

16 Click **Quick Layout** from the Charts Layouts group and then Click **Layout 1**. Your window may look different if it is sized larger. If so just select Layout 1 from the Chart Layouts group.

17 Type **Expense Comparison** as the new chart title.

18 Click **File** and then click **Save As**.

19 Change the file name to include a reference to column charts, and add your name to the file name using the underscore key as you have done previously. In this example, the file will be saved as ch3-01_ Column_Chart_student_name (replace student_name with your name). Be sure to save your file to a location that you can access later.

20 Click **File** and then click **Print**, and, then click **Print** again to print the worksheet with the chart. Your printout should look like Figure 3.13.

Figure 3.13

Printed Income Statement
with Expense Comparison
Chart

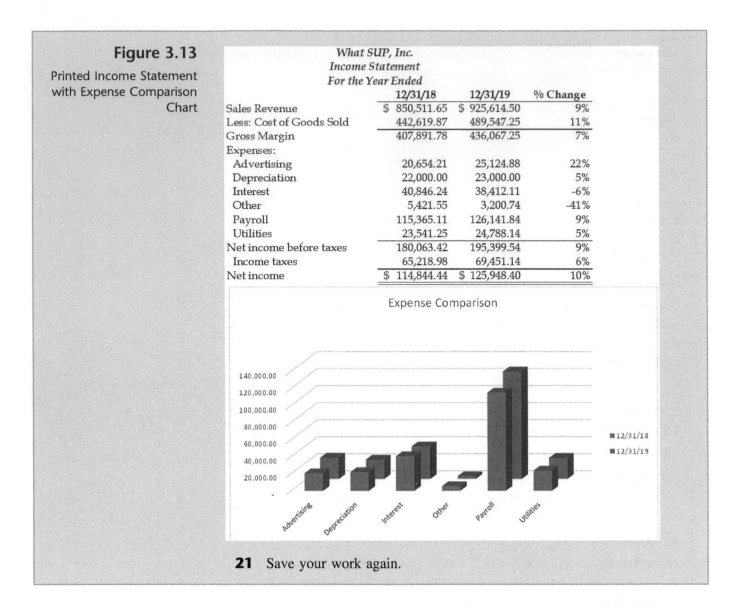

What SUP, Inc.
Income Statement
For the Year Ended

	12/31/18	12/31/19	% Change
Sales Revenue	$ 850,511.65	$ 925,614.50	9%
Less: Cost of Goods Sold	442,619.87	489,547.25	11%
Gross Margin	407,891.78	436,067.25	7%
Expenses:			
Advertising	20,654.21	25,124.88	22%
Depreciation	22,000.00	23,000.00	5%
Interest	40,846.24	38,412.11	-6%
Other	5,421.55	3,200.74	-41%
Payroll	115,365.11	126,141.84	9%
Utilities	23,541.25	24,788.14	5%
Net income before taxes	180,063.42	195,399.54	9%
Income taxes	65,218.98	69,451.14	6%
Net income	$ 114,844.44	$ 125,948.40	10%

21 Save your work again.

"All of this is very interesting," says Nathan. "I'll bet there's more. Am I right?" "Yes, we still need to do a ratio analysis in order to complete our financial statement analyses portfolio," Kyle responds.

Ratio Analysis

Kyle explains that several standard ratios are often used to assess a company's profitability, liquidity, and solvency. Profitability represents the company's ability to generate a profit to investors. Liquidity represents the company's ability to pay its bills currently. Solvency represents the company's ability to stay in business given its debt structure. A chart of each ratio's formula follows.

Profitability

Return on owners' investment	Net income ÷ Average stockholders' equity
Return on total investment	Net income before interest expense ÷ Average total assets
Profit margin	Net income ÷ Sales
Gross margin	Gross margin ÷ Sales

Liquidity

Current ratio	Current assets ÷ Current liabilities
Quick ratio	(Cash + Accounts receivable + Short-term investments) ÷ Current liabilities
Receivable turnover	Sales ÷ Average accounts receivable
Inventory turnover	Cost of goods sold ÷ Average inventory

Solvency

Debt-to-equity	Total liabilities ÷ Total equity
Liability	Total liabilities ÷ Total assets

In Excel, each of these amounts is a part of a given financial statement or can easily be computed. Therefore, you can create a new worksheet that has formulas referencing these amounts. Kyle suggests you create a new worksheet to compute these ratios.

> **To calculate the first financial ratio on a new worksheet (refer to preceding ratio table for the *return on owners' investment* formula):**
>
> **1** Right-click the **Income Statement** tab of your workbook and click **Insert . . .**; then click **Worksheet** and then **OK** to insert a new worksheet.
>
> **2** Double-click the **Sheet1** tab and rename the worksheet **Ratio Analysis**.
>
> **3** Format the Ratio Analysis worksheet like Figure 3.14 with a heading and listing of ratios as shown. To center and merge the title, select the range of cells **A1:B1** and then click the **Merge and Center** button from the Alignment group on the Home tab of the Ribbon. Repeat these steps for the ranges A2:B2 and A3:B3.
>
> **4** Click in cell **B6** and type the following **='Income Statement'!C17/ (('Balance Sheet'!B26+'Balance Sheet'!B27+'Balance Sheet'!C26+ 'Balance Sheet'!C27)/2)** to compute return on owners' investment.
>
> **5** Alternatively, you could utilize multiple worksheet referencing. Type = in cell B6, then activate the income statement worksheet and click cell **C17**.
>
> **6** Type **/((** (the forward slash and two left parentheses, which determine the all-important *order* of calculation).
>
> **7** Activate the balance sheet worksheet and click cell **B26**.
>
> **8** Type **+**, then click cell **C26**.
>
> **9** Type **+**, then click cell **B27**.
>
> **10** Type **+**, then click cell **C27**.

Figure 3.14

Format for Ratio Analysis

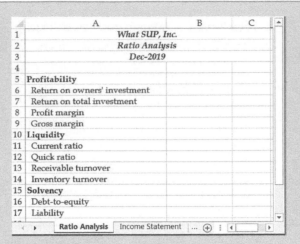

	A	B	C
1	*What SUP, Inc.*		
2	*Ratio Analysis*		
3	*Dec-2019*		
4			
5	**Profitability**		
6	Return on owners' investment		
7	Return on total investment		
8	Profit margin		
9	Gross margin		
10	**Liquidity**		
11	Current ratio		
12	Quick ratio		
13	Receivable turnover		
14	Inventory turnover		
15	**Solvency**		
16	Debt-to-equity		
17	Liability		

‹ ›   **Ratio Analysis**   Income Statement   … ⊕ ⁝ ◄   ►

11 Type)/2) to end the summation of equity accounts and divide the result by 2 to derive an average.

12 Press [**Enter**] to end your formula.

13 Format cell B6 in a percent style.

Trouble? If you choose to type the formula as written here and forget an apostrophe or exclamation point or misspell a word, then Excel will give you an error message and you'll have to debug your formula. Also, if you don't have the correct number of parentheses, Excel will give you an error message. Note that when you edit the formula, Excel changes the color of each set of parentheses so that you can clearly see which is which. Also be careful when typing formulas to use the apostrophe and not the accent key to create formulas. The apostrophe key is usually located next to the Enter key on your keyboard, and the accent key is usually located above the Tab key.

"The point-and-click method of cell referencing on multiple worksheets is sure easier than typing the references themselves," you comment. "Otherwise I would have to type all of those apostrophes and exclamation points. With my typing skills, I would probably forget one of them and create an error in the formula."

"Good point," Kyle says. "Let's finish the profitability ratios next."

To enter remaining formulas for profitability analysis (refer to the ratio table for these formulas):

1 Click cell **B7** and type =.

2 Use the values at cells C17 and C11 on the income statement to compute net income before interest expense, which is the numerator of the *return on total investment* ratio.

3 Use the values at cells B17 and C17 on the balance sheet to add total assets, and then divide the result by 2 to obtain average total assets.

4 Once your formula is typed, press [**Enter**] to compute the ratio. Your formula should look like this: **=('Income Statement'!C17+'Income Statement'!C11)/(('Balance Sheet'!B17+'Balance Sheet'!C17)/2)**. Be careful to use the correct parentheses.

5 Format the cell in percent style.

6 In cell B8, use the values at cells C17 and C5 on the income statement to compute the *profit margin*. (Use the ratio table to enter the appropriate formula.) Your formula should look like this: **='Income Statement'!C17/ 'Income Statement'!C5**.

7 Format the cell in percent style.

8 In cell B9, use the values at cells C7 and C5 on the income statement to compute the *gross margin*. (Use the ratio table to enter the appropriate formula.) Your formula should look like this: **= 'Income Statement'!C7/ 'Income Statement'!C5**.

9 Format the cell in percent style. Your window should look like Figure 3.15.

	A	B
1	*What SUP, Inc.*	
2	*Ratio Analysis*	
3	*Dec-2019*	
4		
5	**Profitability**	
6	Return on owners' investment	45%
7	Return on total investment	23%
8	Profit margin	14%
9	Gross margin	47%

Figure 3.15

Profitability Analysis Completed

10 Click **File** then click **Save As**.

11 Change the file name to include a reference to ratios, and then add your name to the file name using the underscore key as before. In this example, the file will be saved as ch3-01_Ratios_student_name (replace student_name with your name). Be sure to save your file to a safe location.

Remember, profitability ratios measure the company's ability to generate a profit to investors. In this case, Nathan and Meagan are fairly satisfied with their profitability in comparison to other companies of their size and type of business. They are eager to see if their liquidity ratios are equally as positive.

Kyle encourages you to continue with your ratio analysis.

To compute the liquidity ratios:

1 In cell B11, use the values in cells C7 through C11 (current assets) and C22 through C23 (current liabilities) on the balance sheet to compute the *current ratio*. (Use the ratio table to find the appropriate formula.) Your formula could be =('Balance Sheet'!C7+'Balance Sheet'!C8+ 'Balance Sheet'!C9+'Balance Sheet'!C10+'Balance Sheet'!C11)/ ('Balance Sheet'!C22+'Balance Sheet'!C23), where current assets and current liabilities are added up separately; or you could use the SUM function and write the formula as =SUM('Balance Sheet'!C7:C11)/ SUM('Balance Sheet'!C22:C23).

2 Format the cell in comma style.

3 In cell B12, use the values in cells C7–C8 (cash and accounts receivable) and C22–C23 (current liabilities) on the balance sheet to compute the *quick ratio*. (Refer to the ratio table for the appropriate formula.) Your formula could be either =('Balance Sheet'!C7+'Balance Sheet'! C8)/('Balance Sheet'!C22+'Balance Sheet'!C23) or =SUM('Balance Sheet'!C7:C8)/SUM('Balance Sheet'!C22:C23).

4 Format the cell in comma style.

5 In cell B13, use the values in cell C5 (sales revenue) on the income statement and cells B8 and C8 (accounts receivable) on the balance sheet to compute the *receivable turnover* ratio. (Use the ratio table to find the appropriate formula.) Your formula should look like this: ='Income Statement'!C5/(('Balance Sheet'!B8+'Balance Sheet'!C8)/2).

6 Format the cell in comma style.

7 In cell B14, use the values in cell C6 (cost of goods sold) on the income statement and cells B9 and C9 (inventory) on the balance sheet to compute the *inventory turnover* ratio. (Use the ratio table to find the appropriate formula.) Your formula should look like this: ='Income Statement'!C6/(('Balance Sheet'!B9+'Balance Sheet'!C9)/2).

8 Format the cell in comma style.

9 Save your work.

Remember, the liquidity ratios measure the company's ability to pay its bills currently. In this case, Nathan and Meagan are surprised at how good their current and quick ratios are. Usually, their current ratio is around 2:1, which is normal.

The 4.04 current ratio and the 1.65 quick ratio indicate they have plenty of resources to meet their current liabilities. Receivable turnover is fine, given they have 30-day credit terms. Inventory turnover is a little slow at 3.53, but this is fairly common in their business. They are eager to see if the solvency ratios continue the favorable trend.

To compute the solvency ratios:

1 In cell B16, use the values in cells C22 through C24 (accounts payable, payroll liabilities, and long-term debt) and C26 and C27 (common stock and retained earnings) on the balance sheet to compute the *debt-to-equity* ratio. (Refer to the ratio table for the appropriate formula.) Your formula should look like this: **=SUM('Balance Sheet'! C22:C24)/SUM('Balance Sheet'!C27:C26)**.

2 Format the cell in percent style.

3 In cell B17, use the values in cells C22 through C24 (accounts payable, payroll liabilities, and long-term debt) and C17 (total assets) on the balance sheet to compute the *liability* ratio. (Refer to the ratio table for the appropriate formula.) Your formula should look like this: **=SUM('Balance Sheet'!C22:C24)/'Balance Sheet'!C17**.

4 Format the cell in percent style. Your completed work should look like Figure 3.16.

	A	B
1	*What SUP, Inc.*	
2	*Ratio Analysis*	
3	*Dec-2019*	
4		
5	**Profitability**	
6	Return on owners' investment	45%
7	Return on total investment	23%
8	Profit margin	14%
9	Gross margin	47%
10	**Liquidity**	
11	Current ratio	4.04
12	Quick ratio	1.65
13	Receivable turnover	10.96
14	Inventory turnover	3.53
15	**Solvency**	
16	Debt-to-equity	111%
17	Liability	53%

Figure 3.16

Completed Ratio Analysis

5 Save your work.

Now the news is not as good. It turns out the positive liquidity ratio is somewhat offset by the solvency ratios, which indicate that debt is 111 percent of equity. The company is financed heavily with debt, and this can lead to problems if the return on investment doesn't exceed the cost of the debt. The liability ratio reflects the same problem in that 53 percent of the company's assets are financed with debt versus equity. Nathan's business plan calls for a reduction in debt over the next several years as profits provide the necessary cash.

"This is great," Meagan says. "Although the solvency ratios are high, they do reflect our business plan. As long as we continue to generate profits and cash flow, we should be able to improve the solvency ratios."

End Note

You've applied some of what you learned in the first two chapters to create a set of useful worksheets that identify trends and relationships. Plus you've created them in a reusable format for future periods.

In the next chapter, you will learn how to use Excel to perform depreciation calculations and prepare depreciation schedules.

Chapter 3 Questions

1   What is another term for vertical analysis?

2   What base amount is used for vertical analysis of an income statement?

3   What base amount is used for vertical analysis of a balance sheet?

4   What base amount is used for horizontal analysis of both income statements and balance sheets? Give an example.

5   What do profitability ratios represent?

6   What do liquidity ratios represent?

7   What do solvency ratios represent?

8   Why is the point-and-click method of cell referencing easier than typing references directly into worksheet cells?

9   Which ratios are usually formatted as percentages?

10   Which ratios are usually formatted as numbers?

Chapter 3 Assignments

1   Create a Financial Analysis for What SUP, Inc. as of December 31, 2019.

You are to create this financial analysis as of December 31, 2019, from the information found on file ch3-02.xls. This file contains three worksheets, which are labeled Income Statement, Balance Sheet, and Ratios.

Following the Chapter 3 examples, create a vertical analysis of both the income statement and balance sheet for December 31, 2019, only. Then create a horizontal analysis of both the income statement and balance sheet. (*Note:* The horizontal analysis will compare December 31, 2018, with December 31, 2019.) In addition, create a pie chart of expenses for the year ended December 31, 2019; a column chart (in a format of your choice) of expenses for the years ended December 31, 2018, and 2019; and a ratio analysis as of December 31, 2019. Save the file as ch3-02_student_name.xls (replacing student_name with your name).

Print each completed worksheet in Value view, with your name and date printed in the lower left footer and the file name in the lower right footer.

2   Create a Financial Analysis for What SUP, Inc. as of December 31, 2020.

You are to create What SUP's financial analysis as of December 31, 2020, from the information found on file ch3-03.xls. This file contains three worksheets, which are labeled Income Statement, Balance Sheet, and Ratios.

Following the Chapter 3 examples, create a vertical analysis of both the income statement and balance sheet for December 31, 2020, only. Then create a horizontal analysis of both the income statement and balance sheet. (*Note:* The horizontal analysis will compare December 31, 2019, with December 31, 2020.) In addition, create a pie chart of expenses for the year ended December 31, 2020; a column chart (in a format of your choice) of expenses for the years ended December 31, 2019, and 2020; and a ratio analysis as of December 31, 2020. Save the file as ch3-03_student_name.xls (replacing student_name with your name).

Print each completed worksheet in Value view, with your name and date printed in the lower left footer and the file name in the lower right footer.

Chapter 3 Case Problem 1:
KELLY'S BOUTIQUE

You are to create Kelly's Boutique's financial analyses as of December 31, 2018, and as of December 31, 2019. Following the Chapter 3 examples, use the student file ch3-04.xls to create a vertical and horizontal analysis of the balance sheet and income statement in the columns provided. (*Note:* The horizontal analysis will compare December 31, 2018, with December 31, 2019.) Also create a pie chart of expenses for the year ended December 31, 2019; a column chart of expenses for the years ended December 31, 2018, and December 31, 2019; and a ratio analysis as of December 31, 2019. Save the file as ch3-04_student_name.xls (replacing student_name with your name).

Print each completed worksheet in Value view, with your name and date printed in the lower left footer and the file name in the lower right footer.

Chapter 3 Case Problem 2:
WINE DEPOT

You are to create Wine Depot's financial analyses as of December 31, 2020, and as of December 31, 2021. Following the Chapter 3 examples, use the student file ch3-05.xls to create a vertical and horizontal analysis of the balance sheet and income statement in the columns provided. (*Note:* The horizontal analysis will compare December 31, 2020 with December 31, 2021.) Also create a pie chart of expenses for the year ended December 31, 2021; a column chart of expenses for the years ended December 31, 2020, and December 31,

2021; and a ratio analysis as of December 31, 2021. Save the file as ch3-05_student_name.xls (replacing student_name with your name). *Note*: You will have to use Excel's help feature to create the column chart, because the columns are not adjacent to one another as in the chapter example. Use whatever chart layout you prefer.

Print each completed worksheet in Value view, with landscape orientation, scaling to fit to 1 page wide by 1 page tall, and with your name and date printed in the lower left footer and the file name in the lower right footer. Use Excel's help feature to move charts on your worksheet so that they print on a separate page.

Chapter 3 Case Problem 3:
SNICK'S BOARD SHOP

You are to create a financial analysis for Snick's Board Shop as of December 31, 2017, and December 31, 2018. Following the Chapter 3 examples, use the student file ch3-06.xls to create a vertical and horizontal analysis of the balance sheet and income statement in the columns provided. (*Note:* The horizontal analysis will compare December 31, 2017, with December 31, 2018.) Also create a pie chart of expenses for the year ended December 31, 2018, formatted in a manner similar to your chapter work; a column chart of expenses for the years ended December 31, 2017, and December 31, 2018, formatted in a manner similar to your chapter work; and a ratio analysis as of December 31, 2018. Save the file as ch3-06_student_name.xls (replacing student_name with your name). *Note:* You will have to use Excel's help feature to create the column chart, because the columns are not adjacent to one another as in the chapter example. Use whatever chart layout you prefer.

Print each completed worksheet in Value view, with landscape orientation, scaling to fit to 1 page wide by 1 page tall, and with your name and date printed in the lower left footer and the file name in the lower right footer.

Chapter 3 Case Problem 4:
ROSEY'S ROSES

You are to create a financial analysis for Rosey's Roses as of December 31, 2022, and December 31, 2023. Following the Chapter 3 examples, use the student file ch3-07.xls to create a vertical analysis of the balance sheet and income statement as of December 31, 2022, and December 31, 2023—as well as a horizontal analysis of both the income statement and balance sheet comparing December 31, 2022, with December 31, 2023. Place the vertical analysis in columns D and G on the income statement labeled % of Sales in cells D5 and G5. Place the vertical analysis in columns D and G on the balance sheet labeled % of Assets in cells D5 and G5. Place the horizontal analysis in column I labeled % Change in cell I5 for both the income statement and balance sheet.

Also create a pie chart of expenses for the year ended December 31, 2023, formatted in a manner similar to your chapter work; a column chart of expenses for the years ended December 31, 2022, and December 31, 2023, formatted in a manner similar to your chapter work; and a ratio analysis as of December 31, 2023. *Note:* You will have to use Excel's help feature to create the column chart, because the columns are not adjacent to one another as in the chapter example. Use whatever chart layout you prefer.

Save the workbook as ch3-07_student_name (replacing student_name with your name). Print all worksheets in Value view, with your name and date printed in the lower left footer and the file name in the lower right footer.

Depreciation

In this chapter you will learn:

- How to calculate straight-line depreciation using Excel's built-in function
- How to use what-if analysis with the depreciation function
- How to create a depreciation summary for many assets
- How to calculate depreciation using double declining balance and sum-of-the-year's digits methods using Excel's built-in functions
- How to create charts to illustrate depreciation expense
- How to calculate partial year depreciation.

Case: What SUP, Inc.

Worksheets are used for more than financial statement preparation and analysis. For the accountant, worksheets serve a useful supporting schedule role. Nathan and Meagan want to make sure that you are fully trained on all aspects of Excel's use in accounting for their business.

Depreciation Calculations

The financial statements you analyzed in the preceding chapter didn't just appear. They were created using the company's trial balance, which in turn was prepared from the accounts in the general ledger. Prior to financial statement preparation, accounts in the general ledger needed adjustment to properly present accrual accounting. One of those adjustments, of course, is the depreciation of a company's fixed assets.

You recall learning that depreciation is the allocation of a firm's investment in fixed assets in a systematic and rational manner. The easiest of several generally accepted methods of depreciating these assets is called the straight-line method.

"How can Excel help us with depreciation?" Nathan asks.

"Excel has some built-in functions that, when given the appropriate information, can calculate depreciation for you." Kyle responds.

"What about salvage value, useful life, et cetera?" you ask. "Aren't those important factors in determining depreciation?"

"Indeed they are," Kyle says. "That's the appropriate information that I am referring to. In order to calculate depreciation, the Excel function requires information about the asset's cost, estimated salvage value, and economic useful life."

Kyle explains that Excel's built-in function for calculating straight-line depreciation is written as follows: =SLN(Cost, Salvage Value, Useful Life), where

SLN stands for straight-line depreciation. Inside the parentheses are three arguments separated by commas. The first argument identifies the asset's cost, the second its salvage value, the third its useful life. You can type the dollar cost, salvage value, and number of years into the function or you can point the function to the cell locations where the cost, salvage value, and useful life are located. This second alternative is much more effective because the cell references can then be duplicated across several cells.

Kyle suggests that you use a template he's created to compute depreciation for one asset. You are up to the challenge and proceed with the task. The asset you'll depreciate—number 1001, Display Racks—was acquired January 1, 2017, for $25,000. It has no salvage value and has an economic useful life of 5 years.

To calculate depreciation using Excel's built-in function:

1 Start Excel and open file ch4-01.xls.

2 Activate the Asset 1001 worksheet; it should look like Figure 4.1. (*Note:* You'll use the summary worksheet later.)

Figure 4.1

Depreciation Calculation Worksheet

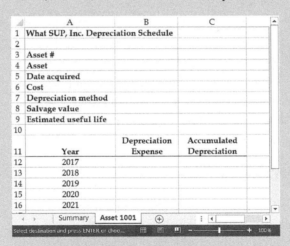

3 Enter the appropriate information on the worksheet: the asset number, date acquired, depreciation method (use S/L for straight-line), salvage value, and estimated useful life.

4 Enter the formula **=SLN($B$6,$B$8,$B$9)** in cell B12, and then press the [**Enter**] key. B6 is the location of the asset's cost, B8 is the location of its salvage value, and B9 is the location of its useful life. (*Note:* Entering these references as absolute values using the $ will help later as we replicate the formula for each year.)

5 Fill the formula in cell B12 down to cells B13 through B16.

6 Enter the formula **=B12** into cell C12.

7 Enter the formula **=C12+B13** into cell C13 and fill this formula down to cells C14 through C16. These formulas create a running total of depreciation over the years. Your worksheet should now look like Figure 4.2.

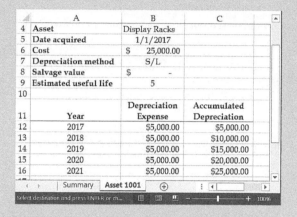

Figure 4.2

Completed Depreciation Calculation Worksheet for Asset 1001

	A	B	C
4	Asset	Display Racks	
5	Date acquired	1/1/2017	
6	Cost	$ 25,000.00	
7	Depreciation method	S/L	
8	Salvage value	$ -	
9	Estimated useful life	5	
10			
11	Year	Depreciation Expense	Accumulated Depreciation
12	2017	$5,000.00	$5,000.00
13	2018	$5,000.00	$10,000.00
14	2019	$5,000.00	$15,000.00
15	2020	$5,000.00	$20,000.00
16	2021	$5,000.00	$25,000.00

Summary   Asset 1001

Select destination and press ENTER or ch...   100%

8 Save your work to ch4-01_SLN_student_name.xls (replacing student_name with your name).

Meagan offers to create another depreciation worksheet. The company purchased chairs on January 1, 2017, for $8,000. These assets were designated as asset #1002, have a $300 salvage value, and were estimated to have a 5-year useful life.

To create another deprecation worksheet:

1 Right-click the **Asset 1001** tab to reveal the Shortcut menu.

2 Click **Move or Copy**.

3 Check the **Create a Copy checkbox**, and then click **OK**.

4 Change the name of the newly created worksheet to Asset 1002.

5 Modify the appropriate information on the worksheet to reflect the new asset: the asset number, date acquired, depreciation method (use S/L for straight-line), salvage value, and estimated useful life. Your completed worksheet should look like Figure 4.3.

Figure 4.3

Depreciation Worksheet
for Asset 1002

	A	B	C
1	What SUP, Inc. Depreciation Schedule		
2			
3	Asset #	1002	
4	Asset	Chairs	
5	Date acquired	1/1/2017	
6	Cost	$ 8,000.00	
7	Depreciation method	S/L	
8	Salvage value	$ 300.00	
9	Estimated useful life	5	
10			
11	Year	Depreciation Expense	Accumulated Depreciation
12	2017	$1,540.00	$1,540.00
13	2018	$1,540.00	$3,080.00
14	2019	$1,540.00	$4,620.00
15	2020	$1,540.00	$6,160.00
16	2021	$1,540.00	$7,700.00
17			

Summary | Asset 1001 | **Asset 1002** ... (+)

Select destination and press ENTER or choos...   100%

6 Save your work.

Meagan asks: "How is using the SLN function and all the cell references different from using a calculator or just typing the values into the function?" Kyle responds that Excel's power is in its sensitivity or *what-if* analysis capability, which he offers to illustrate next.

Conducting a What-If Analysis with the Depreciation Function

What-if analysis helps you determine the consequences of changes in your assumptions or variables. For instance, what if Asset 1001 did have some salvage value. How would that change the depreciation calculation each year?

To utilize the what-if capabilities of Excel:

1 Activate the worksheet for Asset 1001.

2 Change the salvage value in your deprecation worksheet by entering **1000** into cell B8. Note the change in depreciation expense each period and the resulting change in accumulated depreciation.

3 Now change the cost of the asset from $25,000 to $28,000. Note the change in depreciation expense each period and the resulting change in accumulated depreciation.

4 Now change the cost back to $25,000 and the salvage value back to 0; then save your file again.

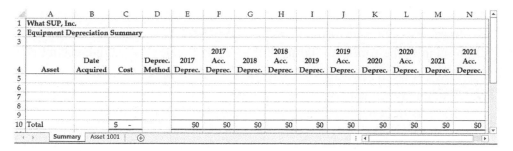

Figure 4.4

Depreciation Summary Worksheet

Kyle explains that the only thing missing is a way for collecting similar asset cost, depreciation, and accumulated depreciation to support the financial statement.

Creating a Depreciation Summary

A depreciation summary is designed to capture all the costs, depreciation, and accumulated depreciation from similar assets and thus facilitate preparation of financial statements on an annual basis. Kyle sketches out a worksheet design (shown in Figure 4.4) that he suggests could be used for this purpose.

Using Excel, Kyle demonstrates how multiple worksheets can be summarized.

To create a depreciation summary worksheet:

1 Activate the Summary worksheet. (*Note:* This worksheet is preformatted for you without formulas. Observe also that your workbook should contain three worksheets: Summary, Asset 1001, and Asset 1002.)

2 In cell A5, enter the formula =**'Asset 1001'!B4**. (Remember from previous chapters that you can either type this formula or type = and then click in the Asset 1001 worksheet at cell **B4** and press [**Enter**].)

3 Using either method, continue the same process to include the date acquired, cost, and depreciation method in cells B5, C5, and D5, respectively. Adjust column widths as needed and format without decimal places.

4 In cell E5, enter the formula =**'Asset 1001'!B12**. This enters the depreciation for 2017 on Asset 1001.

5 In cell F5, enter the formula =**'Asset 1001'!C12**. This enters the accumulated depreciation for Asset 1001 as of the end of 2017.

6 Continue the same process for cells G5 through N5, referencing depreciation and accumulated depreciation for years 2018 through 2021.

7 In cell A6, enter the formula **='Asset 1002'!B4**. (Note that this closely resembles the formula used in cell A5 except now you are referencing a different asset, Asset 1002.)

8 Continue referencing formulas from Asset 1002 to the summary worksheet. Your completed worksheet should look like Figure 4.5.

Figure 4.5

Completed Depreciation Summary Worksheet

	A	B	C	D	E	F	G	H	I	J	K	L	M	N
1	What SUP, Inc.													
2	Equipment Depreciation Summary													
3														
4	Asset	Date Acquired	Cost	Deprec. Method	2017 Deprec.	2017 Acc. Deprec.	2018 Deprec.	2018 Acc. Deprec.	2019 Deprec.	2019 Acc. Deprec.	2020 Deprec.	2020 Acc. Deprec.	2021 Deprec.	2021 Acc. Deprec.
5	Display Racks	1/1/2017	$ 25,000	S/L	$5,000	$5,000	$5,000	$10,000	$5,000	$15,000	$5,000	$20,000	$5,000	$25,000
6	Chairs	1/1/2017	$ 8,000	S/L	$1,540	$1,540	$1,540	$3,080	$1,540	$4,620	$1,540	$6,160	$1,540	$7,700
7														
8														
9														
10	Total		$ 33,000		$6,540	$6,540	$6,540	$13,080	$6,540	$19,620	$6,540	$26,160	$6,540	$32,700
11														

Summary | Asset 1001 | Asset 1002 | Sheet1 | Sheet2 | Sheet3 | ⊕

9 Save your work again.

What SUP uses the straight-line method of depreciation, but Kyle explains that there are alternative methods, such as declining balance and sum-of-the-year's digits.

Calculating Depreciation Using Other Methods

You inform Nathan and Meagan that, even though you are familiar with the declining balance and sum-of-the-year's digits methods, you've never used a worksheet to calculate depreciation.

Kyle explains how easy it is, given that you've already invested the time and energy creating the worksheet itself. He suggests you make a copy of one of the depreciation worksheets and just change the depreciation formula to include the new depreciation function.

To create depreciation worksheets using the declining balance method:

1 Click the **File** menu and select **Save As**.

2 Type **ch4-01_DDB_student_name** as the file name (replacing student_name with your name).

3 Click the **Asset 1001** tab.

4 Change cell B7 to read **DDB** (for double declining balance)

5 Change cell B12 to read **=DDB($B$6,$B$8,$B$9,1)**. Once again, the depreciation function DDB takes arguments located within the parentheses. The first three arguments are the same as the SLN function: cost, salvage value, and useful life. All three of these arguments have been set for absolute referencing so that later, when you copy them down the worksheet, they will continue to reference the appropriate cells. The fourth argument is the period for which the asset is being depreciated (e.g., the first, second, or third period).

6 Change cell B13 to read **=DDB($B$6,$B$8,$B$9,2)**. Note that the only difference between B13 and B12 is the fourth argument.

7 Continue to place the DDB formula in cells B14, B15, and B16, changing only the last argument. This is best accomplished by filling down the formula and then going back to edit each cell individually. Upon completion, your worksheet should look like Figure 4.6.

Figure 4.6

Initial Calculation of Declining Balance Depreciation for Asset 1001

	A	B	C
1	What SUP, Inc. Depreciation Schedule		
2			
3	Asset #	1001	
4	Asset	Display Racks	
5	Date acquired	1/1/2017	
6	Cost	$ 25,000.00	
7	Depreciation method	DDB	
8	Salvage value	$ -	
9	Estimated useful life	5	
10			
11	Year	Depreciation Expense	Accumulated Depreciation
12	2017	$10,000.00	$10,000.00
13	2018	$6,000.00	$16,000.00
14	2019	$3,600.00	$19,600.00
15	2020	$2,160.00	$21,760.00
16	2021	$1,296.00	$23,056.00

Summary | **Asset 1001** | Asset 1002 ...

8 Save your work.

You, however, raise a question. "I remember that when using the double declining balance depreciation method we ignore the salvage value, but in this case shouldn't your accumulated depreciation at the end of 5 years be equal to the cost, since your salvage value was zero?"

"Right you are," Kyle responds. "Generally accepted accounting principles for this method of depreciation require that we switch to straight-line depreciation once that method would calculate depreciation expense greater than that calculated by the double declining balance method. That then assures us that the asset is fully depreciated to its salvage value."

Kyle explains that he'll have to modify the existing worksheet to include a calculation of what the straight-line deprecation would be for each year based on the asset's cost (less salvage value) divided by its remaining useful life. Then he will create a "switch" column that will test to see if the straight-line depreciation method produces a higher depreciation amount than the double declining balance method. Then he will create a new depreciation expense column that will establish if the previous period required a switch or not. If it did, then the depreciation expense will be that previously calculated by the straight-line method. If not, the formula will indicate if a switch should take place in the current period. If a switch is appropriate, then the straight-line depreciation amount will be entered; otherwise, the double declining balance depreciation amounts previously calculated will be used. Kyle will then add a new accumulated depreciation column based on the new depreciation expense calculations.

To do all this, Kyle will need to use a built-in Excel function called IF. The IF function tests a condition and returns a value of "true" if the test is true or a value if "false" if the test is not true. The formula is written =IF(condition, value if true, value if false) where the three arguments result in some value. For example =IF(10>4,5A,6A) would return 5A since 10 is greater than 4.

Kyle points out that he can use the basic IF function to determine if a switch is necessary by comparing calculated depreciation amounts. To determine which amount to use will depend on two things. First, he will have to determine whether the switch was made in the previous period or not. Second, he will have to determine whether it is appropriate to switch in the current period. This will require the use of what are known as *nested* IF statements.

"This is getting pretty complicated!" you comment.

"I agree, but it's well worth the trouble once we're finished," Kyle responds.

Kyle offers to show you how to modify this worksheet to calculate the proper depreciation method using the double declining balance method.

To modify this worksheet to properly calculate double declining depreciation:

1 Change the width of column D to 18 pixels.

2 Type **Straight-Line Test** in cell E11.

3 Type **Switch** in cell F11.

4 Type **Depreciation Expense** in cell G11.

5 Type **Accumulated Depreciation** in cell H11.

6 Increase the column width of columns E, F, G, and H to that all values are visible.

7 Type **=SLN($B$6,$B$8,$B$9)** into cell E12. (Note that this is the same calculation we performed before to calculate straight-line depreciation expense.)

8 Type **=SLN($B$6-C12,$B$8,$B$9-1)** into cell E13. (This is the same calculation we performed before to calculate straight-line depreciation expense minus the previous period's accumulated depreciation and with one less year of useful life.)

9 Type **=SLN($B$6-C13,$B$8,$B$9-2)** into cell E14. (Again, this is the same calculation as for straight-line depreciation expense minus the previous period's accumulated depreciation and with one less year of useful life.)

10 Type **=SLN($B$6-C14,$B$8,$B$9-3)** into cell E15.

11 Type **=SLN($B$6-C15,$B$8,$B$9-4)** into cell E16. Your window should look like Figure 4.7.

	A	B	C	D	E
1	What SUP, Inc. Depreciation Schedule				
2					
3	Asset #	1001			
4	Asset	Display Racks			
5	Date acquired	1/1/2017			
6	Cost	$ 25,000.00			
7	Depreciation method	DDB			
8	Salvage value	$ -			
9	Estimated useful life	5			
10					
11	Year	Depreciation Expense	Accumulated Depreciation		Straight-Line Test
12	2017	$10,000.00	$10,000.00		$5,000.00
13	2018	$6,000.00	$16,000.00		$3,750.00
14	2019	$3,600.00	$19,600.00		$3,000.00
15	2020	$2,160.00	$21,760.00		$2,700.00
16	2021	$1,296.00	$23,056.00		$3,240.00

Summary | **Asset 1001** | Asset 1002 | Sheet1 | She ...

Figure 4.7

DDB Depreciation Schedule with Straight-Line Test

12 Observe that straight-line depreciation is greater than the calculated double declining balance depreciation in 2020. Type **=IF(E12>B12, "X","-")** in cell F12 to determine if the straight-line depreciation method produces an expense greater than from the double declining balance depreciation method. (*Note:* Kyle has chosen to place an X in the Switch column if this is true and a dash (hyphen) in the Switch column if the condition is not true. The quotes indicate that the entry is text, not a number.)

13 Format cell F12 to center the text by clicking the **Center text** button in the Alignment group of the Ribbon.

14 Fill that formula down from cell F12 to cell F16. (*Note:* Kyle points out that an X appears in the 2020 and 2021 rows.)

15 Type **=IF(F12="X",E12,B12)** in cell G12 and format the cell as Currency. (This will test to see if a switch to straight-line depreciation method is appropriate for the current period.)

16 Fill that formula down from cell G12 to G13.

17 Edit the formula in G13 so that it reads exactly as follows: **=IF(F12="X",G12,IF(F13="X",E13,B13))**. (*Note:* Here we test to see if we used straight-line deprecation in the previous year. If we did, then we'll use that same amount for the current year; otherwise, we'll use the amount calculated by testing to see if a switch is necessary for the current year.)

18 Fill this new formula down from cell G13 to G16.

19 Type **=G12** in cell H12, and then type **=H12+G13** into cell H13.

20 Fill down the formula in H13 to cell H16 and then format columns G and H as currency. Your screen should look like Figure 4.8.

Figure 4.8

DDB Depreciation Schedule with New Depreciation Amounts

	A	B	C	D	E	F	G	H
1	What SUP, Inc. Depreciation Schedule							
2								
3	Asset #	1001						
4	Asset	Display Racks						
5	Date acquired	1/1/2017						
6	Cost	$ 25,000.00						
7	Depreciation method	DDB						
8	Salvage value	$ -						
9	Estimated useful life	5						
10								
11	Year	Depreciation Expense	Accumulated Depreciation		Straight-Line Test	Switch	Depreciation Expense	Accumulated Depreciation
12	2017	$10,000.00	$10,000.00		$5,000.00	-	$10,000.00	$10,000.00
13	2018	$6,000.00	$16,000.00		$3,750.00	-	$6,000.00	$16,000.00
14	2019	$3,600.00	$19,600.00		$3,000.00	-	$3,600.00	$19,600.00
15	2020	$2,160.00	$21,760.00		$2,700.00	X	$2,700.00	$22,300.00
16	2021	$1,296.00	$23,056.00		$3,240.00	X	$2,700.00	$25,000.00

Summary | **Asset 1001** | Asset 1002 | Sheet1 | Sheet2 | Sheet3 | +

21 Follow the same steps to modify Asset 1002 for double declining balance depreciation. Your completed screen for Asset 1002 should look like Figure 4.9. (Observe that a switch was also necessary in this case.)

Figure 4.9

DDB Depreciation Schedule for Asset 1002

	A	B	C	D	E	F	G	H
1	What SUP, Inc. Depreciation Schedule							
2								
3	Asset #	1002						
4	Asset	Chairs						
5	Date acquired	1/1/2017						
6	Cost	$ 8,000.00						
7	Depreciation method	DDB						
8	Salvage value	$ 300.00	(Ctrl) ▾					
9	Estimated useful life	5						
10								
11	Year	Depreciation Expense	Accumulated Depreciation		Straight-Line Test	Switch	Depreciation Expense	Accumulated Depreciation
12	2017	$3,200.00	$3,200.00		$1,540.00	-	$3,200.00	$3,200.00
13	2018	$1,920.00	$5,120.00		$1,125.00	-	$1,920.00	$5,120.00
14	2019	$1,152.00	$6,272.00		$860.00	-	$1,152.00	$6,272.00
15	2020	$691.20	$6,963.20		$714.00	X	$714.00	$6,986.00
16	2021	$414.72	$7,377.92		$736.80	X	$714.00	$7,700.00

Summary | Asset 1001 | **Asset 1002** | Sheet1 | Sheet2 | Sheet3 | +

22 Save your work and then close the workbook.

A third common depreciation method is called *sum-of-the-year's digits*. Like the double declining balance method, this is an accelerated method that places more depreciation expense in the first few years of use than in later years. For a 5-year asset, the method sums up the years: $1 + 2 + 3 + 4 + 5 = 15$. In the first year of depreciation, 5/15 of the depreciable cost is recorded as depreciation expense; in the next year, 4/15 of the depreciable cost is recorded; and so forth. Kyle offers to show you how to create a worksheet to calculate the depreciation using the sum-of-the-year's digits method built into Excel.

To create a sum-of-the-year's digits depreciation schedule:

1 Open the straight-line depreciation workbook you created earlier in the chapter named ch4-01_SLN_student_name.xls.

2 Save this workbook with a new name: **ch4-01_SYD_student_name.xls** (replacing student_name with your name).

3 Activate the Asset 1001 worksheet.

4 Type **SYD** in cell B7.

5 Change cell B12 to read **=SYD($B$6,$B$8,$B$9,1)**. Once again, the depreciation function SYD takes arguments located within the parentheses. The first three arguments are the same as the SLN function: cost, salvage value, and useful life. All three of these arguments have been set for absolute referencing so that later, when you copy them down the worksheet, they will continue to reference the appropriate cells. The fourth argument is the period for which the asset is being depreciated: the first, second, third, etc.

6 Change cell B13 to read **=SYD($B$6,$B$8,$B$9,2)**. Note that the only difference between B13 and B12 is the fourth argument.

7 Continue to place the SYD formula in cells B14, B15, and B16, changing only the last argument. This is best accomplished by filling down the formula and then going back to edit each cell individually. Upon completion, your worksheet should look like Figure 4.10.

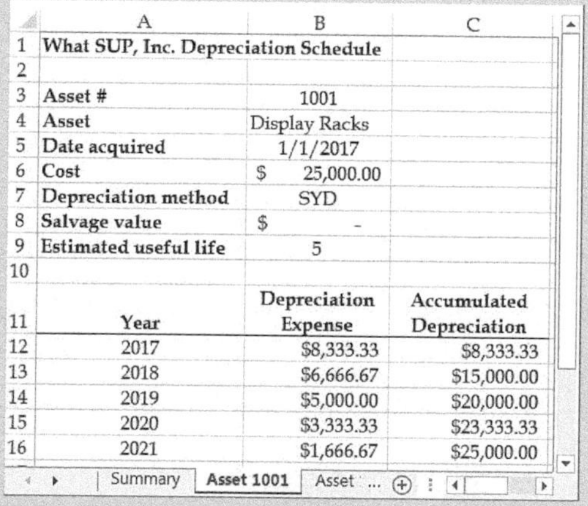

	A	B	C
1	What SUP, Inc. Depreciation Schedule		
2			
3	Asset #	1001	
4	Asset	Display Racks	
5	Date acquired	1/1/2017	
6	Cost	$ 25,000.00	
7	Depreciation method	SYD	
8	Salvage value	$ -	
9	Estimated useful life	5	
10			
11	Year	Depreciation Expense	Accumulated Depreciation
12	2017	$8,333.33	$8,333.33
13	2018	$6,666.67	$15,000.00
14	2019	$5,000.00	$20,000.00
15	2020	$3,333.33	$23,333.33
16	2021	$1,666.67	$25,000.00

◄ ► Summary | **Asset 1001** | Asset ... ⊕

Figure 4.10

SYD Depreciation Schedule for Asset 1001

8 Save your work.

9 Follow the same steps for Asset 1002. When complete, your worksheet should look like Figure 4.11.

Figure 4.11

SYD Depreciation
Schedule for
Asset 1002

	A	B	C
1	What SUP, Inc. Depreciation Schedule		
2			
3	Asset #	1002	
4	Asset	Chairs	
5	Date acquired	1/1/2017	
6	Cost	$ 8,000.00	
7	Depreciation method	SYD	
8	Salvage value	$ 300.00	
9	Estimated useful life	5	
10			
11	Year	Depreciation Expense	Accumulated Depreciation
12	2017	$2,566.67	$2,566.67
13	2018	$2,053.33	$4,620.00
14	2019	$1,540.00	$6,160.00
15	2020	$1,026.67	$7,186.67
16	2021	$513.33	$7,700.00

10 Save your work.

"This makes calculating depreciation fairly easy!" you say.

"That's the idea," Kyle responds.

Kyle points out that the charting feature you've used previously can also be used to help illustrate the effects of different depreciation methods.

Charting Depreciation Expense

You have created three files calculating depreciation expense for Asset 1001. Kyle states that, by using the charting feature of Excel, you can easily see the accounting impacts of the three different methods: straight-line, double declining balance, and sum-of-the-year's digits. First he suggests you create a simple chart illustrating the straight-line depreciation of Asset 1001.

To create a chart illustrating the straight-line depreciation of Asset 1001:

1 Open all three workbooks: ch4-01_SLN_student_name, ch4-01_DDB_student_name, and ch4-01_SYD_student_name.

2 Click **File** and then select **New**.

3 Double-click Blank Workbook to create a new workbook.

4 Save the workbook as ch4-01_Chart_student_name (replacing student_name with your name).

5 Click the **Insert** tab and then click the **Line** icon from the Charts group.

6 Click the **3-D Line** chart.

7 Click **Select Data** from the Data group.

8 Click **Add** from the Legend Entries (Series) section.

9 Type **SL** (to represent straight-line depreciation) in the Series name: text box.

10 Delete whatever text is in the Series values: text box and then select the **Select Range** icon in the Series values: text box.

11 Make the ch4-01_SLN_student_name window active.

12 Select cells **B12** through **B16** from the Asset 1001 worksheet located in the ch4-01_SLN_student_name workbook. Your screen should look like Figure 4.12.

	A	B	C	D	E
1	What SUP, Inc. Depreciation Schedule				
2					
3	Asset #	1001			
4	Asset	Display Racks			
5	Date acquired	1/1/2017			
6	Cost	$ 25,000.00			
7	Depreciation method	S/L			
8	Salvage value	$ -			
9	Estimated useful life	5			
10					
11	Year	Depreciation Expense	Accumulated Depreciation		
12	2017	$5,000.00	$5,000.00		
13	2018	$5,000.00	$10,000.00		
14	2019	$5,000.00	$15,000.00		
15	2020	$5,000.00	$20,000.00		
16	2021	$5,000.00	$25,000.00		
17					

Edit Series

='[ch4-01_SLN_student_name.xlsx]Asset 1001'!$B$12:$B$16

Summary | **Asset 1001** | Asset 1002 | Sheet1 | Sheet2

Figure 4.12
Creating a Line Chart

13 Press [**Enter**] and then click **OK** in the Edit Series window.

14 Click **Edit** in the Horizontal (Category) Axis Labels section of the Select Data Source window.

15 Once again make the ch4-01_SLN_student_name window active.

16 Select cells **A12** through **A16** from the Asset 1001 worksheet located in the ch4-01_SLN_student_name file.

17 Press [**Enter**] and then click **OK** in the Axis Labels window and then click **OK** in the Select Data Source window.

18 Move the chart to fit in the upper left-hand corner of the worksheet.

19 Click and hold the mouse in the lower right-hand corner of the chart, and then drag it down and to the right until it covers the range from cell A1 to H16.

20 With the chart still selected, click **Layout 3** from the Chart Layouts group as shown in Figure 4.13. Then change the name of the worksheet to Asset 1001. Your window make look different if it is larger. If so, just select Layout 3 from the Chart Layouts group.

Figure 4.13

Asset 1001 Straight-Line Depreciation Chart

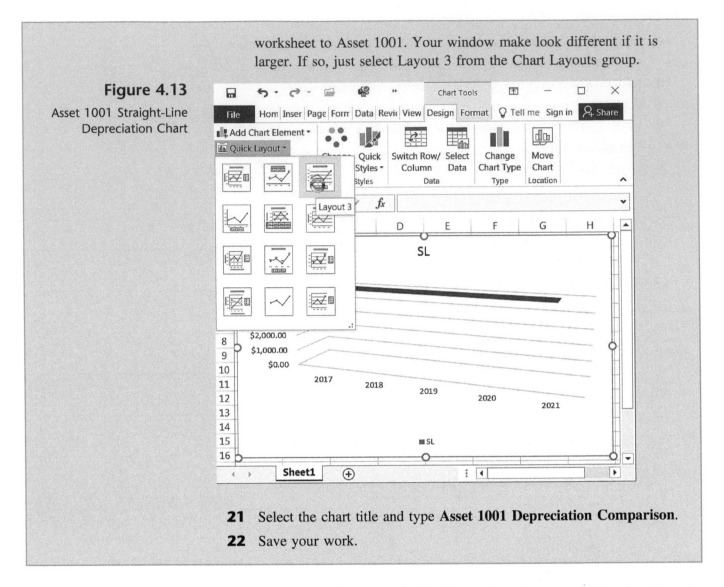

21 Select the chart title and type **Asset 1001 Depreciation Comparison**.

22 Save your work.

Kyle then explains how to make the depreciation chart comparative. Once the original chart is created, all that is needed is to add lines that depict depreciation based on the double declining balance and sum-of-the-year's digits methods. Adding a new series of data to an existing chart is simple: first you select the chart and then, using Chart Tools, you add data from existing workbooks you've already created.

Kyle suggests that you now add data from the double declining and sum-of-the-year's digits files that you saved before.

To modify an existing chart to show comparative depreciation methods:

1 Click and select the chart you created previously.

2 From the Design tab, click **Select Data** from the Data Group as you did before.

3 Click **Add** from the Legend Entries (Series) section.

4 Type **DDB** (for double declining balance depreciation) in the Series name: text box.

5 Delete whatever text appears in the Series values: text box.

6 Select the **Range icon** like you've done before, then make the ch4-01_DDB_student_name window active.

7 Select cells **G12** through **G16** from the Asset 1001 worksheet located in the ch4-01_DDB_student_name workbook.

8 Press [**Enter**] and then click **OK** in the Edit Series window.

9 Click **Add** from the Legend Entries (Series) section.

10 Type **SYD** (for sum-of-the-year's digits depreciation) in the Series name: text box.

11 Delete whatever text appears in the Series values: text box.

12 Select the **Range icon** like you've done before, then make the ch4-01_SYD_student_name window active.

13 Select cells **B12** through **B16** from the Asset 1001 worksheet located in the ch4-01_SYD_student_name workbook.

14 Press [**Enter**] and then click **OK** in the Edit Series window.

15 Click **OK** in the Select Data Source window.

16 Your new comparative depreciation chart should look like Figure 4.14.

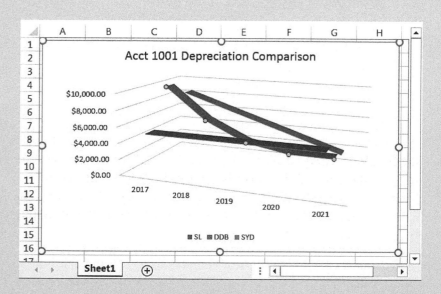

Figure 4.14

Asset 1001 Comparative Depreciation Chart

17 With the chart still selected, click **File**.

18 Click **Print**.

19 Make sure that Print Selected Chart is selected in the Settings section and then click **Print** to print the chart.

20 Save your work and close all windows.

"That's just like I remember from my college classes," you comment.

Kyle points out that straight-line depreciation will always produce a horizontal line, reflecting a constant depreciation expense. The double declining balance method will always produce a curved line, reflecting larger depreciation in the first years with declines thereafter. Finally, sum-of-the-year's digits always produces a straight line that goes down from left to right, reflecting larger depreciation in the first years with a constant decline each year thereafter.

Partial Year Depreciation

The preceding examples calculating depreciation were done using full-year depreciation, assuming that companies purchased their long-term assets on January 1 of the year of acquisition. That, of course, is rarely the case. Usually assets are acquired throughout the year, and thus depreciation schedules should account for this fact.

One key piece of information already included in the depreciation schedule is the date of acquisition. From that you can calculate the number of days of depreciation to be calculated for the first year. An additional year needs to be added to the schedule to account for the depreciation not recorded in the initial year of acquisition.

To modify your previously created worksheet for straight-line depreciation to accommodate partial year depreciation:

1 Open your previously saved file ch04-01_SLN_student_name.xlsx.

2 Click the **File** menu, then click **Save As**, then type **ch4-01_SLN_PY_student_name.xlsx** as the new file name and click **Save**.

3 Select the **Asset 1001** tab.

4 Type **3/1/17** in cell B5 as the new date acquired and then press **[Enter]**.

5 Right-click row 10 and select **Insert** to add a new row.

6 Type **Days in 1ˢᵗ year** into cell A10.

7 Type **=Date(2017,12,31)–B5** into cell B10 and then press **[Enter]**. (This equation will calculate the number of days between 3/1/17 and 12/31/17.)

8 Select cell **B10** and select **General** to format the cell into a numerical value.

9 Select cell **B13** and type **=SLN($B$6,$B$8,$B$9) * (B10/365)** as the new formula. (This adds the percent of a year the asset was used in 2017 to the previous formula.)

10 Type **2022** into cell A18.

11 Type **=SLN($B$6,$B$8,$B$9)-B13** into cell B18.

12 Copy the formula in C17 down to cell C18.

13 Click **File** and then click **Save**. Your worksheet should look like Figure 4.15.

	A	B	C
1	What SUP, Inc. Depreciation Schedule		
2			
3	Asset #	1001	
4	Asset	Display Racks	
5	Date acquired	3/1/2017	
6	Cost	$ 25,000.00	
7	Depreciation method	S/L	
8	Salvage value	$ -	
9	Estimated useful life	5	
10	Days in 1st year	305	
11			
12	Year	Depreciation Expense	Accumulated Depreciation
13	2017	$4,178.08	$4,178.08
14	2018	$5,000.00	$9,178.08
15	2019	$5,000.00	$14,178.08
16	2020	$5,000.00	$19,178.08
17	2021	$5,000.00	$24,178.08
18	2022	$821.92	$25,000.00

Summary | **Asset 1001** | Asset 1 …

Figure 4.15

Partial Year Straight-Line Depreciation for Asset 1001

14 Perform a similar process to modify Asset 1002 with a date acquired of 11/1/17. Your worksheet for Asset 1002 should look like Figure 4.16.

	A	B	C
1	What SUP, Inc. Depreciation Schedule		
2			
3	Asset #	1002	
4	Asset	Chairs	
5	Date acquired	11/1/2017	
6	Cost	$ 8,000.00	
7	Depreciation method	S/L	
8	Salvage value	$ 300.00	
9	Estimated useful life	5	
10	Days in 1st year	60	
11			
12	Year	Depreciation Expense	Accumulated Depreciation
13	2017	$253.15	$253.15
14	2018	$1,540.00	$1,793.15
15	2019	$1,540.00	$3,333.15
16	2020	$1,540.00	$4,873.15
17	2021	$1,540.00	$6,413.15
18	2022	$1,286.85	$7,700.00

… | Asset 1001 | **Asset 1002** | Sheet' …

Figure 4.16

Partial Year Straight-Line Depreciation for Asset 1002

15 Save your work.

A similar process is used to calculate partial year depreciation using the declining balance method. However, this method requires you to parcel the normal depreciation calculation into each period. For example, an asset acquired on October 1 would require 3 months (Oct, Nov, Dec) of year 1's declining balance amount (25%) to be reported in the first year of asset ownership. In the second year of ownership, 9 months (75%) of year 1's declining balance amount would be added to 3 months (25%) of year 2's declining balance amount. You decide to demonstrate this using your previously created declining balance worksheets.

To modify your previously created worksheet for declining balance depreciation to accommodate partial year depreciation:

1 Open your previously saved file ch04-01_DDB_student_name.xlsx.

2 Click the **File** menu, then click **Save As**, then type **ch4-01_DDB_PY_student_name.xlsx** as the new file name and click **Save**.

3 Select the **Asset 1001** tab.

4 Type **4/1/17** in cell B5 as the new date acquired and then press [**Enter**].

5 Right-click row 10 and select **Insert** to add a new row.

6 Type **Days in 1st year** into cell A10.

7 Type **=Date(2017,12,31)–B5** into cell B10 and then press [**Enter**]. (This equation will calculate the number of days between 4/1/17 and 12/31/17.)

8 Select cell **B10** and select **General** to format the cell into a numerical value.

9 Format cell B10 to be centered if it is not already formatted.

10 Type **Partial Year Schedule** in cell A19.

11 Type **2017** through **2022** into cells A20 through A25, respectively.

12 Type **=G13*($B$10/365)** into cell G20. Format the cell as currency.

13 Type **=G13 - (G13*($B$10/365))** into cell G21. Format the cell as currency if it is not already formatted. This places the first-year declining balance depreciation not allocated to 2017 into the cell. You still have to add the allocated portion of the second-year declining balance depreciation to the formula for 2018.

14 Type **=G13 - (G13*($B$10/365)) + (G14*($B$10/365))** into cell G21.

15 Fill down the formula in G21 to cells G22 through G25.

16 Copy the formulas at H13 and H14 to cells H20 and H21.

17 Fill down the formula in H21 to cells H22 through H25. Your worksheet should look like Figure 4.17.

Figure 4.17

Partial Year Declining Balance Depreciation for Asset 1001

	A	B	C	D	E	F	G	H
1	What SUP, Inc. Depreciation Schedule							
2								
3	Asset #	1001						
4	Asset	Display Racks						
5	Date acquired	4/1/2017						
6	Cost	$ 25,000.00						
7	Depreciation method	DDB						
8	Salvage value	$ -						
9	Estimated useful life	5						
10	Days in 1st year	274						
11								
12	Year	Depreciation Expense	Accumulated Depreciation	Straight-Line Test	Switch	Depreciation Expense	Accumulated Depreciation	
13	2017	$10,000.00	$10,000.00	$5,000.00	-	$10,000.00	$10,000.00	
14	2018	$6,000.00	$16,000.00	$3,750.00	-	$6,000.00	$16,000.00	
15	2019	$3,600.00	$19,600.00	$3,000.00	-	$3,600.00	$19,600.00	
16	2020	$2,160.00	$21,760.00	$2,700.00	X	$2,700.00	$22,300.00	
17	2021	$1,296.00	$23,056.00	$3,240.00	X	$2,700.00	$25,000.00	
18								
19	Partial Year Schedule							
20	2017					$ 7,506.85	$7,506.85	
21	2018					$ 6,997.26	$14,504.11	
22	2019					$ 4,198.36	$18,702.47	
23	2020					$ 2,924.38	$21,626.85	
24	2021					$ 2,700.00	$24,326.85	
25	2022					$ 673.15	$25,000.00	

Summary | **Asset 1001** | Asset 1002 | Sheet1 | Sheet2 | Sheet3

18 Perform a similar process to modify Asset 1002 with a date acquired of 9/1/17. Your worksheet for Asset 1002 should look like Figure 4.18.

	A	B	C	D	E	F	G	H
1	What SUP, Inc. Depreciation Schedule							
2								
3	Asset #	1002						
4	Asset	Chairs						
5	Date acquired	9/1/2017						
6	Cost	$ 8,000.00						
7	Depreciation method	DDB						
8	Salvage value	$ 300.00						
9	Estimated useful life	5						
10	Days in 1st year	121						
11								
12	Year	Depreciation Expense	Accumulated Depreciation	Straight-Line Test	Switch	Depreciation Expense	Accumulated Depreciation	
13	2017	$3,200.00	$3,200.00	$1,540.00	-	$3,200.00	$3,200.00	
14	2018	$1,920.00	$5,120.00	$1,125.00	-	$1,920.00	$5,120.00	
15	2019	$1,152.00	$6,272.00	$860.00	-	$1,152.00	$6,272.00	
16	2020	$691.20	$6,963.20	$714.00	X	$714.00	$6,986.00	
17	2021	$414.72	$7,377.92	$736.80	X	$714.00	$7,700.00	
18								
19	Partial Year Schedule							
20	2017					$ 1,060.82	$1,060.82	
21	2018					$ 2,775.67	$3,836.49	
22	2019					$ 1,665.40	$5,501.90	
23	2020					$ 1,006.80	$6,508.70	
24	2021					$ 714.00	$7,222.70	
25	2022					$ 477.30	$7,700.00	

Summary | Asset 1001 | **Asset 1002** | Sheet1 | Sheet2 | Sheet3

Figure 4.18

Partial Year Declining Balance Depreciation for Asset 1002

A similar process is used to calculate partial year depreciation using the sum-of-the-year digits method. However, this method requires you to parcel the normal depreciation calculation into each period. You decide to demonstrate this using your previously created sum-of-the-years digits worksheets.

To modify your previously created worksheet for created sum-of-the-year's digits depreciation to accommodate partial year depreciation:

1 Open your previously saved file ch04-01_SYD_student_name.xlsx.

2 Click the **File** menu, then click **Save As**, then type **ch4-01_SYD_PY_student_name.xlsx** as the new file name and click **Save**.

3 Select the **Asset 1001** tab.

4 Type **6/1/17** in cell B5 as the new date acquired and then press [**Enter**].

5 Right-click row 10 and select **Insert** to add a new row.

6 Type **Days in 1st year** into cell A10.

7 Type **=Date(2017,12,31)–B5** into cell B10 and then press [**Enter**]. (This equation will calculate the number of days between 6/1/17 and 12/31/17.)

8 Select cell **B10** and select **General** to format the cell into a numerical value.

9 Format cell B10 to be centered.

10 Type **Partial Year Schedule** in cell A19.

11 Type **2017** through **2022** into cells A20 through A25, respectively.

12 Type **=B13*($B$10/365)** into cell B20. Format the cell as currency.

13 Type **=B13 - (B13*($B$10/365))** into cell B21. Format the cell as currency. This places the first-year declining balance depreciation not allocated to 2017 into the cell. You still have to add the allocated portion of the second-year declining balance depreciation to the formula for 2018.

14 Type **=B13 - (B13*($B$10/365)) + (B14*($B$10/365))** into cell B21.

15 Fill down the formula in B21 to cells B22 through B25.

16 Copy the formulas at C13 and C14 to cells C20 and C21.

17 Fill down the formula in C21 to cells C22 through C25. Your worksheet should look like Figure 4.19.

	A	B	C
1	**What SUP, Inc. Depreciation Schedule**		
2			
3	**Asset #**	1001	
4	**Asset**	Display Racks	
5	**Date acquired**	6/1/2017	
6	**Cost**	$ 25,000.00	
7	**Depreciation method**	SYD	
8	**Salvage value**	$ -	
9	**Estimated useful life**	5	
10	**Days in 1st year**	213	
11			
12	**Year**	**Depreciation Expense**	**Accumulated Depreciation**
13	2017	$8,333.33	$8,333.33
14	2018	$6,666.67	$15,000.00
15	2019	$5,000.00	$20,000.00
16	2020	$3,333.33	$23,333.33
17	2021	$1,666.67	$25,000.00
18			
19	Partial Year Schedule		
20	2017	$4,863.01	$4,863.01
21	2018	$7,360.73	$12,223.74
22	2019	$5,694.06	$17,917.81
23	2020	$4,027.40	$21,945.21
24	2021	$2,360.73	$24,305.94
25	2022	$694.06	$25,000.00

Summary | **Asset 1001** | Asset 1002 ...

Figure 4.19

Partial Year Sum-of-the-Year's Digits Depreciation for Asset 1001

18 Perform a similar process to modify Asset 1002 with a date acquired of 2/1/17. Your worksheet for Asset 1002 should look like Figure 4.20.

	A	B	C
1	**What SUP, Inc. Depreciation Schedule**		
2			
3	**Asset #**	1002	
4	**Asset**	Chairs	
5	**Date acquired**	2/1/2017	
6	**Cost**	$ 8,000.00	
7	**Depreciation method**	SYD	
8	**Salvage value**	$ 300.00	
9	**Estimated useful life**	5	
10	**Days in 1st year**	333	
11			
12	**Year**	**Depreciation Expense**	**Accumulated Depreciation**
13	2017	$2,566.67	$2,566.67
14	2018	$2,053.33	$4,620.00
15	2019	$1,540.00	$6,160.00
16	2020	$1,026.67	$7,186.67
17	2021	$513.33	$7,700.00
18			
19	Partial Year Schedule		
20	2017	$2,341.64	$2,341.64
21	2018	$2,098.34	$4,439.98
22	2019	$1,585.00	$6,024.99
23	2020	$1,071.67	$7,096.66
24	2021	$558.34	$7,655.00
25	2022	$45.00	$7,700.00

Figure 4.20

Partial Year Sum-of-the-Year's Digits Depreciation for Asset 1002

19 Click **Save** and then close Excel.

Kyle explains that the only method that's a bit difficult is declining balance. Otherwise, calculating partial year depreciation is fairly logical.

End Note

You've applied some of what you learned in the first three chapters to a specific accounting problem, the depreciation of fixed assets. In the next chapter, you will learn how to use Excel to create loan amortization schedules.

Chapter 4 Questions

1   What function is built-into Excel to help you calculate straight-line depreciation?

2   What arguments does the SLN function take?

3   Should the arguments in the SLN function be values or references?

4   Why should the arguments in the SLN function be values or references?

5   Should references used as arguments to the SLN function be absolute or relative?

6   What is the purpose of a depreciation summary?

7   What other depreciation functions are built into Excel?

8   What additional argument is added for these depreciation functions?

9   How do you add a new series of data to an existing chart?

10   Describe the shape of the three lines in a depreciation comparison chart depicting straight-line, double declining balance, and sum-of-the-year's digits depreciation.

Chapter 4 Assignments

1   Modify What SUP's Straight-Line Depreciation Schedule

You are to add another depreciation schedule for What SUP. Use the ch4-01_SLN_student_name.xls worksheet you created in this chapter. Add a new depreciation worksheet, labeled Asset 1003, using the Move or Copy Shortcut menu. The asset to be depreciated is a forge purchased on January 1, 2018, for $85,000. It has an estimated salvage value of $4,000 and is to be depreciated over 3 years using the straight-line method. Update the summary worksheet to include information on this new asset. (Be careful to note the date this asset was acquired.) Save the file as ch4-02_SLN_student_name (replacing student_name with your name).

Print the newly completed worksheet for Asset 1003 and the modified Summary worksheet in Value view, with your name and date printed in the lower left footer and the file name in the lower right footer.

2   Modify What SUP's Double Declining Balance Depreciation Schedule

You are to add another depreciation schedule for What SUP. Use the ch4-01_DDB_student_name worksheet you created in this chapter. Add a new depreciation worksheet, labeled Asset 1003, using the Move or Copy Shortcut menu. The asset to be depreciated is the forge purchased on January 1, 2018, for $85,000 (again, its estimated salvage value is $4,000). The forge is to be depreciated (over 3 years) using the double declining balance method. Update the summary worksheet to include information on this asset. (Be careful to note the date this asset was acquired.) Save the file as ch4-02_DDB_student_name (replacing student_name with your name).

Print the newly completed worksheet for Asset 1003 and the modified Summary worksheet (showing only 2017–2019) in Value view, with your name and date printed in the lower left footer and the file name in the lower right footer.

3   Modify What SUP's Sum-of-the-Year's Digits Depreciation Schedule

You are to add another depreciation schedule for What SUP. Use the ch4-01_SYD_student_name worksheet you created in this chapter. Add a new depreciation worksheet, labeled Asset 1003, using the Move or Copy Shortcut menu. The asset to be depreciated is the forge purchased on January 1, 2018, for $85,000 (again, its estimated salvage value is $4,000). The forge is to be depreciated (over 4 years) using the sum-of-the-year's digits method. Update the summary worksheet to include information on this asset. (Be careful to note the date this asset was acquired.) Save the file as ch4-02_SYD_student_name (replacing student_name with your name).

Print the newly completed worksheet for Asset 1003 and the modified Summary worksheet (showing only 2017–2019) in Value view, with your name and date printed in the lower left footer and the file name in the lower right footer.

4   What SUP's Depreciation Comparison Chart for Asset 1002

You are to add another depreciation chart for What SUP. Use the ch4-01_Chart_student_name workbook you created in this chapter. Add a new depreciation chart by changing the name of Sheet2 to Asset 1002. Following the steps shown in the chapter, create a new chart comparing straight-line, double declining balance, and sum-of-the-year's digit depreciation amounts for Asset 1002. Save the workbook as ch4-02_Asset 1002_Chart_student_name (replacing student_name with your name). Print then newly created chart.

5   What SUP's Depreciation Comparison Chart for Asset 1003

You are to create a depreciation chart for What SUP for Asset 1003. After completing assignments 1, 2, and 3, and following the steps shown in the chapter, create a new chart comparing straight-line, double declining balance, and sum-of-the-year's digits depreciation amount for Asset 1003. Save the workbook as ch4-02_Asset 1003_Chart_student_name (replacing student_name with your name). Then print the newly created chart.

6   What SUP Partial Year Straight-Line Depreciation for Asset 1004

Create a new worksheet to calculate depreciation for a table purchased on August 1, 2017, for $95,000. It has an estimated salvage value of $2,000 and is to be depreciated over 10 years using the straight-line method. Follow the same process used in the chapter to calculate depreciation for partial periods. Save the workbook as ch4-07 SLN_PY_student_name (replacing student_name with your name). Print the newly created worksheet.

7   What SUP Partial Year Double Declining Balance Depreciation for Asset 1004

Create a new worksheet to calculate depreciation for a table purchased on August 1, 2017, for $95,000. It has an estimated salvage value of $2,000 and is to be depreciated over 10 years using the double declining balance method. Follow the same process used in the chapter to calculate depreciation for partial periods. Save the workbook as ch4-08 DDB_PY_student_name (replacing student_name with your name). Print the newly created worksheet.

8   What SUP Partial Year Sum of the Year's Digits Depreciation for Asset 1004

Create a new worksheet to calculate depreciation for a table purchased on August 1, 2017, for $95,000. It has an estimated salvage value of $2,000 and is to be depreciated over 10 years using the sum-of-the-year's digits method. Follow the same process used in the chapter to calculate depreciation for partial periods. Save the workbook as ch4-09 SYD_PY_student_name (replacing student_name with your name). Print the newly created worksheet.

Chapter 4 Case Problem 1:
KELLY'S BOUTIQUE

Kelly's Boutique owned the following fixed assets as of December 31, 2018:

Description

Asset #	101	102	103
Asset	Building	Computer System	Phone System
Date acquired	1/1/15	1/1/17	1/1/17
Cost	$625,000	$95,000	$84,000
Salvage value	$25,000	$4,000	$5,000
Estimated useful life	25 years	4 years	5 years

You are to create a fixed asset depreciation summary and individual depreciation worksheets for Kelly's Boutique using the straight-line depreciation method based on the information tabulated above. Be sure to pay close attention to the date of purchase for each asset so that your summary sheet is correct. The summary sheet need only include depreciation from 2015 through 2018. Individual assets must show depreciation over their entire useful life. Follow the text examples for formatting. Label your worksheets as follows: Summary SL, Asset 101 SL, Asset 102 SL, and Asset 103 SL.

In the same workbook, create Kelly's Boutique's fixed asset depreciation summary and individual depreciation worksheets using the double declining balance method and based on the tabulated information. Again, pay close attention to the date of purchase for each asset so that your summary sheet is correct. Label your worksheets: Summary DDB, Asset 101 DDB, Asset 102 DDB, and Asset 103 DDB.

In the same workbook, next create Kelly's Boutique's fixed asset depreciation summary and individual depreciation worksheets using the sum-of-the-year's digits method and based on the tabulated information. Pay close attention to the date of purchase for each asset so that your summary sheet is correct. Label your worksheets: Summary SYD, Asset 101 SYD, Asset 102 SYD, and Asset 103 SYD.

In the same workbook, you should now create a chart of Asset 101's depreciation (over its 25-year estimated useful life) that compares the straight-line, double declining balance, and sum-of-the-year's digits methods of calculating depreciation. Label this worksheet: Chart. Choose any 2D line chart and chart layout that you like.

Save the workbook as ch4-03_student_name (replacing student_name with your name). Print all worksheets in Value view, with your name and date printed in the lower left footer and the file name in the lower right footer.

Chapter 4 Case Problem 2:
WINE DEPOT

The Wine Depot owned the following fixed assets as of December 31, 2018:

Description			
Asset #	101	102	103
Asset	Equipment	Truck	Portable
Date acquired	1/1/15	1/1/16	1/1/17
Cost	$689,115	$150,000	$198,412
Salvage value	$15,000	$8,000	$23,000
Estimated useful life	5 years	10 years	15 years

You are to create Wine Depot's fixed asset depreciation summary and individual depreciation worksheets using the straight-line depreciation method and based on the information in the preceding table. Be sure to pay close attention to the date of purchase for each asset so that your summary sheet is correct. The summary sheet need only include depreciation from 2015 through 2018. Individual assets must show depreciation over their entire useful life. Follow the text examples for formatting. Label your worksheets as follows: Summary SL, Asset 101 SL, Asset 102 SL, and Asset 103 SL.

In the same workbook, create Wine Depot's fixed asset depreciation summary and individual depreciation worksheets using the double declining balance method and based on the same tabulated information. Again, pay close attention to the date of purchase for each asset so that your summary sheet is correct. Label your worksheets: Summary DDB, Asset 101 DDB, Asset 102 DDB, and Asset 103 DDB.

In the same workbook, next create Wine Depot's fixed asset depreciation summary and individual depreciation worksheets using the sum-of-the-year's digits method and based on the tabulated information. Be sure to pay close attention to the date of purchase for each asset so that your summary sheet is correct. Label your worksheets: Summary SYD, Asset 101 SYD, Asset 102 SYD, and Asset 103 SYD.

In the same workbook, you should now create a chart of Asset 103's depreciation (over its 15-year estimated useful life) that compares the straight-line, double declining balance, and sum-of-the-year's digits methods of calculating depreciation. Label this worksheet: Chart. Choose any 2D line chart and chart layout that you like.

Save the workbook as ch4-04_student_name (replacing student_name with your name). Print all worksheets in Value view, with your name and date printed in the lower left footer and the file name in the lower right footer.

Chapter 4 Case Problem 3:
SNICK'S BOARD SHOP

Snick's Board Shop owned the fixed assets shown below as of December 31, 2018:

Asset #	Shelving	Cash Register	Computer
Date acquired	1/1/16	1/1/16	1/1/16
Cost	$8,000	$6,500	$24,000
Salvage value	$500	$300	$1,900
Estimated useful life	10 years	8 years	3 years

You are to create Snick's fixed asset depreciation worksheets using the straight-line depreciation method and based on the information in the preceding table. No summary sheet is required. Individual assets must show depreciation over their entire useful life. Follow the text examples for formatting. Label each worksheet Shelving SL, Cash Register SL, and Computer SL.

In the same workbook, create Snick's fixed asset depreciation worksheets using the double declining balance method and based on the same table. No summary sheet is required. Individual assets must show depreciation over their entire useful life. Follow the text examples for formatting. Label each worksheet Shelving DDB, Cash Register DDB, and Computer DDB.

In the same workbook, create Snick's fixed asset depreciation worksheets using the sum-of-the-year's-digits method and based on the same table. No summary sheet is required. Individual assets must show depreciation over their entire useful life. Follow the text examples for formatting. Label each worksheet Shelving SYD, Cash Register SYD, and Computer SYD.

In the same workbook, you should now create a chart of each asset's depreciation that compares the straight-line, double declining balance, and sum-of-the-year's digits methods of calculating depreciation. Label each worksheet Shelving Chart, Cash Register Chart, and Computer Chart. Choose any line chart and chart layout that you like.

Save the workbook as ch4-05_student_name (replacing student_name with your name). Print all worksheets in Value view, with your name and date printed in the lower left footer and the file name in the lower right footer.

Chapter 4 Case Problem 4:
ROSEY'S ROSES

Rosey's Roses owned the fixed assets shown below as of December 31, 2019:

Asset	Building #1	Building #2	Equipment
Date acquired	1/1/18	1/1/19	1/1/18
Cost	$74,000	$24,000	$9,500
Salvage value	$4,000	$1,000	$500
Estimated useful life	15 years	5 years	4 years

This assignment has no beginning student file. You are to create Rosey's fixed asset depreciation worksheets using the straight-line depreciation method and based on the information in the preceding table. No summary sheet is required. Individual assets must show depreciation over their entire useful life. Follow the text examples for formatting. Label each worksheet Building #1 SL, Building #2 SL, and Equipment SL.

In the same workbook, create Rosey's fixed asset depreciation worksheets using the double declining balance method and based on the same table. No summary sheet is required. Individual assets must show depreciation over their entire useful life. Follow the text examples for formatting. Label each worksheet Building #1 DDB, Building #2 DDB, and Equipment DDB.

In the same workbook, create Rosey's fixed asset depreciation worksheets using the sum-of-the-year's-digits method and based on the same table. No summary sheet is required. Individual assets must show depreciation over their entire useful life. Follow the text examples for formatting. Label each worksheet Building #1 SYD, Building #2 SYD, and Equipment SYD.

In the same workbook, you should now create a chart of each asset's depreciation that compares the straight-line, double declining balance, and sum-of-the-year's-digits methods of calculating depreciation. Label each worksheet Building #1 Chart, Building #2 Chart, and Equipment Chart. Choose any line chart and chart layout that you like.

Save the workbook as ch4-06_student_name (replacing student_name with your name). Print all worksheets in Value view, with your name and date printed in the lower left footer and the file name in the lower right footer.

Loan and Bond Amortization

In this chapter you will learn:

- How to use the payment function to calculate payments to retire a loan
- How to create a loan amortization schedule
- How to use a what-if analysis with the payment function
- How to use names in a worksheet
- How to use the present value function to calculate the proceeds of a bond
- How to create a bond amortization schedule
- How to use Excel's what-if analysis and goal-seeking capabilities with the present value function
- How to use Excel's Scenario Manager
- How to integrate monthly periods into loan or bond amortization analyses

Case: **What SUP, Inc.**

Nathan and Meagan have been contemplating the prospect of opening several new locations. They are somewhat strapped for cash and are interested in looking into their financing alternatives. On the one hand, they could borrow funds from their local banker. Alternatively, they could borrow money by issuing bonds to local investors. They are curious whether Excel could help them analyze the alternatives or at least help them determine the payments required to pay back a loan or bond.

"Can Excel perform these types of loan calculations?" Meagan asks.

"Yes," Kyle responds, "not only can Excel help you with the calculations, it can also help you with what-if sensitivity analyses to determine interest costs, loan payments, and balances."

Loan Calculations

Kyle explains that loans usually involve some constant periodic payment that pays both interest and principal over a specified period of time. Banks usually want to see some principal payment rather than the interest-only payments often associated with bonds. Excel has a built-in function that calculates the payment on a loan given three variables: interest rate, period, and loan amount. The PMT function takes three arguments and is written =PMT (rate, nper, pv), where *rate* is the periodic interest rate, *nper* is the number of periods, and *pv* is the present value (usually the loan amount). Kyle suggests that you create a worksheet to calculate the annual payment necessary on a 3-year, $100,000 loan at an interest rate of 10 percent.

To calculate a loan payment using Excel's built-in function:

1 Start Excel and open file ch5-01. The worksheet should look like Figure 5.1.

Figure 5.1

Loan Worksheet

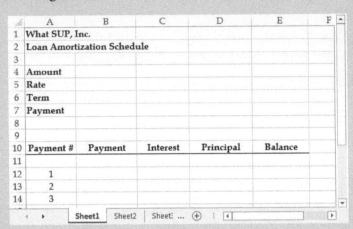

2 Type **100000** in cell B4, **10** in cell B5, and **3** in cell B6.

3 Type **=PMT(B5,B6,B4)** in cell B7, and then press [**Enter**]. Note that the resulting amount is a negative number. This is Excel's way of indicating that cash must be paid out to repay the loan proceeds received.

4 Place a negative sign in front of the function PMT so that the formula reads as follows: **=−PMT(B5,B6,B4)**. This has the effect of making the payment a positive number.

5 Save your work to ch5-01_student_name (replacing student_name with your name).

Thus, a payment of $40,211.48, when made at the end of each year for 3 years, will repay the loan and interest charges.

"How much of those payments is interest and how much principal?" Nathan asks.

"Good question." Kyle responds. "That's why it is helpful to create a loan amortization schedule with each worksheet."

Loan Amortization Schedule

Kyle explains how a loan amortization schedule answers Nathan's question. The schedule breaks down each payment into the components of interest and principal. You remind Kyle that interest expense, based on the accrual accounting principal, is calculated as the balance owed multiplied by the periodic interest rate. The amount of payment that exceeds the interest owed is applied to the principal and so reduces the loan amount.

"I can do that," you say.

To add a loan amortization schedule to your worksheet:

1 Type =**B4** in cell E11. This places the loan amount at the beginning of the schedule.

2 Type =**$B$7** in cell B12. This places the loan payment in the schedule. (This reference is absolute so that it can be replicated later.)

3 Type =**E11*$B$5** in cell C12. This formula calculates interest expense as the loan amount multiplied by the interest rate. (The reference to the interest rate is absolute so that it can be replicated later.)

4 Type =**B12–C12** in cell D12. This formula calculates the amount of the payment that reduces the loan amount, otherwise known as principal.

5 Type =**E11–D12** in cell E12. This formula calculates the new loan balance after the loan payment as the previous loan balance less principal reduction.

6 Replicate formulas located at cells B12 through E12 down through row 14.

7 The resulting worksheet should look like Figure 5.2.

	A	B	C	D	E
1	What SUP, Inc.				
2	Loan Amortization Schedule				
3					
4	Amount	$ 100,000.00			
5	Rate	10%			
6	Term	3			
7	Payment	$40,211.48			
8					
9					
10	Payment #	Payment	Interest	Principal	Balance
11					$100,000.00
12	1	$40,211.48	$10,000.00	$30,211.48	$ 69,788.52
13	2	$40,211.48	$ 6,978.85	$33,232.63	$ 36,555.89
14	3	$40,211.48	$ 3,655.59	$36,555.89	$ -
15					

Sheet1 Sheet2 ... ⊕

Figure 5.2

Loan Amortization Schedule for a $100,000 Loan at 10%

8 Save your work.

Kyle points out that, at the end of the loan period, the balance should (of course) be zero, which it is in the worksheet.

"What is the payment if the interest rate is higher or lower?" Meagan asks.

"Another good question," Kyle comments. "That leads us into the sensitivity features of Excel that we've worked on previously."

What-If Analysis and the Payment Function

Kyle explains that, because you built the loan amortization worksheet with cell references, a what-if analysis is easy. To investigate the effects of changing interest rates or different loan balances, Kyle suggests he determine the effect on the loan payment of interest rates of 11 percent and 9 percent as well as loan balances of $150,000 or $75,000.

Using Excel, Kyle demonstrates how these variable changes affect the loan payment.

To perform a what-if analysis using the payment function:

1 Type **11** in cell B5, and then press [**Enter**]. Note the change in payment.

2 Type **9** in cell B5, and then press [**Enter**]. Again, note the change in payment. Your worksheet should look like Figure 5.3.

Figure 5.3

Loan Amortization Schedule for a $100,000 Loan at 9%

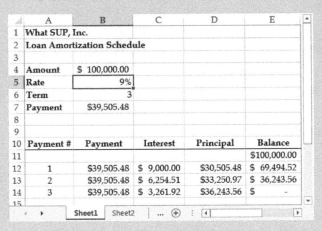

	A	B	C	D	E
1	What SUP, Inc.				
2	Loan Amortization Schedule				
3					
4	Amount	$ 100,000.00			
5	Rate	9%			
6	Term	3			
7	Payment	$39,505.48			
8					
9					
10	Payment #	Payment	Interest	Principal	Balance
11					$100,000.00
12	1	$39,505.48	$ 9,000.00	$30,505.48	$ 69,494.52
13	2	$39,505.48	$ 6,254.51	$33,250.97	$ 36,243.56
14	3	$39,505.48	$ 3,261.92	$36,243.56	$ -
15					

Sheet1   Sheet2   ... (+)

3 Type **10** in cell B5, and then press [**Enter**].

4 Type **150000** in cell B4, then press [**Enter**]. Note the change in payment.

5 Type **75000** in cell B4, then press [**Enter**]. Note the change in payment. Your worksheet should look like Figure 5.4.

Figure 5.4

Loan Amortization Schedule for a $75,000 Loan at 10%

	A	B	C	D	E
1	What SUP, Inc.				
2	Loan Amortization Schedule				
3					
4	Amount	$ 75,000.00			
5	Rate	10%			
6	Term	3			
7	Payment	$30,158.61			
8					
9					
10	Payment #	Payment	Interest	Principal	Balance
11					$ 75,000.00
12	1	$30,158.61	$ 7,500.00	$22,658.61	$ 52,341.39
13	2	$30,158.61	$ 5,234.14	$24,924.47	$ 27,416.92
14	3	$30,158.61	$ 2,741.69	$27,416.92	$ (0.00)
15					

Sheet1   Sheet2   ... (+)

"Fascinating!" Meagan exclaims. "This is a great tool!"

"Yes, but these formulas get a bit confusing," Nathan comments. "I have trouble understanding what the payment function is doing with B5, B6, and B4. Isn't there a better way of describing the arguments to functions or what these cell references mean?"

Kyle decides to introduce the concept of named ranges to you, Nathan, and Meagan. He explains that cell references can also be named for clearer analysis.

Names in a Worksheet

Excel provides a naming feature in every worksheet that allows you to define a cell or cells with a name that can then be used elsewhere in the worksheet. There are two steps involved in changing an existing worksheet from cell references to named references. Step 1 is defining cell names; Step 2 is applying those names throughout the worksheet. Kyle suggests that you first name the variables Amount, Rate, Term, and Payment and then apply those names throughout the loan amortization worksheet.

To use names in the loan amortization worksheet:

1 Select the cell range **A4** through **B7**.

2 Click **Create from Selection** from the Defined Names group of the Formulas tab.

3 Click in the check box next to Left column as shown in Figure 5.5. (*Note:* This will name the cells in B4 through B7 with the corresponding name in the left column.)

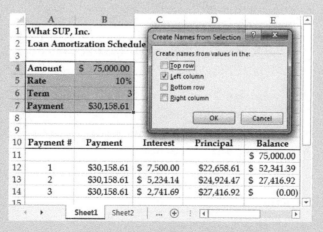

Figure 5.5

Creating Names

4 Click **OK**.

5 Click in cell **E11**.

6 Click **Use in Formula** from the Defined Names group on the Formulas tab.

7 Click **Amount** and then press [**Enter**]. (*Note:* This action only replaces the reference to B4 in cell E11 with the newly defined name Amount.)

8 Click in cell **B12**. Click **Use in Formula** like you did before and this time click **Payment** and then press **[Enter]**. Then fill this new formula down to cell B14.

9 Click in any blank cell and then click the down arrow next to Define Name and then click **Apply Names** and then click **OK** from the Apply Names window. (*Note:* This action replaces all references to B4, B5, B6, and B7 with the respective new names of Amount, Rate, Term, and Payment.)

10 Click in cell **B7**. Observe that the new argument references the payment function: =−PMT(Rate,Term,Amount).

11 Save your work.

Kyle explains that not all cell references will be replaced, since you defined only four cells. However, all references to those cells will now refer to the names instead of specific cells such as B4 and B5.

"This looks much better," Nathan says. "Now I can clearly see that the payment function takes three arguments: Rate, Term, and Amount."

Kyle further explains that these named cells can be used in other ways as well. For example, Excel provides you with a Name Box that lists all the named cells and ranges on the worksheet. He suggests that you explore the use of names further.

To explore the use of named cells and ranges:

1 Click on the drop-down arrow of the Name box located next to the formula text box to reveal the named cells on the worksheet. Then highlight Rate but don't click.

2 Now click **Rate**. (Note how Excel now positions the active cell as B5, the location of the name Rate.) See Figure 5.6.

Figure 5.6

Name Box

				fx	10%		
Rate							
Amount			B	C	D	E	
Payment		Inc.					
Rate		rtization Schedule					
Term							
4	Amount	$ 75,000.00					
5	Rate	10%					
6	Term	3					
7	Payment	$30,158.61					
8							
9							
10	Payment #	Payment	Interest	Principal	Balance		
11					$ 75,000.00		
12	1	$30,158.61	$ 7,500.00	$22,658.61	$ 52,341.39		
13	2	$30,158.61	$ 5,234.14	$24,924.47	$ 27,416.92		
14	3	$30,158.61	$ 2,741.69	$27,416.92	$ (0.00)		

3 Save and close this file.

Once names have been created, they can be used throughout the worksheet as you'll see in the next section. Kyle suggests that you now explore the use of worksheets as tools for bond calculations.

Present Value and Bonds

You recall having lots of trouble with present value and bonds while in school and are leery of using them in a worksheet. However, Kyle calms your fears by explaining how the use of a worksheet actually helped him better understand bonds and the concept of present value.

"Whoa now!" Meagan comments. "Why should I learn about present values?"

"Present values are very helpful to an accountant and businessperson," Kyle explains. "In fact, you were using present value concepts when you computed the loan payment above!"

Kyle reminds you that bonds are financial instruments that usually require constant interest payments to the bondholder and then a lump-sum payment equal to the bond's face value at the end of a specified term. The proceeds from a bond's sale, however, depend on the market interest rate at the time of sale.

Kyle explains that Excel's present value function can compute those proceeds based on the following variables: market interest rate, term, periodic interest payment, and lump-sum face value payment. The present value function is written: PV(rate,nper,pmt,fv), where rate is the market rate of interest, nper is the number of periods, pmt is the periodic interest payment, and fv is the future value that is paid at the end of the bond term.

You recall that, if the stated rate of interest on a bond differs from the market rate of interest, then the bond's proceeds won't match its face value. If the stated rate is lower than the market rate, then buyers will pay less than the face value, resulting in a discount; if the stated rate is higher than the market rate, then buyers will pay more than the face value, resulting in a premium.

Kyle suggests you use Excel to calculate proceeds of a $100,000 bond paying 10 percent per year for 5 years, given an 11 percent market interest rate at the time of the bond's issuance.

To calculate bond proceeds:

1 Open file ch5-02. The worksheet should look like Figure 5.7.

2 Type **100000** in cell B4 to identify the bond face value.

3 Type **10** in cell B5 to identify the bond's stated interest rate.

4 Type **11** in cell B6 to identify the market interest rate.

Figure 5.7

Bond Worksheet

	A	B	C	D	E	F
1	What SUP, Inc.					
2	Bond Amortization Schedule					
3						
4	Amount					
5	Stated Rate					
6	Market Rate					
7	Term					
8	Interest Payment					
9	Proceeds					
10	(Discount) / Premium					
11						
12	Payment #	Interest Payment	Interest Expense	Amortization	(Discount) Premium	Carrying Value
13						
14	1					
15	2					
16	3					
17	4					
18	5					

Sheet1   Sheet2   Sheet3   (+)

5 Type **5** in cell B7 to identify the bond term.

6 Type **=B4*B5** in cell B8 to calculate annual interest payment.

7 Type **=−PV(B6,B7,B8,B4)** in cell B9 to calculate bond proceeds. (Don't forget the minus sign in front of PV to make the proceeds positive.)

8 Type **=B9–B4** in cell B10 to calculate the bond discount or premium. Your worksheet should look like Figure 5.8.

Figure 5.8

Calculating Bond Proceeds

	A	B
1	What SUP, Inc.	
2	Bond Amortization Schedule	
3		
4	Amount	$ 100,000.00
5	Stated Rate	10.00%
6	Market Rate	11.00%
7	Term	5
8	Interest Payment	$10,000.00
9	Proceeds	$96,304.10
10	(Discount) / Premium	($3,695.90)

9 Name the cells located at B4 through B10.

10 Apply the names you just defined. (*Hint:* If you need help doing this, review the Names in a Worksheet section of this chapter.)

11 Click on cell **B9**. The new formula should read as follows: =−PV(Market_Rate,Term,Interest_Payment,Amount).

12 Save the file as ch5-02_student_name (replacing student_name with your name).

Next you need to create a bond amortization schedule to summarize interest payments, interest expense, bond amortization, and remaining carrying value.

Bond Amortization Schedule

A bond amortization schedule is, in essence, a reconciliation of interest payments and bond accounting. Interest expense, usually recorded using the "effective interest" method, is based on the market rate of interest and the carrying value of the debt.

Kyle suggests that you complete the bond amortization table using the named cell ranges that you've already created. In addition to the effective interest formula described previously, you'll need to compute the bond discount/premium amortization as the difference between the interest expense recorded and the interest payment. The ending carrying value for each period will then be the previous period carrying value plus or minus the remaining discount or premium amortization.

To create the bond amortization schedule:

1 Select cell **E13**.

2 Click **Use in Formula** from the Defined Names group of the Formulas tab.

3 Click **Discount_Premium** from the drop-down list of names and then press [**Enter**]. (*Note:* This is one way to use previously defined names.)

4 Type =**Amount+E13** in cell F13. Then replicate this formula down to cell F18. This calculation represents the sum of the discount or premium left to be amortized plus the face value of the note. (*Note:* Typing a name is another way of using previously defined names.)

5 Type =**Interest_Payment** in cell B14. Replicate this formula down to cell B18.

6 Type =**F13*Market_Rate** in cell C14. Replicate this formula down to cell C18. These cells will calculate interest expense as the previous period carrying value multiplied by the market rate of interest.

7 Type =**B14–C14** in cell D14. Replicate this formula down to cell D18. These cells will calculate the amortization for the period as the amount by which interest expense differs from the interest payment.

8 Type =**E13–D14** in cell E14. Replicate this formula down to cell E18. These cells will calculate the remaining amount of bond discount or premium to be amortized in future periods.

9 Type **=SUM(B14:B18)** in cell B19 to sum interest payments.

10 Format the cell with a top and double bottom border.

11 Replicate the formula to cell D19 to sum interest expense and amortization.

12 Select cell **B19**, then click **Define Name** from the Defined Names group on the Formulas tab of the Ribbon.

13 Type **Total_Interest_Payments** in the Name: text box and then click **OK**.

14 Select cell **C19**, then click **Define Name** from the Defined Names group on the Formulas tab of the Ribbon.

15 Type **Total_Interest_Expense** in the Name: text box and then click **OK**. (*Note:* You'll use this name later.)

16 The resulting amortization table should look like Figure 5.9.

Figure 5.9

Bond Amortization at a Market Rate of 11%

	A	B	C	D	E	F
1	What SUP, Inc.					
2	Bond Amortization Schedule					
3						
4	Amount	$ 100,000.00				
5	Stated Rate	10.00%				
6	Market Rate	11.00%				
7	Term	5				
8	Interest Payment	$10,000.00				
9	Proceeds	$96,304.10				
10	(Discount) / Premium	($3,695.90)				
11						
12	Payment #	Interest Payment	Interest Expense	Amortization	(Discount) Premium	Carrying Value
13					($3,695.90)	$96,304.10
14	1	$10,000.00	$10,593.45	($593.45)	($3,102.45)	$96,897.55
15	2	$10,000.00	$10,658.73	($658.73)	($2,443.71)	$97,556.29
16	3	$10,000.00	$10,731.19	($731.19)	($1,712.52)	$98,287.48
17	4	$10,000.00	$10,811.62	($811.62)	($900.90)	$99,099.10
18	5	$10,000.00	$10,900.90	($900.90)	$0.00	$100,000.00
19		$50,000.00	$53,695.90	($3,695.90)		

17 Save the file.

"I'll bet we can use this schedule to do some what-if analyses like we did with the loan amortization schedule," you suggest.

"Exactly!" Kyle responds. "Let's see the impact of changing the effective interest rate on bond proceeds and interest expense."

What-If Analysis and Goal Seeking

Nathan is curious about the impact that different market interest rates will have on the proceeds from a bond issuance and on the company's interest expense. He suggests you try interest rates of 9 percent and 12 percent.

To assess the effect of different market rates:

1 Type **9** into cell B6. Note the effect on bond proceeds and total interest expenses, as shown in Figure 5.10.

	A	B	C	D	E	F
1	What SUP, Inc.					
2	Bond Amortization Schedule					
3						
4	Amount	$ 100,000.00				
5	Stated Rate	10.00%				
6	Market Rate	9.00%				
7	Term	5				
8	Interest Payment	$10,000.00				
9	Proceeds	$103,889.65				
10	(Discount) / Premium	$3,889.65				
11						
12	Payment #	Interest Payment	Interest Expense	Amortization	(Discount) Premium	Carrying Value
13					$3,889.65	$103,889.65
14	1	$10,000.00	$9,350.07	$649.93	$3,239.72	$103,239.72
15	2	$10,000.00	$9,291.57	$708.43	$2,531.29	$102,531.29
16	3	$10,000.00	$9,227.82	$772.18	$1,759.11	$101,759.11
17	4	$10,000.00	$9,158.32	$841.68	$917.43	$100,917.43
18	5	$10,000.00	$9,082.57	$917.43	$0.00	$100,000.00
19		$50,000.00	$46,110.35	$3,889.65		

Figure 5.10

Bond Amortization at a Market Rate of 9%

2 Type **12** into cell B6. Note the effect on bond proceeds and total interest expenses.

"Wow, that sure is useful." Nathan says. "We can use this information for our accounting record keeping as well as for financial planning."

"Quite true," Kyle responds. "Excel also has a goal seek feature to help determine a stated rate given needed bond proceeds. Let's assume the company wants to issue a 5-year, $100,000 bond when the market interest rate is 8 percent. If the company needs at least $95,000 from the proceeds, what must be the bond's stated rate of interest?"

"I'll use the existing worksheet and try different stated rates to see how close I can get to $95,000," you comment.

"Not necessary," Kyle explains. "We can use the existing worksheet formulas and simply use Excel's goal seek feature. First you change the variable information, such as the market rate of interest. Then you invoke the goal seek command, set the location of the desired value (B9), specify the desired value (95,000), and identify the location of the variable that should be changed to achieve the desired value (B5). In this case, that location is the cell containing the stated interest rate."

"I'll try that," Meagan says.

To use the goal seek feature:

1 Type **8** into cell B6. Observe the effect on bond proceeds (the old stated rate of 10% implied payment of a bond premium).

2 Now click **What-If Analysis** from the Data Tools group of the Data tab of the Ribbon.

3 Select **Goal Seek** from the drop-down menu.

4 Type **Proceeds** in the Set cell: edit box. (Alternatively, you could click in the **Set cell: edit** box and then click cell **B9**.)

5 Type **95000** in the To value: edit box.

6 Type **Stated_Rate** in the By changing cell: edit box, as shown in Figure 5.11.

Figure 5.11

Goal Seek Window

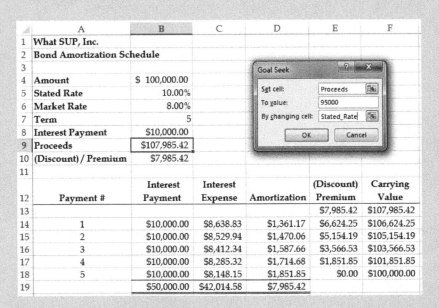

7 Click **OK**. The Goal Seek Status window should appear as shown in Figure 5.12, indicating that a solution has been found.

8 Click **OK** in the Goal Seek Status window.

9 Save your work.

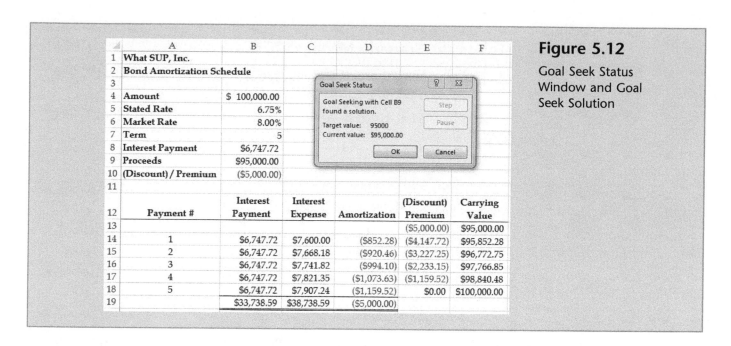

Figure 5.12

Goal Seek Status Window and Goal Seek Solution

Kyle remarks that the goal seek solution indicates that a stated rate of 6.75 percent yields the $95,000 proceeds needed, given an 8 percent market rate for a 5-year, $100,000 bond. In reality, the stated rate necessary to produce exactly $95,000 in proceeds is slightly smaller than 6.75. The B5 cell is formatted to show only two decimal places. If you formatted the cell to read additional decimal places it would have shown 6.74771772716582%. However, Kyle contends that 6.75 percent is close enough!

"This is very cool," Nathan comments, "but I wish I could see the effects of the different market rates on the bond proceeds in one worksheet at one time."

Kyle responds: "Sounds like I need to demonstrate the Scenario Manager to you."

Scenario Manager

Scenarios are part of a suite of commands called *what-if analysis tools*. When you use scenarios, you are performing what-if analysis. As we've seen, what-if analysis is the process of changing the values in cells to see how those changes will affect the outcome of formulas on the worksheet. The values in cells are independent variables but formulas, by their very nature, yield dependent variables. That is, the value generated by a formula is dependent on the values in the worksheet's cells that are specified in that formula. You can use scenarios to create and save different sets of independent variable values and switch between them. You can also create a scenario summary report, which combines all the scenarios into one worksheet.

Kyle suggests you use the Scenario Manager to create a scenario describing the effects a change in the market interest rate (an independent variable) on the proceeds from issuing a bond (a dependent variable) and the related total interest expense (another dependent variable) over the term of the bond.

To use the Scenario Manager:

1 Leave **100000** in cell B4, and then type **10** in cell B5, and **11** in cell B6 to return to the original bond proposal.

2 Click **What-If-Analysis** from the Forecast Tools group of the Data tab on the Ribbon.

3 Click **Scenario Manager**.

4 Click **Add** to add a new scenario.

5 Type **1** in the Scenario name: text box.

6 Type **Market_Rate** in the Changing cells: text box. Your window should look like Figure 5.13.

Figure 5.13

Adding a Scenario

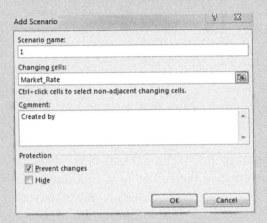

7 Click **OK**.

8 Type **0.12** for the Market_Rate, as shown in Figure 5.14. (*Note:* 0.12 represents interest at 12 percent.)

Figure 5.14

Entering Scenario Values

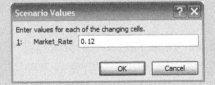

9 Click **OK**.

10 Continue the same process by adding scenarios 2, 3, and 4, which change the Market_Rate cell to 0.10, 0.09, and 0.08 respectively. Your window should now look like Figure 5.15.

11 Click **Summary**.

12 Select the Scenario summary option button and then type **Proceeds, Total_Interest_Expense** in the Result cells text box. (*Note:* This action specifies the target variables affected by the change in interest rate—namely, bond proceeds, located in cell B9, and total interest expense, located in cell C19.) See Figure 5.16.

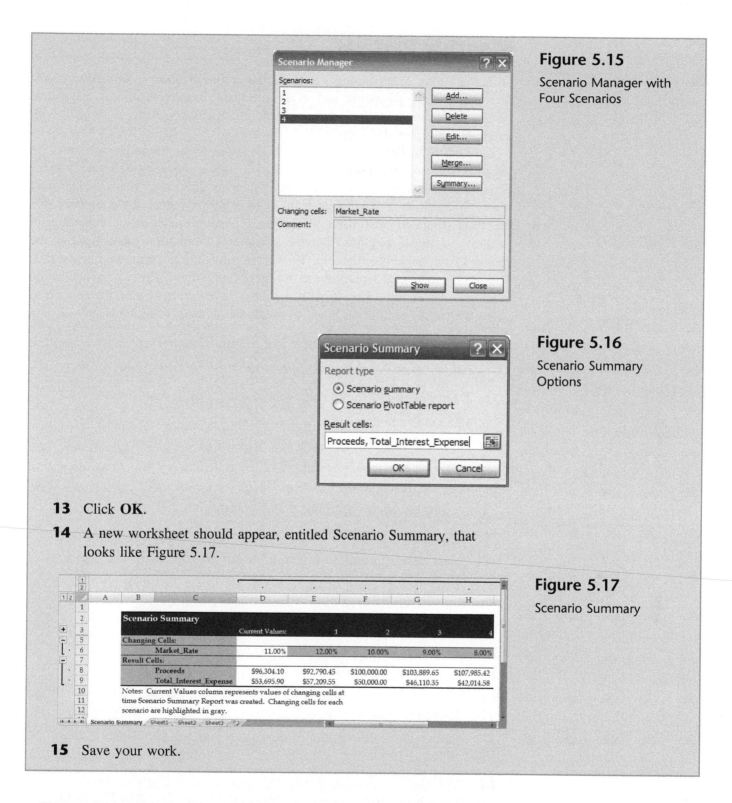

Figure 5.15

Scenario Manager with Four Scenarios

Figure 5.16

Scenario Summary Options

13 Click **OK**.

14 A new worksheet should appear, entitled Scenario Summary, that looks like Figure 5.17.

Figure 5.17

Scenario Summary

15 Save your work.

You explain to Nathan and Meagan how the Scenario Manager is just an extension of the what-if analysis capabilities of Excel. The ability to compare alternative outcomes based on variations in market rates should prove most helpful in planning and future decision making.

Monthly Periods

So far you have created annual loan and bond amortization schedules and have determined loan payments and bond proceeds based on annual payments. Nathan is curious how this analysis would change if you were confronted with a monthly payment situation.

Kyle offers to help you modify your worksheets for monthly payments. He suggests you take the previous loan workbook you created—a 3-year loan of $75,000 with interest at 10 percent and payments due every year—and convert it to a 3-year loan at 10 percent with 36 monthly payments. Kyle explains that the PMT function was used to determine annual payments; converting to monthly payments requires that the arguments in the payment function be changed from annual to monthly. The first argument is the periodic interest rate. The annual rate is 10 percent, so we need only divide by 12 to obtain the monthly interest rate. The second argument is the term. Since the term is 3 years, we simply multiply 3 by 12 to obtain the number of monthly periods: 36.

To modify your worksheets from annual to monthly:

1 Open your previously saved workbook, ch5-01_student_name.

2 Change the name of Sheet1 to **Annual**.

3 Right-click the **Annual** sheet tab and then click **Move or Copy**.

4 Select the **Create a copy** check box and then select **Sheet2** to insert a copy of your worksheet before Sheet2; then click **OK**.

5 Change the name of Annual (2) to **Monthly**.

6 Type =**−PMT(Rate/12,Term*12,Amount)** as the formula for cell B7.

7 Select cells A13 and A14, then fill down the column so that payment numbers 1 through 36 show.

8 Type =**E11*Rate/12** as the new formula in cell C12

9 Fill that formula down to cell C14.

10 Select cells B14 through E14.

11 Fill the formulas in those cells down through B47 through E47.

12 Click **File** and then click **Print** to view a print preview.

13 Click **Page Setup** and click the **Page** tab (if it is not already selected) then choose the **Fit to:** option to scale the worksheet to 1 page wide by 1 page tall.

14 Click **OK** and then click **Print**. Your printout should look like Figure 5.18.

15 Save your work.

The interest rate here is expressed in years, however the interest rate used in the formulas below is .083333 per month as calculated by dividing the 10% by 12 months.

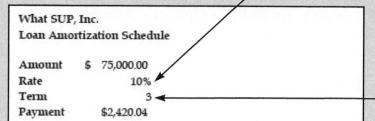

What SUP, Inc.
Loan Amortization Schedule

Amount	$	75,000.00
Rate		10%
Term		3
Payment		$2,420.04

Figure 5.18

Printed Monthly Loan Amortization Worksheet

The term here is expressed in years, however the term used in the formulas below is 36 months as calculated by multiplying the 3 years times 12 months.

Payment #	Payment	Interest	Principal	Balance
				$ 75,000.00
1	$2,420.04	$ 625.00	$1,795.04	$ 73,204.96
2	$2,420.04	$ 610.04	$1,810.00	$ 71,394.96
3	$2,420.04	$ 594.96	$1,825.08	$ 69,569.88
4	$2,420.04	$ 579.75	$1,840.29	$ 67,729.59
5	$2,420.04	$ 564.41	$1,855.63	$ 65,873.97
6	$2,420.04	$ 548.95	$1,871.09	$ 64,002.88
7	$2,420.04	$ 533.36	$1,886.68	$ 62,116.20
8	$2,420.04	$ 517.63	$1,902.40	$ 60,213.79
9	$2,420.04	$ 501.78	$1,918.26	$ 58,295.53
10	$2,420.04	$ 485.80	$1,934.24	$ 56,361.29
11	$2,420.04	$ 469.68	$1,950.36	$ 54,410.93
12	$2,420.04	$ 453.42	$1,966.61	$ 52,444.31
13	$2,420.04	$ 437.04	$1,983.00	$ 50,461.31
14	$2,420.04	$ 420.51	$1,999.53	$ 48,461.78
15	$2,420.04	$ 403.85	$2,016.19	$ 46,445.59
16	$2,420.04	$ 387.05	$2,032.99	$ 44,412.60
17	$2,420.04	$ 370.11	$2,049.93	$ 42,362.67
18	$2,420.04	$ 353.02	$2,067.02	$ 40,295.65
19	$2,420.04	$ 335.80	$2,084.24	$ 38,211.41
20	$2,420.04	$ 318.43	$2,101.61	$ 36,109.80
21	$2,420.04	$ 300.91	$2,119.12	$ 33,990.67
22	$2,420.04	$ 283.26	$2,136.78	$ 31,853.89
23	$2,420.04	$ 265.45	$2,154.59	$ 29,699.30
24	$2,420.04	$ 247.49	$2,172.54	$ 27,526.75
25	$2,420.04	$ 229.39	$2,190.65	$ 25,336.11
26	$2,420.04	$ 211.13	$2,208.90	$ 23,127.20
27	$2,420.04	$ 192.73	$2,227.31	$ 20,899.89
28	$2,420.04	$ 174.17	$2,245.87	$ 18,654.01
29	$2,420.04	$ 155.45	$2,264.59	$ 16,389.43
30	$2,420.04	$ 136.58	$2,283.46	$ 14,105.97
31	$2,420.04	$ 117.55	$2,302.49	$ 11,803.48
32	$2,420.04	$ 98.36	$2,321.68	$ 9,481.80
33	$2,420.04	$ 79.01	$2,341.02	$ 7,140.77
34	$2,420.04	$ 59.51	$2,360.53	$ 4,780.24
35	$2,420.04	$ 39.84	$2,380.20	$ 2,400.04
36	$2,420.04	$ 20.00	$2,400.04	$ 0.00

"I see," Nathan says. "Not only is the payment reduced, but the loan is fully amortized after the 36th payment."

"Exactly," responds Kyle. "Note how the interest portion of each payment diminishes with each payment while the principal portion increases."

Meagan and Nathan are impressed with Excel's robust features and functionality. You and Kyle point out that you've barely scratched the surface and that more is to come.

End Note

You've applied some of what you learned in the first four chapters to better understand how Excel can be used to analyze loans and bonds. In addition, you've learned some new functions—payment (PMT) and present value (PV)— as well as two new features, goal seeking and Scenario Manager. In the next chapter, you'll explore cash flow budgets.

Chapter 5 Questions

1 Explain the difference between a loan and a bond.

2 What function is used to calculate a loan payment?

3 What arguments does the loan payment function take?

4 Why does the payment function result in a negative number?

5 What does a loan amortization schedule do?

6 Describe the formula for computing interest expense each period for a loan.

7 What function is used to calculate bond proceeds, and what arguments does that function take?

8 Describe the formula computing interest expense each period for a bond.

9 Describe the goal seek process.

10 Describe the Scenario Manager.

Chapter 5 Assignments

1 Create a new What SUP Loan Amortization Schedule

Using the ch5-03 file to start your work, create a worksheet (similar to the one created in this chapter) that calculates the required annual payment for an $850,000, 7-year loan at 5 percent and includes a loan amortization schedule. (Be sure to use names in the worksheet, as illustrated in the chapter. You will also need to format the cells.) Save your file as ch5-03_student_name (replacing student_name with your name).

a. Print the newly completed worksheet in Value view, with your name and date printed in the lower left footer and the file name in the lower right footer.

b. Use the Scenario Manager to create a scenario using rates of 10, 9, 7, and 6 percent to calculate alternative payments. Print the resulting summary worksheet.

c. Use Excel's goal seek feature to calculate the amount the company could borrow if it could afford a payment of $120,000 per year assuming the original loan assumptions. Print the resulting worksheet in Value view, with your name and date printed in the lower left footer and the file name in the lower right footer.

2 Create a new What SUP Bond Amortization Schedule

Using the ch5-04 file to start your work, create a worksheet (similar to the one created in this chapter) that calculates the bond proceeds for a $2,500,000, 10-year, 4 percent stated interest bond issued when the market interest rate is 5 percent. Include a bond amortization schedule and use names in the worksheet, as illustrated in the chapter (You will also need to format the cells.) Save your file as ch5-04_student_name (replacing student_name with your name).

a. Print the newly completed worksheet in Value view, with your name and date printed in the lower left footer and the file name in the lower right footer.

b. Use the Scenario Manager to create a scenario using stated rates of 3, 3.5, 4.5, and 6 percent to calculate alternative annual interest payments and bond proceeds. Print the resulting summary worksheet.

c. Use Excel's goal seek feature to calculate the stated interest rate it would have to pay under the original bond analysis (in part a) to achieve bond proceeds of $2,600,000. Print the resulting worksheet in Value view, with your name and date printed in the lower left footer and the file name in the lower right footer.

Chapter 5 Case Problem 1:
KELLY'S BOUTIQUE

Kelly's Boutique is contemplating several alternative means of financing an expansion. One alternative is to borrow $425,000 from a local bank; another alternative is to borrow this amount from investors by issuing bonds. Both alternatives involve a 5-year debt period. Modify the workbook file ch5-05 to compute a loan and bond analysis. Name and format cell ranges as appropriate. Assume an initial loan rate of 3 percent, an initial bond stated rate of 3 percent, and a market interest rate of 3.5 percent.

a. Print the newly completed loan and bond worksheets in Value view, with your name and date printed in the lower left footer and the file name in the lower right footer.

b. Use the Scenario Manager to create two loan scenarios called Best Case and Worst Case. In the Best Case, the rate would be 2.8 percent and the loan amount would be $450,000; in the Worst Case, the rate would be 3.2 percent and the loan amount would be $400,000. (*Hint:* You'll need to place two cell references, separated by a comma, in the Changing cells: text box.) The resulting comparison values you're trying to predict are Payment, Total Payments, and Total Interest. Print the resulting summary worksheet.

c. Use the Scenario Manager to create two bond scenarios called Best Case and Worst Case. In the Best Case, the market rate would be 2.9 percent and the stated rate would be 2 percent; in the Worst Case, the market rate would be 3.8 percent and the stated rate would be 4 percent. (Again, you'll need to place two cell references, separated by a comma, in the Changing cells: text box.) The resulting comparison values you're trying to predict are Proceeds, Total Interest Payments, and Total Interest Expense. Print the resulting summary worksheet.

d.   Use Excel's goal seek feature to calculate the interest rate that the company would have to negotiate under the original loan analysis (in part a) to achieve a payment of $90,000. Round the interest rate to two decimal places. Print the resulting worksheet in Value view, with your name and date printed in the lower left footer and the file name in the lower right footer.

e.   Use Excel's goal seek feature to calculate the market rate necessary to achieve bond proceeds of $430,000. Round the interest rate to two decimal places. Print the resulting worksheet in Value view, with your name and date printed in the lower left footer and the file name in the lower right footer.

Chapter 5 Case Problem 2:
WINE DEPOT

Wine Depot is considering several alternative means of financing an expansion. One alternative is to borrow $500,000 from a local bank, but another alternative is to borrow this amount from investors by issuing bonds. Both alternatives involve a 3-year debt period with quarterly payments. Modify the workbook ch5-06 to compute a loan and bond analysis, naming and formatting cell ranges as appropriate. Assume an annual loan rate of 3 percent, an annual bond stated rate of 3 percent, and a market annual interest rate of 3.5 percent.

a.   Print the newly completed loan and bond worksheets in Value view, with your name and date printed in the lower left footer and the file name in the lower right footer.

b.   Use the Scenario Manager to create two loan scenarios called Best Case and Worst Case. In the Best Case, the rate would be 2.5 percent and the loan amount would be $550,000; in the Worst Case, the rate would be 3.5 percent and the loan amount would be $450,000. (*Hint:* You'll need to place two cell references, separated by a comma, in the Changing cells: text box.) The resulting comparison values you're trying to predict are Payment, Total Payments, and Total Interest. Print the resulting summary worksheet.

c.   Use the Scenario Manager to create two bond scenarios called Best Case and Worst Case. In the Best Case, the market rate would be 2.9 percent and the stated rate would be 2 percent. In the Worst Case, the market rate would be 4.0 percent and the stated rate would be 3.9 percent. (Again, you'll need to place two cell references, separated by a comma, in the Changing cells: text box.) The resulting comparison values you're trying to predict are Proceeds, Total Interest Payments, and Total Interest Expense. Print the resulting summary worksheet.

d. Use Excel's goal seek feature to calculate the interest rate the company would have to negotiate under the original loan analysis (in part a) to achieve a quarterly payment of $42,000. Round the interest rate to two decimal places. Print the resulting worksheet in Value view, with your name and date printed in the lower left footer and the file name in the lower right footer.

e. Use Excel's goal seek feature to calculate the market rate necessary to achieve bond proceeds of $495,000. Round the interest rate to two decimal places. Print the resulting worksheet in Value view, with your name and date printed in the lower left footer and the file name in the lower right footer.

Chapter 5 Case Problem 3:
SNICK'S BOARD SHOP

Snick's Board Shop is considering several alternative means of financing an expansion. One alternative is to borrow $65,000 from a local bank, but another alternative is to borrow this amount from investors by issuing bonds. Both alternatives involve a 2-year debt period with monthly payments. Modify the workbook ch5–07 to compute a loan and bond analysis, naming and formatting cell ranges as appropriate. Assume an initial loan rate of 6 percent, an initial bond stated rate of 6 percent, and a market interest rate of 5.5 percent.

a. Print the newly completed loan and bond worksheets in Value view, with your name and date printed in the lower left footer and the file name in the lower right footer.

b. Use the Scenario Manager to create two loan scenarios called Best Case and Worst Case. In the Best Case, the rate would be 5 percent and the loan amount would be $75,000; in the Worst Case, the rate would be 7 percent and the loan amount would be $60,000. (*Hint:* You'll need to place two cell references, separated by a comma, in the Changing cells: text box.) The resulting comparison values you're trying to predict are Payment, Total Payments, and Total Interest. Print the resulting summary worksheet.

c. Use the Scenario Manager to create two bond scenarios called Best Case and Worst Case. In the Best Case, the market rate would be 4 percent and the stated rate would be 5 percent. In the Worst Case, the market rate would be 7.5 percent and the stated rate would be 7 percent. (Again, you'll need to place two cell references, separated by a comma, in the Changing cells: text box.) The resulting comparison values you're trying to predict are Proceeds, Total Interest Payments, and Total Interest Expense. Print the resulting summary worksheet.

d. Use Excel's goal seek feature to calculate the interest rate that the company would have to negotiate under the original loan analysis (in part a) to achieve a monthly payment of $2,750. Round the interest rate to two decimal places. Print the resulting worksheet in Value view, with your name and date printed in the lower left footer and the file name in the lower right footer.

e. Use Excel's goal seek feature to calculate the market rate necessary to achieve bond proceeds of $67,000. Round the interest rate to two decimal places. Print the resulting worksheet in Value view, with your name and date printed in the lower left footer and the file name in the lower right footer.

Chapter 5 Case Problem 4:
ROSEY'S ROSES

Rosey's Roses is considering several alternative means of financing an expansion. One alternative is to borrow $100,000 from a local bank, but another alternative is to borrow this amount from investors by issuing bonds. Both alternatives involve a 10-year debt period with annual payments. Modify the workbook ch5–08 to compute a loan and bond analysis, naming and formatting cell ranges as appropriate. Assume an initial loan rate of 10 percent, an initial bond stated rate of 10 percent, and a market interest rate of 9 percent.

a. Print the newly completed loan and bond worksheets in Value view, with your name and date printed in the lower left footer and the file name in the lower right footer.

b. Use the Scenario Manager to create two loan scenarios called Best Case and Worst Case. In the Best Case, the rate would be 9 percent and the loan amount would be $125,000; in the Worst Case, the rate would be 11 percent and the loan amount would be $90,000. The resulting comparison values you're trying to predict are Payment, Total Payments, and Total Interest. Print the resulting summary worksheet.

c. Use the Scenario Manager to create two bond scenarios called Best Case and Worst Case. In the Best Case, the market rate would be 8 percent and the stated rate would be 7 percent. In the Worst Case, the market rate would be 10 percent and the stated rate would be 12 percent. The resulting comparison values you're trying to predict are Proceeds, Total Interest Payments, and Total Interest Expense. Print the resulting summary worksheet.

d. Use Excel's goal seek feature to calculate the interest rate that the company would have to negotiate under the original loan analysis (in part a) to achieve an annual payment of $15,000. Round the interest rate to two decimal places. Print the resulting worksheet in Value view, with your name and date printed in the lower left footer and the file name in the lower right footer.

e. Use Excel's goal seek feature to calculate the market rate necessary to achieve bond proceeds of $110,000. Round the interest rate to two decimal places. Print the resulting worksheet in Value view, with your name and date printed in the lower left footer and the file name in the lower right footer.

6

Cash Budgeting

In this chapter you will learn:

- How to prepare a budget for operating activities that includes a
- Sales budget
- Operating cash receipts budget
- Purchases budget
- Sales and administrative expenses budget
- Operating cash payments budget
- How to prepare a budget for investing and financing activities
- How to finalize and format the cash budget with grouping
- How to utilize what-if analysis and goal seeking with a cash budget

Case: **What SUP, Inc.**

Nathan and Meagan have been contemplating an expansion of their business to include stand up paddle board repair, which will require some new equipment. Nathan is certain they don't have the cash resources necessary to pull it off. Meagan believes that, with the right financing, they'll be okay. At Kyle's suggestion, they have contacted their bankers, who recommended that they prepare a budget for the next year that specifically addresses their cash needs.

"You'll need to complete an operating activities budget that includes forecasts of sales, purchases, selling and administrative expenses, operating cash receipts, and operating cash payments for the year," Kyle informs them. "In addition, you'll need to budget for investing activities such as equipment purchases and sales as well as a budget for financing activities such as loan proceeds and repayments."

"I'll bet we could use Excel to help us!" Meagan responds. "However, since I'm not much of an accountant, I'll need help."

"I did some budgeting in my accounting classes," you comment. "If Kyle can help me get started I'm sure this can be done on Excel."

"The first place to start is with the operating activities budget," Kyle says.

Operating Activities Budget

Kyle explains that the operating activities budget will include an operating cash receipts budget and an operating activities cash payments budget. However, before you can complete either, you must first determine your sales and purchases budgets.

"What is the difference between operating cash receipts and sales?" Meagan asks.

"The sales budget will estimate the service revenues you expect to earn and the products you expect to sell during the year; however, not all of those revenues will be collected in cash during the year. Also, some of the sales you made on account in the previous year will be collected in the current year," Kyle answers. "So the first thing we need to do is create a sales budget."

Sales Budget

Kyle explains that most budgets are broken into periods smaller than a year. He suggests that you prepare a quarterly budget with an annual summary column. He reminds you that you'll need to plan for both product and repair revenue and that no cost of goods sold or expenses will appear on this part of the sales budget.

Nathan estimates product sales revenue to be $425,000, $400,000, $375,000, and $450,000 for the first through fourth quarters, respectively. During these periods, Nathan thinks he'll bill 1,500, 1,600, 1,700, and 1,800 hours of stand-up paddle board repair (respectively) at $50 per hour.

Kyle suggests that you place most of your assumptions that you might consider changing at a later date in a special section of the worksheet called Assumptions. This makes it easy to locate these assumptions in case you want to do some what-if analysis after the budget is created.

To prepare the sales portion of the cash budget:

1 Start Excel and open file ch6-01. The worksheet should look like Figure 6.1.

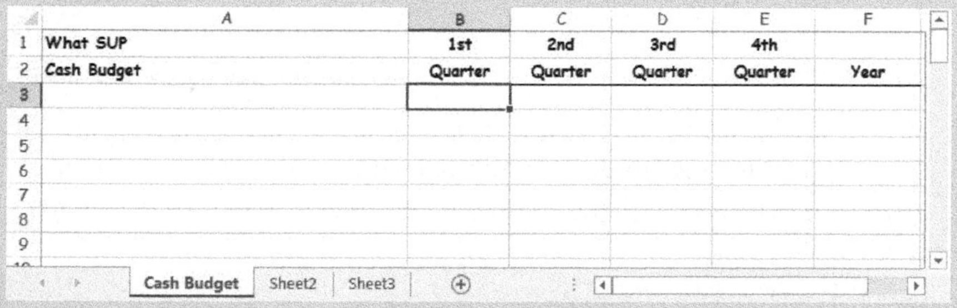

Figure 6.1

Cash Budget Worksheet

2 Type **Operating activities** in cell A4 and then type **Operating cash receipts** into cell A5. Then type **Estimated repair hours** into cell A6.

3 Type **1500** into cell B6, **1600** into cell C6, **1700** into cell D6, and **1800** into cell E6.

4 Type **=SUM(B6:E6)** into cell F6 and then press [**Enter**] to sum estimated repair hours.

5 Format cells B6 to F6 with commas and no decimals. (*Hint:* Use the comma style and decimal tools.)

6 Format cells B6 to F6 with a bottom border by selecting those cells, clicking the **Border** tool located in the Font group of the Home tab of the Ribbon, and then selecting the **Bottom Border** tool. (*Note:* This is done to indicate that the number is not summed in later formulas.)

7 Type **Assumptions** in cell A41 and then type **Hourly repair rate** in cell A42.

8 Type **50** into cell B42 and format that cell with commas and no decimals.

9 Define cell B42 as the Hourly repair rate by selecting cells **A42** to **B42**. From the Defined Names group in the Formula tab of the Ribbon, click **Create from Selection**. With the Left column check box checked, click **OK**.

10 Type **Professional services revenue** in cell A7.

11 Type =**B6*** into cell B7 but do *not* press the [Enter] key.

12 From the Defined Names group in the Formulas tab of the Ribbon, click **Use in Formula**, select **Hourly_repair_rate**, and then press [**Enter**] to compute professional services revenue. (Observe how the formatting from B6 is transferred to cell B6.) Fill the formula across to cells B7 through E7.

13 Type =**SUM(B7:E7)** into cell F7 and then press [**Enter**] to sum estimated repair hours.

14 Type **Product sales revenue** into cell A8.

15 Type the product sales revenue estimates **425000**, **400000**, **375000**, and **450000** into cells B8 through E8, respectively.

16 Type =**SUM(B8:E8)** into cell F8 and then press [**Enter**] to sum Professional services revenues.

17 Format cells B8 to F8 with commas and no decimals and a bottom border.

18 Type **Total revenue** into cell A9.

19 Type the formula =**B7+B8** into cell B9 to calculate total revenue. Fill the formula across to cells C9 through E9.

20 Type =**SUM(B9:E9)** into cell F9 and then press [**Enter**] to sum revenues.

21 Format cells B9 to F9 with commas and no decimals and a bottom border.

22 The completed worksheet should look like Figure 6.2.

23 Save your work to ch6-01_student_name (replacing student_name with your name as before).

⊿	A	B	C	D	E	F
1	What SUP	1st	2nd	3rd	4th	
2	Cash Budget	🖺 (Ctrl) ▾	Quarter	Quarter	Quarter	Year
3						
4	Operating activities					
5	Operating cash receipts					
6	Estimated repair hours	1,500	1,600	1,700	1,800	6,600
7	Professional services revenue	75,000	80,000	85,000	90,000	330,000
8	Product sales revenue	425,000	400,000	375,000	450,000	1,650,000
9	Total revenue	500,000	480,000	460,000	540,000	1,980,000

Figure 6.2

Sales Budget

Now that you have created the sales budget, you can create the operating cash receipts budget.

Operating Cash Receipts Budget

Kyle explains that the operating cash receipts budget must account for the timing of revenue collection. Whenever a company offers terms to customers (i.e., payment at other than the time of sale, such as "net 30"), the budget must take into consideration when revenue will actually be collected.

"Based on the last two years, our customers usually pay 80 percent of what we've invoiced them in the quarter when sales were earned and 20 percent in the next quarter" says Nathan. "At the end of last year we had a balance of $81,000 in accounts receivable."

Kyle suggests that you use that information, along with the data provided in the sales budget, to calculate an operating cash receipts budget.

To create the operating cash receipts budget:

1   To add the new assumptions just discussed, type **Pct. collections in current quarter** in cell A43.

2   Type **80%** in cell B43.

3   Type **Pct. collections in subsequent quarter** in cell A44.

4   Type **20%** in cell B44.

5   Type **Beginning accounts receivable** in cell A45.

6   Type **81000** in cell B45 and then format the cell in comma format with no decimals.

7   Define names for cells B43 through B45 as you have done before.

8   Type **Current quarter collections** in cell A10.

9   Type **Subsequent quarter collections** in cell A11.

10   Type **Operating cash receipts** in cell A12.

11   Type **=B9*** into cell B10 but do *not* press the [Enter] key.

12 From the Defined Names group in the Formulas tab of the Ribbon, click **Use in Formula**, select **Pct._collections_in_current_quarter**, and then press [**Enter**] to compute current quarter collections. Fill the formula across to cells C10 through E10.

13 Type =**SUM(B10:E10)** into cell F10 and then press [**Enter**] to sum current quarter collections.

14 Type = into cell B11 but do *not* press the [Enter] key.

15 From the Defined Names group in the Formulas tab of the Ribbon, click **Use in Formula**, select **Beginning_accounts_receivable**, and then press [**Enter**]. Format the cell in comma format with no decimals.

16 Type =**B9*** into cell C11 but do *not* press the [Enter] key.

17 From the Defined Names group in the Formulas tab of the Ribbon, click **Use in Formula**, select **Pct._collections_in_subsequent_quarter**, and then press [**Enter**] to compute subsequent quarter collections. Fill the formula across to cells C11 through E11.

18 Type =**SUM(B11:E11)** into cell F11 and then press [**Enter**] to sum subsequent quarter collections.

19 Place a bottom border in cells B11 through F11.

20 Type =**B10+B11** into cell B12 and then fill this formula across to cells C12 through E12.

21 Type =**SUM(B12:E12)** into cell F12 and then press [**Enter**] to sum operating cash receipts.

22 Place a bottom border in cells B12 through F12. Your cash budget so far should look like Figure 6.3.

Figure 6.3

Cash Budget of Operating Cash Receipts

	A	B	C	D	E	F
1	What SUP	1st	2nd	3rd	4th	
2	Cash Budget	Quarter	Quarter	Quarter	Quarter	Year
3						
4	**Operating activities**					
5	Operating cash receipts					
6	Estimated repair hours	1,500	1,600	1,700	1,800	6,600
7	Professional services revenue	75,000	80,000	85,000	90,000	330,000
8	Product sales revenue	425,000	400,000	375,000	450,000	1,650,000
9	Total revenue	500,000	480,000	460,000	540,000	1,980,000
10	Current quarter collections	400,000	384,000	368,000	432,000	1,584,000
11	Subsequent quarter collections	81,000	100,000	96,000	92,000	369,000
12	Operating cash receipts	481,000	484,000	464,000	524,000	1,953,000

23 Save your work.

Kyle explains that now it is time to move on to budgeting operating cash payments. It is important first to budget purchases to meet sales demand and then to contemplate when those purchases will be paid for and then to consider what other operating cash payments must be made, such as selling and administrative expenses.

Purchases Budget

Nathan and Meagan explain that quarterly purchases are dependent on beginning inventory, the cost of expected sales, and the desired amount of ending inventory. They give the following example. Assume a beginning inventory of $500 and expected merchandise sales of $1,500 (that cost them $900). Further, assume they would like to keep an inventory of $400 on hand for next month's sales. Hence they will need to purchase $800 of inventory during the quarter. This is computed using the following formula: cost of expected sales ($900) + desired ending inventory ($400) – beginning inventory ($500) = required purchases ($800).

Nathan estimates that the cost of most of his inventory is 60 percent of sales. For example, a necklace Coast sells for $100 cost them $60. Further, he would like to maintain an inventory on hand each month of 80 percent of expected sales in the following month. Inventory at the beginning of the year was $125,000, and product sales in the first quarter of the next year are expected to be $500,000.

Kyle recommends that you take a shot at producing the desired purchases budget while explaining the process to Meagan and Nathan.

To create a purchases budget:

1 Type **Operating cash payments** in cell A13 and format this cell bold.

2 Type **Purchases** in cell A14.

3 To add the new assumptions discussed above, type **Cost of expected sales** in cell A46.

4 Type **60%** in cell B46.

5 Type **Required ending inventory** in cell A47.

6 Type **80%** in cell B47.

7 Type **Beginning inventory** in cell A48.

8 Type **125000** in cell B48 in comma style format.

9 Type **Product sales 1st quarter of next year** in cell A49.

10 Type **500000** in cell B49 in comma style format.

11 Define names for cells B46 through B49 and format them as you have done before.

12 Type **Cost of expected sales** in cell A15.

13 Type **Required ending inventory** in cell A16.

14 Type **Beginning inventory** in cell A17.

15 Type **Purchases** in cell A18.

16 Type **=B8*** into cell B15 but do *not* press the [Enter] key. (*Note:* This is not total revenue but just product sales revenue.)

17 From the Defined Names group in the Formulas tab of the Ribbon, click **Use in Formula**, select **Cost_of_expected_sales**, and then press [**Enter**] to compute the cost of expected sales for the quarter.

18 Fill the formula across to cells C15 through E15.

19 Type =**SUM(B15:E15)** into cell F15 and then press [**Enter**] to sum the cost of expected sales for the year.

20 Type =**C15*** into cell B16 but do *not* press the [Enter] key.

21 From the Defined Names group in the Formulas tab of the Ribbon, click **Use in Formula,** select **Required_ending_inventory,** and then press [**Enter**] to compute the required ending inventory for the quarter. Fill the formula across to cells C16 through D16.

22 Type = into cell E16 but do *not* press the [Enter] key.

23 From the Defined Names group in the Formulas tab of the Ribbon, click **Use in Formula**.

24 Click **Cost_of_expected_sales**, then type *****. Continue the same process of selecting the Use in Formula command to insert names. When complete your formula in cell E16 should be=Cost_of_expected_sales *Required_ending_inventory* Product_sales_1st_quarter_of_next_year. After entering the formula press [**Enter**]. Use comma style format.

25 Type =**E16** in cell F16 to indicate that the required ending inventory for the year is the same as the required ending inventory for the fourth quarter.

26 Type =− in cell B17, and then click **Use in Formula** from the Defined Names group on the Formulas tab of the Ribbon. (*Note:* Be sure you type the equals sign *and* the minus sign here to indicate you are going to make this value negative.)

27 Select **Beginning_inventory** and then press [**Enter**]. Format the cell.

28 Type =−**B16** in cell C17 and then press [**Enter**] to indicate that the current quarter's beginning inventory is equal to the previous quarter's ending inventory. Fill this formula across from cell D17 to E17.

29 Type =**B17** in cell F17 to indicate that the beginning inventory for the year was the same as the beginning inventory for the first quarter.

30 Place a bottom border in cells B17 through F17.

31 Type =**SUM(B15:B17)** in cell B18 to calculate the first quarter's purchases. Fill this formula across to cell C18 to F18.

32 Place a bottom border in cells B18 through F18. Your completed cash budget, including purchases, should look like Figure 6.4.

	A	B	C	D	E	F
1	What SUP	1st	2nd	3rd	4th	
2	Cash Budget	Quarter	Quarter	Quarter	Quarter	Year
3						
4	Operating activities					
5	Operating cash receipts					
6	Estimated repair hours	1,500	1,600	1,700	1,800	6,600
7	Professional services revenue	75,000	80,000	85,000	90,000	330,000
8	Product sales revenue	425,000	400,000	375,000	450,000	1,650,000
9	Total revenue	500,000	480,000	460,000	540,000	1,980,000
10	Current quarter collections	400,000	384,000	368,000	432,000	1,584,000
11	Subsequent quarter collections	81,000	100,000	96,000	92,000	369,000
12	Operating cash receipts	481,000	484,000	464,000	524,000	1,953,000
13	Operating cash payments					
14	Purchases					
15	Cost of expected sales	255,000	240,000	225,000	270,000	990,000
16	Required ending inventory	192,000	180,000	216,000	240,000	240,000
17	Beginning inventory	(125,000)	(192,000)	(180,000)	(216,000)	(125,000)
18	Purchases	322,000	228,000	261,000	294,000	1,105,000

Figure 6.4

Cash Budget of Operating Cash Receipts Through Purchases

33 Save your work.

"As you can see, the purchases budget is based on the sales budget we had previously created and some additional facts and assumptions, such as the relationship between sales and costs of goods sold," Kyle notes.

"How does all this relate to cash flow?" you ask.

"We must now factor in the relationship between when we purchase merchandise and when we actually pay for it," Kyle answers. "Thus, we have to adjust purchases for our payment expectations."

Operating Cash Payments for Purchases

Kyle explains that, whenever a vendor or supplier does not require immediate payment, the budget must take into consideration when payment is actually paid. In this case, it is expected that 75 percent of purchases are paid in the month of purchase and 25 percent are paid in the month following purchases. He also points out that, at the beginning of the year, the company's accounts payable amount to $16,000, which must be paid in the first quarter. He suggests you add the assumptions he just made to your cash budget and incorporate them into your calculation of cash payments for purchases.

To create a cash payments for purchases budget:

1 Type **Current quarter payments** in cell A19.

2 Type **Subsequent quarter payments** in cell A20.

3 Type **Cash payments for purchases** in cell A21.

4 To add the new assumptions just discussed, type **Beginning accounts payable** in cell A50.

5 Type **16000** in cell B50. Format the cell.

6 Type **Pct. of purchases paid in current quarter** in cell A51.

7 Type **75%** in cell B51.

8 Type **Pct. of purchases paid in subsequent quarter** in cell A52.

9 Type **25%** in cell B52.

10 Define names for cells B50 through B52 as you have done before.

11 Type **=B18*** into cell B19 but do *not* press the [Enter] key.

12 From the Defined Names group in the Formulas tab of the Ribbon, click **Use in Formula**, select **Pct._of_purchases_paid_in_current_quarter**, and then press [**Enter**].

13 Fill the formula across to cells C19 through E19.

14 Type **=SUM(B19:E19)** into cell F19 and then press [**Enter**] to sum the current quarter payments for the year.

15 Type **=** into cell B20 but do *not* press the [Enter] key.

16 From the Defined Names group in the Formulas tab of the Ribbon, click **Use in Formula**, select **Beginning_accounts_payable**, and then press [**Enter**].

17 Format the cell in comma format with no decimals.

18 Type **=B18*** into cell C20 but do *not* press the [Enter] key.

19 From the Defined Names group in the Formulas tab of the Ribbon, click **Use in Formula**, select **Pct._of_purchases_paid_in_subsequent_quarter**, and then press [**Enter**].

20 Fill the formula across to cells D20 through E20.

21 Type **=SUM(B20:E20)** into cell F20 and then press [**Enter**] to sum the subsequent quarter payments for the year.

22 Place a bottom border in cells B20 through F20.

23 Type **=B19+B20** in cell B21 to sum payments made in the quarter, and then fill the formula across to cells C21 through F21.

24 Place a bottom border in cells B21 through F21. Your modified cash budget should look like Figure 6.5.

⬜	A	B	C	D	E	F
1	What SUP	1st	2nd	3rd	4th	
2	Cash Budget	Quarter	Quarter	Quarter	Quarter	Year
3						
4	**Operating activities**					
5	Operating cash receipts					
6	Estimated repair hours	1,500	1,600	1,700	1,800	6,600
7	Professional services revenue	75,000	80,000	85,000	90,000	330,000
8	Product sales revenue	425,000	400,000	375,000	450,000	1,650,000
9	Total revenue	500,000	480,000	460,000	540,000	1,980,000
10	Current quarter collections	400,000	384,000	368,000	432,000	1,584,000
11	Subsequent quarter collections	81,000	100,000	96,000	92,000	369,000
12	Operating cash receipts	481,000	484,000	464,000	524,000	1,953,000
13	Operating cash payments					
14	Purchases					
15	Cost of expected sales	255,000	240,000	225,000	270,000	990,000
16	Required ending inventory	192,000	180,000	216,000	240,000	240,000
17	Beginning inventory	(125,000)	(192,000)	(180,000)	(216,000)	(125,000)
18	Purchases	322,000	228,000	261,000	294,000	1,105,000
19	Current quarter payments	241,500	171,000	195,750	220,500	828,750
20	Subsequent quarter payments	16,000	80,500	57,000	65,250	218,750
21	Cash payments for purchases	257,500	251,500	252,750	285,750	1,047,500

25 Save your work.

Figure 6.5

Cash Budget with Cash Payments for Purchases

"Operating cash flow encompasses cash inflow from sales as well as cash outflow for purchases and expenses," Kyle explains. "Next up is budget for sales and administrative expenses. The nice thing about these expenses is that they are usually paid in the same period they are incurred."

Sales and Administrative Expenses Budget

Kyle explains to you, Nathan, and Meagan that the sales and administrative expense budget won't be linked to either sales or purchases. Instead, the budget will be based on expected costs to be incurred for advertising, depreciation, payroll, and utilities. Nathan thinks that advertising expense will be $25,000 in the first quarter and then increase $5,000 per quarter over the year. Depreciation will be $8,000 in the first quarter and then increase $1,000 per quarter over the year based on new equipment purchases. Payroll will vary based on the expected expansion of business and seasonal sales but is expected to be $125,000 the first quarter, $150,000 in the first and second quarter, and then $185,000 in the fourth quarter. Utilities will be based on the prior year's actual results, which were $15,000, $18,000, $17,500, and $19,000 in the first through fourth quarters, respectively.

"How does depreciation affect our cash budget?" you ask. "Isn't depreciation a noncash outlay?"

"As a matter of fact, it is," Kyle answers. "It is still an expense, but we won't include it in our selling and administrative expense budget."

Kyle suggests that you prepare the sales and administrative expense budget based on the data provided—excluding depreciation, as you so aptly pointed out.

To create the selling and administrative expense portion of your cash budget:

1 Type **Selling and administrative expenses** in cell A22.

2 Type **Advertising expense** in cell A23.

3 Type **Payroll expense** in cell A24.

4 Type **Utilities expense** in cell A25.

5 Type **Selling and administrative expenses** in cell A26.

6 Enter the expense information provided by Nathan into cells B23 through E25.

7 Enter formulas to sum quarterly expenses in cells B26 through E26. Use comma style format.

8 Enter formulas to sum expenses in cells F23 through F26. Use comma style format.

9 Place a bottom border in cells B25 through F25.

10 Place a bottom border in cells B26 through F26. Your modified cash budget should look like Figure 6.6.

Figure 6.6

Cash Budget with Cash Payments for Expenses

	A	B	C	D	E	F
1	What SUP	1st	2nd	3rd	4th	
2	Cash Budget	Quarter	Quarter	Quarter	Quarter	Year
3						
4	**Operating activities**					
5	Operating cash receipts					
6	Estimated repair hours	1,500	1,600	1,700	1,800	6,600
7	Professional services revenue	75,000	80,000	85,000	90,000	330,000
8	Product sales revenue	425,000	400,000	375,000	450,000	1,650,000
9	Total revenue	500,000	480,000	460,000	540,000	1,980,000
10	Current quarter collections	400,000	384,000	368,000	432,000	1,584,000
11	Subsequent quarter collections	81,000	100,000	96,000	92,000	369,000
12	Operating cash receipts	481,000	484,000	464,000	524,000	1,953,000
13	Operating cash payments					
14	Purchases					
15	Cost of expected sales	255,000	240,000	225,000	270,000	990,000
16	Required ending inventory	192,000	180,000	216,000	240,000	240,000
17	Beginning inventory	(125,000)	(192,000)	(180,000)	(216,000)	(125,000)
18	Purchases	322,000	228,000	261,000	294,000	1,105,000
19	Current quarter payments	241,500	171,000	195,750	220,500	828,750
20	Subsequent quarter payments	16,000	80,500	57,000	65,250	218,750
21	Cash payments for purchases	257,500	251,500	252,750	285,750	1,047,500
22	Selling and administrative expenses					
23	Advertising expense	25,000	30,000	35,000	40,000	130,000
24	Payroll expense	125,000	150,000	150,000	185,000	610,000
25	Utilities expense	15,000	18,000	17,500	19,000	69,500
26	Selling and administrative expenses	165,000	198,000	202,500	244,000	809,500

11 Save your work.

Operating Cash Payments Budget

Kyle remarks that you must now put all the pieces together in order to complete the operating cash payments budget. The budget will consist of the sum of payments made for purchases and payments made for selling and administrative expenses.

To finalize the operating cash payments budget:

1 Type **Operating cash payments** in cell A27.

2 Type **=B21+B26** in cell B27 to add the first-quarter cash payments for purchases to the first-quarter cash payments for selling and administrative expenses together.

3 Fill this formula across to cells C27 through F27.

4 Place a bottom border in cells B27 through F27.

To finalize the operating portion of the cash budget, all that is left is to subtract the operating cash payments from the operating cash receipts.

To finalize the operating cash budget:

1 Type **Cash from (to) operating activities** in cell A28.

2 Type **=B12−B27** in cell B28 to subtract the first-quarter cash payments from the first-quarter cash receipts.

3 Fill this formula across to cells C28 through F28.

4 Place a bottom border in cells B28 through F28. Your completed cash budget for operating activities is shown in Figure 6.7.

	A	B	C	D	E	F
1	What SUP	1st	2nd	3rd	4th	
2	Cash Budget	Quarter	Quarter	Quarter	Quarter	Year
3						
4	**Operating activities**					
5	Operating cash receipts					
6	Estimated repair hours	1,500	1,600	1,700	1,800	6,600
7	Professional services revenue	75,000	80,000	85,000	90,000	330,000
8	Product sales revenue	425,000	400,000	375,000	450,000	1,650,000
9	Total revenue	500,000	480,000	460,000	540,000	1,980,000
10	Current quarter collections	400,000	384,000	368,000	432,000	1,584,000
11	Subsequent quarter collections	81,000	100,000	96,000	92,000	369,000
12	Operating cash receipts	481,000	484,000	464,000	524,000	1,953,000
13	Operating cash payments					
14	Purchases					
15	Cost of expected sales	255,000	240,000	225,000	270,000	990,000
16	Required ending inventory	192,000	180,000	216,000	240,000	240,000
17	Beginning inventory	(125,000)	(192,000)	(180,000)	(216,000)	(125,000)
18	Purchases	322,000	228,000	261,000	294,000	1,105,000
19	Current quarter payments	241,500	171,000	195,750	220,500	828,750
20	Subsequent quarter payments	16,000	80,500	57,000	65,250	218,750
21	Cash payments for purchases	257,500	251,500	252,750	285,750	1,047,500
22	Selling and administrative expenses					
23	Advertising expense	25,000	30,000	35,000	40,000	130,000
24	Payroll expense	125,000	150,000	150,000	185,000	610,000
25	Utilities expense	15,000	18,000	17,500	19,000	69,500
26	Selling and administrative expenses	165,000	198,000	202,500	244,000	809,500
27	Operating cash payments	422,500	449,500	455,250	529,750	1,857,000
28	Cash from (to) operating activities	58,500	34,500	8,750	(5,750)	96,000

Figure 6.7

Completed Cash Budget from Operating Activities

5 Save your work.

"That was interesting," you comment. "I have prepared a statement of cash flows before but never a budget that looked like a statement of cash flows!"

"Ah, but there is more," Kyle responds. "Remember, the other two components of cash flow are investing and financing activities."

Investing and Financing Activities Budgets

You recall that investing activities usually involve not only the purchase or sale of such long-term assets as land, buildings, and equipment but also the purchase or sale of long-term investments. You also know that financing activities usually involve borrowings or repayment of borrowings, the sale or repurchase of stock, and/or the payment of dividends.

"What are your plans for the coming year?" Kyle asks.

"Well, I'd like to purchase some new equipment in the second quarter for about $300,000," Nathan says. "The bank is willing to lend me $250,000, provided these budgets support the stories I've been telling them about the business. The quarterly payment on the loan, which includes interest, is about $20,000 starting in the third quarter."

"That's all the information we need to create the investing and financing portion of our cash budget," Kyle says. "Let's have our student here finalize the budget."

To create the investing and financing portion of our cash budget:

1 Type **Investing activities** in cell A29.

2 Verify that this cell is formatted bold.

3 Type **Equipment purchases** in cell A30.

4 Type **Equipment sales** in cell A31.

5 Type **Cash from (to) investing activities** in cell A32.

6 Type **Financing activities** in cell A33.

7 Verify that this cell is formatted bold.

8 Type **Loan proceeds** in cell A34.

9 Type **Loan payments** in cell A35.

10 Type **Cash from (to) financing activities** in cell A36.

11 Type **−300000** in cell C30 to reflect the equipment purchase in the second quarter.

12 Type **250000** in cell C34 to reflect the proceeds from the loan in the second quarter.

13 Type **−20000** in cells D35 and E35 to reflect payments on the loan made in the third and fourth quarter.

14 Format all cells in the range B30 to F36 in comma format with no decimals.

15 Type =**SUM(B30:E30)** in cell F30.

16 Type =**SUM(B31:E31)** in cell F31.

17 Place a bottom border in cells B31 through F31.

18 Type =**B30+B31** in cell B32 and then fill this formula across from cell C32 to F32.

19 Place a bottom border in cells B32 through F32.

20 Place a bottom border in cells B35 through F35.

21 Type =**SUM(B34:E34)** in cell F34.

22 Type =**SUM(B35:E35)** in cell F35.

23 Type =**B34+B35** in cell B36 and then fill this formula across from cell C36 to F36.

24 Place a bottom border in cells B36 through F36. The investing and financing portion of your cash budget should look like Figure 6.8.

	A	B	C	D	E	F
29	**Investing activities**					
30	Equipment purchases		(300,000)			(300,000)
31	Equipment sales					-
32	Cash from (to) investing activities	-	(300,000)	-	-	(300,000)
33	**Financing activities**					
34	Loan proceeds		250,000			250,000
35	Loan payments			(20,000)	(20,000)	(40,000)
36	Cash from (to) financing activities	-	250,000	(20,000)	(20,000)	210,000

Figure 6.8

Investing and Financing Portion of the Cash Budget

25 Save your work.

You are very close to completing the cash budget.

Finalizing and Formatting the Cash Budget

"To finalize the cash budget we need to compute the net change in cash and compare it to beginning cash to determine our forecasted ending cash balance for the year," comments Kyle. "How much cash will you have at the beginning of the budgeted period?" Kyle asks.

"Right now my best estimate is about $25,000," Nathan responds.

To finalize the cash budget:

1 To add the new assumptions discussed above, type **Beginning cash** in cell A53.

2 Type **25000** in cell B53. Format the cell in comma format with no decimals.

3 Define a name for cell B53 as you've done before.

4 Type **Change in cash** in cell A37.

5 Type **Beginning cash** in cell A38.

6 Type **Ending cash** in cell A39.

7 Type **=B28+B32+B36** in cell B37 to add operating, investing, and financing cash activities for the first quarter.

8 Fill that formula across from cell C37 to F37.

9 Click in cell **B38**, click **Use in Formula** from the Defined Names group on the Formulas tab of the Ribbon, click **Beginning_cash,** and then press [**Enter**]. Format the cell in comma format with no decimals.

10 Type **=B37+B38** in cell B39.

11 Fill that formula across from cell C39 to F39.

12 Type **=B39** in cell C38 to reference ending cash from the first quarter to beginning cash in the second quarter.

13 Fill that formula across from cell D38 to E38.

14 Type **=B38** in cell F38 to reference beginning cash from the first quarter to beginning cash for the year.

15 Place a bottom border in cells B38 through F38.

16 Place a bottom double border in cells B39 through F39.

17 Save your work.

18 Click **File** and then click **Print**.

19 Click **OK** to print the cash budget (two pages) shown in Figure 6.9 and Figure 6.10.

20 Press the [**Ctrl**] and [] (grave accent key) keys simultaneously to switch to Formula view. Part of your window should look like Figure 6.11.

21 Click the **Microsoft Office** button and then click **Print**.

22 Click **Preview** and then click **Page Setup**.

23 Choose the **Landscape** option for orientation and then click the **Fit to:** scaling option.

24 Set scaling to 1 page wide by 1 tall and then click **OK** in the Page Setup window.

25 Click **Print** in the Print Preview window and then click **OK** to print the cash budget in Formula view.

What SUP Cash Budget	1st Quarter	2nd Quarter	3rd Quarter	4th Quarter	Year
Operating activities					
Operating cash receipts					
Estimated repair hours	1,500	1,600	1,700	1,800	6,600
Professional services revenue	75,000	80,000	85,000	90,000	330,000
Product sales revenue	425,000	400,000	375,000	450,000	1,650,000
Total revenue	500,000	480,000	460,000	540,000	1,980,000
Current quarter collections	400,000	384,000	368,000	432,000	1,584,000
Subsequent quarter collections	81,000	100,000	96,000	92,000	369,000
Operating cash receipts	481,000	484,000	464,000	524,000	1,953,000
Operating cash payments					
Purchases					
Cost of expected sales	255,000	240,000	225,000	270,000	990,000
Required ending inventory	192,000	180,000	216,000	240,000	240,000
Beginning inventory	(125,000)	(192,000)	(180,000)	(216,000)	(125,000)
Purchases	322,000	228,000	261,000	294,000	1,105,000
Current quarter payments	241,500	171,000	195,750	220,500	828,750
Subsequent quarter payments	16,000	80,500	57,000	65,250	218,750
Cash payments for purchases	257,500	251,500	252,750	285,750	1,047,500
Selling and administrative expenses					
Advertising expense	25,000	30,000	35,000	40,000	130,000
Payroll expense	125,000	150,000	150,000	185,000	610,000
Utilities expense	15,000	18,000	17,500	19,000	69,500
Selling and administrative expenses	165,000	198,000	202,500	244,000	809,500
Operating cash payments	422,500	449,500	455,250	529,750	1,857,000
Cash from (to) operating activities	58,500	34,500	8,750	(5,750)	96,000
Investing activities					
Equipment purchases		(300,000)			(300,000)
Equipment sales					-
Cash from (to) investing activities	-	(300,000)	-	-	(300,000)
Financing activities					
Loan proceeds		250,000			250,000
Loan payments			(20,000)	(20,000)	(40,000)
Cash from (to) financing activities	-	250,000	(20,000)	(20,000)	210,000
Change in cash	58,500	(15,500)	(11,250)	(25,750)	6,000
Beginning cash	25,000	83,500	68,000	56,750	25,000
Ending cash	83,500	68,000	56,750	31,000	31,000

Figure 6.9

Completed Cash Budget

Assumptions	
Hourly repair rate	50
Pct. collections in current quarter	80%
Pct. collections in subsequent quarter	20%
Beginning accounts receivable	81,000
Cost of expected sales	60%
Required ending inventory	80%
Beginning inventory	125,000
Product sales 1st quarter of next year	500,000
Beginning accounts payable	16,000
Pct. of purchases paid in current quarter	75%
Pct. of purchases paid in subsequent quarter	25%
Beginning cash	$25,000

Figure 6.10

Cash Budget Assumptions

26 Press the [**Ctrl**] and [ ] (grave accent key) keys simultaneously to switch back to Value view.

27 Double-click between each column to resize that column to fit its contents.

28 Save your work.

Figure 6.11

Partial Formula View of the Cash Budget

Double-click here to resize column A to fit its contents

	A	B
1	What SUP	1st
2	Cash Budget	Quarter
3		
4	**Operating activities**	
5	Operating cash receipts	
6	Estimated repair hours	1500
7	Professional services revenue	=B6*Hourly_repair_rate
8	Product sales revenue	425000
9	Total revenue	=B7+B8
10	Current quarter collections	=Pct._collections_in_current_quarter*B9
11	Subsequent quarter collections	=Beginning_accounts_receivable
12	Operating cash receipts	=B10+B11
13	Operating cash payments	
14	Purchases	
15	Cost of expected sales	=Cost_of_expected_sales*B8
16	Required ending inventory	=Required_ending_inventory*C15
17	Beginning inventory	=-Beginning_inventory
18	Purchases	=SUM(B15:B17)
19	Current quarter payments	=Pct._of_purchases_paid_in_current_quarter*B18
20	Subsequent quarter payments	='Cash Budget'!B50
21	Cash payments for purchases	=SUM(B19:B20)
22	Selling and administrative expenses	
23	Advertising expense	25000
24	Payroll expense	125000
25	Utilities expense	15000
26	Selling and administrative expenses	=SUM(B23:B25)
27	Operating cash payments	=B21+B26
28	Cash from (to) operating activities	=B12-B27

"I like using names in Excel," says Nathan. "It is much easier to follow the formula logic when I see descriptions of what is going on rather that just cell references."

"I agree," responds Meagan. "It's not much of a hassle to create and use the names, because Excel gives you the 'Create from Selection' option for naming cells and the 'Use in Formula' option for using names."

Excel also has a grouping feature that can dramatically change the way this budget is viewed. Kyle explains that the entire budget can be summarized horizontally (by rows) down to the entries for cash from (to) operating, investing, and financing activities, the net change in cash, beginning cash, and ending cash. The budget can also be grouped vertically to collapse columns and show only the year amounts. Kyle offers to show you Excel's grouping feature by creating five different levels of grouping.

To use Excel's grouping feature on the cash budget:

1 Click and select rows **6**, **7**, and **8**, as shown in Figure 6.12, to group total revenues.

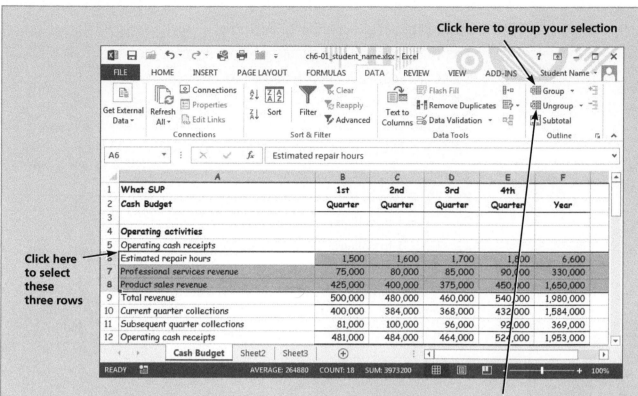

Click here to group your selection

Click here to select these three rows

Click here to ungroup your selection

Figure 6.12

Grouping

2 Click **Group** in the Outline group on the Data tab of the Ribbon and then click **Group** again.

Trouble? What if you accidently group the wrong rows? No problem, just reselect those rows that you grouped and then click Ungroup from the Outline group on the Data tab of the Ribbon.

3 Click and select rows **5** through **11** to group operating cash receipts.

4 Click **Group** in the Outline group on the Data tab of the Ribbon.

5 Click and select rows **14** through **17** to group purchases.

6 Click **Group** in the Outline group on the Data tab of the Ribbon.

7 Click and select rows **14** through **20** to group cash payments for purchases.

8 Click **Group** in the Outline group on the Data tab of the Ribbon.

9 Click and select rows **22** through **25** to group selling and administrative expenses.

10 Click **Group** in the Outline group on the Data tab of the Ribbon.

11 Click and select rows **13** through **26** to group operating cash payments.

12 Click **Group** in the Outline group on the Data tab of the Ribbon.

13 Click and select rows **4** through **27** to group operating activities.

14 Click **Group** in the Outline group on the Data tab of the Ribbon.

15 Click and select rows **29** through **31** to group investing activities.

16 Click **Group** in the Outline group on the Data tab of the Ribbon.

17 Click and select rows **33** through **35** to group financing activities.

18 Click **Group** in the Outline group on the Data tab of the Ribbon.

19 Click and select columns **B** through **E** to group quarters.

20 Click **Group** in the Outline group on the Data tab of the Ribbon.

21 Click **1** to collapse the column group to the first level.

22 Click **1** to collapse the row group to the first level. Your worksheet should look like Figure 6.13.

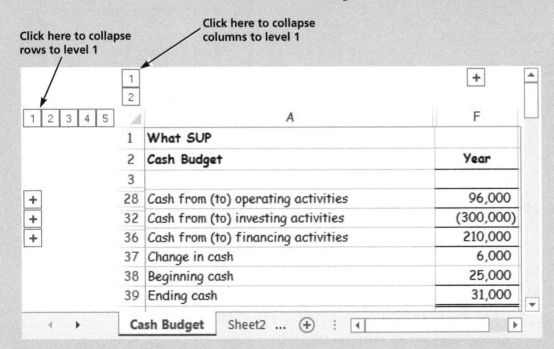

Click here to collapse columns to level 1

Click here to collapse rows to level 1

Figure 6.13

Cash Budget Grouped at Level-1 Rows and Level-1 Columns

23 Click **2** to collapse the column group to the second level.

24 Click **2** to collapse the row group to the second level. Your worksheet should look like Figure 6.14.

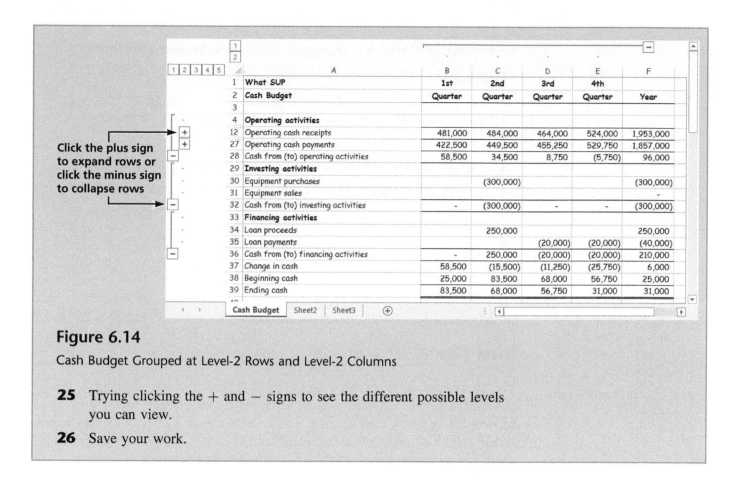

	A	B	C	D	E	F
1	What SUP	1st	2nd	3rd	4th	
2	Cash Budget	Quarter	Quarter	Quarter	Quarter	Year
3						
4	**Operating activities**					
12	Operating cash receipts	481,000	484,000	464,000	524,000	1,953,000
27	Operating cash payments	422,500	449,500	455,250	529,750	1,857,000
28	Cash from (to) operating activities	58,500	34,500	8,750	(5,750)	96,000
29	**Investing activities**					
30	Equipment purchases		(300,000)			(300,000)
31	Equipment sales					-
32	Cash from (to) investing activities	-	(300,000)	-	-	(300,000)
33	**Financing activities**					
34	Loan proceeds		250,000			250,000
35	Loan payments			(20,000)	(20,000)	(40,000)
36	Cash from (to) financing activities	-	250,000	(20,000)	(20,000)	210,000
37	Change in cash	58,500	(15,500)	(11,250)	(25,750)	6,000
38	Beginning cash	25,000	83,500	68,000	56,750	25,000
39	Ending cash	83,500	68,000	56,750	31,000	31,000

Click the plus sign to expand rows or click the minus sign to collapse rows

Cash Budget | Sheet2 | Sheet3 | (+)

Figure 6.14

Cash Budget Grouped at Level-2 Rows and Level-2 Columns

25 Trying clicking the + and − signs to see the different possible levels you can view.

26 Save your work.

The resulting cash budget leaves the company with only $31,000 at the end of the fourth quarter—which, as Nathan explains, is not acceptable. "We must have done something wrong. I'm sure the bank will reject my application if I present them this budget," he says.

Using What-If Analysis and Goal Seeking with the Cash Budget

"Perhaps we can use Excel's What-If feature to manipulate the budget and give us a better ending balance?" Meagan says. "I propose we increase the hourly rate we charge for repairs from $50 to $75 per hour."

"We can also use the goal seek feature we used before to determine what changes need to be made to achieve a certain target value for ending cash," you suggest. "For instance, if we want an ending cash balance of $50,000, what cost of expected sales percentage could you use?"

Kyle suggests you experiment with your newly created cash budget by using what-if analysis and goal seeking for the two scenarios described.

To use what-if analysis and goal seeking with the cash budget:

1 Change the hourly rate charged for repairs to $75 in cell B42.

2 The result should be ending cash of $187,000, assuming the change in hourly rate had no effect on the projected repair hours.

3 Change the hourly rate charged for repairs back to $50.

4 Use goal seek by setting cell F39 (ending cash) on the cash budget to $50,000 by changing cell B46 (the cost of expected sales). The result should be a percent cost of sales of 59 percent (actually, 59.0142671854734 percent before rounding).

5 Close the workbook without saving changes.

"Now, that is a powerful tool." Nathan says. "I think I can shave off a little on the percentage of cost of sales by increasing my markup slightly."

End Note

You've applied some of what you learned in the first five chapters to better understand how Excel can be used to create a cash budget. In doing so, you created an operating cash receipts budget based on budgeted sales and a predicted pattern of expected cash collections. You also created an operating cash payments budget based on budgeted purchases and a pattern of expected cash payments. To round out the cash budget you created a budget for investing and financing activities and pulled it all together with Excel's grouping feature to create a complete annual cash budget. In addition, you applied the what-if analysis and goal seek features of Excel to answer common questions posed when analyzing budgets. Finally, you used names extensively to better understand formulas and calculations in Excel. In the next chapter, you'll explore some additional ways in which Excel is used in accounting.

Chapter 6 Questions

1 Why should you locate budget assumptions in a special section of the worksheet?

2 What information is provided in the operating cash receipts portion of the cash budget?

3 Why does the typical cash budget spread collection of sales revenue over more than one month?

4 What information is provided in the operating cash payments portion of the cash budget?

5 What factors determine monthly purchases in the cash budget?

6 Why does the typical cash budget spread payment of purchases over more than one month?

7 What information is provided in the investing activities portion of the cash budget?

8 What information is provided in the financing activities portion of the cash budget?

9 How is the goal seeking feature used in this chapter?

10 How is grouping used with the cash budget?

Chapter 6 Assignments

1 Create a new What SUP Operating Cash Receipts Budget

Using the ch6-02 file to start your work, create a worksheet similar to the one created in this chapter to budget operating cash receipts by month for 3 months. Place assumption information in the cells provided, and define and use names extensively. The company expects to incur repair hours of 800, 900, and 950 in January, February, and March (respectively) at an expected hourly rate of $80. Product sales revenue of $150,000, $165,000, and $175,000 is expected in January, February, and March, together with interest revenue of $15,000, $12,000, and $10,000, respectively. Professional service revenue and interest revenue are all collected in the month earned. It is anticipated that 70 percent of product sales revenue will be collected in the same month as earned, 20 percent collected in the next month, and 10 percent in the following month. Product sales revenue last November was $180,000 and last December was $190,000. (*Hint:* Use these amounts in your budget to determine cash collections in the current

3 months of January, February, and March as a function of prior product sales. Use Excel's grouping feature to group "revenues" rows together and to group the three monthly columns together. Save your file as ch6-02_student_name (replacing student_name with your name).

a. Print the newly completed worksheet in Value view, with your name and date printed in the lower left footer and the file name in the lower right footer.

b. Collapse all rows and columns and then print the worksheet in Value view, with your name and date printed in the lower left footer and the file name in the lower right footer. Print only the total cash budget, no assumptions.

c. Expand all rows and columns. Use what-if analysis to calculate operating cash receipts if 85 percent of product sales revenue were collected in the same month as earned, 10 percent in the next month, and 5 percent in the following month. Print the resulting worksheet in Value view, with your name and date printed in the lower left footer and the file name in the lower right footer.

d. Reset the collection expectations to their original values (of 70, 20, and 10 percent). Use goal seek to determine what number of repair hours must be worked in January in order to achieve operating cash receipts of $220,000 in January. Print the resulting cash budget, no assumptions in Value view, with your name and date printed in the lower left footer and the file name in the lower right footer.

2 Create a new What SUP Operating Cash Payments Budget

Using the ch6-03 file to start your work, create a worksheet similar to the one created in this chapter to budget operating cash payments by month for 3 months. Place assumption information in the cells provided, and define and use names extensively. Product sales revenue of $150,000, $165,000, $175,000, and $180,000 is expected in January, February, March, and April respectively. Purchases cost 60 percent of product sales. The company would like to maintain an ending inventory equal to 50 percent of the next month's cost of sales. At the beginning of January, the company had $75,000 in inventory and $15,000 in accounts payable; 90 percent of a month's purchases are paid in the current month, with the remaining paid in the following month. Selling expenses are expected to be $6,000, $7,000, and $8,000 in January, February, and March (respectively), while general and administrative expenses are expected to remain constant at $40,000 per month. All expenses are paid in the month incurred. Use Excel's grouping feature to group purchases, payments for purchases, and expense rows together and to group the three monthly columns together. Save your file as ch6-03_student_name (replacing student_name with your name).

a. Print the newly completed worksheet in Value view, with your name and date printed in the lower left footer and the file name in the lower right footer.

b. Collapse all rows and columns and then print the worksheet, no assumptions in Value view, with your name and date printed in the lower left footer and the file name in the lower right footer.

c. Expand all rows and columns. Use what-if analysis to calculate operating cash payments if 70 percent of purchases are paid in the current month and 30 percent are paid in the following month. Print the resulting worksheet in Value view, with your name and date printed in the lower left footer and the file name in the lower right footer.

d. Reset the payments expectations to the original 90 percent and 10 percent values. Use goal seek to determine what cost of expected sales percentage would cause the operating cash payments to be $500,000 for the quarter. Print the resulting worksheet in Value view, with your name and date printed in the lower left footer and the file name in the lower right footer.

Chapter 6 Case Problem 1:
KELLY'S BOUTIQUE

Kelly's Boutique is contemplating several means of financing their acquisition of $200,000 in special equipment. One alternative is to borrow $200,000 from a local bank for 10 years at 12 percent per annum. The bank has asked them to produce a 1-year cash budget broken down by quarters. Sales of $40,000 are expected in the first quarter, with each quarter thereafter increasing 2 percent. Purchases are based on an expected cost of sales of 55 percent and a required ending inventory of 70 percent of next quarter's cost of sales. Beginning inventory was $11,000. Sales for the first quarter next year are expected to be $50,000. Sales in the previous year's fourth quarter were $28,000. Sales in the previous year's third quarter were $30,000. Expenses include advertising expense of $900, depreciation expense of $800, interest expense of $1,000, payroll expense of $8,000, supplies expense of $500, and utilities expense of $600 per quarter throughout the year. All expenses except depreciation are paid in the quarter during which they are incurred. Collections in the quarter of sale are expected to be 80 percent, collections in the first quarter following a sale 15 percent, and in the second quarter 5 percent. Payments in the quarter of purchase are expected to be 85 percent, payments in the first quarter following a purchase 10 percent, and payments in the second quarter to be 5 percent. Purchases in the previous year's fourth quarter were $20,000. Purchases in the previous year's third quarter were $17,000. Proceeds from the $200,000 loan are expected in the second quarter and $200,000 of equipment will be purchased in the third quarter. Quarterly payments of $4,200 on the loan also begin in the third quarter. The beginning cash balance in the first quarter was $15,000.

Using the ch6-04 file to start your work, create a cash budget (as you did in the chapter) that is based on the assumptions listed in the previous paragraph. Use Excel's grouping feature to group operating cash receipts, operating cash payment, cash from (to) operating activities, cash from (to) investing activities, and cash from (to) financing activities and also to group the four quarterly columns together. Save your file as ch6-04_student_name (replacing student_name with your name). Define names as appropriate.

a. Print the newly completed worksheet in Value view, with your name and date printed in the lower left footer and the file name in the lower right footer.

b. Collapse rows to level 2 and columns to level 1, and then print the worksheet in Value view with your name and date printed in the lower left footer and the file name in the lower right footer. Print cash budget only, no assumptions.

c. Expand rows to level 3 and columns to level 2, and then use what-if analysis to calculate end-of-year cash if the sales growth each quarter were 4 percent and payroll expense were $18,000 per quarter. Print the resulting worksheet in Value view, with your name and date printed in the lower left footer and the file name in the lower right footer. Print cash budget only, no assumptions.

d. Undo the what-if analysis performed in part c. Use goal seek to determine what sales growth would be needed to produce an ending cash balance of $50,000. Print the resulting worksheet in Value view with your name and date printed in the lower left footer and the file name in the lower right footer. Print cash budget and assumptions.

Chapter 6 Case Problem 2:
WINE DEPOT

The Wine Depot is contemplating several alternative means of financing their annual acquisition of $70,000 in equipment. One option is to borrow $300,000 from a local bank for 5 years at 11 percent per annum. The bank has asked them to produce a 4-year cash budget broken down by year (Year 1 through Year 4). Sales of $650,000 are expected in year 1, with sales increasing each year thereafter by 10 percent. Sales in the previous year were $600,000. Purchases are based on an expected cost of sales of 30 percent and a required ending inventory of 10 percent of next year's sales. Purchases in the previous year were $200,000, and beginning inventory was $32,000. Annual expenses include advertising expense of $10,000, marketing expense of $6,000, depreciation expense of $8,000, interest expense of $35,000, salaries expense of $250,000, wages expense of $65,000, supplies expense of $7,500, and utilities expense of $10,000. All expenses except depreciation are paid in the year in which they are incurred and are expected to increase 5 percent each year. Collections in the year of sale are expected to be 92 percent, with the remaining 8 percent collected in the next year. Payments in the year of purchase are expected to be

93 percent, with the remaining 7 percent paid in the next year. Proceeds from the $300,000 loan are expected in year 1 and $75,000 of facilities will be purchased each year. Proceeds from expected equipment sales each year are expected to amount to $10,000. Annual payments of $81,171 on the loan also begin in year 1. The beginning cash balance in year 1 was $20,000.

Using the ch6-05 file to start your work, create a cash budget (as you did in the chapter) based on the assumptions just provided. Use Excel's grouping feature to group operating cash receipts, operating cash payment, cash from (to) operating activities, cash from (to) investing activities, and cash from (to) financing activities. Save your file as ch6-05_student_name (replacing student_name with your name). Define names as appropriate.

a. Print the newly completed worksheet in Value view, with your name and date printed in the lower left footer and the file name in the lower right footer.

b. Collapse rows to level 2; then print the worksheet in Value view, with your name and date printed in the lower left footer and the file name in the lower right footer. Print cash budget only, no assumptions.

c. Collapse rows to level 2, and then use what-if analysis to calculate end-of-year cash if the sales growth each year were 4 percent. Print the resulting worksheet in Value view, with your name and date printed in the lower left footer and the file name in the lower right footer. Print cash budget only, no assumptions.

d. Undo the what-if analysis performed in part d. Collapse rows to level 2, and then use goal seek to determine what annual sales growth would be needed to produce an ending cash balance of $100,000 in year 4. Print the resulting worksheet in Value view, with your name and date printed in the lower left footer and the file name in the lower right footer. Print cash budget and assumptions.

Chapter 6 Case Problem 3:
SNICK'S BOARD SHOP

Snick's Board Shop is contemplating several alternative means of financing their acquisition of $350,000 in new equipment in year 1. One option is to borrow $300,000 from a local bank. The bank has asked them to produce a 3-year cash budget broken down by year (Year 1, 2, and 3). Sales in the prior year were $300,000 and are expected to increase 3 percent each year. Year 1 beginning cash was $97,450 and beginning inventory was $30,000. Purchases are based on an expected cost of sales of 40 percent and a required ending inventory of 25 percent of next year's sales. Prior year expenses included advertising expense of $2,500, depreciation expense of $1,000, wages expense of $46,000, supplies expense of $450, and utilities expense of $1,600. All expenses except depreciation are paid in the year in which they are incurred and are expected to increase 8 percent each year. Interest expense is expected to remain constant at $15,000 each year for years 1–3. Collections in the year of sale are expected to be 90 percent, with the remaining 10 percent collected in the next year. Payments in the year of purchase are expected to be 95 percent, with the remaining 5 percent paid in the next year. Proceeds from the $300,000 loan are expected in year 1, and $350,000 of equipment will be purchased during year 1. In subsequent years equipment purchases are expected to be $1,000 each year. Proceeds from projected equipment sales each year are expected to amount to $200. Annual payments of $110,000 on the loan also begin in year 1.

Using the ch6-06 file to start your work, create a cash budget (as you did in the chapter) based on the assumptions just provided. Use Excel's grouping feature to group operating cash receipts, operating cash payment, cash from (to) operating activities, cash from (to) investing activities, and cash from (to) financing activities. Define names as appropriate.

Save your file as ch6-06_student_name (replacing student_name with your name).

a. Print the newly completed worksheet in Value view, with your name and date printed in the lower left footer and the file name in the lower right footer. Print the resulting worksheet in Value view, with your name and date printed in the lower left footer and the file name in the lower right footer. Print cash budget and assumptions.

b. Collapse rows to level 2. Print the resulting worksheet in Value view, with your name and date printed in the lower left footer and the file name in the lower right footer. Print cash budget with no assumptions.

c. Expand to view all rows and then use what-if analysis to calculate end-of-year cash if the sales growth each year were 7 percent. Print the resulting worksheet in Value view, with your name and date printed in the lower left footer and the file name in the lower right footer. Print cash budget and assumptions.

d. Undo the what-if analysis performed in part c. Use goal seek to determine what annual sales growth would be needed to produce an ending cash balance of $50,000 in year 3. Print the resulting worksheet in Value view, with your name and date printed in the lower left footer and the file name in the lower right footer. Print cash budget and assumptions.

Chapter 6 Case Problem 4:
ROSEY'S ROSES

Rosey's Roses is contemplating several alternative means of financing their acquisition of $100,000 in new equipment in year 1. One option is to borrow $80,000 from a local bank. The bank has asked them to produce a 3-year cash budget broken down by year (Year 1, 2, and 3). Sales of $250,000 were earned in the prior year and are expected to increase each year thereafter by 15 percent. Prior year purchases were $195,500. Future purchases are based on an expected cost of sales of 75 percent and a required ending inventory of 20 percent of next year's sales. Prior year expenses included advertising expense of $15,000, depreciation expense of $1,000, wages expense of $20,000, supplies expense of

$1,000, and utilities expense of $3,300. All expenses except depreciation and interest expense are paid in the year in which they are incurred and are expected to increase 5 percent each year. Interest expense is paid in the year incurred and is expected to remain constant at $4,000 each year for years 1–3. Collections in the year of sale are expected to be 85 percent, with the remaining 15 percent collected in the next year. Payments in the year of purchase are expected to be 90 percent, with the remaining 10 percent paid in the next year. Proceeds from the $80,000 loan are expected at the beginning of year 1, and $100,000 of equipment will be purchased during year 1. In subsequent years, equipment purchases are expected to be $2,000 each year. Proceeds from projected equipment sales each year are expected to amount to $500. Annual payments of $10,360 on the loan occur at the end of each year. Cash and Inventory at the beginning of year 1 were $20,200 and $58,000 respectively.

Using the ch6–07 file to start your work, create a cash budget (as you did in the chapter) based on the assumptions just provided. Use Excel's grouping feature to group operating cash receipts, operating cash payment, cash from (to) operating activities, cash from (to) investing activities, and cash from (to) financing activities. Define names as appropriate.

Save your file as ch6-07_student_name (replacing student_name with your name).

a. Print the newly completed worksheet in Value view, with your name and date printed in the lower left footer and the file name in the lower right footer. Print the resulting worksheet in Value view, with your name and date printed in the lower left footer and the file name in the lower right footer. Print cash budget and assumptions.

b. Collapse rows to level 2, and then print the worksheet in Value view, with your name and date printed in the lower left footer and the file name in the lower right footer. Print the cash budget, no assumptions.

c. Expand all rows and then use what-if analysis to calculate end-of-year cash if the sales growth each year were 0 percent. Print the resulting worksheet in Value view, with your name and date printed in the lower left footer and the file name in the lower right footer. Print cash budget and assumptions.

d. Undo the what-if analysis performed in part c. Use goal seek to determine what annual sales growth would be needed to produce an ending cash balance of $50,000 in year 3. Print the resulting worksheet in Value view, with your name and date printed in the lower left footer and the file name in the lower right footer. Print cash budget and assumptions.

Other Topics: Present/ Future Values, Predicting Costs, and Allowance for Uncollectible Accounts

In this chapter you will learn:

- How to use Excel to prepare a present/future value analysis
- How to use Excel to predict costs
- How to use Excel to calculate an allowance for uncollectible accounts

Case: What SUP, Inc.

Nathan and Megan are aware that there are other accounting issues that may be aided by using Excel. Kyle explains that this week they will look at how Excel can help them calculate present and future values based on assumptions about interest rates, time, and financial needs. They will also look at predicting future costs based on trends experienced in the current year. They will utilize Excel's ability to visualize cost behaviors: fixed and variable costs based on past experience and Excel's charting ability to examine patterns of cost behavior. Lastly they will look at using Excel to calculate uncollectible accounts expense and an allowance for uncollectible accounts using both the percentage of sales and aging methods.

As the recent accounting graduate in the group, you offer to lend your accounting expertise to using Excel to solve these common business problems.

Present/Future Value Analysis

The first additional accounting issue Nathan and Megan agree to tackle is the calculation of present and future values. Kyle suggests that they consider using Excel to help them calculate how much they should invest now to be able to meet an expected future equipment purchase need. In this case Excel will calculate the present value of a lump sum payment in the future. Alternatively, they could put some funds away at the end of each year to save up for the equipment purchase. Kyle explains that that approach requires that they calculate an annuity payment they would make into a fund so that at the end of a certain period they would have funds for the purchase.

"This is perfect," says Megan. "We anticipate having to replace equipment we currently use with more modern and efficient equipment in 5 years. We expect it will cost about $50,000 at that time."

"Excellent," says Kyle. "We'll approach this problem from both angles: calculating a lump sum to be invested now and calculating an annuity to help save for this future purchase."

You explain that all present value problems have five variables: (1) interest rate, (2) term, (3) annuity payment, (4) future value, and (5) present value. If you know four of the variables, you can always calculate the fifth. Interest rates are currently 6 percent, and Megan indicated the term of 5 years and future cost of $50,000. Under scenario 1, the company wants to know what amount should be invested now to have $50,000 in 5 years assuming a 6 percent return on their investment.

The present value function in Excel is written PV(rate,nper,pmt,fv,type). PV stands for present value. The arguments to that function are contained within the parentheses. The rate is the periodic interest rate, nper is the number of periods, pmt is the periodic annuity payment, fv is the lump sum future value, and type represents ordinary annuity or annuity due which basically indicates whether payments are made at the beginning or ending of the period in question. We will assume all payments are made at the end of the period. For this problem the fv = $50,000, rate = 6%, and the nper = 5 years.

To calculate a present value of a lump sum:

1 Open Excel.

2 Enter the information with correct formats, as shown in Figure 7.1.

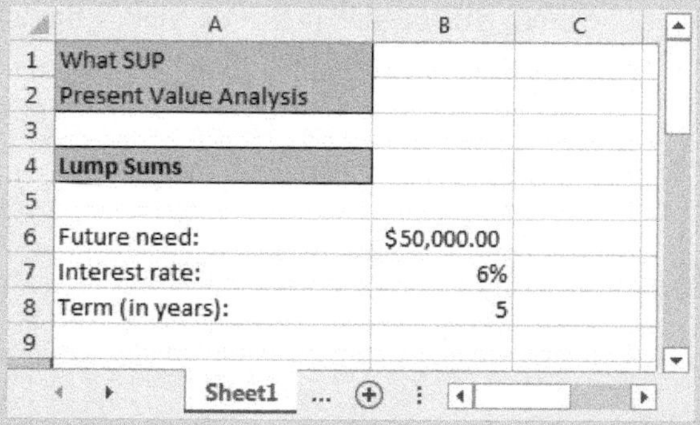

Figure 7.1

Creating a Lump Sums Worksheet

3 In cell A10 type **Invest now:**

4 In cell B10 type the formula =**PV(B7,B8,0,B6)**. B7 is the first argument to the PV function since it is where we have stored the rate. B8 is the second argument since it is where we have stored the number of periods, 0 is the third argument since this problem doesn't require an annuity payment, and B6 is the fourth argument since that is where we have stored the future value. Now press [**Enter**].

5 Your screen should look like Figure 7.2 Keep it open.

Figure 7.2

Adding an Invest Now Formula

	A	B	C
1	What SUP		
2	Present Value Analysis		
3			
4	Lump Sums		
5			
6	Future need:	$50,000.00	
7	Interest rate:	6%	
8	Term (in years):	5	
9			
10	Invest now:	($37,362.91)	

Sheet1 ... ⊕ ⦂ ◄

"Why is the amount negative?" Nathan asks.

"Well," you explain, "that is the amount we have to give up now to have $50,000 in 5 years if we can earn 6 percent per year."

"You'll have to prove that to me," Nathan retorts.

"Ok," you answer. "I'll create a column for the year, interest earned, and investment value. I always start with year 0 since that represents the end of last year and the beginning of this year. In the interest column I'll be entering the interest earned each year at 6 percent of the investment balance held during the year. In the final column I'll be entering the end of year balance in the investment, which will be the previous year's balance plus interest earned during the current year.

To prove the increase in value over the 5 years:

1 Create a table in Excel like the one shown in Figure 7.3.

Figure 7.3

Creating a Proof of Lump Sums Calculations

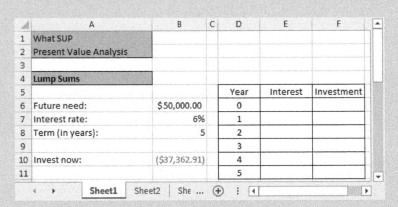

	A	B	C	D	E	F
1	What SUP					
2	Present Value Analysis					
3						
4	Lump Sums					
5				Year	Interest	Investment
6	Future need:	$50,000.00		0		
7	Interest rate:	6%		1		
8	Term (in years):	5		2		
9				3		
10	Invest now:	($37,362.91)		4		
11				5		

Sheet1 Sheet2 She ... ⊕ ⦂ ◄

2 Type =−**B10** in cell F6 since that is the beginning of the year investment. (Be sure to include the minus sign in front of the cell reference so that values all come out positive).

3 Type **=F6*$B$7** in cell E7. This will calculate the interest earned each year by multiplying the rate (always located in cell B7) times the beginning of year investment.

4 Fill the formula written in cell E7 down to cell E11.

5 Type **=E7+F6** in cell F7. This will calculate the end of the year balance in the investment account.

6 Fill the formula written in cell F7 down to cell F11.

7 Your screen should look like Figure 7.4.

	A	B	C	D	E	F
1	What SUP					
2	Present Value Analysis					
3						
4	Lump Sums					
5				Year	Interest	Investment
6	Future need:	$50,000.00		0		$37,362.91
7	Interest rate:	6%		1	$2,241.77	$39,604.68
8	Term (in years):	5		2	$2,376.28	$41,980.96
9				3	$2,518.86	$44,499.82
10	Invest now:	($37,362.91)		4	$2,669.99	$47,169.81
11				5	$2,830.19	$50,000.00

Sheet1 · Sheet2 · Sh ...

Figure 7.4

Completed Proof of Lump Sum Calculations

8 Press **[Ctrl]** and **[~]** at the same time to switch to formula view. Your screen should look like Figure 7.5.

	A	B	C	D	E	F
1	What SUP					
2	Present Value Analysis					
3						
4	Lump Sums					
5				Year	Interest	Investment
6	Future need:	50000		0		=-B10
7	Interest rate:	0.06		1	=F6*$B$7	=E7+F6
8	Term (in years):	5		2	=F7*$B$7	=E8+F7
9				3	=F8*$B$7	=E9+F8
10	Invest now:	=PV(B7,B8,0,B6)		4	=F9*$B$7	=E10+F9
11				5	=F10*$B$7	=E11+F10

Sheet1 · Sheet2 · Sh ...

Figure 7.5

Formula View of Completed Proof of Lump Sum Calculations

9 Press **[Ctrl]** and **[~]** at the same time to switch back to value view.

10 Save your file with the name Ch7PV.

After calculating a lump sum to be invested now to achieve a future need, you now turn your attention to calculating an annuity to help save for this future purchase. An annuity is a constant payment either received or paid over a specific period of time. Excel helps you solve this with the payment function (PMT).

The PMT function in Excel is written PMT(rate,nper,pv,[fv],[type]). The arguments to that function are contained within the parentheses. The rate is the periodic interest rate, nper is number of payments, pv is the lump sum present value, fv is the lump sum future value, and type represents ordinary annuity or annuity due which basically indicates whether payments are made at the beginning or ending of the period in question. We will assume all payments are made at the end of the period. For this problem the pv is 0, fv = $50,000, rate = 6%, and the nper = 5 years.

To calculate the annuity payment required to meet a future need:

1 Start a new worksheet (don't close the current file) and then enter the information as shown in Figure 7.6.

Figure 7.6

Creating an Annuities Worksheet

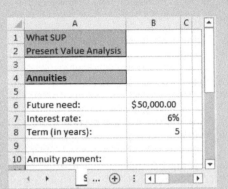

2 Type =**PMT(B7,B8,0,B6)** into cell B10, being sure to type zero (**0**) in the third argument to indicate no present value payment is made in this analysis.

3 Press [**Enter**]. Your resulting worksheet should look like Figure 7.7.

Figure 7.7

Calculated Annuity

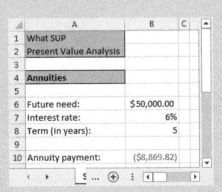

4 To prove that an annual payment of $8,869.82 earning interest at 6 percent per year will yield the $50,000 future value, set up the table below on your worksheet, as shown in Figure 7.8.

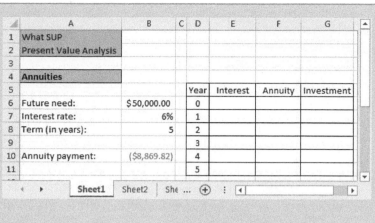

Figure 7.8

Annuity Table

5 Type **0** in cell G6 since there is no beginning investment amount.

6 Type **=G6*$B$7** in cell E7 which multiplies the interest rate times the end of year investment amount. Format the cell using the Currency format.

7 Fill the formula just created in E7 down through cell E11.

8 Type **=–$B$10** in cell F7 to place the annuity payment in this cell. (Putting the minus sign in front is done to reflect a positive value).

9 Fill the formula just created in F7 down through cell F11.

10 Type **=G6+E7+F7** in cell G7 to sum the previous year's investment with the current year's interest and annuity payment.

11 Fill the formula just created in G7 down through cell G11. Your worksheet should look like Figure 7.9.

	A	B	C	D	E	F	G
1	What SUP						
2	Present Value Analysis						
3							
4	Annuities						
5				Year	Interest	Annuity	Investment
6	Future need:	$50,000.00		0			0
7	Interest rate:	6%		1	$ -	$8,869.82	$8,869.82
8	Term (in years):	5		2	$ 532.19	$8,869.82	$18,271.83
9				3	$ 1,096.31	$8,869.82	$28,237.96
10	Annuity payment	($8,869.82)		4	$ 1,694.28	$8,869.82	$38,802.06
11				5	$ 2,328.12	$8,869.82	$50,000.00

Sheet1   Sheet2   Sheet3

Figure 7.9

Completed Annuity Table

12 Save your file with the name Ch7PVAN.

"Now," you explain, "you know that you can either invest $37,362.91 today or you can invest $8,869.82 annually to achieve your $50,000 in 5 years at 6 percent.

"What if I can only earn a 5 percent return?" Nathan asks.

"I'll show you." you answer. "This requires a what-if analysis. All you have to do is change the interest rate from 6 percent to 5 percent."

Nathan decides to try this himself by typing **5%** in cell B7 of the Ch7PVAN and Ch7PV worksheet files. His resulting worksheet looks like Figures 7.10 and 7.11 below.

Figure 7.10

Required Investment at 5%

	A	B	C	D	E	F
1	What SUP					
2	Present Value Analysis					
3						
4	**Lump Sums**					
5				Year	Interest	Investment
6	Future need:	$50,000.00		0		$39,176.31
7	Interest rate:	5%		1	$1,958.82	$41,135.12
8	Term (in years):	5		2	$2,056.76	$43,191.88
9				3	$2,159.59	$45,351.47
10	Invest now:	($39,176.31)		4	$2,267.57	$47,619.05
11				5	$2,380.95	$50,000.00

Sheet1   Sheet2   She ...

Figure 7.11

Required Annuity at 5%

	A	B	C	D	E	F	G
1	What SUP						
2	Present Value Analysis						
3							
4	**Annuities**						
5				Year	Interest	Annuity	Investment
6	Future need:	$50,000.00		0			0
7	Interest rate:	5%		1	$ -	$9,048.74	$9,048.74
8	Term (in years):	5		2	$ 452.44	$9,048.74	$18,549.92
9				3	$ 927.50	$9,048.74	$28,526.15
10	Annuity payment	($9,048.74)		4	$ 1,426.31	$9,048.74	$39,001.20
11				5	$ 1,950.06	$9,048.74	$50,000.00

Sheet1   Sheet2   Sheet3

"That makes sense," Nathan comments. "If I can only earn 5 percent I need to invest more now, $39,176.31 versus $37,262.91 assuming a 6 percent return. Alternatively, I would have to make a larger annuity payment of $9,048.74 assuming a 5 percent return versus $8,869.82 assuming a 6 percent return."

"What about working the other way around?" Meagan asks. "I would like to know how much I would have in 5 years if I was able to invest either $10,000 right now or $1,000 per year assuming a 5 percent return on my investment."

You explain that that requires the use of another of Excel's built-in functions. The FV function takes very similar arguments to the PV function you just described. It is written FV(rate,per,pmt,pv,type) where pv and type are optional.

"Let's create a new worksheet for future values," you suggest.

To create a future value worksheet and table:

1 Create a new worksheet like that shown in Figure 7.12.

Figure 7.12

Beginning Your Future Value Worksheet

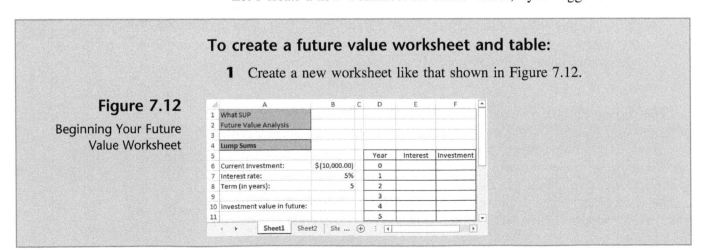

	A	B	C	D	E	F
1	What SUP					
2	Future Value Analysis					
3						
4	Lump Sums					
5				Year	Interest	Investment
6	Current Investment:	$(10,000.00)		0		
7	Interest rate:	5%		1		
8	Term (in years):	5		2		
9				3		
10	Investment value in future:			4		
11				5		

Sheet1   Sheet2   She ...

2   Type the formula **=FV(B7,B8,0,B6)** into cell B10. This sets the rate at 5%, which is in cell B7; the period to 5, which is in cell B8; the annuity payment to zero since this part of the problem has no annuity payment; and the present value to the current investment shown in cell B6.

3   Press [**Enter**].

4   Type **=–B6** into cell F15

5   Type **=F6*$B$7** into cell E16 and then fill the formula down to cell E11. This cell calculates the interest earned on the investment balance at the end of the previous year.

6   Type **=E7+F6** into cell F16 to add the current year interest and prior year investment amounts together and then fill the formula down to cell F11. Your resulting worksheet should look like Figure 7.13. Save your file with the name Ch7FV.

	A	B	C	D	E	F
1	What SUP					
2	Future Value Analysis					
3						
4	**Lump Sums**					
5				Year	Interest	Investment
6	Current Investment:	$(10,000.00)		0		$10,000.00
7	Interest rate:	5%		1	$ 500.00	$10,500.00
8	Term (in years):	5		2	$ 525.00	$11,025.00
9				3	$ 551.25	$11,576.25
10	Investment value in future:	$12,762.82		4	$ 578.81	$12,155.06
11				5	$ 607.75	$12,762.82

Sheet1   Sheet2   She …   ⊕

Figure 7.13

Future Value of a Lump Sum

7   Create another new worksheet like that shown in Figure 7.14.

	A	B	C	D	E	F	G
1	What SUP						
2	Future Value Analysis						
3							
4	**Annuities**						
5				Year	Interest	Annuity	Investment
6	Current annuity investment:	$ (1,000.00)		0			
7	Interest rate:	5%		1			
8	Term (in years):	5		2			
9				3			
10	Investment value in future:			4			
11				5			

Sheet1   Sheet2   Sheet3   ⊕

Figure 7.14

Future Value of an Annuity

8   Type the formula **=FV(B7,B8,B6)** into cell B10. This sets the rate at 5%, which is in cell B7; the period to 5, which is in cell B8; and the annuity payment to $1,000, which is in cell B6.

9   Press [**Enter**].

10   Type **0** into cell G6.

11   Type **=G6*$B$7** into cell E7 and then fill the formula down to cell E11. This cell calculates the interest earned on the investment balance at the end of the previous year.

12   Type **=–$B$6** into cell F7 and then fill the formula down to F11. This places the annual payment into the cell.

13 **Type =G6+E7+F7** into cell G7 to add the current year interest, current year annuity payment, and prior year investment amounts together and then fill the formula down to cell G11. Your resulting worksheet should look like Figure 7.15. Save your file with the name Ch7FVAN.

Figure 7.15

Future Value of an Annuity

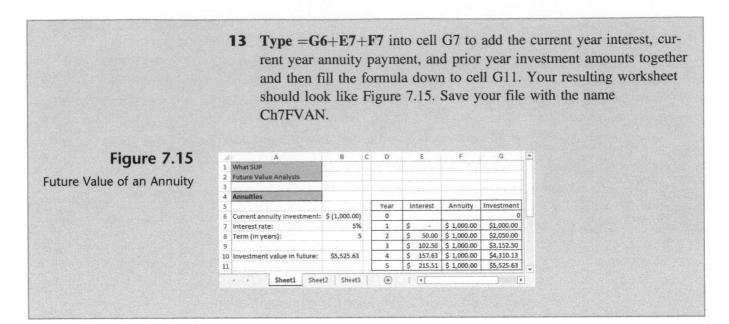

	A	B	C	D	E	F	G
1	What SUP						
2	Future Value Analysis						
3							
4	**Annuities**						
5				Year	Interest	Annuity	Investment
6	Current annuity investment:	$ (1,000.00)		0			0
7	Interest rate:	5%		1	$ -	$ 1,000.00	$1,000.00
8	Term (in years):	5		2	$ 50.00	$ 1,000.00	$2,050.00
9				3	$ 102.50	$ 1,000.00	$3,152.50
10	Investment value in future:	$5,525.63		4	$ 157.63	$ 1,000.00	$4,310.13
11				5	$ 215.51	$ 1,000.00	$5,525.63

Meagan and Nathan are both very pleased with their worksheet creation, which tells them the future value of a lump sum investment and the future value of an annual annuity.

"Can we change the interest rates to see the effect of earning either a higher or lower rate?" Meagan asks.

"Sure," you respond.

You change the Interest rates to 7 percent for both the annuity and lump sum to get the results, as shown in Figure 7.16 and 7.17.

Figure 7.16

Future Value of an Initial Investment of $10,000 at 7% for 5 years

	A	B	C	D	E	F
1	What SUP					
2	Future Value Analysis					
3						
4	**Lump Sums**					
5				Year	Interest	Investment
6	Current Investment:	$ (10,000.00)		0		$10,000.00
7	Interest rate:	7%		1	$ 700.00	$10,700.00
8	Term (in years):	5		2	$ 749.00	$11,449.00
9				3	$ 801.43	$12,250.43
10	Investment value in future:	$14,025.52		4	$ 857.53	$13,107.96
11				5	$ 917.56	$14,025.52

Figure 7.17

Future Value of an Annual Annuity Investment of $1,000 at 7% for 5 years

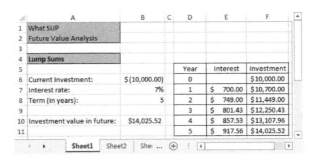

	A	B	C	D	E	F	G
1	What SUP						
2	Future Value Analysis						
3							
4	**Annuities**						
5				Year	Interest	Annuity	Investment
6	Current annuity investment:	$ (1,000.00)		0			0
7	Interest rate:	7%		1	$ -	$ 1,000.00	$1,000.00
8	Term (in years):	5		2	$ 70.00	$ 1,000.00	$2,070.00
9				3	$ 144.90	$ 1,000.00	$3,214.90
10	Investment value in future:	$5,750.74		4	$ 225.04	$ 1,000.00	$4,439.94
11				5	$ 310.80	$ 1,000.00	$5,750.74

Predicting Future Costs

Another issue facing What SUP is predicting future costs. They know that, based on past experiences, certain expenses tend to be constant over time while others vary from month to month. Megan explains that her monthly operating expenses seem to vary according to how many days the store is open, and she asks you whether Excel can help predict costs based on this previous cost behavior.

You explain that accountants use two basic methods to predict costs: the Hi-Lo method and the Least Squares/ Regression method.

"The Hi-Lo method is the easiest but least accurate, while the Least Squares/ Regression method is a bit more complicated but much more accurate," you comment. "Excel can do both and we can create a chart to graphically represent the pattern of cost behavior."

You start by gathering data on past experiences. Nathan provides you with the following information showing monthly expenses and days open by month, as shown in Figure 7.18.

Month	Days Open	Expense
Jan	20	4,500
Feb	18	4,200
Mar	21	4,600
Apr	16	3,800
May	22	4,800
Jun	23	5,000
Jul	25	6,000
Aug	26	6,100
Sep	22	5,000
Oct	18	4,300
Nov	17	4,100
Dec	16	4,000

Figure 7.18

Expenses and Days Open by Month

You decide to enter this information into Excel and then perform a Hi-Lo method analysis. To do so, you first need to enter the data into a new worksheet, calculate the high and low expense and days open, calculate the difference, and then determine the variable and fixed cost behaviors.

"The difference in cost between months must be attributed to a change in variable cost since each month should continue to have the same fixed cost," you explain. "That is the basis of the Hi-Lo method. We'll use the Min and Max functions built-in to Excel to help calculate the high and low costs and days open and then calculate the variable and fixed costs. (Note, the Min and Max functions work in these examples because the highest and lowest activity also equals the highest and lowest costs incurred.) The variable cost can be calculated by dividing the difference in the high and low costs by the difference in the high and low days open. The fixed costs can be calculated by subtracting variable costs from total costs. After that we'll be able to predict costs in a future month based on the number of days open."

To create a Hi-Lo method analysis:

1 Open Excel and start a new worksheet.

2 Enter the information with correct formats, as shown in Figure 7.19.

Figure 7.19

Expenses Entered into Excel

	A	B	C	D	E
1	What SUP				
2	Predicting Costs				
3					
4			Month	Days Open	Expense
5			Jan	20	4,500
6			Feb	18	4,200
7			Mar	21	4,600
8			Apr	16	3,800
9			May	22	4,800
10			Jun	23	5,000
11			Jul	25	6,000
12			Aug	26	6,100
13			Sep	22	5,000
14			Oct	18	4,300
15			Nov	17	4,100
16			Dec	16	4,000

Sheet1   Sheet2   ...   ⊕

3 Type **High Expense** in cell A18 as a label.

4 Type **Low Expense** in cell A19 as a label.

5 Type **Difference** in cell A20 as a label.

6 Type **Hi-Lo Method** in cell A22 as a label.

7 Type **Variable cost/day open** in cell A23 as a label.

8 Type **Fixed cost** in cell A24 as a label.

9 Type **=MAX(D5:D16)** in cell D18 to calculate the highest number of days open.

10 Type **=MAX(E5:E16)** in cell E18 to calculate the highest amount of expense.

11 Type **=MIN(D5:D16)** in cell D19 to calculate the lowest number of days open.

12 Type **=MIN(E5:E16)** in cell E19 to calculate the lowest amount of expense.

13 Type **=D18-D19** in cell D20 to calculate the difference between the highest and lowest days open.

14 Type **=E18-E19** in cell E20 to calculate the difference between the highest and lowest expense.

15 Type **=E20/D20** in cell C23 to calculate the variable cost per day open.

16 Type **=E18–(C23*D18)** in cell C24 to calculate the fixed cost per month.

17 Type **Prediction of expense if open** in cell A26.

18 Type **20** in cell B26.

19 Type **days =** in cell C26.

20 Type **=(B26*C23)+C24** in cell D26 to calculate the total costs assuming a fixed cost as calculated in cell C24, a variable cost as calculated in cell C23, and a number of days open as stated in cell B26.

21 Format your worksheet like the completed worksheet shown in Figure 7.20.

22 Save your work using file name Ch7HiLo.xlsx.

	A	B	C	D	E
1	What SUP				
2	Predicting Costs				
3					
4			Month	Days Open	Expense
5			Jan	20	4,500
6			Feb	18	4,200
7			Mar	21	4,600
8			Apr	16	3,800
9			May	22	4,800
10			Jun	23	5,000
11			Jul	25	6,000
12			Aug	26	6,100
13			Sep	22	5,000
14			Oct	18	4,300
15			Nov	17	4,100
16			Dec	16	4,000
17					
18	High Expense			26	6,100
19	Low Expense			16	3,800
20	Difference			10	2,300
21					
22	Hi-Lo Method				
23	Variable cost/day open		$ 230.00		
24	Fixed cost		$ 120.00		
25					
26	Prediction of expense if open	20	days =	$ 4,720	

Sheet1 Sheet2 ...

Figure 7.20

Hi-Lo Method Worksheet

Megan is delighted with your new worksheet. You explain that by varying the value of cell B26 you can calculate the expected costs for any future month based on the number of days she expects to be open.

"How can we graphically illustrate this pattern of cost behavior?" Meagan asks.

"Easy," you retort, "let me show you."

To create a chart of cost behavior:

1   Select the range of cells from D4 to E16.

2   Click the **Scatter** chart from Charts group on the Insert tab of the Ribbon, and then select **Scatter with only markers**. (Office 365 users select **Scatter Chart**.)

3   Select the **Expense** legend and press the [**Delete**] key to remove it.

4   Double-click the horizontal axis of the chart and select **Axis Options**.

5   Set the minimum axis by selecting **Fixed** and typing **15.0** as the minimum. (Office 365 users will have to enter the range in bounds for this step as well as steps 6, 11, and 12.)

6   Set the maximum axis by selecting **Fixed** and typing **27.0** as the maximum.

7   With the chart selected, click **Axis Titles** from the Labels group of the Layout tab of the Ribbon. (Office 365 users will have to select **Add Chart Element** and then **Axis Titles** from Charts Layout for this step and step 13.)

8   Select **Primary Horizontal Axis Title** and then select **Title Below Axis**.

9   Type **Days Open** as the horizontal axis title.

10   Double-click the vertical axis of the chart and select **Axis Options**.

11   Set the minimum axis by selecting **Fixed** and typing **3000** as the minimum.

12   Set the maximum axis by selecting **Fixed** and typing **6500** as the maximum.

13   With the chart selected click **Axis Titles** from the Labels group of the Layout tab of the Ribbon.

14   Select **Primary Vertical Axis Title** and then select **Vertical Title**.

15   Type **Expense** as the vertical axis title.

16   Select the chart title and change the name by typing **Expense/Days Open**.

17   On the Layout tab in the Analysis group, click **Trendline** and then select **Linear Trendline**. (Office 365 users will have to select **Add Chart Element** in the Charts Layout group.) Your chart should look like Figure 7.21.

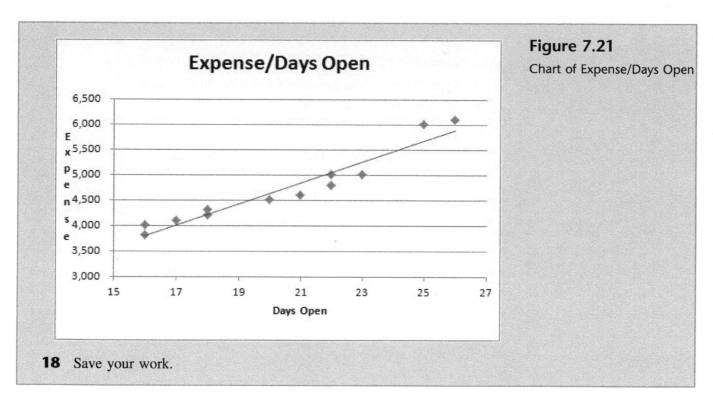

Figure 7.21

Chart of Expense/Days Open

18 Save your work.

You explain to Nathan and Megan that this trend line uses all 12 data points to predict costs, which is exactly what the Least Squares/Regression method does. The trick now is to determine the slope of that line (otherwise known as the variable cost per unit) and the vertical axis intercept (otherwise known as fixed costs).

"The Slope and Intercept functions of Excel are used in the Least Squares/ Regression method. The Slope function provides the slope of a line (in other words, variable costs per unit) defined by two arguments: known y's and known x's. In our case the known y's are the actual costs and the known x's are actual days open. Both are located on our worksheet in an array of cells located at E5 to E16 and D5 to D16 respectively. The Intercept function takes the same two arguments and provides the value of costs incurred when the days open are zero (in other words, fixed costs)."

To calculate the variable cost per day open and fixed costs using Excel:

1 Type **Least Squares/ Regression Method** as a label in cell G22.

2 Type **Variable cost/day open** as a label in cell G23.

3 Type **Fixed cost** as a label in cell G24.

4 Type **=SLOPE(E5:E16,D5:D16)** in cell I23 to calculate the variable cost per unit by using the data provided on the worksheet.

5 Type =INTERCEPT(E5:E16,D5:D16) in cell I24 to calculate the fixed costs by using the data provided on the worksheet.

6 Type **Prediction of expense if open** in cell G26 as a label.

7 Type **20** in cell H26.

8 Type **days =** in cell I27 as a label.

9 Type =TREND(E5:E16,D5:D16,H26) to calculate the predicted costs assuming 20 open days.

10 Format your worksheet like Figure 7.22. Save your work.

Figure 7.22

Completed Predicting
Costs Worksheet

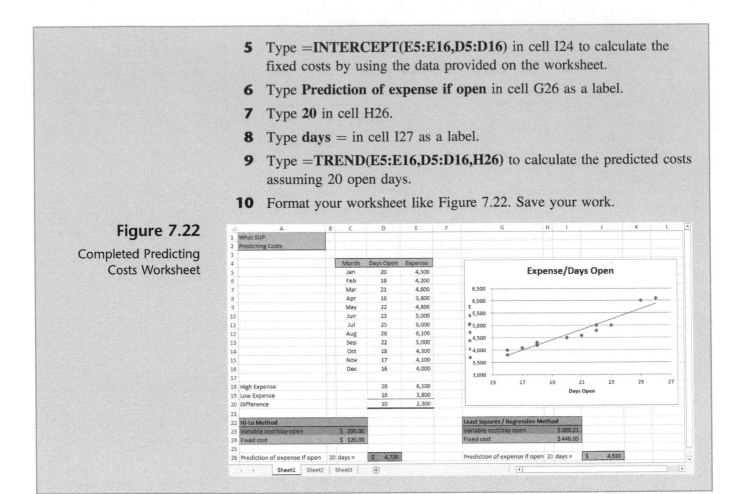

Megan notes that the two methods predict different expense amounts for 20 open days. She speculates that the Least Squares/ Regression method is more accurate since it used 12 data points whereas the Hi-Lo method, used only two.

You agree and conclude that although the Least Squares/Regression method uses some functions like trend, slope, and intercept (which sound too mathematical to Megan) it does produce the more accurate predictions.

Calculating an Allowance for Uncollectible Accounts

An additional accounting issue that What SUP is confronting is the need for an allowance for uncollectible accounts. Two years ago Megan had recommended that the business extend credit to customers, which gave them 30 days to pay for their purchases. In doing so she realized the risk associated with granting credit and that some customers, for a variety of reasons, may end up not paying their bills. They have been collecting data on their experience with non-payment and know that, according to generally accepted accounting principles, they needed to establish an allowance for uncollectible accounts and record some uncollectible accounts expense in the current accounting period.

"There are two common methods for estimating the expense and allowance," you say. "You can either use the percent of sales method or an aging method. Excel can help us with the calculations since in both cases all we are doing is multiplying an estimated uncollectible accounts percentage times either sales or an aging of accounts receivable balances."

Megan provides last year's receivable and sales information. The beginning balance in receivables was $500,000. During the year the company had sales of $5,600,000 and collections of $5,280,000. They wrote off $20,000 in accounts receivable during the year. She created an estimate of the allowance at the end of last year of $25,000.

To calculate the allowance using the percent of sales method:

1 Open Excel and start a new worksheet.

2 Enter the information with correct formats as shown in Figure 7.23.

	A	B	C	D	E	F	G	H
1	What SUP							
2	Allowance for Uncollectible Accounts							
3								
4	Percentage of Sales Method							
5								
6	Accounts receivable balance (beg)	500,000						
7	Sales on account	5,600,000						
8	Write-offs of accounts receivable	(20,000)						
9	Collections on account	(5,280,000)						
10	Accounts receivable balance (end)	800,000						
11								
12	Past experience ratio							
13								
14	Allowance for Uncollectible accounts (beg)	25,000						
15	Write-offs of accounts receivable	(20,000)						
16	Uncollectible accounts expense							
17	Allowance for Uncollectible accounts (end)							
18								
19								
20	Aging Method							
21				Current	0 - 30 Days Past Due	31 - 60 Days Past Due	61 - 90 Days Past Due	> 90 Days Past Due
22	Accounts receivable balance (beg)	500,000						
23	Sales on account	5,600,000						
24	Write-offs of accounts receivable	(20,000)						
25	Collections on account	(5,280,000)						
26	Accounts receivable balance (end)	800,000	=	600,000	100,000	50,000	30,000	20,000
27								
28	Past experience ratio			2.00%	3.50%	6.50%	13.00%	25.00%
29								
30	Allowance for Uncollectible accounts (beg)	25,000						
31	Write-offs of accounts receivable	(20,000)						
32	Uncollectible accounts expense							
33	Allowance for Uncollectible accounts (end)							

Sheet1 Sheet2 Sheet3 (+)

Figure 7.23

Beginning Your Allowance for Uncollectible Accounts Worksheet

3 Type **.50%** as the past experience ratio in cell B12.

4 Type **=B12*B7** in cell B16 to calculate uncollectible accounts expense as current period sales times the past experience ratio.

5 Type **=SUM(B14:B16)** in cell B17 to find the balance of allowance for uncollectible accounts.

"That was easy," comments Nathan. "How do we use the Aging method?"
"I'll show you," you answer.

To calculate the allowance using the aging method:

1 Continuing from your previous work, type **=(D26*D28)+(E26*E28)+(F26*F28)+(G26*G28)+(H26*H28)** into cell B33. (This adds up the past experience rate for each category of accounts receivable times the amount of accounts receivable in each category.) The result is the required ending balance in the allowance for uncollectible accounts.

2 Type **=B33-(B30+B31)** into cell B32 to determine the amount of uncollectible accounts expense necessary to give you the balance in the allowance you calculated above.

3 The completed worksheet should look like Figure 7.24.

Figure 7.24

Completed Allowance for Uncollectible Accounts

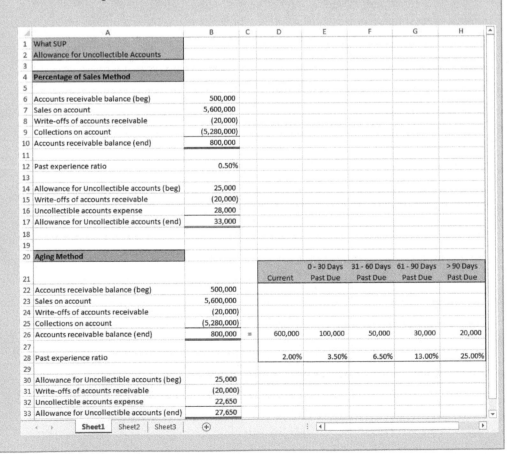

	A	B	C	D	E	F	G	H
1	What SUP							
2	Allowance for Uncollectible Accounts							
3								
4	**Percentage of Sales Method**							
5								
6	Accounts receivable balance (beg)	500,000						
7	Sales on account	5,600,000						
8	Write-offs of accounts receivable	(20,000)						
9	Collections on account	(5,280,000)						
10	Accounts receivable balance (end)	800,000						
11								
12	Past experience ratio	0.50%						
13								
14	Allowance for Uncollectible accounts (beg)	25,000						
15	Write-offs of accounts receivable	(20,000)						
16	Uncollectible accounts expense	28,000						
17	Allowance for Uncollectible accounts (end)	33,000						
18								
19								
20	**Aging Method**							
21					Current	0 - 30 Days Past Due	31 - 60 Days Past Due	61 - 90 Days Past Due	> 90 Days Past Due
22	Accounts receivable balance (beg)	500,000						
23	Sales on account	5,600,000						
24	Write-offs of accounts receivable	(20,000)						
25	Collections on account	(5,280,000)						
26	Accounts receivable balance (end)	800,000	=	600,000	100,000	50,000	30,000	20,000
27								
28	Past experience ratio			2.00%	3.50%	6.50%	13.00%	25.00%
29								
30	Allowance for Uncollectible accounts (beg)	25,000						
31	Write-offs of accounts receivable	(20,000)						
32	Uncollectible accounts expense	22,650						
33	Allowance for Uncollectible accounts (end)	27,650						

Sheet1 Sheet2 Sheet3

You explain that the two methods are basically the same. The percent of sales method calculates the uncollectible accounts expense, which then dictates the ending allowance for the uncollectible accounts balance. On the other hand, the aging method calculates the ending allowance for the uncollectible accounts balance, which then dictates the uncollectible accounts expense.

"Sweet," comments Nathan. "I'm assuming we can reuse these worksheets in future months?" he asks.

"Yes," you respond. "Now that we have set them up we can just change the data and generate new results."

End Note

In this chapter you have created worksheets to calculate present and future values, predict future costs based on past experience, and calculate an allowance for uncollectible accounts under both the percent of sales and aging methods.

Chapter 7 Questions

1 Identify the five variables in present value problems.

2 Describe the PV function in Excel and its arguments.

3 Describe the PMT function in Excel and its arguments.

4 Describe the FV function in Excel and its arguments.

5 Describe the Excel functions used in the Hi-Lo method of predicting costs.

6 Describe the Excel functions used in the Least Squares/Regression method of predicting costs.

7 Describe how to create a trend line for a chart.

8 Describe how Excel can be used to calculate an allowance for uncollectible accounts using the percent of sales method.

9 Describe how Excel can be used to calculate an allowance for uncollectible accounts using the aging method.

10 Compare the percent of sales and aging methods of determining uncollectible accounts expense and the ending allowance for the uncollectible accounts balance.

Chapter 7 Assignments

1 Create a new What SUP Present Value Analysis

a. Using the ch7-01 file to start your work, modify that worksheet to do the following:

i. Calculate the annuity payment required at the end of each year for the next 4 years at 4 percent such that the value in 4 years is $95,000 and illustrate the annual value of that investment.

ii. Calculate the future value of an investment of $20,000 invested for 4 years at a rate of 3 percent and illustrate the annual value of that investment.

iii. Calculate the future value of an investment of $8,500 each year for 4 years at a rate of 3 percent and illustrate the annual value of that investment.

iv. Calculate the initial investment required to obtain a future value of $10,500, assuming a rate of 3 percent for 4 years and illustrate the annual value of that investment.

    b.   Save the file as ch7-01_student_name (replacing student_name with your name).

    c.   Print the resulting worksheet.

2   Create a new What SUP Cost Analysis

    a.   Using the ch7-02 file to start your work, create a worksheet to do the following:

        i.   Calculate the Hi-Lo Method variable cost/hour open and fixed cost.

        ii.   Predicted expense under the Hi-Lo Method assuming 2,000 open hours.

        iii.   Calculate the Least Squares/Regression Method variable cost/ hour open and fixed cost.

        iv.   Predicted expense under the Least Squares/Regression Method assuming 2,000 open hours.

        v.   Display a chart of Expense/Hours Open with a trend line. (be sure to modify each axis so your scatter diagram is better displayed as you did in the chapter)

    b.   Save the file as ch7-02_student_name (replacing student_name with your name).

    c.   Print the resulting worksheet.

3   Create a new What SUP Allowance for Uncollectible Accounts Analysis

    a.   Using the ch7-03 file to start your work, create a worksheet to do the following:

        i.   Calculate uncollectible accounts expense and the allowance for uncollectible accounts using the percent of sales method.

        ii.   Calculate uncollectible accounts expense and the allowance for uncollectible accounts using the aging method.

    b.   Save the file as ch7-03_student_name (replacing student_name with your name).

    c.   Print the resulting worksheet.

Chapter 7 Case Problem 1:
KELLY'S BOUTIQUE

Kelly's Boutique has several questions for you that Excel can help answer.

1 Kelly is planning for the future and would like you to prepare a present value analysis. Using the file ch7-04 complete a present value analysis for the following situations. Save the file as ch7-04_student_name (replacing student_name with your name). Print this completed worksheet. Kelly would like to know the following:

a. How much she would have to pay at the end of each year, assuming a 5 percent rate of return, to yield $150,000 at the end of 10 years.

b. How much she would have at the end of 10 years if she invested $75,000 today, earning 5 percent per year.

c. How much she would have at the end of 10 years if she invested $4,785 at the end of each year, earning 5 percent per year.

d. How much she would have to invest today to have $204,530 in 10 years, earning 5 percent per year.

2 Kelly has a very fluctuating workforce based on seasonal demand. She's ranged from having 10 employees in one month to 35 employees in another month. Some employees are paid a salary, others are paid hourly. She would like to know more about how these costs behave. Use the file ch7-05 to complete a cost prediction worksheet. Save the file as ch7-05_student_name (replacing student_name with your name). The worksheet should do the following:

a. Calculate variable cost per employee, fixed costs, and a prediction of payroll cost with 43 employees using the Hi-Lo method.

b. Calculate variable cost per employee, fixed costs, and a prediction of payroll cost with 43 employees using the Least Squares/Regression method.

c. Display a chart of payroll/employees with a trend line. (Be sure to modify each axis so your scatter diagram is better displayed, as you did earlier in this chapter)

3 During a recent year Kelly's Boutique had sales on account of $6,025,000, collections of $5,800,000, write-offs of $50,000, a beginning balance in accounts receivable of $500,000, and a beginning balance in the allowance for uncollectible accounts of $37,000. At year end, $600,000 of accounts receivable were current, $39,000 were 0–30 days past due, $18,000 were 31–60 days past due, $10,000 were 61–90 days past due, and $8,000 were over 90 days past due. The company believes .8 percent of sales will not be collected. They also have experience that suggests that 4 percent of all current receivables, 8 percent of receivables 0–30 days past due, 20 percent of receivables 31–60 days past due, 25 percent of receivables 61–90 days past due, and 75 percent of receivables over 90 days past due will not be collected. Using the file ch7-06, complete the allowance for uncollectible accounts analysis for both standard methods. Save the file as ch7-06_student_name (replacing student_name with your name). Print this completed worksheet.

Chapter 7 Case Problem 2:
WINE DEPOT

Wine Depot has several questions for you that Excel can help answer.

1 The Wine Depot is planning for the future and would like you to prepare a present value analysis. Using the file ch7-07, complete a present value analysis for the following situations. Save the file as ch7-07_student_name (replacing student_name with your name). Print this completed worksheet. The Wine Depot would like to know the following:

    a. How much they would have to pay at the end of each year, assuming a 3 percent rate of return, to yield $85,000 at the end of 7 years.

    b. How much they would have at the end of 7 years if they invested $8,000 today earning 3 percent per year.

    c. How much they would have at the end of 7 years if they invested $550 at the end of each year earning 3 percent per year.

    d. How much they would have to invest today to have $12,500 in 7 years, earning 3 percent per year.

2 The Wine Depot is trying to better understand the behavior of their selling expenses. They have accumulated selling expenses over the last 6 months and believe units sold are a good predictor of expense behavior. Selling expenses include commissions on sales and advertising. Use the file ch7-08 to complete a cost prediction worksheet. Save the file as ch7-08_student_name (replacing student_name with your name). The worksheet should do the following:

    a. Calculate variable cost per unit sold, fixed costs, and a prediction of selling expense when 19,000 units are sold using the Hi-Lo method.

    b. Calculate variable cost per unit sold, fixed costs, and a prediction of selling expense when 19,000 units are sold using the Least Squares/ Regression method.

    c. Display a chart of selling expense/units sold with a trend line. (Be sure to modify each axis so your scatter diagram is better displayed as you did earlier in this chapter.)

3 During a recent year, the Wine Depot had sales on account of $1,601,542, collections of $1,523,541, write-offs of $23,487, a beginning balance in accounts receivable of $758,271, and a beginning balance in the allowance for uncollectible accounts of $25,121. At year end, $734,539 of accounts receivable were current, $45,812 were 0–30 days past due, $21,012 were 31–60 days past due, $6,422 were 61–90 days past due, and $5,000 were over 90 days past due. The company believes 2.1 percent of sales will not be collected. They also have experience that suggests that 3 percent of all current receivables, 8 percent of receivables 0–30 days past due, 15 percent of receivables 31–60 days past due, 20 percent of receivables 61–90 days past due, and 40 percent of receivables over 90 days past due will not be collected. Using the file ch7-09, complete the allowance for uncollectible accounts analysis for both standard methods. Save the file as ch7-09_ student_name (replacing student_name with your name). Print this completed worksheet.

Chapter 7 Case Problem 3:
SNICK'S BOARD SHOP

Snick's Board Shop has several questions for you that Excel can help answer.

1 The company is planning for the future and would like you to prepare a present value analysis. Using the file ch7-10, complete a present value analysis for the following situations. Save the file as ch7-10_student_name (replacing student_name with your name). Print this completed worksheet. They would like to know the following:

    a. How much they would have to pay at the end of each year, assuming a 4 percent rate of return, to yield $80,000 at the end of 5 years.

    b. How much they would have at the end of 5 years if they invested $73,500 today, earning 4 percent per year.

    c. How much they would have at the end of 5 years if they invested $1,850 at the end of each year, earning 4 percent per year.

    d. How much they would have to invest today to have $25,100 in 5 years, earning 4 percent per year.

2 Snick's Board Shop is trying to better understand the behavior of their utility expenses. They have accumulated utility expenses over the last 9 months and believe hours open per month are a good predictor of expense behavior. Utility expenses include electricity, gas, and water. Use the file ch7-11 to complete a cost prediction worksheet. Save the file as ch7-11_student_name (replacing student_name with your name). The worksheet should do the following:

    1. Using the Hi-Lo method, calculate variable cost per unit sold, fixed costs, and a prediction of utility expense when they are open 230 hours in a month.

    2. Using the Least Squares/Regression method, calculate variable cost per unit sold, fixed costs, and a prediction of utility expense when they are open 230 hours in a month.

    3. Display a chart of selling expense/units sold with a trend line. (Be sure to modify each axis so your scatter diagram is better displayed, as you did earlier in this chapter.)

3 During a recent year, Snick's Board Shop had sales on account of $45,000, collections of $45,500, write-offs of $800, a beginning balance in accounts receivable of $5,000, and a beginning balance in the allowance for uncollectible accounts of $300. At year end $2,400 of accounts receivable were current, $700 were 0–30 days past due, $300 were 31–60 days past due, $200 were 61–90 days past due, and $100 were over 90 days past due. The company believes 1.5 percent of sales will not be collected. They also have experience suggesting that 2 percent of all current receivables, 11 percent of receivables 0–30 days past due, 16 percent of receivables 31–60 days past due, 25 percent of receivables 61–90 days past due, and 50 percent of receivables over 90 days past due will not be collected. Using the file ch7-12, complete the allowance for uncollectible accounts analysis for both standard methods. Save the file as ch7-12_student_name (replacing student_name with your name). Print this completed worksheet.

Chapter 7 Case Problem 4:
ROSEY'S ROSES

Rosey's Roses has several questions for you that Excel can help answer. Use student file ch7-13 to solve 3 of these problems. This file has three worksheets labeled: Present and Future Values, Cost Prediction, and Allowance for Uncollectibles. Complete the file answering the questions below and then save the file as ch7-13_student_name (replacing student_name with your name). Print each worksheet. (*Note:* This file has three worksheets.)

1 Present and Future Values (Calculate the answer and then provide a table for each question. Use the first worksheet of the workbook to answer this problem.):

    a.   How much they would have to pay at the end of each year, assuming a 2 percent rate of return, to yield $15,000 at the end of 4 years.

    b.   How much they would have at the end of 4 years if they invested $1,000 at the end of each year, earning 2 percent per year.

    c.   How much they would have to invest today to have $15,000 in 4 years, earning 2 percent per year.

    d.   How much they would have at the end of 4 years if they invested $4,000 today, earning 2 percent per year.

2 Rosey's Roses is trying to better understand the behavior of their delivery expenses. They have accumulated the delivery expenses over the last 24 months and believe that miles driven per month are a good predictor of expense behavior. Use the second worksheet of the workbook to answer this problem:

    a.   Using the Hi-Lo method, calculate variable cost per mile, fixed costs, and a prediction of delivery expense when they travel 12,000 miles in a month.

b. Using the Least Squares/Regression method, calculate variable cost per mile, fixed costs, and a prediction of delivery expense when they travel 12,000 miles in a month.

c. Display a chart of delivery expense and miles driven with a trend line. (Be sure to modify each axis so your scatter diagram is better displayed, as you did earlier in this chapter.)

3 During a recent year, Rosey's Roses had sales on account of $345,000, collections of $337,000, write-offs of $3,700, a beginning balance in accounts receivable of $37,000, and a beginning balance in the allowance for uncollectible accounts of $1,200. At year end, $34,000 of accounts receivable were current, $4,900 were 0–30 days past due, $1,500 were 31–60 days past due, $500 were 61–90 days past due, and $400 were over 90 days past due. The company believes 1.0 percent of sales will not be collected. They also have experience suggesting that 3 percent of all current receivables, 5 percent of receivables 0–30 days past due, 15 percent of receivables 31–60 days past due, 20 percent of receivables 61–90 days past due, and 40 percent of receivables over 90 days past due will not be collected. Use the third worksheet of the workbook to answer this problem:

a. Complete an allowance for uncollectible accounts analysis using the percentage of sales method.

b. Complete an allowance for uncollectible accounts analysis using the aging method.

Access for Accounting

part

2

Access Tour

In this chapter you will learn:

- Access's capabilities and new features
- How to start, navigate, and work with Access files
- How to use Access help
- How Access is used in accounting

Case: **What SUP, Inc.**

Nathan and Meagan have expressed an interest in other software that might be able to help them in their business. Kyle asks them what kinds of records they keep for customer orders and inventory control.

"We keep records by hand now, and it is very tedious and problematic," Meagan responds. "I have a file for customers, suppliers, products, et cetera, but often they get misplaced and are frequently out of date. It's difficult to keep track of it all!"

"Well, perhaps a database management system might help you out," suggests Kyle.

"What's a database management system?" asks Nathan.

Kyle explains that, as their business grows, the information available to them will increase as well. A database management system (DBMS) can help. "Essentially, a DBMS is a tool for storing, retrieving, and interpreting information in an effective and useful way. These days, Microsoft's Access program, a relational database management system, has proven to be a very successful tool in combating information overload."

"Hold on," warns Nathan. "What is a relational database?"

"Ok, let's go slowly," responds Kyle. "Let me walk you and our student assistant through the basics and I'll define relational database then."

"Great," you respond. "I know businesses use databases every day, and this way I can get a better insight on how they are created and used."

Understanding Access's Capabilities and New Features

Access is a DBMS that organizes a collection of related information used for a specific purpose. For example, information about What SUP's customers, its suppliers, and its products could be three different databases in and of themselves.

A relational database is one in which information is divided into separate stacks of logically related information, each of which is stored in a separate table in the file. Thus, tables are a critical part of a DBMS, and the relations among the tables are key to its success.

Tables can be related in three different ways: one-to-many, one-to-one, and many-to-many. For instance, the supervisor of an accounting department may have many employees who work under her; however, all the employees who work for her have only one supervisor. This would be a one-to-many relationship: one supervisor to many employees. Another example is the chief financial officer (CFO), who reports to the chief executive officer (CEO). This is a one-to-one relationship because there is only one CEO and one CFO. Still another example is the construction worker who works on many different jobs and each job requires many different workers. This is an example of a many-to-many relationship. The most common of these, and the ones you'll experience here, are the one-to-many relationships.

The DBMS includes more than just tables, of course. Queries, forms, and reports based on the data stored in tables are what make up the management component of DBMS. Before you get too far, Kyle suggests you learn how to start Access.

So what's new in Access 2016? You'll notice a text box on the ribbon in Access 2016 that says Tell me what you want to do. This is a text field where you can enter words and phrases related to what you want to do next and quickly get to features you want to use or actions you want to perform. You can also choose to get help related to what you're looking for.

Can't find a button? Click inside the Tell Me box (it's the box at the top, with the light bulb). Type a button or command, like "filter," and you'll see all of your filter-related options listed for you.

There are now two Office themes that you can apply to the Access program: Colorful and White. To access these themes, go to File > Options > General, and then click the drop-down menu next to Office Theme.

Lastly, the default height of the Show Table dialog has been increased so you can easily see more table and query names in your database.

To view the Show Table dialog in queries, click Create > Query Design. The Show Table dialog opens by default. You can also open this dialog in queries by clicking Design > Show Table. To view the Show Table dialog in the Relationships window, click Database Tools > Relationships. The Show Table dialog opens by default. You can also open this dialog in the Relationship window by clicking Design > Show Table.

Starting, Navigating, and Working with Access Files

Kyle asks you if you are familiar with starting programs in Windows 7. Nathan and Meagan don't know much about computers, so you offer to demonstrate. First you explain that starting Access is the same regardless of whether the computer's operating system is Windows 7, 8, 10 or XP, and then you offer to demonstrate the process for starting Access in Windows 7.

To start Access:

1 Click the **Start** button. Your window may look like Figure 8.1.

2 Click **Access 2016** to start the application.

T r o u b l e ? Your start menu may be completely different from that shown in Figure 8.1. See your instructor or lab personnel for instructions on starting Access.

Figure 8.1

Starting Access

3 Double-click **Blank desktop database**.

Nathan's laptop has Access installed as well, so he has been duplicating Kyle's actions on his own computer, whose screen looks somewhat different than Kyle's—in particular, Kyle's Quick Access Toolbar and Ribbon seem different. Kyle explains that screen size can change the appearance of the Ribbon and that, just like Access itself, both its Ribbon and Quick Access Toolbar can be customized.

To illustrate, Kyle starts Access and creates a new blank database file named Database1. He has captured his Access window (see Figure 8.2) and provided callouts and an explanation of the Access window characteristics. He reminds you that the user interface described here is similar to Excel's interface, so much of this will sound familiar.

File Menu – The File menu is where you manage your files and the data about them-creating, saving, inspecting for hidden metadata or personal information, and setting options. In short, it is everything that you do to a file that you don't do in the file.

Quick Access Toolbar – At the top of the Access window is the Quick Access Toolbar, which is designed to provied an easy way to execute the commands used most often. The default setting in Access provides access to the Save, Undo, and Redo commands.

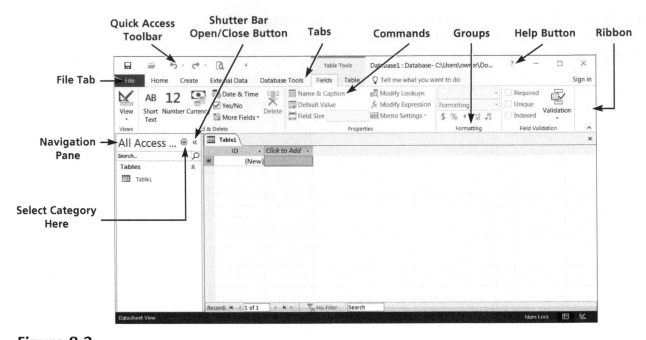

Figure 8.2

The Access Window

Ribbon – There are three basic components of the Ribbon.

1 Tabs: There are several of them across the top depending on whether you have added any add-ins to Access; each represents core tasks you do in Access.

2 Groups: Each tab has groups that show related items together.

3 Commands: A command is a button, a box to enter information, or a menu.

The principal commands in Access are gathered on the second tab, the Home tab. The commands on this tab are those that Microsoft has identified as the most commonly used when people do basic tasks with databases. For example, the Paste, Cut, and Copy commands are arranged first on the Home tab, in the Clipboard group. Font formatting commands are in the Font group. Groups pull together all the commands you're likely to need for a particular type of task, and throughout the task they remain on display and readily available, instead of being hidden within menus. These vital commands are visible above your work space.

The commands on the Ribbon are the ones you use the most. Instead of showing every command all the time, Access 2016 shows some commands in response to an action you take. When you see an arrow (called the Dialog Box Launcher) in the lower right corner of a group, there are more options available for the group. Click the arrow, and you'll see a dialog box or a task pane.

Navigation Pane – At the left of the Access window is the Navigation Pane. New in Microsoft Office Access 2016. It is a central location from which you can easily view and access all database objects such as tables, queries, forms, and reports. The Navigation Pane replaces the Database window, which was used in earlier versions of Access.

Other Access Window Items – Like all Windows screens, scroll bars control your view of the worksheet (horizontal and vertical).

To demonstrate some of Access's features, Kyle suggests you follow along while he opens an Access file:

1   Click the **File** menu and then double-click **Open**.

2   Click **Browse** and then navigate the Open window to the location of this text's student files. (The location would either be somewhere on your computer lab's server or wherever you downloaded your student files from Cengage.)

3   Double-click the file **ch8-01**, which should be located in a Ch 08 folder.

4   Click the **Shutter Bar Open/Close** button a few times to see how it opens and closes the Navigation pane.

5   With the Shutter Bar Open, select **All Access Objects** and **Object Type** as the category.

6   Click the **Table** header a few times to see how you hide or show its contents. (*Note:* This works for all group headers like tables, queries, forms, and reports. The navigation pane does not display empty groups; if this database did not have any reports, the group header would not display.)

7   Double-click the **Table Products** table. The table shown in Figure 8.3 should appear.

8   Click the **File** tab and then click the text Save As. Then click the **Save Database As** button and then select **Access Database (*.accdb)** as the Database File Type. (This is done to keep your original student file available, in case you need it again, and also to provide a unique name for your file.)

T r o u b l e ? The action above was designed to save the entire database with a different file name. It is not the same as clicking the Save Object command, which only saves the current object (table, query, form, report etc.).

Figure 8.3

Sample Table

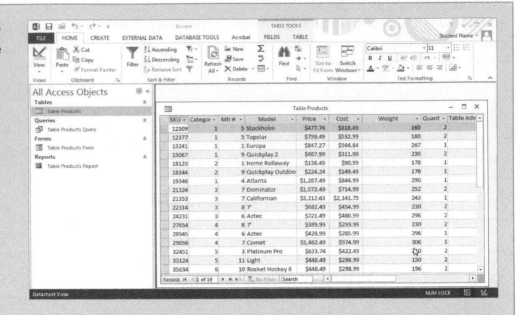

9   Click **Save As** and then click **Yes** when asked if you want Access to close all open objects.

10 Add your name to the file name using the underscore key, as shown in Figure 8.4. In this example the file will be saved as ch8-01_student_name into a folder called My Access Files. You should replace "student_name" with your name.

Figure 8.4

Saving a Database

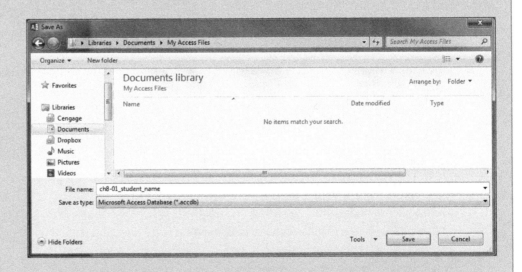

11 Click **Save**.

Now that you've had a brief view of how to start, navigate, and work with Access files, it's time to become familiar with Access's help features.

Getting Access Help

Access's help features are quite extensive. Whenever you are working with Access and are not certain how to create tables, queries, forms or reports you should press the [F1] function key or click the blue and white question mark on the Tab bar. To illustrate, Kyle decides to show you Access's help feature while trying to create a new table.

To view Access's help to create a new table:

1 Press the [**F1**] function key or click the blue and white question mark to open Access's help window, as shown in Figure 8.5.

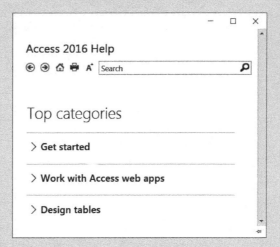

Figure 8.5

Access's Help Window

Trouble? You do not have to be connected to the Internet to get Access help. However, the online help is much more extensive.

2 Click **Design tables** and then click **Introduction to tables** from the Access Help window.

3 Click the text **Overview** to expand the help text. The help window shown in Figure 8.6 should appear.

Figure 8.6

Access Help for Tables

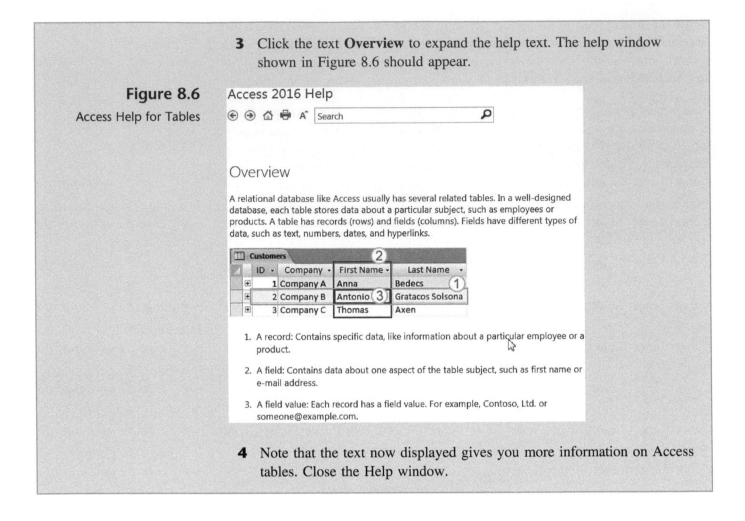

4 Note that the text now displayed gives you more information on Access tables. Close the Help window.

Now that you're familiar with Access's help feature, Kyle thinks it would be a good idea to explore how Access is used in the accounting field.

Examples of How Access Is Used in Accounting

There are an unlimited number of ways Access can be used in accounting. This text will focus on how Access can be used to track inventory, but of course that is just one example.

Accounting programs like QuickBooks and Peachtree are nothing more than sophisticated databases. Each organizes information by accounts, such as assets (cash, accounts receivable, inventory, etc.), liabilities (e.g., accounts payable), and equities (common stock and retained earnings). Revenue and expense transactions are also organized by accounts. A user who wants to create an income statement is simply creating a query that says, in essence, "give me the sum of all revenues and all expenses that occurred for a specific period." Thus the transactions are filtered by date and by account types.

All the major asset and liability accounts are supported by a database. For example, the accounts receivable balance sheet account is supported by a detailed subsidiary ledger that can explain how much each customer owes at any point in time, and a query can be generated that filters the information by date and by customer. Fixed assets accounts (e.g., furniture and fixtures, equipment, buildings) are supported by a detailed subsidiary ledger that can explain the cost of each asset, its economic useful life, its accumulated depreciation, and so forth. The accounts payable balance sheet account is supported by a detailed subsidiary ledger that can explain how much the company owes each vendor at any point in time; a query can be generated that filters the information by date and by vendor. Figure 8.7 shows a report that summarizes a firm's sales for the year. This report was created from an Access database designed to capture business events for a firm. Figure 8.8 illustrates a query of inventory on order the same Access database.

Yearly Sales Report

Saturday, November 16, 2013

2006

Product	Q1	Q2	Q3	Q4	Total
Northwind Traders Coffee	$14,720.00	$230.00	$0.00	$0.00	$14,950.00
Northwind Traders Beer	$1,400.00	$5,418.00	$0.00	$0.00	$6,818.00
Northwind Traders Marmalade	$0.00	$3,240.00	$0.00	$0.00	$3,240.00
Northwind Traders Mozzarella	$0.00	$3,132.00	$0.00	$0.00	$3,132.00
Northwind Traders Clam Chowder	$1,930.00	$868.50	$0.00	$0.00	$2,798.50
Northwind Traders Curry Sauce	$680.00	$1,920.00	$0.00	$0.00	$2,600.00
Northwind Traders Chocolate	$1,402.50	$1,147.50	$0.00	$0.00	$2,550.00
Northwind Traders Boysenberry Spread	$250.00	$2,250.00	$0.00	$0.00	$2,500.00
Northwind Traders Crab Meat	$0.00	$2,208.00	$0.00	$0.00	$2,208.00
Northwind Traders Dried Apples	$530.00	$1,590.00	$0.00	$0.00	$2,120.00
Northwind Traders Ravioli	$0.00	$1,950.00	$0.00	$0.00	$1,950.00

Figure 8.7

Sales Report

Payroll is supported by a database as well. Information is collected from employees that includes Social Security number, address, pay rate, exemptions, and deductions. Time-keeping databases collection information about how many hours an employee worked on a particular job, day, or area. All of this information is stored in employee tables and payroll time tables and is then used to compute payroll expenses, withholding, paychecks, and cost distributions. Figure 8.9 shows a form used to collect time data.

The list of database applications for accounting is unlimited, and the illustrations given here are just the tip of the iceberg. However, the goal of this text is to introduce you to the fundamentals of database design and use, so we will focus on how to create tables, queries, forms, and reports that are related to inventory control only.

Figure 8.8

Sample Query

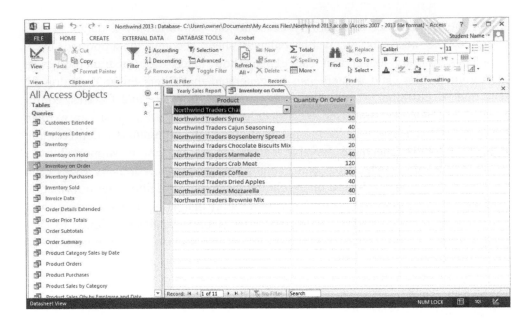

Figure 8.9

Sample Form

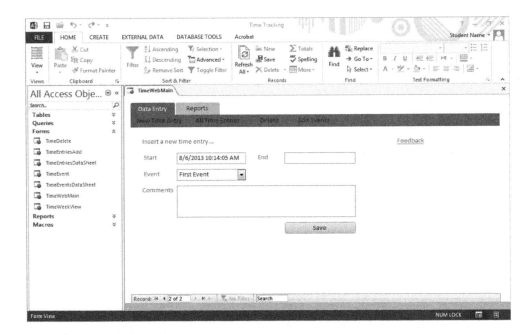

End Note

The three of you are impressed by your first exposure to Access and pleased with your accomplishments so far. You've learned some of Access's capabilities and new features; how to start, navigate, and work with Access files; how to use Access help; and how Access is used in accounting.

In the next chapter you will learn how to create tables, queries, forms, and reports as well as how to print in Access.

Chapter 8 Questions

1 What is a DBMS?

2 What is a relational database?

3 How are tables related?

4 Identify some new features in the 2016 version of Access.

5 Why would you use the File menu in Access?

6 What and where is the Quick Access Toolbar?

7 Describe the Ribbon.

8 What and where is the navigation pane?

9 What is the quickest way to access help while in Access?

10 Describe ways in which Access is used in Accounting.

Access Basics

9

- How to create and print tables
- How to create and print queries
- How to create and print forms
- How to create and print reports

Case: **What SUP, Inc.**

Kyle explains to Nathan, Meagan, and you that the key to understanding how to create and use a database is to understand a database's elements: tables, queries, forms, and reports.

Tables store like information together. Once a table is designed with fields and attributes, information is then collected into tables for later queries, forms, and reports.

Queries allow the database user to ask questions of the information stored in tables. For example, a database user might want to know what inventory balances are for each item as of a particular date or how many units of a particular item were sold to a particular customer.

Forms allow the database user to view, update, add, and delete information stored in tables but organized in traditional forms or source documents like sales invoices, inventory cards, purchase orders, and so forth. Change management experts agree that users of databases prefer information presented in traditional formats even though the raw data might be stored in a different manner (i.e., in tables).

Reports allow the database user to communicate information stored in the database in more usable formats. This might include sorting the information in a certain way—for example, from largest value to smallest value. It might also include grouping the information in a certain way: by customer, salesperson, or product. Finally, reports allow us to "filter" the information and so view only what is needed; examples include sales for a particular month, inventory balances as of a particular date, and accounts receivables for certain specified customers.

Kyle suggests you practice by creating some tables, queries, formats, and reports for What SUP's inventory system.

Tables

Step 1 in the creation of any database is developing an understanding of the business and its information needs. Initially, this will take the form of table creation and separation. Rather than placing all information in one table, it's important to separate information into manageable "chunks," or tables. In our inventory example, What SUP has information about its products, product suppliers, and product categories that could be combined. However, since every product has one supplier but some suppliers provide more than one product, a one-to-many relation exists between suppliers and products. Likewise, every product falls under one category, but most categories include many products. Thus, we should separate product, supplier, and category information into three separate tables with the common relationship being the supplier identification (ID) number and category ID number.

Step 2 is deciding what information we need for each table, what form (or data type) that information takes, and what properties exist for each field. This means that, for each table (product, supplier, and category), we must identify fields where information is to be stored. A common technique in database creation is to establish a unique ID number field for each record. This field will also be identified as our *Primary Key* field, which by definition holds data that uniquely identifies each record in a table. Thus, our first field, common to all information entered into the table, is a product ID. Next would be a product name, description, and so on. For each field, a corresponding data type (number, text, currency, etc.) must be established and, depending on the data type, properties for each field must be identified (field size, format, caption, etc.).

Step 3 is inputting the information into the tables. This is where we gather information about each product, supplier, and category. "How about running all that by me one more time?" you ask.

"I'll do you one better," responds Kyle. "I'll let you watch me create the product table."

Creating the Product Table

Kyle explains that—in addition to creating fields for a product ID, name, and description—he will create fields that link the product to a specific inventory category supplier and that identify the product's serial number, unit price, reorder level, and required lead time.

To create the product table:

1 Start Access.

2 Click **Blank desktop database** to create a new database file.

3 Type **ch9-01_student_name** (replacing "student_name" with your name, as before) into the File Name: text box as shown in Figure 9.1. (In the figure, the file is being saved into the Documents folder on a computer's "C" drive in a folder called My Databases. You should place your newly created file into a folder and drive you will be able to access later. Do this by clicking the folder icon next to the text box and navigating to your desired location.

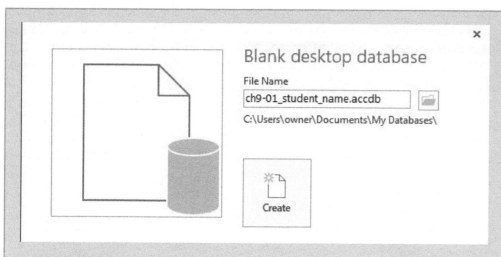

Figure 9.1

Creating a New Blank Database

4 Click **Create**. A new blank database should open with a new table and with the table tools showing in the ribbon, as shown in Figure 9.2.

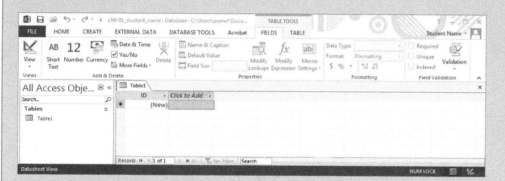

Figure 9.2

New Database Window

5 Click **View**.

6 Type **Product Table** as the name of the new table you are about to create and then click **OK**.

7 Change the first field name from ID to ProductID, then change the Data Type from AutoNumber to Number.

8 Enter the additional field information shown in Figure 9.3 exactly as typed. (*Note:* Each data type has different field property characteristics, but all allow you to specify a caption. Be sure to separate the field name for clarification and enter it as each field's caption; see Figure 9.3, Product ID, for an example.) Continue with the rest of the fields, changing captions ProductName to Product Name, SupplierID to Supplier ID, et cetera. *Note:* When adding field name Length as a data type number you'll need to specify the field size property as Single, and the decimal places property as 2.

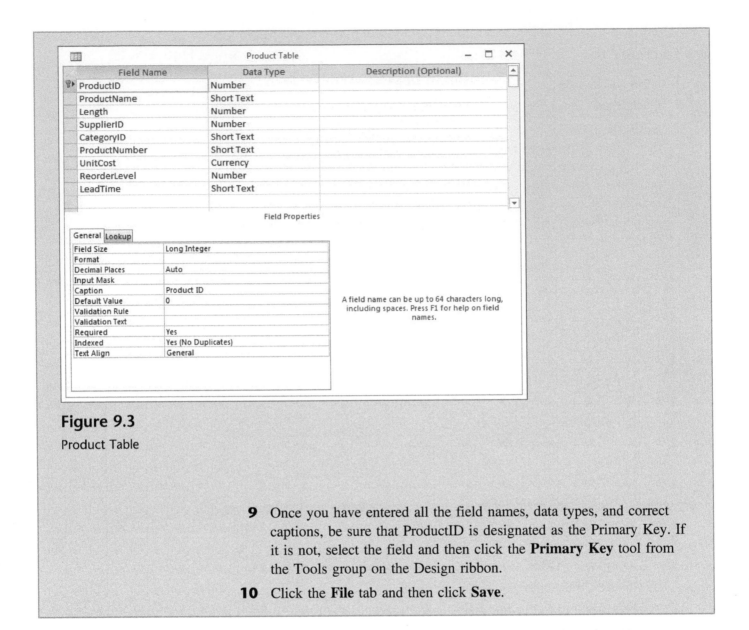

Figure 9.3

Product Table

9 Once you have entered all the field names, data types, and correct captions, be sure that ProductID is designated as the Primary Key. If it is not, select the field and then click the **Primary Key** tool from the Tools group on the Design ribbon.

10 Click the **File** tab and then click **Save**.

You have created a placeholder for product information. Now it's time to create a placeholder for supplier information.

Creating the Supplier Table

As with the product table creation, once again several fields will be required to capture information about each supplier. A supplier ID, supplier name, and contact name are just a few of the critical pieces of information necessary. In addition, Kyle suggests you should also include information about the contact's title, address, and phone and fax numbers.

To create the supplier table:

1 Click the **Create** tab on the ribbon.

2 Click **Table Design** from the Tables group on the ribbon.

3 Enter the information shown in Figure 9.4 exactly as typed. (*Note:* Each data type has different field property characteristics, but all allow you to specify a caption. Be sure to separate the field name for clarification and enter it as each field's caption.) Continue with the rest of the fields, changing SupplierName to Supplier Name, ContactName to Contact Name, and so forth. (Observe that changing a field's caption does not change the field's name.)

Figure 9.4

Supplier Table

4 Once you have entered all the field names, data types, and correct captions, click the **SupplierID** field name and then click the **Primary Key** tool on the ribbon.

5 Click the **File** tab and then click **Save**.

6 Type **Supplier Table** as the table name in the Save As text box and then click **OK**.

You have now created a placeholder for supplier information. All that is left is to create a table with category information so that you can separate products into identifiable categories.

Creating a Category Table

The final table necessary to complete the inventory database is a category table, which will consist of only two fields: a category ID and a category name. "Why not just add the category to each product in the product table?" you ask.

"Because," Kyle responds, "in a relational database we try to conserve space and eliminate redundancy."

To create a category table:

1 Click the **Create** tab on the ribbon.

2 Click **Table Design** from the Tables group on the ribbon.

3 Create two fields: CategoryID as Short Text data type and CategoryName as a Short Text data type.

4 Set the CategoryID field as the primary field

5 Click the **File** tab and then click **Save** and then type **Category Table** in the Save As text box and then click **OK**.

Your table structure is complete. All you need now is information.

Entering Data into Tables

With the table structure complete, you volunteer to enter information about the company's products, suppliers, and categories. Nathan provides the information for each category, product, and supplier.

To enter data into the three tables:

1 Double-click the **Category Table**.

2 Type **A** as the first Category ID and then type **Flatwater** as the first Category Name. After you type each record, press the [**Enter**] key to begin a new category.

3 Type additional categories as shown below in Figure 9.5.

Figure 9.5

Completed Category Table

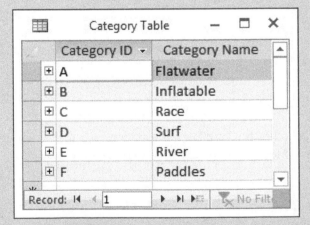

4 Close the Category Table window after you have typed all the information.

5 Click **Yes** if asked to save changes.

6 Click the **Supplier Table** tab and then click **View** from the Ribbon.

7 Enter the information as specified in Table 9.1. After you type each record, press the [**Enter**] key to begin a new supplier.

Table 9.1 Supplier Table Information

Supplier ID	1	2	3	4	5
Supplier Name	Academy	Naish	Bark	Infinity	Ron House
Contact Name	Ben Nimitz	Sara Munoz	Nancy Bearfoot	Paul Moo	Kelly O'Leary
Contact Title	VP Sales	Sales director	Western sales	Salesman	Regional sales
Address	100 8th Ave.	909 S. Washington	111 Macarthur Blvd.	24382 Del Prado	571 Mount Pleasant
City	New York	Pilot Pt.	Mahwah	Dana Point	Dover
Postal Code	10035	76258	07430	92629	07801
State Or Province	NY	TX	NJ	CA	NJ
Country	USA	USA	USA	USA	USA
Phone Number	212-555-1354	940-555-0817	201-555-5730	949-555-4166	201-555-3215
Fax Number	212-555-6874	940-555-1187	201-555-3872	949-555-9718	201-555-8741

8 Close the Supplier Table after you have typed all the information.

9 Double-click the **Product Table**.

10 Enter the information as specified in Table 9.2. After you type each record, press the [**Enter**] key to begin a new product.

11 Close the Product Table window after you have typed all the information.

"Remember," Kyle says, "in this case every product has one category, but every category may have multiple products. Thus we have a one-to-many relationship."

Next up: establishing relationships among the three tables.

Establishing Table Relationships

One final step is necessary when you create multiple tables: creating relationships between the tables. Recall our previous discussion (see Chapter 8) about one-to-one, one-to-many, and many-to-many relationships. In the What SUP database you created three tables, and now you must define each relationship. For example, every product belongs in a particular category and has a supplier. Thus, there is a one-to-many relationship between the supplier table and the product table and a one-to-many relationship between the category table and the product table.

Kyle suggests you establish those relationships using Access's relationship tool.

To establish relationships between tables:

1 Select the **Relationships** tool from the Database Tools tab on the Ribbon.

2 Click each table in the Show Table window and click the **Add** button so that all three tables appear in the Relationships window.

Table 9.2 Product Table Information

Product ID	101	102	103	104	105	106	107	108	109	110	111	112	113	114
Product Name	Veneer Raven	Nalu	Shubu X	Nalu Air	Candice Appleby	Glide GS	Slater Trout	Hollow Carbon	Joy Ride	Badfish	Badfish	Clear Wood	Makani	BW Hybrid
Length	11.5	12.5	10	10	12.5	12.5	10	14	11	7	9	12.5	8	9
Supplier ID	1	2	1	2	3	2	4	5	1	3	3	4	2	1
Category ID	A	A	B	B	C	C	D	C	E	D	E	C	F	F
Product Number	136305	NA321	137814	NA841	CA392	GS233	ST23141	234	514102	BD741	BD241	CW94355	NA112	415333
Unit Cost	700.00	800.00	500.00	625.00	1,150.00	810.00	690.00	1,700.00	626.00	410.00	685.00	975.00	135.00	110.00
Reorder Level	5	2	2	2	2	1	2	2	2	2	3	1	10	20
Lead Time	10	11	14	10	15	30	30	25	18	10	7	12	3	2

3 Click **Close** in the Show Table window.

4 Resize the Product table and the Supplier Table so that all fields are visible and the vertical scroll bars disappear, as shown in Figure 9.6.

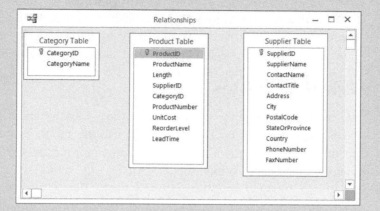

Figure 9.6
Relationships Window

5 Click on the **Category ID** field in the Category Table. Hold the mouse button down and drag to the **Category ID** field in the Product Table, and then release the mouse button.

6 When the Edit Relationships window appears, click **Create**.

7 Click on the **Supplier ID** field in the Supplier Table. Hold the mouse button down and drag to the **Supplier ID** field in the Product Table; then release the mouse button.

8 When the Edit Relationships window appears, click **Create**. The Relationships window should now show lines connecting the common fields between each table, as shown in Figure 9.7.

9 Click the **Relationship Report** tool in the Tools group of the Design tab on the Ribbon. Click **Open** if a Microsoft Access Security Notice appears.

10 Click **Print** and then click **OK** to print the relationships report.

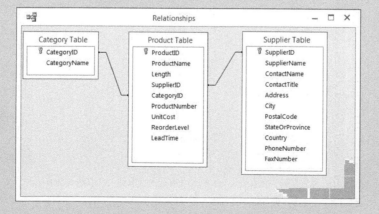

Figure 9.7
Established Relationships

11 Close the Relationships report and click **No** when asked if you want to save changes to the report.

12 Close the Relationships window and click **Yes** if asked to save the changes to the relationships.

Now that relations have been established, you can create queries, reports, and forms that use information from one or more tables. However, it is always important to have a physical copy of your tables for backup and reference.

Printing Tables

Occasionally you may want to print the tables to make sure information has been entered correctly. Later you will use the report feature of Access to print specific information available in the tables in a format that more effectively provides the needed information.

To print all three tables:

1 Double-click the **Category Table**.

2 Click the **File** tab and then click **Print** and then click **Print Preview** to view a reduced-size version of the table to be printed.

3 Click once in the table to zoom to a larger size. (*Note:* You may have to move the scroll bars around to find the table to be printed.) Your screen should look like Figure 9.8.

4 Click the **Print** button on the Print Preview tab to print a copy of the table, and then click **OK** to print.

5 Click the **Close Print Preview** button and then close the Category Table window.

Figure 9.8

Print Preview of the
Category Table

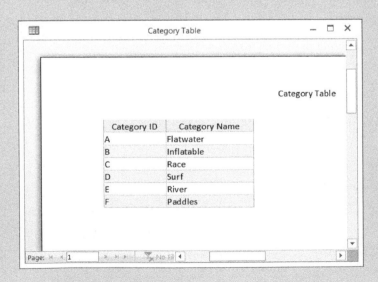

6 Double-click the **Product Table**.

7 Click the **File** tab and then click **Print** and then click **Print Preview** to view a reduced-size version of the table to be printed.

8 Click the **Print** button on the Print Preview tab to print a copy of the table, and then click **OK** to print.

9 Click the **Close Print Preview** button and then close the Product Table window.

10 Double-click the **Supplier Table**.

11 Click the **File** tab and then click **Print** and then click **Print Preview** to view a reduced-size version of the table to be printed.

12 Click the **Print** button on the Print Preview tab to print a copy of the table, and then click **OK** to print.

13 Click the **Close Print Preview** button and then close the Supplier Table window.

Queries

Queries are essentially questions about the information stored in the database, such as: What products do we sell? From whom do we buy products? For any query, it is important to identify where the information can be found, what information is required, what criteria have been established, and how the information is reported.

Creating a Query

Kyle explains that, for each query, tables are identified that contain the information to be requested. He suggests you create a query to list all products. Specifically, he wants you to provide the category name, product name, unit price, supplier name, and supplier phone number.

To create a query:

1 Click the **Create** tab on the Ribbon.

2 Click **Query Wizard** from the Queries group on the Create tab.

3 Select **Simple Query Wizard** from the New Query window and then click **OK**. Click **Open** if a Microsoft Access Security Notice appears.

4 Select **Table: Category Table** from the Table/Queries drop-down list.

5 Click the field **CategoryName** from the list of available fields, then click the > button. This action will place the field CategoryName into the list of selected fields; see Figure 9.9.

Figure 9.9

Simple Query Wizard

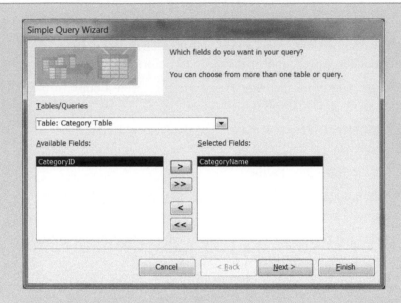

Trouble? If you select the wrong field or click the wrong buttons, you can use the > or < buttons to move fields back and forth between the list of available fields and the list of selected fields.

6 Select **Table: Product Table** from the Table/Queries drop-down list.

7 Click the field **ProductName** from the list of available fields, then click the > button. This action will place the field ProductName into the list of selected fields.

8 Click the field **UnitCost** from the list of available fields, then click the > button. This action will place the field UnitCost into the list of selected fields.

9 Select **Table: Supplier Table** from the Table/Queries drop-down list.

10 Click the field **SupplierName** from the list of available fields, then click the > button. This action will place the field SupplierName into the list of selected fields.

11 Click **Next** in the Simple Query Wizard window.

12 Make sure the Detail button is selected in the window presented, and then click **Next**.

13 Type **Products Query** as the title, click the **Open the query to view information** button, and then click **Finish**.

14 The resulting query lists all products, as shown in Figure 9.10.

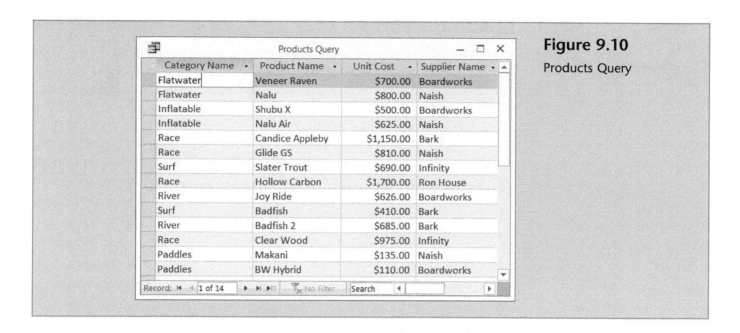

Figure 9.10

Products Query

Printing a Query

Occasionally you may want to print the query to make sure information has been properly selected. Later you will use the report feature of Access to print specific information available from a query in a format that more effectively provides the needed information.

To print a query:

1 Double-click **Products Query**.

2 Click the **File** tab and then click **Print** and then click **Print Preview** to view a reduced-size version of the query to be printed.

3 Click the **Print** button on the Print Preview tab to print a copy of the table, and then click **OK** to print.

4 Click the **Close Print Preview** button, and then close the Products Query window.

Access has another helpful feature, called *forms*, for capturing or viewing information in a database.

Forms

Forms have a variety of purposes. One purpose is to provide a dialog box for access to predesigned queries, other forms, or reports. Another purpose is to provide a dialog box to capture new information and use it to carry out an action.

Creating a Form

Kyle suggests that you use a form to capture information about additional What SUP's products. He reminds you that entering information into a form automatically updates the table containing such information. The form itself is just a means to update the table either by editing existing information or by adding new information like a new record.

To create a form to capture additional products:

1 Click the **Create** tab on the Ribbon.

2 Click **Form Wizard**

3 Select **Table: Product Table** from the Table/Queries drop-down list.

4 Click the >> button to select all the fields available, and then click **Next**.

5 Select the **Columnar** layout, and then click **Next**.

6 Type **Product Form** as the new form title, and then click **Finish**. The resulting form should look like Figure 9.11.

   Trouble? If you receive an error message you most likely didn't close the Product Table you were working on previously. If so, delete the form you just created, close the Product Table, then use the Form Wizard again to create the new form.

7 Do not close this form.

Figure 9.11

Products Form

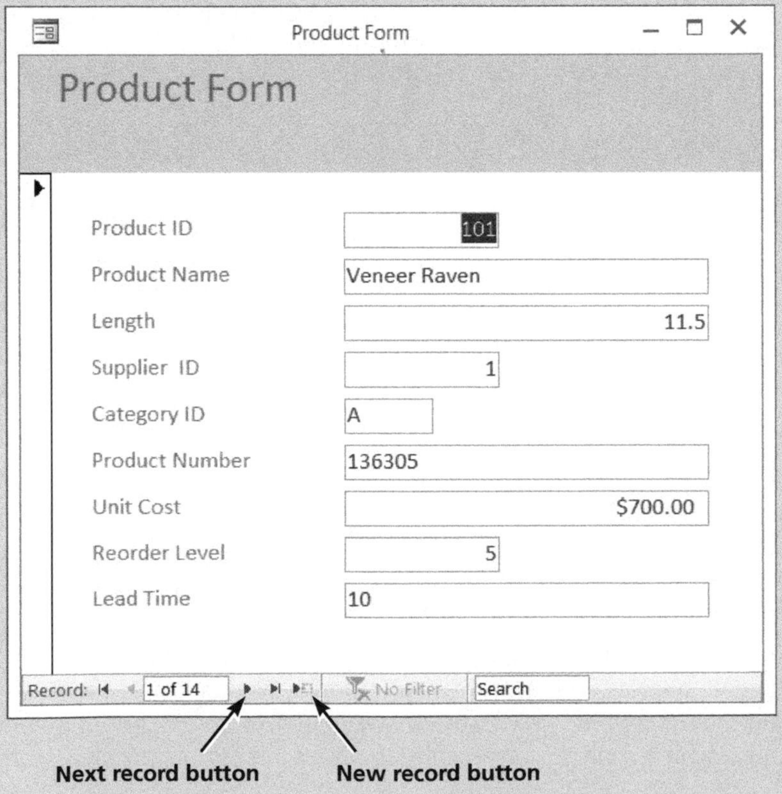

Product Form	— □ ×
Product Form	

Product ID	101
Product Name	Veneer Raven
Length	11.5
Supplier ID	1
Category ID	A
Product Number	136305
Unit Cost	$700.00
Reorder Level	5
Lead Time	10

Record: I◀ ◀ 1 of 14 ▶ ▶I ▶⊟ 🍸 No Filter Search

Next record button   **New record button**

Using a Form to View, Edit, or Add Information

This newly created form can be used to enter new information, edit existing information, and view existing information for each product. Nathan offers to try out the new form by viewing each record. He also volunteers to enter a new product and edit a reorder level for one product.

To use a form to view and edit existing products and add an additional product:

1 Click the **Next record** button (the right arrow) at the bottom of the Products form and view each product. Continue to view each record until you reach record 5, Product ID 105.

2 Click in the **Reorder Level** edit box and change the reorder level from 2 to 3.

3 Click the **New record** button (the right arrow with the asterisk).

4 Click in the Product Name field.

5 Type **115** as the Product ID and then type **Blaster** as the Product Name.

6 Complete the form as shown in Figure 9.12.

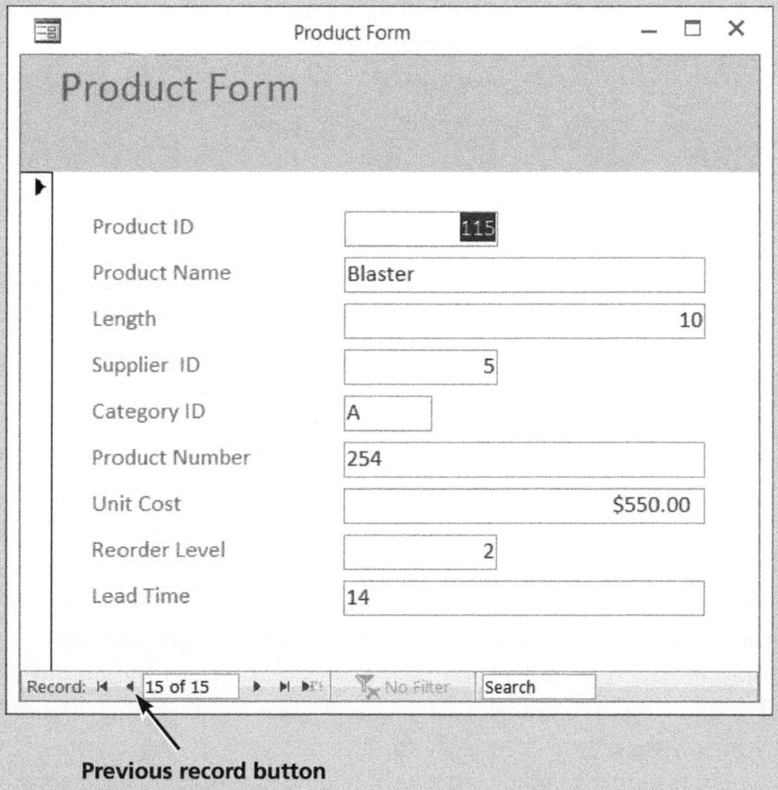

Figure 9.12

Product Form with New Record

Previous record button

7 Do not close this form.

Nathan has completed the form and, in so doing, has edited an existing record and added a new one. This new product is now a part of the product table and will be present for future queries or reports. Most of the information in a form comes from an underlying record source. For What SUP this includes some of the product information derived from the product table. Using graphical objects called *controls*, Nathan created a link between the form and its record source, the product table. He used the most common type of control used to display and enter data: a text box.

Other information in the form is stored in the form's design. In the What SUP form just created, this includes the descriptive text (such as headers and footers) as well as graphic elements (such as the horizontal rule). In other forms this might include a calculation that comes from an expression stored in the form's design.

Printing a Form

Occasionally you may want to print a single form.

To print a single form:

1 Click the **Previous record** button until you reach Record 2.

2 Click the **File** tab, click **Print**, and then click **Print** again.

3 Click **Selected Record(s)** to print the form of record 2. Note that only record 2 will be printed, because you were in record 2 when you activated the Print window.

4 Click **OK** to print the selected record.

5 Close the Products form.

"How do I get a report of the information in my new database?" asks Nathan. "Good question," Kyle answers. "Let's generate a report for you now."

Reports

Reports are a way for a user to get information out of a database in a format that helps the analytical process. To be useful, reported information needs to be properly formatted, sorted, and/or grouped. Reports are more than listings of information. For instance, a user may want to create mailing labels, which would require a different level of formatting than a report of items grouped in particular categories. Your report may need a chart, a logo, subtotals, or grand totals. It may need a date, a special title, headers and footers by item or category, et cetera. Finally, your requirements may necessitate the reporting of only certain items in your database that meet specific criteria, such as those items that cost more than a certain dollar amount or those items from a particular category only.

Creating a Report

Kyle suggests that your first report utilize Access's Reports Wizard and simply list, by product number, all the products together with their product ID, product name, and unit price. There are five steps to creating a report:

- Identify which fields you want in your report and in what tables those fields are present.

- Specify grouping levels, if any.

- Specify sort order, if any.

- Specify a report layout.

- Specify a report style.

To create a report of all products listed by product number:

1 Click the **Create** tab on the Ribbon.

2 Click **Report Wizard** from the Reports group. Click **Open** if a Microsoft Access Security Notice appears.

3 Click **Table: Product Table** from the list of Tables/Queries.

4 Click **ProductID** from the list of Available Fields; then click the > button to move ProductID from the list of Available Fields to the list of Selected Fields. Your screen should look like Figure 9.13.

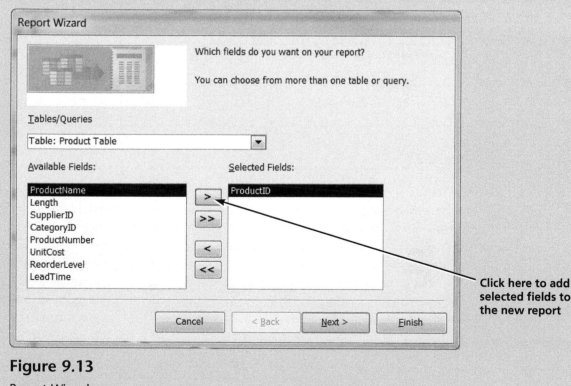

Figure 9.13

Report Wizard

5 Click **ProductName** from the list of Available Fields, then click the
> button to move ProductName from the list of Available Fields to
the list of Selected Fields.

6 Click **UnitCost** from the list of Available Fields, then click the
> button to move UnitCost from the list of Available Fields to the list
of Selected Fields.

7 Click the **Next** button.

8 Click the **Next** button again, since no grouping is required for this report.

9 Select **ProductID** in the first sort order list box. Make sure the sort
order is Ascending, as shown in Figure 9.14, and then click **Next**.

10 Click **Tabular** Layout, **Portrait** Orientation, and make sure the
Adjust the field width so that all fields fit on a page check box is
checked; then click **Next**.

11 Type **Products by Product ID** as the name of the report. Select the
Preview the Report option button, and then click **Finish**. Your
window should look like the one shown in Figure 9.15.

12 Click **Close Print Preview** to reveal the report's design view, as
shown in Figure 9.16.

13 Leave the resulting report design view window open.

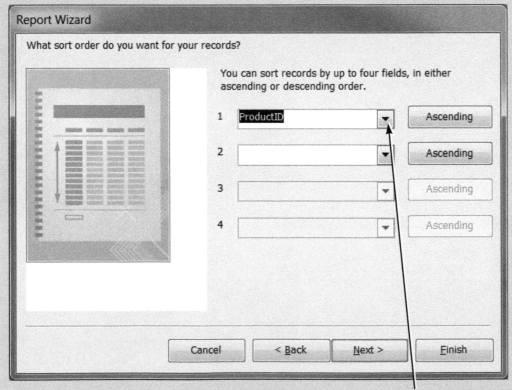

Click here to select sort order

Figure 9.14
Selecting the Sort Order for a New Report

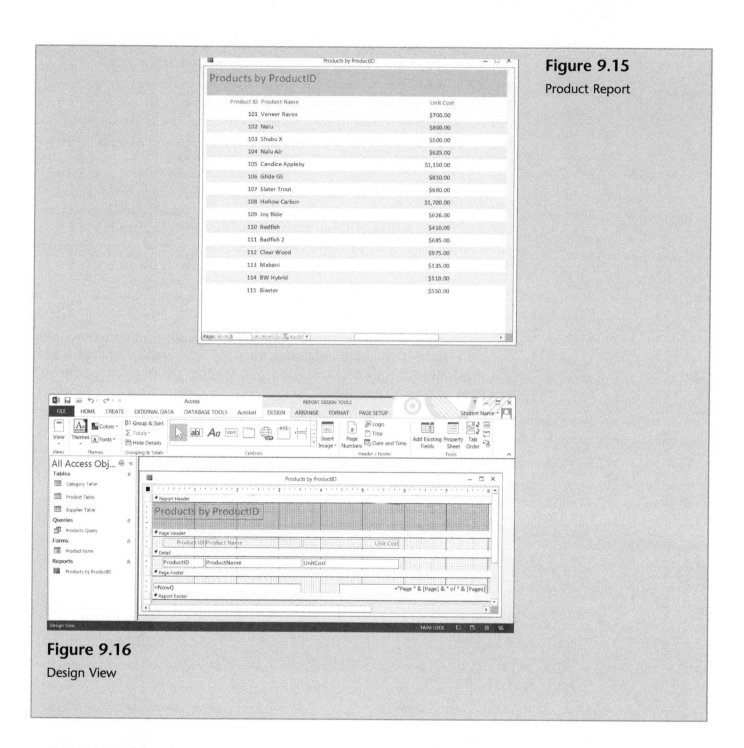

Figure 9.15

Product Report

Figure 9.16

Design View

Editing a Report

You can edit this report at any point and change its characteristics. When you closed the Report window, a Design View window appeared. You can switch between Report, Layout, and Design view by clicking on the View tool.

The *Design view* gives you a more detailed view of the structure of your report. You can see the header and footer bands for the report, page, and groups. The report is not actually running in Design view, so you cannot see the underlying data while working; however, there are certain tasks you can perform more easily in Design view than in Layout view. You can add a wider variety of controls to your report, such as labels, images, lines, and rectangles. You can also edit text-box control sources in the text boxes themselves (without using the property sheet) and change certain properties that are not available in Layout view.

The *Layout view* is the most intuitive view to use for report modification, and it can be used for nearly all the changes you would want to make to a report in Office Access 2016. In Layout view the report is actually running, so you can see your data much as it will appear when printed. Nonetheless, you can still make changes to the report design in this view. Because you can see the data while you are modifying the report, it's a useful view for setting column widths, adding grouping levels, or performing almost any other task that affects the appearance and readability of the report.

Meagan suggests that the report just generated could be improved be centering the product ID title and data, narrowing the width of the unit price field, and narrowing the horizontal rule. You offer to make the changes she has suggested by using the Design view.

To edit the "Products by Product ID" report:

1 Change to the Layout view by clicking the **View** button tool and clicking **Layout View**. Note the differences between the Layout view shown here in Figure 9.17 below and the Design view shown previously in Figure 9.16. (More on this later.)

Figure 9.17

Layout View

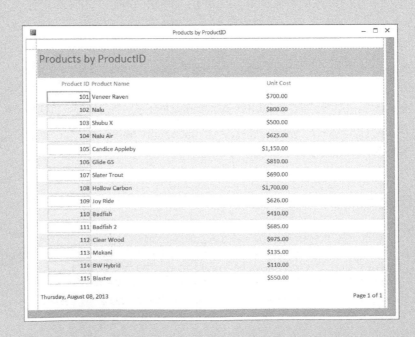

2 Change back to the Design view by clicking the **View** button tool and clicking **Design View**.

3 Click **ProductID** (located in the Page Header section), then click the **Center** tool in the Text Formatting group in the Home tab of the Ribbon.

4 Click **ProductID** (in the Detail section) and then click the **Center** tool.

5 Click **ProductName** (in the Page Header section). Hold the Shift key down and click **ProductName** in the Detail section as well. (*Note:* Holding the Shift key down allows you to select both the header and the detail field at the same time.)

6 Click the right side on the **ProductName** field and drag to the left until the rightmost edge of both the ProductName field and header are lined up with the 3-inch marker on the ruler. Repeat the same process for the UnitCost field and header so that they are lined up as shown in Figure 9.18.

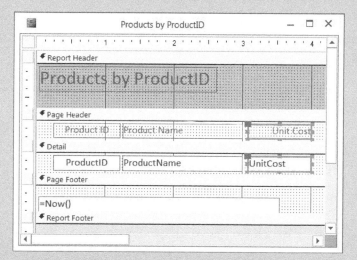

Figure 9.18

Resizing Fields in a Report

7 Click anywhere in the Report window to unselect the Unit Cost fields.

8 Scroll to the far lower right-hand side of the report and then click the **Pages** text box located in the Page Footer.

9 Click the right side of the **Pages** text box and drag to the left until the rightmost edge of text box is lined up with the 5½-inch marker on the ruler.

10 Click the right side of the report and drag to the left until the rightmost edge of the report is lined up with the 6-inch marker on the ruler.

11 Click the **View** tool and then click **Report View** to see the effects of these changes on the final report. Your report should now look like Figure 9.19.

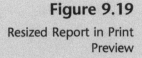

Figure 9.19

Resized Report in Print Preview

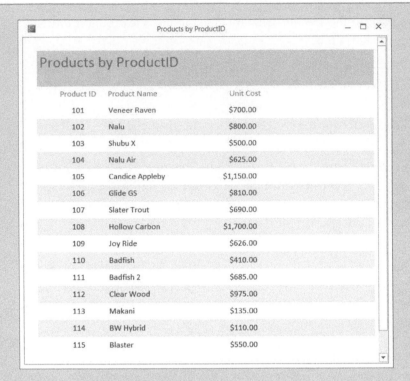

12 Close the Products by ProductID report.

13 When prompted, click **Yes** to save the changes in the Products by ProductID report.

Printing a Report

Often you will want to print the reports created.

To print the "Products by Product ID" report:

1 Double-click the **Products by Product ID** report.

2 Click the **File** tab, click **Print**, and then click **Print Preview**.

3 Click the **Print** button and then click **OK** to print the report. Your report should look like Figure 9.20.

Figure 9.20

Printed Products by
Product ID Report

Products by ProductID

Product ID	Product Name	Unit Cost
101	Veneer Raven	$700.00
102	Nalu	$800.00
103	Shubu X	$500.00
104	Nalu Air	$625.00
105	Candice Appleby	$1,150.00
106	Glide GS	$810.00
107	Slater Trout	$690.00
108	Hollow Carbon	$1,700.00
109	Joy Ride	$626.00
110	Badfish	$410.00
111	Badfish 2	$685.00
112	Clear Wood	$975.00
113	Makani	$135.00
114	BW Hybrid	$110.00
115	Blaster	$550.00

4 Close the Products by ProductID report window.

Nathan and Meagan are both pleased with your changes and impressed with your skills. They recognize that they have just scratched the surface of what Access can do for their business and are anxious to learn more.

End Note

In this chapter you have learned about some basics of the Access program, some features of the help system, and how to work with tables, queries, forms, and reports. There is much more to the Access program and much more to know about tables, queries, forms, and reports. The following four chapters will elaborate on each of these, bringing you a keener understanding of how Access is used in accounting.

Chapter 9 Questions

1 Why isn't all information entered into a single table?

2 Identify and describe the first three steps followed in the creation of a database.

3 Which tool is used to establish relationships between tables?

4 What are queries?

5 What facts must be identified for each query?

6 What questions are asked by the Simple Query Wizard?

7 What are the purposes of forms?

8 From where does most of the information in a form come?

9 How are controls used to create forms?

10 Are headers and footers also a part of the record source?

11 What questions does the Simple Form Wizard ask?

12 What are reports?

13 To be useful, how should reports be organized?

14 What questions does the Report Wizard ask?

15 What are the five steps necessary to create a report?

16 How do you switch between the Design view and the Layout view when creating reports?

Chapter 9 Assignments

1 Create new queries for What SUP (use the Ch9-02 file)

   a. Create and print a query for What SUP that lists the supplier name, contact name, and phone number of every supplier. (*Note:* Be sure to use the supplier table to locate field names.) Save the query as Supplier Query 1.

   b. Create and print another query for What SUP that lists the supplier name, address, city, and state of every supplier. (*Note:* Be sure to use the supplier table to locate field names.) Save the query as Supplier Query 2.

2 Create new forms for What SUP (use the Ch9-02 file)

   a. Create and print a form for What SUP that lists all fields from the supplier table in a columnar format. (*Note:* Once again, use the supplier table to locate field names.) Save the form as Supplier Form, and print the first record only.

   b. Create and print a form for What SUP that lists all fields from the category table in a columnar format. (*Note:* Use the category table to locate field names.) Save the form as Category Form, and print the first record only.

3 Create new reports for What SUP (use the Ch9-02 file)

   a. Create and print a report for What SUP that lists the supplier ID, supplier name, and city from the supplier table. (Use the supplier table to locate field names.) The report should have no grouping, be sorted by supplier ID in ascending order, and be formatted in a tabular layout with portrait orientation. Save the report as Suppliers by Supplier ID. Make sure all field information is visible.

   b. Create and print a report for What SUP that lists the supplier name, contact name, contact title, and phone number from the supplier table. (Use the supplier table to locate field names.) The report should have no grouping, be sorted by supplier name in ascending order, and be formatted in a tabular layout with portrait orientation. Save the report as Suppliers by Supplier Name. Make sure all field information is visible.

4 Create and edit tables for What SUP (use the Ch9-02 file)

   a. Create a new table for What SUP that includes fields BuyerID, BuyerName, and BuyerPhone. The first field (BuyerID) is a Number data type; the rest are Short Text data types. All should have captions that separate each word (e.g., Buyer ID). Set the Buyer ID field as the Primary Key and save the new table as Buyers Table. Enter the following buyer information into the Buyers table, and then print the new table.

Buyer ID	Buyer Name	Buyer Phone
601	Frankenstein	555-7894
602	Ng	555-1324
603	Fortier	555-9137

   b. Add a field to the Product table called BuyerID, a Number data type. Add the specific BuyerID information to the following products in the Products table and then print the new table.

Product ID	Buyer ID
101	603
102	603
103	602
104	601
105	602
106	603
107	601
108	602
109	603
110	602
111	602
112	601
113	601
114	603
115	601

c. Establish a one-to-many relationship between the Buyers table and the Product table using BuyerID as the related field. Print the relationships report.

d. Create and print a query for What SUP that lists the product name, buyer name, and buyer phone number for every product. (*Note:* Be sure to use both the product and buyer tables to locate field names.) Save the query as Product Buyer Query.

Chapter 9 Case Problem 1:
KELLY'S BOUTIQUE

Recall from Chapter 2 that Kelly's Boutique sells books as well as women's shoes. Kelly's son Casey, a college accounting student who is home for the holidays, is eager to help his mom incorporate computers in her business. In this chapter (and in those that follow), Casey will try teaching Kelly the use of Access as it applies to her accounting and business needs.

Casey suggests that Kelly use a database to keep a record of her book inventory. Kelly has a partial list of books she has purchased that she thinks should be part of the database. This list includes each book's ISBN, department name, related supervisor and phone number of the supervisor, book title, publisher, publisher contact, publisher phone number, author, and list price.

Create a new database file using the following information and name the file ch9-03_student_name (replacing student_name with your name).

a. Use the information below to create a book table, department table, and publisher table in Access. Then print each table.

Table Structure:

Table	Field Name	Data Type
Book	ISBN	Number
	Dept	Short Text
	BookTitle	Short Text
	PubNum	Number
	Author	Short Text
	ListPrice	Currency
Dept Table	Dept	Short Text
	Supervisor	Short Text
	Phone	Short Text
Product	PubNum	Number
	Publisher	Short Text
	Contact	Short Text
	Phone	Short Text

Book Table

ISBN	Dept	Book Title	PubNum	Author	ListPrice
684872153	Adult	Angela's Ashes	7	McCourt	$ 7.99
60244151	Children	Betsy–Tacy	1	Lovelace	$ 35.95
670175919	Children	Blueberries for Sal	5	McCloskey	$ 16.99
27136701	Children	Caddie Woodlawn	4	Brink	$ 17.00
140286276	Adult	Deep End of the Ocean	3	Mitchard	$ 12.95
60173289	Adult	Divine Secrets of the YaYa Sisterhood	2	Wells	$ 24.00
394800168	Children	Green Eggs and Ham	6	Seuss	$ 7.99
439064864	Children	Harry Potter and the Chamber of Secrets	9	Rowling	$ 17.95
439136350	Children	Harry Potter and the Prisoner of Azkaban	9	Rowling	$ 17.95
590353403	Children	Harry Potter and the Sorcerer's Stone	9	Rowling	$ 17.95

Dept Table

Dept	Supervisor	Phone
Adult	Rexford Merlot	555-9754
Children	Barbara Manchester	555-1974

Publisher Table

Pub Num	Publisher	Contact	Phone
1	Cengage	Smith	555-9745
2	Harper Collins	Potter	555-7481
3	Penguin	Frued	555-8974
4	Simon & Schuster	Gonzalez	555-9874
5	Viking Press	Hu	555-1654
6	Random House	Ouimet	555-9144
7	Scholastic Press	Salazar	555-9888
8	Touchstone Books	Chi	555-1112
9	Arthur A. Levine Books	Robinson	555-5118

b. Establish the appropriate relationship between each table. Print the relationships report.

c. Create and print a query that lists department, book title, author, supervisor, publisher, and contact. Save this query as Books by Department.

d. Create a form that shows all fields from the book table in a columnar format with. Save it as Book Form, and print the first record.

e. Create and print a report that contains the book title, ISBN, publisher, and phone number. The report should have no grouping, be sorted by book title in ascending order, and be formatted in a tabular portrait layout and the title Book Report. All field information should be visible.

f. Make sure you keep a copy of this file for use in the next chapter.

Chapter 9 Case Problem 2:
WINE DEPOT

The Wine Depot is interested in more effectively managing their inventory. Barbara would like you to put together a database of their current wine inventory. Create a new database file using the following information and name the file ch9-04_student_name (replacing student_name with your name).

a. Use the following information to create and print a wine products table, a buyer table, and a winery table. Use the field Name in the Buyer and Winery tables even when you are warned against using a reserved name.

Table Structure:

Table	Field Name	Data Type
Buyer	Buyer	Number
	Name	Short Text
	Phone	Short Text
Wine Products	SKU	Number
	Type	Short Text
	Winery	Number
	Price	Currency
	Cost	Currency
	Size	Number
	Vintage	Number
	Quantity	Number
Winery	Winery	Number
	Name	Short Text
	Location	Short Text
	Buyer	Number

SKU	Type	Winery	Price	Cost	Size	Vintage	Quantity
13883	Chardonnay	7	41.00	24.60	750	2013	12
14539	Merlot	8	36.00	21.60	750	2014	5
15347	Cabernet Sauvignon	3	120.00	72.00	750	2014	7
15966	Pinot Noir	2	65.00	39.00	750	2014	24
16528	Chardonnay	15	30.00	18.00	750	2016	12
16554	Sauvignon Blanc	18	21.00	12.60	750	2016	8
16716	Chardonnay	11	20.00	12.00	750	2016	10
16739	Chardonnay	17	75.00	45.00	750	2014	50
16769	Syrah	6	34.00	20.40	750	2015	10
16874	Syrah	5	35.00	21.00	750	2015	15
17024	Sauvignon Blanc	4	22.00	13.20	750	2016	10
17275	Sauvignon Blanc	14	16.00	9.60	750	2017	1
17425	Zinfandel	10	28.00	16.80	750	2016	7
17454	Sauvignon Blanc	13	15.00	9.00	750	2017	24
17521	Chardonnay	1	24.00	14.40	750	2016	4
17539	Cabernet Sauvignon	19	75.00	45.00	750	2015	3
17549	Zinfandel	9	22.00	13.20	750	2015	3
17578	Cabernet Sauvignon	12	11.00	6.60	750	2016	2
17840	Red Chianti	16	32.00	19.20	750	2014	12

Buyer	Name	Phone
101	James Taylor	555-1245
102	Johnny Rivers	555-8794
103	Michael Jackson	555-9743
104	David Bowie	555-2914

Winery	Name	Location	Buyer
1	Babcock	America	101
2	Bass Phillip	Australia	104
3	Beringer	America	101
4	Brander	America	101
5	Cafaro	America	101
6	Carhartt	America	101
7	Clarendon	Australia	104
8	Gainey	America	102
9	Gary Farrell	America	102
10	Joel Gott	America	102
11	Melville	America	102
12	Miguel Torres	Chile	104
13	MudHouse	New Zealand	104
14	Neil Ellis	South Africa	103
15	Neyers	America	103
16	San Vincenti	Italy	104
17	Uber	America	103
18	Voss	America	103
19	Woodward	America	103

b. Establish the appropriate relationship between each table and then print the relationships report.

c. Create and print a query that lists SKU, Type, Winery, Buyer, and Buyer Phone for all products. (Save as Wine Products Query 1.)

d. Create and print a form for entering new products; use whatever style you'd like. (Save the form as Wine Products Form 1, and print the first record only.)

e. Create and print a report with the fields Type, Name (Name of Winery), Vintage, and Price for all products. The report should be sorted by Type in ascending order and be formatted in a Tabular layout with Portrait orientation. (Save the report as Wine Products Report 1.) All field information should be visible.

f. Make sure you keep a copy of this file for use in the next chapter.

Chapter 9 Case Problem 3:
SNICK'S BOARD SHOP

Snick's Board Shop is interested in more effectively managing their inventory. Casey and Caitlin would like you to put together a database of their current inventory. Create a new database file using the information below. Name the file ch9-05_student_name (replacing student_name with your name).

a. Use the information below to create and print a products table, a manufacturer table, and a category table as you did earlier in this chapter.

Table Structure:

Table	Field Name	Data Type
Category	CategoryID	Number
	CategoryName	Short Text
Manufacturer	ManufacturerID	Short Text
	ManufacturerName	Short Text
Product	ProductID	Short Text
	ProductName	Short Text
	CategoryID	Number
	ManufacturerID	Short Text
	Price	Currency
	Style	Short Text
	Quantity	Number

Category Table

CategoryID	CategoryName
1	Complete
2	Ramp
3	Longboards
4	Protective Gear
5	Rails

Manufacturer Table

ManufacturerID	ManufacturerName
BPR	Boardpusher
EMT	Element
GC	Goldcoast
MOJ	Mojo
KRO	Krooked
SC	Santa Cruz
S9	Sector 9
888	Triple 8
0	Zero

Product Table

ProductID	ProductName	CategoryID	ManufacturerID	Price	Style	Quantity
61-16758	Element Flat Bar Grind Rail	5	EMT	109.99	Black	10
61-23116	Zero Switchblade Rail	5	0	119.99	Silver	10
61-36447	Zero 6 Foot Flat Bar Grind Rail	5	0	99.99	Red	10
65-00011	Mojo Wedge Ramp	2	MOJ	179.99	Black/Blue	8
65-00335	Almost Mullen OC Impact V4	1	BPR	119.99	Orange/Teal	10
65-00358	Element Section	1	EMT	89.99	Black/Red	10
65-00981	Almost Mullen Day Glow	1	BPR	169.99	Black/Yellow	25
65-01135	Macon Helmet	4	888	59.99	White	10
65-01400	Krooked Eyes	1	KRO	89.99	Pink/Blue	10
65-01783	Santa Cruz Landshark	3	SC	99.99	Blue/White	10
65-01786	Santa Cruz Tiger Shark	3	SC	129.99	Orange/Black	10
65-01837	Element Launch Ramp	2	EMT	179.99	Black/Red	5
65-01967	Sector 9 Sand Wedge	3	S9	189.99	Black/White	10
65-01970	Goldcoast Venice	3	GC	149.99	Green/Yellow	10
65-23174	Little Tricky Helmet	4	888	34.99	Black	10

b. Establish the appropriate relationship between each table and then print the relationships report.

c. Create and print a query using the Simple Query Wizard that lists ProductName, CategoryName, and ManufacturerName for all product sorted by CategoryName. (Save Query 1.)

d. Create and print a form using the Form Wizard for entering new products that lists all the available fields in the product table; use whatever style you'd like. (Save the form as Form 1, and print the first record only.)

e. Create and print a report using the Report Wizard with the fields ProductID, Style, Quantity, and ManufacturerName for all products. The report should be viewed by Manufacturer sorted by ProductID in ascending order and be formatted in a Tabular layout with Portrait orientation and no grouping. (Save the report as Report 1.) All field information should be visible.

f. Make sure you keep a copy of this file for use in the next chapter.

Chapter 9 Case Problem 4:
ROSEY'S ROSES

Rosey's Roses is interested in more effectively managing their inventory. They would like you to put together a database of their current inventory. Create a new database file using the information below. Name the file ch9-06_student_name (replacing student_name with your name).

    a.   Use the information below to create and print three tables—Products, Type, and Grower—as you did earlier in this chapter.

Table Structure:

Table	Field Name	Data Type	Primary Key?
Product	ID	Number	Yes
	Type	Short Text	
	Description	Short Text	
	Quantity	Number	
	Cost/Unit	Currency	
	Grower ID	Number	
Type	Type	Short Text	Yes
	Description	Long Text	
Grower	Grower ID	Number	Yes
	Grower Name	Short Text	
	Contact	Short Text	

Products:

ID	Type	Description	Quantity	Cost/Unit	Grower ID
1	Shrub	Abraham Darby #5	25	$39.99	100
2	Shrub	Be My Baby #5	30	$18.99	100
3	Shrub	Deja Blu #5	18	$25.99	200
4	Shrub	Mongo	38	$47.99	300
5	Shrub	Peach Drift #10	33	$12.99	200
6	Shrub	Red Drift #10	15	$ 6.99	100
7	Shrub	Sedona #5	3	$14.99	200
8	Shrub	Sweet Intoxication #5	17	$ 9.99	300
9	Shrub	Wing Ding #5	30	$11.99	300
10	Climber	Climbing Orange Crush #7	16	$32.99	100
11	Climber	Don Juan Climber #5	25	$37.99	200
12	Tree	Barbara Streisand 36in Tree	50	$52.99	300
13	Tree	Firefighter 36in Tree	14	$55.99	200
14	Tree	Trumpeter 36in Tree	4	$65.99	100

Type:

Type	Description
Climber	Climbing roses that are trained upright will tend to bloom only at the tips, and will not generate laterals. Other terms that are commonly used are climbers, ramblers, pillar roses, etc. There is no "official" definition of these terms. Generally, climbing roses are repeat blooming roses with large, stiff canes.
Shrub	Rose shrubs that are not classified under the common varieties are known as shrub roses. Shrub roses are available in many different varieties, colors, and sizes.
Tree	A rose tree is a rose bush that is pruned and grafted to grow as a tree. It has a long trunk with foliage and flower growth in a rounded mass at the top of the trunk.

Grower:

Grower ID	Grower Name	Contact
100	Jackson & Perkins	Nate Rexford
200	Passion Growers	Kyle Said
300	Passion Heights	Casey Crawford

b. Establish the appropriate relationship between each table and then print the relationships report.

c. Create and print a query using the Simple Query Wizard that lists the product description, type, and grower name for all products. (Save as Query 1.)

d. Create and print a form using the Form Wizard for entering new products that lists all the available fields in the product table; use whatever style you'd like. (Save the form as Form 1, and print the first record only.)

e. Create and print a report using the Report Wizard with the fields ID, type, description, and grower name for all products. The report should be viewed by grower sorted by ID in ascending order and be formatted in a Stepped layout with Portrait orientation. (Save the report as Report 1.) All field information should be visible.

f. Make sure you keep a copy of this file for use in the next chapter.

10

Tables

Case: **What SUP, Inc.**

Nathan and Meagan are impressed with the features of Access as a database program. Kyle cautions them that there is a lot more to Access than what they have seen so far. He explains that the tables they have created can be structured in different ways and that each field can be set up with specific formats, default values, validation rules, and so on.

"Wait just a minute," exclaims Nathan. "This sounds more complicated than what we might need!"

"On the contrary," responds Kyle. "These table features—and the ones I'll explain later for queries, forms, and reports—are important to the validity of the data included in your database and helpful in making your database useful."

"Let's just take it one step at a time," says Meagan.

Kyle then enlightens them both on the importance of data validity and integrity. He explains that information in your database is of little use if it is incorrect, incomplete, or in an inconsistent format. Over the next few days he plans on explaining tables in more detail. Let's begin by reviewing the basic procedures for adding, changing, or deleting records from a table.

Add, Change, and Delete Records

In this section, you will learn how to add, change, and delete records from tables. This process can also be done via forms, which will be discussed in Chapter 12.

Add Records

You have already added records to the inventory database in Chapter 8 but decide to practice it again. Kyle observes your input of adding one more record to the Product table.

To add a new record to a table:

1 Start Access.

2 Click the **File** tab button and then click **Open**.

3 Navigate the Open window to the location of this text's student files. (The location would be the CD provided with the text or from your computer lab's server.)

4 Double-click **ch10-01**, which should be located in a Ch 10 folder. (This is the completed What SUP Inventory file from Chapter 9 with a few modifications.)

5 Click the **Enable Content** button.

6 Click the **File** tab, then click **Save As**, then click **Save Database As** and then click **Save As**.

7 Navigate the Save As window to the location you wish to save this file and type **Ch10-01_student_name** in the File Name: text box (replacing "student_name" with your name).

8 Click **Save**.

9 Double-click **Product Table**.

10 Type **116** as the new product's Product ID and **Zoomer** as the new product's Product Name.

11 Press the [**Tab**] key and type **9.5** as the Length.

12 Press the [**Tab**] key and type **4** as the Supplier ID.

13 Press the [**Tab**] key and type **E** as the Category ID.

14 Press the [**Tab**] key and type **Z23111** as the Product Number.

15 Press the [**Tab**] key and type **2000** as the Unit Cost.

16 Press the [**Tab**] key and type **3** as the Reorder Level.

17 Press the [**Tab**] key and type **10** as the Lead Time.

18 Press the [**Tab**] key and type **605** as the Buyer ID.

19 Press the [**Tab**] key again and note that a new record (product) has been added to the table, as shown in Figure 10.1.

20 Do not close this file.

Figure 10.1

Partial View of Updated Product Table

Change Records

Changing records in the table is equally as easy. Kyle suggests you change the supplier for the product you just entered from **3** to **2** and change the buyer from **1** to **3**.

To change a record in a table:

1 Double-click the **Supplier ID** field for the Product ID 116 you just entered. Type **2** to replace the 4 currently listed in this field.

2 Double-click the **Buyer ID** field for the Diamond Pendant you just entered. Type **603** to replace the 605 currently listed in this field. You may have to use the horizontal scroll bars at the bottom of the table to view this field.

3 Press the [**Tab**] key to move to a new record.

Changing fields for a particular record in a table is easy. So is the procedure for deleting a record.

Delete Records

Kyle warns you that deleting records in a table is a permanent act. It is important to be sure you want to delete a record before proceeding. Access will warn you of this and give you an opportunity to undo your deletion.

To delete a record from a table:

1 Click on the far left side of the table next to the row containing information on Product ID 107.

2 With the Product ID 107 record selected, right-click anywhere in that record to bring up a shortcut menu.

3 Point your mouse to the text Delete Record as shown in Figure 10.2.

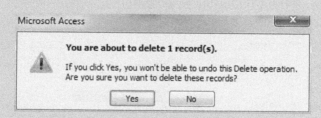

Product ID ▾	Product Name ▾	Length ▾	Supplier ID ▾	Category ID ▾	Product Number ▾	Unit Cost ▾	Reorder Level ▾	Lead Time ▾	BuyerID ▾	Cli
101	Veneer Raven	11.5	1	A	136305	$700.00	5	10	603	
102	Nalu	12.5	2	A	NA321	$800.00	2	11	603	
103	Shubu X	10	1	B	137814	$500.00	2	14	602	
104	Nalu Air	10	2	B	NA841	$625.00	2	10	601	
105	Candice Appleby	12.5	3	C	CA392	$1,150.00	3	15	602	
106	Glide GS	12.5	2	C	GS233	$810.00	1	30	603	
107	Slater Trout	10			ST23141	$690.00	2	30	601	
108	Sleeping One	12		New Record	234	$1,500.00	2	10	605	
109	Joy Ride	11		Delete Record	514102	$626.00	2	18	603	
110	Badfish	7		Cut	BD741	$410.00	2	10	602	
111	Badfish 2	9		Copy	BD241	$685.00	3	7	602	
112	Clear Wood	12.5		Paste	CW94355	$975.00	1	12	601	
113	Makani	8		Row Height...	NA112	$135.00	10	3	601	
114	BW Hybrid	9			415333	$110.00	20	2	603	
115	Blaster	10	5	A	254	$550.00	2	14	601	
116	Zoomer	9.5	2	E	Z23111	$2,000.00	3	10	603	
*	0	0							0	

Record: H ◀ 7 of 16 ▶ H ▶▶ No Filter   Search ◀

Figure 10.2

Deleting a Record from a Table

4 Click **Delete Record**.

5 An Access dialog warning box appears asking if you are sure you want to delete this record. See Figure 10.3.

> Microsoft Access ⬛ X
>
> ⚠ **You are about to delete 1 record(s).**
>
> If you click Yes, you won't be able to undo this Delete operation. Are you sure you want to delete these records?
>
> [Yes]   [No]

Figure 10.3

Delete Warning

6 Click **Yes**, and the record is deleted.

"That was easy," you comment. "Let's continue."

Add a Picture with an OLE Field

In this section, you will add a special field to the table and insert pictures to enhance the database. The process requires two steps. Step 1 is adding a new field to the table; step 2 is adding a picture to each record.

Add an OLE Field to a Table

Kyle decides to add a picture field to the Product table. The picture—in this case, pictures of the stand-up paddle boards and products that What SUP sells—is created either by taking a digital picture of each product or by scanning a picture of each product. Nathan has taken digital pictures of each product and saved them as bitmaps (.bmp) files. Because these objects were created with another application, they need to be inserted as objects into the database. OLE (Object Linking/Embedding) is the integration of objects from other applications.

To add an OLE field to the Product table:

1 Click **View** and then click **Design View**.

2 Scroll down the Design view and click in the **blank field name** under Buyer ID.

3 Type **Picture** as the new field name.

4 Press [**Tab**] to move the cursor to the Data Type column.

5 Select **OLE Object** from the drop-down list of data types as shown in Figure 10.4.

Figure 10.4

Adding a New OLE Field

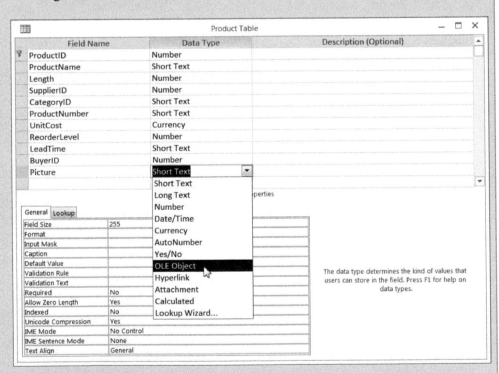

6 Save the modified table by clicking the **Save** tool on the Quick Access toolbar.

The table is now ready for additional data. You will need to switch from the design view of the table back to the datasheet view in order to add pictures of each product.

Add Pictures to the Table

To add pictures to the table you will need your student disk, which contains all the bitmap files that you'll need to insert into the Product table.

To add a picture to the Product table:

1 Click **View** and then click **Datasheet View**.

2 Scroll to the right of the table to view the Picture field.

3 Right-click the **Picture** field on the first record to reveal the Shortcut menu; then click **Insert Object**, as shown in Figure 10.5.

Unit Cost ▾	Reorder Level ▾	Lead Time ▾	BuyerID ▾	Picture ▾	Click to Add ▾
$700.00	5	10	603		
$800.00	2	11	603		
$500.00	2	14	602		
$625.00	2	10	601		
$1,150.00	3	15	602		
$810.00	1	30	603		
$1,500.00	2	10	605		
$626.00	2	18	603		
$410.00	2	10	602		
$685.00	3	7	602		
$975.00	1	12	601		
$135.00	10	3	601		
$110.00	20	2	603		

Product Table

Shortcut menu: Cut, Copy, Paste, Sort Ascending, Sort Descending, Clear filter from Picture, Is Not Blank, Insert Object...

Record: 1 of 15   No Filter   Search

Figure 10.5

Inserting an Object

4 Click the **Create from File** option.

5 Click **Browse**.

6 Navigate the Browse window to the location of this text's Images folder. (The location would be the CD provided with the text or from your computer lab's server.)

7 Several images should be available, as shown in Figure 10.6.

8 Double-click on **101** to insert that picture into the Product ID 101 record.

9 Click **OK** in the Insert Object window. This window should then close, and the table should now contain the words Paintbrush Picture in the Picture field of the Product ID 101 record. (*Note:* Instead, the words Bitmap Image, Package, or some other words may appear here. It all depends on what program your computer uses to manage images.)

10 Follow the same procedures to add pictures to the next *three* products.

11 Close the Product table. If asked click **Yes** to save the layout of the Product Table.

Figure 10.6

Images Available

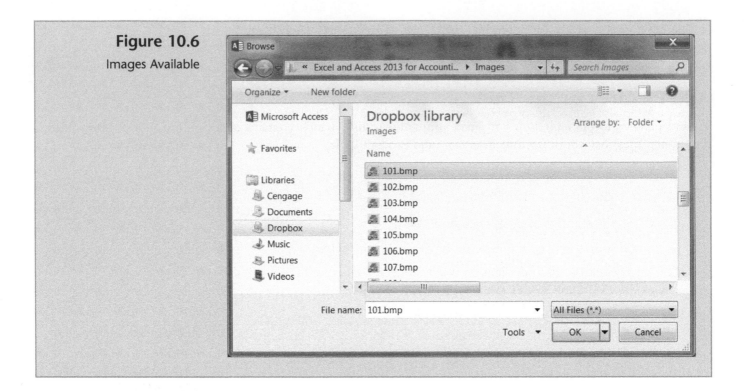

You have now added both a placeholder and some data for the picture field. You will enter more pictures later.

"Why don't I see the pictures in the table?" Meagan asks.

"The pictures are there, they are just not shown." Kyle responds. "Instead, all you'll see in the table under the Picture field are the words Bitmap Image."

"You'll need to add the picture field to a form to view each picture. We can do that next week when we spend time modifying and creating new forms."

Change the Structure of a Database

When you initially created the Inventory database, you defined its structure by specifying the names, data type, and sizes of all the fields in each table. Often, as when you added a picture field, you will need to change the structure of the database. In addition to adding fields, you may also need to change the field size, resize the field rows or columns, or change the data type. Additional changes that affect the validity of the data entered include the creation or modification of field validation rules, default values, and field formats.

"That is an important issue for us," says Nathan. "We can't use this database if the information isn't accurate and reliable. We also need to make it easier for our employees to enter data into the database."

"Exactly the reason for validation rules, default value, and field formats!" Kyle replies.

Change a Field Size, Row Height, Column Width, and Data Type

Recall that, when you first created the Inventory tables, every field you created with a Data Type = Text set the initial field size to 50. That means that a maximum of 50 characters could be entered into that field. In some cases, limiting the field size helps prevent errors. For instance, the supplier table has a field for State or Province. If you wanted only a two-character designation for each State or Province, you could set the field size to 2.

To change a field size:

1 Double-click the **Supplier Table**.

2 Click **View** and then click **Design View**.

3 Click the **State Or Province** field name.

4 Under Field Size for the StateOrProvince field, type **2** (replacing 50). See Figure 10.7.

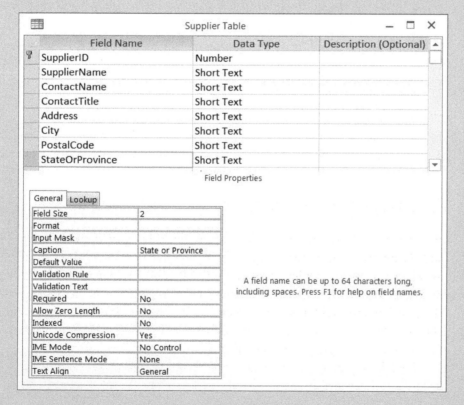

Figure 10.7

Changing a Fields Field Size Property

5 Click **Save**.

6 A warning should appear. Click **Yes** to continue.

7 Click **View** and then click **Datasheet View**.

8 Scroll across Ron House under the StateOrProvince field. Try to type **New Jersey**. Note that you are restricted to two characters.

9 Type **NJ** into the StateOrProvince field for Supplier ID 5.

10 Close the Supplier table.

Viewing data in table format is a quick way to look at all the information available in the table without generating a query or report. Sometimes, however, the information in a table is not very readable. Take, for instance, the Supplier table. Only part of the address is viewable. That is easily fixed by modifying the column width of each record.

"There is also a lot of wasted space in those tables where the columns are too wide as well," remarks Meagan.

"Sometimes the problem is the number of characters in the field and sometimes it's the column title," says Kyle. "I'll show you how to fix both."

Kyle then explains that it's very important to keep field names the same in tables as you may have referred to this field name in a relationship or in a query, form, or report. Thus to resize a column that is too large due to its title, you'll first need to change the field's caption.

To modify the Supplier table's row height and column width:

1 Double-click **Supplier table**.

2 Place the cursor between the Address field and City columns. Double-click the vertical line separating the Address and City column titles. The Address column should expand so that each supplier's address is visible in the column.

3 Now place the cursor between the Supplier Name column title and the Contact Name column title. Once again, double-click the vertical line separating the two columns. The Supplier Name column should contract so that the extra space in the column is eliminated, as shown in Figure 10.8. Notice how the cursor changed its appearance once it was over the line separating each column.

Figure 10.8

Partial View of Supplier Table after Resizing a Field's Column Width

	Supplier ID ▾	Supplier Name ▾	Contact Name ▾	Contact Title ▾	Address ▾	City ▾
⊞	1	Boardworks	Ben Nimitz	VP Sales	100 8th Ave.	New York
⊞	2	Naish	Sara Munoz	Sales director	909 S. Washington	Pilot Pt.
⊞	3	Bark	Nancy Bearfoot	Western sales	111 Macarthur Blvd.	Mahwah
⊞	4	Infinity	Paul Moo	Salesman	24382 Del Prado	Dana Point
⊞	5	Ron House	Kelly O'Leary	Regional sales	571 Mount Pleasant	Dover
*	0					

Record: ◄ ◄ 1 of 5 ► ►I ►⊞ 🔽 No Filter   Search ◄

4 Note in Figure 10.8 the first column (Supplier ID) only has one character in the date but is rather wide due to the number of characters in the column title (otherwise known as the field caption). In the design view, type **ID** in the Caption field property, which will change the column title of the SupplierID field to ID.

5 Repeat the same process to change the caption of the SupplierName field to Supplier, the ContactName field to Contact, the ContactTitle field to Title, the PostalCode field to Zip, the StateOrProvince field to ST, the PhoneNumber field to Phone, and finally the FaxNumber field to FAX.

6 Return to the Datasheet View and be sure to save the table.

7 Resize all columns using the double-click process described above. The newly resized and titled Supplier Table is shown in its entirety in Figure 10.9.

ID	Supplier	Contact	Title	Address	City	Zip	ST	Country	Phone	Fax
1	Boardworks	Ben Nimitz	VP Sales	100 8th Ave.	New York	10035	NY	USA	212-555-1354	212-555-6874
2	Naish	Sara Munoz	Sales director	909 S. Washington	Pilot Pt.	76258	TX	USA	940-555-0817	940-555-1187
3	Bark	Nancy Bearfoot	Western sales	111 Macarthur Blvd.	Mahwah	07430	NJ	USA	201-555-5730	201-555-3872
4	Infinity	Paul Moo	Salesman	24382 Del Prado	Dana Point	92629	CA	USA	949-555-4166	949-555-9718
5	Ron House	Kelly O'Leary	Regional sales	571 Mount Pleasant	Dover	07801	NJ	USA	201-555-3215	201-555-8741

Figure 10.9

Supplier Table after Changing the Caption of Some Fields

8 Close the Supplier Table.

Kyle notes that while you have changed the caption of many fields, you did not change the field names, which is very important.

"I have a question," says Meagan. "When I was watching you create the Product table, I noticed you set up the LeadTime field as a data-type text. Why isn't it considered a number?"

"Good question," Kyle responds. "If we plan to use the lead time information as just information for each product, then it doesn't matter whether we set it up as a Number data type or as a Text data type. However, if we later on want to use this field in a calculation, the Text data type wouldn't work. I'll show you how easy it is to change a field's data type."

To change a field's data type:

1 Open the Product Table in Design View.

2 Scroll down the fields listed and click in the Data Type column next to the field name LeadTime.

3 Select **Number** from the drop-down arrow as the new data type for this field, as shown in Figure 10.10.

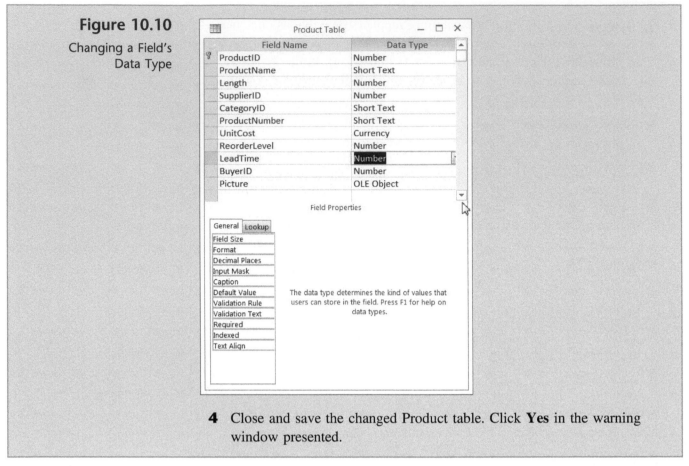

Figure 10.10

Changing a Field's Data Type

4 Close and save the changed Product table. Click **Yes** in the warning window presented.

By changing a table's row height and column width or by editing a field's data type and field size, you change the basic structure of a database. We next address additional changes that can be made to a table: establishing validation rules, default values, and formats.

Create Validation Rules

Kyle explains that validation rules improve data integrity and validity. Validation rules check information entered into the database (e.g., into a field) and test the entry to see if it meets certain criteria. If the information entered passes the test, the entry is allowed. If the entry fails the test, a warning appears and the entry is rejected.

"For example, in the Product table, every product should have a unit price entered and every price should be reasonable. You wouldn't want to have a unit price of $0.00 or something greater than $5,000.00," says Kyle.

"This would then prevent someone from entering an unreasonable price but it wouldn't prevent entering an incorrect price, right?" asks Nathan.

"Right," Kyle responds. "Validation rules can test for limits like greater than 0 and less than 1,000, or just greater than 100." Kyle explains that, in addition to validating a user's entry into a database, the validation rule can also provide specific feedback to a user concerning why the validation test failed. He suggests that you help Meagan and Nathan establish the unit cost restriction for the Product table and ensure that a price is entered for every product.

To create a validation rule:

1 Double-click **Product table**.

2 Click **View** and then click **Design View**.

3 Select the **UnitCost** field.

4 With the UnitCost field selected, click in the Validation Rule text box and type **>0 and <5000**.

5 With the UnitCost field still selected, click in the Validation Text text box and type **Unit Cost must be > $0 and < $5,000**, as shown in Figure 10.11.

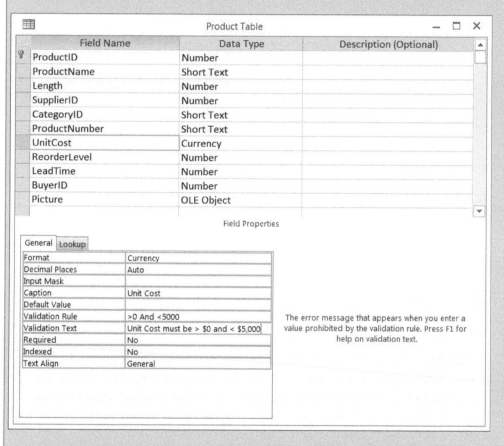

Figure 10.11

Validation Rules and Text

6 Save your changes to the table by clicking on the **Save** tool on the Quick Access toolbar.

7 Before Access will allow you to save the changes in validation rules, it will first ask if you want to test the existing data in the table (specifically, the UnitCost field) to see if it meets the new rule. See Figure 10.12.

Figure 10.12

Warning Window

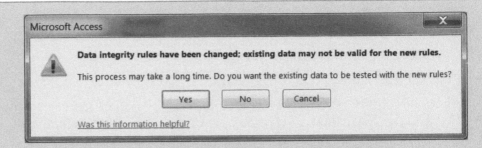

8 Click **Yes** to check the validity of existing information.

9 With the UnitCost field still selected, select **Yes** from the drop-down list in the Required text box. (This will require that all new records in the Product table have a unit cost entered.)

10 Click **View** and then click **Datasheet View**.

11 Click **Yes** in the dialog box provided to save the revised table design.

12 Click **Yes** in the next dialog box provided to once again test whether existing data meets the new rules.

13 Type **5500** as the new unit cost of Product ID 101 and then press [**Tab**].

14 The dialog box shown in Figure 10.13 should appear.

Figure 10.13

Validation Rule
Dialog Box

15 Click **OK**.

16 Type **700** as the unit cost of Product ID 101 and then press [**Tab**].

17 Select the unit cost of Product ID 102; then press [**Backspace**] and to remove the existing $800 unit cost then [**Tab**]. The dialog box shown in Figure 10.14 should appear, stating that an entry is required in this field.

Figure 10.14

Required Value
Dialog Box

18 Click **OK**.

19 Type **800** as the unit cost of Product ID 102 and then press [**Tab**].

20 Close the Product Table.

You've now established validation rules, text, and field requirement rules, which will help you maintain data integrity. Another way to ensure that valid information is entered into the database is to create default values.

Create Default Values

Default values, as the name implies, provides the person entering data into a database with pre-existing information for certain fields. This helps ensure the validity of entered data and also speeds up the process of entering information into a database.

"Repetitive information or information that is present in many or most records is ideal for Access's Default Value option," Kyle explains.

"For example, if most of your suppliers are located in New York, then you could set the default value for the state field of the supplier table to 'NY'."

"But what if a supplier is not actually located in New York?" you ask.

"Then you simply type over the default value," Kyle answers. "However, since most of your suppliers are in the state of New York, that won't happen very often."

"Could we also set the default value for country, given that most of our suppliers are also located in the United States?"

"Now you're catching on!" Kyle responds.

Kyle instructs you to add a new supplier after you establish NY as the default value for the state field and USA as the default value for the country field of the Supplier table.

To create default values:

1 Double-click **Supplier Table**.

2 Click **View** and then click **Design View**.

3 Click the **State Or Province** field.

4 Click in the **Default Value** text box, type **NY**, and then press **[Tab]**. Note that Access automatically adds the quotes around NY. The Field Properties section of your screen should look like Figure 10.15.

General	Lookup	
Field Size	2	
Format		
Input Mask		
Caption	ST	
Default Value	"NY"	
Validation Rule		...
Validation Text		
Required	No	
Allow Zero Length	No	
Indexed	No	
Unicode Compression	Yes	
IME Mode	No Control	
IME Sentence Mode	None	
Text Align	General	

Figure 10.15

Entering a Default Value for a Field

5 Select the **Country** field.

6 With the Country field selected, click the **Default Value** text box and type **USA**.

7 Close the Supplier table and click **Yes** to save your changes.

"Now that should save us some time as we enter more suppliers," you comment.

Kyle remarks that formats and input masks also help ensure valid data entry while making information more meaningful.

Create Formats and Input Masks

Kyle explains that format properties in tables vary depending on the data type assigned to each field. For example, a Number data type can be pre-formatted as currency ($1,234.56), fixed decimal (1234.56), standard decimal (1,234.56), percent (123%), or other formats. A Date/Time data type can be pre-formatted as a short date (1/23/15), a long date (Sunday, January 25, 2015), et cetera. On the other hand, a Text data type is not usually subject to a particular format.

"I'd like to add a date to our supplier table so that I know how long I've been doing business with each supplier," Nathan comments. "Can that date be formatted like you mentioned?"

"Certainly," Kyle responds.

"How about formatting phone numbers?" Meagan asks. "Can we format phone numbers so that the area code, prefix, and number are always displayed the same?"

"The best way to solve that issue is by using another Access feature called *input masks*," Kyle answers.

He explains that input masks are used to control how data is entered. This is quite different from the format property referred to previously, which affects only how a value is displayed, not how it is stored in the table. A display format is not applied until the data entered is saved—nothing is displayed in the field to suggest or control the format in which data is entered. If you need to control how data is entered, Kyle suggests you use an input mask in addition to (or instead of) a data display format in those cases.

An input mask ensures that the data will fit in the format you define, and only the kind of values specified can be entered in each blank. In Meagan's example, an input mask would require that all entries contain exactly enough digits to make up a U.S. area code and telephone number and also that only digits (not alphabetic characters) be entered in each blank.

Kyle instructs you to work with Nathan and Meagan by adding a "first purchase date" field to the Supplier table and have it displayed in a short date format. In addition, he suggests you modify the Supplier table: phone number field using a phone number mask.

To utilize the format and input mask capabilities of Access:

1 Double-click **Supplier table**.

2 Click **View** and then click **Design View**.

3 Create a new field by clicking in the field name text box located under the last field titled FaxNumber.

4 Type **Firstpurchasedate** as the new field name and then press [**Tab**].

5 Select **Date/Time** as the data type for the new field.

6 Select **Short Date** as the format for the new field.

7 Type **First Purchase** as the caption for the new field. Your screen should look like Figure 10.16.

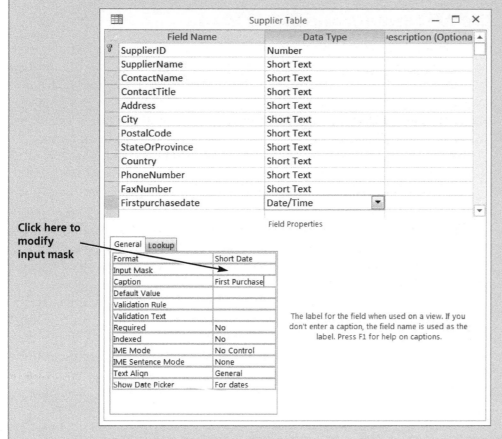

Click here to modify input mask

Figure 10.16
Modified Supplier Table

8 Click **Save** from the Quick Access toolbar.

9 Click the **PhoneNumber** field.

10 With the PhoneNumber field selected, click in the Input Mask text box and select the button on the far right to activate the Input Mask Wizard. If a security warning appears, click **Open**.

T r o u b l e ? The input mask feature may not be installed on your version of Access. If not installed, a message may pop up asking if you want to install it now. If you are in a lab environment, please check with your lab administrator before proceeding. If you are at your own computer, have your installation disk handy and follow the instructions to install this feature.

11 Click **Phone Number** input mask, as shown in Figure 10.17, and then click **Next**.

Figure 10.17

Input Mask Wizard

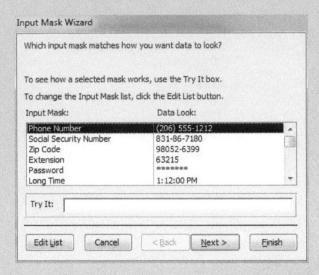

12 Click **Next** two times to accept the default input mask for a phone number; then click **Finish**.

13 The Field Properties section of the PhoneNumber field should look like Figure 10.18.

Figure 10.18

Input Mask for the
PhoneNumber Field

General	Lookup	
Field Size	50	
Format		
Input Mask	!\(999") "000\-0000;;_	...
Caption	Phone	
Default Value		
Validation Rule		
Validation Text		
Required	No	
Allow Zero Length	No	
Indexed	No	
Unicode Compression	Yes	
IME Mode	No Control	
IME Sentence Mode	None	
Text Align	General	

14 Click **Save** from the Quick Access toolbar.

15 Click **View** and then click **Datasheet View**.

16 Type **1/1/15** in the First Purchase field of Supplier ID 1.

17 Click in the **First Purchase** field of Supplier ID 2. Note that the date displayed for Supplier ID 1 has changed to 1/1/2015.

18 Type **February 12, 2015** in the First Purchase field of Supplier ID 2.

19 Click in the **First Purchase** field of Supplier ID 3. Note that the date displayed for Supplier ID 2 has changed to 2/12/2015.

20 Type **Mar 20, 2015** in the First Purchase field of Supplier ID 3.

21 Click in the **First Purchase** field of Supplier ID 4. Note that the date displayed for Supplier ID 3 has changed to 3/20/2015.

22 Type **4/30/15** in the First Purchase field of Supplier ID 4 and 5. Part of your screen should look like Figure 10.19.

Figure 10.19

Partial View of Modified Supplier Table

23 Add a new supplier to the Supplier table by typing **6** in the ID column and **Fanatic** in the Supplier column and then pressing [**Tab**].

24 Type **Paula Lyon** as the Contact, then press [**Tab**].

25 Type **Sales associate** as the Title, then press [**Tab**].

26 Type **10332 5th Avenue** as the Address, then press [**Tab**].

27 Type **New York** as the City, then press [**Tab**].

28 Type **10003** as the Postal Code, then press [**Tab**].

29 Press [**Tab**] twice to accept the default State and Country values of NY and USA.

30 Type **2125551345** as the Phone Number, then press [**Tab**]. Note the input mask will place the parentheses and dashes accordingly. (Although the input mask will affect future entries into this field, it will not affect the form of *existing* entries—e.g., by placing the area code in parentheses.)

31 Type **2125551346** as the Fax Number, then press [**Tab**]. Observe that, in the absence of an input mask, the data is accepted as is.

32 Go back to the Fax Number field and reenter the fax number as **212-555-1346** (to be consistent with previous entries); then press [**Tab**].

33 Type **6/1/15** as the First Purchase field.

34 Click **Save** from the Quick Access toolbar.

35 Close the Supplier table.

You have witnessed the affects and benefits of default values, display formatting, and input masks. Perhaps now is a good time to see how Access can enforce additional constraints on data entry to ensure that only valid data from database tables are entered as a part of a record.

Referential Integrity

In the previous chapter you established relationships between the product, supplier, category, and buyer tables. This action identified the common fields between each table. You can further define that relationship by using referential integrity.

Kyle explains that referential integrity is a system of rules that Microsoft Access uses to ensure not only that relationships between records in related tables are valid but also that you don't accidentally delete or change related data. When referential integrity is enforced, you must observe the following rules.

- You cannot enter a value in the Foreign Key field of the related table that does not exist in the Primary Key of the primary table. A *Foreign Key* is a field that refers to the Primary Key field in another table and indicates how the tables are related: the data in the Foreign Key and Primary Key fields must match, although the field names need not be the same.

- You cannot delete a record from a primary table if matching records exist in a related table.

- You cannot change a Primary Key value in the primary table if that record has related records. If you want Microsoft Access to enforce these rules for a relationship, you should select the Enforce Referential Integrity check box when you create or edit the relationship. If referential integrity is in force and you break one of the rules while changing related tables, Microsoft Access displays an error message and does not allow the change.

"Wait just a minute!" Nathan exclaims. "Primary key, foreign key, referential integrity, I'm confused!"

"I know," responds Kyle. "Let me give you an example. Once I show you how this affects our product, supplier, category, and buyer tables, I think you will have a better understanding."

Kyle explains that one of the foreign keys he was referring to included the SupplierID field located in the Product table. It is considered a Foreign Key field because it refers to a Primary Key field in another table. In this case, the Primary Key to which it refers is the SupplierID field located in the Supplier table. Kyle also notes that this field, SupplierID, is the Primary Key field in the Supplier table as can be seen in Figure 10.20.

"Further," Kyle explains, "to ensure validity in the Product table we should enforce referential integrity. In doing so, every entry in the SupplierID field of the Product table will have to match one of the records in the SupplierID field of the Supplier table."

"This is still a bit baffling," says Meagan.

"Just watch as I establish referential integrity for the SupplierID field and test it by adding another record," responds Kyle.

To establish referential integrity:

1 Click the **Database Tools** tab on the Ribbon.

2 Click the **Relationships** tool in the Relationships group.

3 Expand the tables as needed, so they match Figure 10.20, by clicking the title bar of each window and then dragging it to a new location.

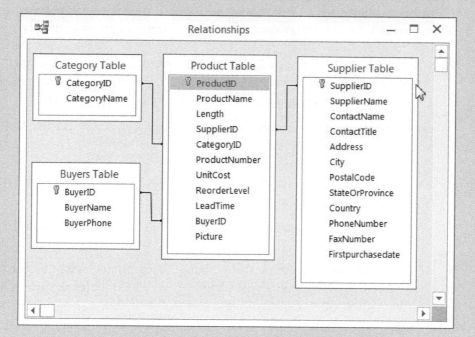

Figure 10.20
Relationships Window

4 Double-click the line that connects the SupplierID field of the Product table with the SupplierID field of the Supplier table.

5 Click the **Enforce Referential Integrity** check box in the Edit Relationships window as shown in Figure 10.21; then click **OK**.

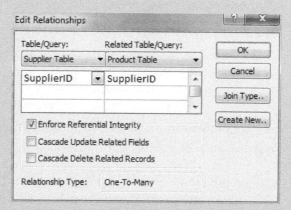

Figure 10.21
Edit Relationships Window

6 Note the changed line connecting the two tables. In particular, note the one-to-many reference shown by the dark line, the 1, and the infinity symbol.

7 Click **Relationship Report** from the Tools group of the Design tab on the Ribbon. If a security notice appears, click **Open**.

8 Click **Print** and then click **OK** to print the Relationships Report as shown in Figure 10.22.

Figure 10.22

Printed Relationships
Report

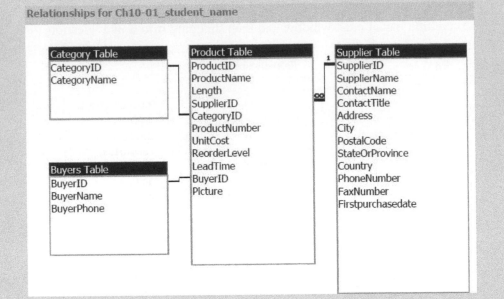

Relationships for Ch10-01_student_name

9   Close the Relationships Report window and click **No** when asked if you want to save changes to the design of Report1.

10 Close the Relationships window and then click **Yes** if asked to save changes to relationships.

11 Double-click the **Product Table**.

12 Enter a new record by typing **117** as the ProductID in the last line of the Product Table, press [**Tab**], type **Allwave** as the ProductName in the Product Name field, and then press [**Tab**].

13 Type **8.6.** in the Length field; then press [**Tab**].

14 Type **7** in the Supplier ID field, then press [**Tab**].

15 Type **G** in the Category ID field, then press [**Tab**].

16 Type **F98** in the Product Number field, then press [**Tab**].

17 Type **750** in the Unit Cost field, then press [**Tab**].

18 Type **1** in the Reorder Level field, then press [**Tab**].

19 Type **14** in the Lead Time field, then press [**Tab**].

20 Type **604** in the Buyer ID field, then press [**Tab**].

21 Insert image 117.bmp for this product like you've done before, and then press [**Tab**].

22 Note that the last Tab completes the entry for this new product. However, since you established referential integrity, an error message (see Figure 10.23) appears. This occurred because there is no Supplier ID 7 in the Supplier table and so Access rejected your entry. Click **OK** in the error message to return to the Product table.

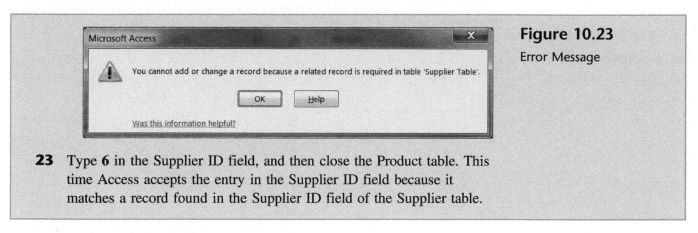

Figure 10.23

Error Message

23 Type **6** in the Supplier ID field, and then close the Product table. This time Access accepts the entry in the Supplier ID field because it matches a record found in the Supplier ID field of the Supplier table.

"That makes more sense now," Meagan and Nathan agree.

Documenting a Database

"Now that we've made all these changes to our database, how do we document them?" Nathan asks.

"Good question" responds Kyle. "Access has a feature called the Database Documenter that will provide a list of table, query, form, and report attributes."

Kyle suggests you document some of the changes you made to the product and supplier tables. In particular, he would like to see documentation of the unit price field in the Product table (where you added a validation rule) and documentation of the phone number field in the Supplier table (where you added an input mask).

To document the information requested:

1 Click **Database Documenter** from the Analyze group of the Database Tools tab on the Ribbon.

2 Click the **Tables** tab in the Documenter window.

3 Click the **Supplier Table** check box as shown in Figure 10.24.

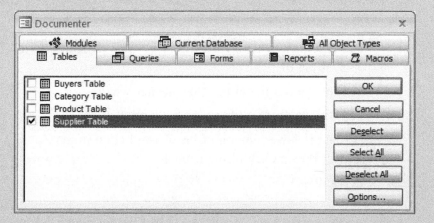

Figure 10.24

Documenter Window

4 Click the **Options** button.

5 Check or uncheck boxes and select option buttons as per Figure 10.25.

Figure 10.25

Print Table Definition

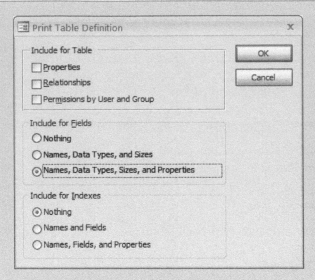

6 Click **OK** in the Print Table Definitions window, and then click **OK** in the Documenter window.

7 Click in the lower portion of the **Zoom** button in the Zoom group of the Print Preview tab of the Ribbon.

8 Click **150%**.

9 Navigate to page 4 of the report by clicking the arrows located in the lower left-hand corner of the Print Preview window, and locate information on the PhoneNumber field.

Trouble? Page 4 on your screen may not contain information on the PhoneNumber field. If not, look on pages 3 or 5 to find it and then change the page you print in step 10 accordingly.

10 Click **Print**, click **Pages** in the Print window, and then type **4** in the From and then type 5 in the To: text boxes and then click **OK** to print. Your resulting printout should contain the information shown in Figure 10.26.

11 Click **Close Print Preview**.

12 Click **Database Documenter** from the Analyze group of the Database Tools tab on the Ribbon.

13 Click the **Tables** tab in the Documenter window.

14 Click the **Product Table** check box and then click **OK**.

15 Click in the lower portion of the **Zoom** button in the Zoom group of the Print Preview tab of the Ribbon.

16 Click **150%**.

17 Navigate to page 3 of the report by clicking the arrows located in the lower left-hand corner of the Print Preview window, and locate information on the UnitCost field.

Trouble? Page 3 on your screen may not contain information on the UnitCost field. If not, look on pages 2 or 4 to find it and then change the page you print in step 18 accordingly.

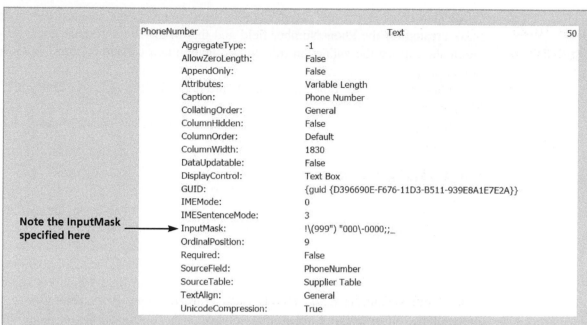

```
PhoneNumber                                    Text                                    50
                  AggregateType:         -1
                  AllowZeroLength:       False
                  AppendOnly:            False
                  Attributes:            Variable Length
                  Caption:               Phone Number
                  CollatingOrder:        General
                  ColumnHidden:          False
                  ColumnOrder:           Default
                  ColumnWidth:           1830
                  DataUpdatable:         False
                  DisplayControl:        Text Box
                  GUID:                  {guid {D396690E-F676-11D3-B511-939E8A1E7E2A}}
                  IMEMode:               0
                  IMESentenceMode:       3
Note the InputMask →  InputMask:         !\(999") "000\-0000;;_
specified here        OrdinalPosition:   9
                  Required:              False
                  SourceField:           PhoneNumber
                  SourceTable:           Supplier Table
                  TextAlign:             General
                  UnicodeCompression:    True
```

Figure 10.26

Database Documenter Information on the Phone Number Field of the Supplier Table

18 Click **Print**. click **Pages** in the Print window, and then type **3** in the From and To: text boxes. Your resulting printout should contain the information shown in Figure 10.27.

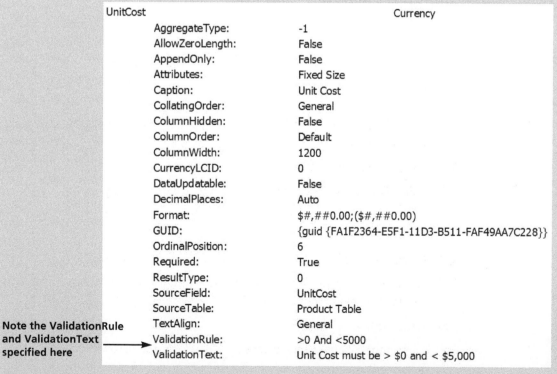

```
UnitCost                                            Currency
                  AggregateType:         -1
                  AllowZeroLength:       False
                  AppendOnly:            False
                  Attributes:            Fixed Size
                  Caption:               Unit Cost
                  CollatingOrder:        General
                  ColumnHidden:          False
                  ColumnOrder:           Default
                  ColumnWidth:           1200
                  CurrencyLCID:          0
                  DataUpdatable:         False
                  DecimalPlaces:         Auto
                  Format:                $#,##0.00;($#,##0.00)
                  GUID:                  {guid {FA1F2364-E5F1-11D3-B511-FAF49AA7C228}}
                  OrdinalPosition:       6
                  Required:              True
                  ResultType:            0
                  SourceField:           UnitCost
                  SourceTable:           Product Table
Note the ValidationRule  TextAlign:      General
and ValidationText →  ValidationRule:    >0 And <5000
specified here        ValidationText:    Unit Cost must be > $0 and < $5,000
```

Figure 10.27

Database Documenter Information on the Unit Cost Field of the Product Table

19 Click **Close Print Preview**.

Meagan notes that in the Supplier table documentation she can see the input mask created for the PhoneNumber field and that in the Product table documentation she can see the validation rule and validation text created for the UnitCost field.

"What about all the other information provided for the fields in question?" Meagan asks.

"Helpful," comments Kyle, "but not that important for us right now. It's time to practice!"

End Note

In this chapter, you have learned more about the use of tables in the Access program. You have learned how to add, change, and delete records; how to add a picture with an OLE field; and how to change the structure of a database, which included changing field data types and column widths and changing record row heights. You have also learned how to create field validation rules, default values, and formats. Finally, you learned about the advantages and functionality of specifying referential integrity. In the next chapter you will experience more of the query process.

Chapter 10 Questions

1 Describe the process for deleting a record from a table.

2 Define OLE.

3 What can you do in Access to change the structure of a database?

4 Why would you want to change the column width and/or row height of a table?

5 What do validation rules do?

6 What is the process for adding a validation rule to a field?

7 Why would you establish default values for a field?

8 What are input masks?

9 What is referential integrity?

10 What rules must be followed if referential integrity is enforced?

Chapter 10 Assignments

1 Add, change, and delete records to the What SUP database (use the Ch10-02 file)

    a. Add the following record to the Buyers table: BuyerID 605, Farley, 555-7187.

    b. Add G as a CategoryID with a CategoryName of Women's as a category to the Category table.

    c. Delete the following record from the Buyers table: BuyerID 601.

    d. Change the buyer for the following Product IDs from buyer 601 to buyer 605: Product ID 104, 108, 113, and 115.

    e. Print the first page of the product, buyers, and category tables as modified in a landscape orientation.

    f. Save your file as Ch10-02_01_student_name (replacing student_name with your name).

2 Add pictures to the What SUP database (use the Ch10-02 file; **do not use the file you just updated in Assignment 1**)

    a. Add pictures for the remaining products in the Product table using the picture files provided. Each product has a picture associated with it and is labeled with the product ID number.

b.   Print the second page of the Product table as modified in landscape orientation.

c.   Save your file as Ch10-02_02_student_name (replacing student_name with your name).

3   Change the structure of the What SUP database (Use the Ch10-02 file; **do not use the file you just updated in Assignment 1 or 2.**)

a.   Add the following product to the Product table. ProductID: 117; ProductName: LadyG; Length: 8.5; SupplierID: 6; CategoryID: F; ProductNumber: 3983AE; UnitCost: 620; Reorder Level: 1; Lead Time: 3; Buyer ID: 604; Picture: 117.bmp.

b.   Modify the caption and re-size the column width of each field of the Product table so that the table will fit on one page when printed in landscape orientation.

c.   Print the Product table in landscape orientation.

d.   Create a validation rule for the Reorder Level field of the Product table, making the field a required one and making sure the reorder level is greater than 0 and less than 25 units. Create your own feedback statement and insert it as the validation text.

e.   Establish 7 as the default value for the Lead Time field of the Product table.

f.   Establish a phone number input mask for the BuyerPhone field of the Buyers table.

g.   Enforce referential integrity between the Product table and the Buyer and Category tables.

h.   Print a Relationships report.

i.   Print documentation on the properties of the Reorder Level and Lead Time fields of the Product table and the BuyerPhone field of the Buyers table.

j.   Save your file as Ch10-02_03_student_name (replacing student_name with your name).

Chapter 10 Case Problem 1:
KELLY'S BOUTIQUE

Note: You must have completed Case 1 in the previous chapter in order to continue working on this case.

In Chapter 9 you created a database for Kelly's Boutique consisting of a Book table, a Department table, and a Publisher table. You also created an initial form, query, and report. Kelly would now like you to make some adjustments to the tables previously created by adding and deleting some records, adding some OLE fields and pictures, and changing the structure of the database. Make the following changes for Kelly using the ch9-03_student_name file you created in Chapter 9. (*Note:* Open your ch9-03_student_name file first, save it as ch10-03_student_name, and then make the listed changes.)

a. Add Warner as the tenth publisher to the Publisher table with a contact Yee and phone 555-7894.

b. Add the following records to the Book table:

ISBN	Dept	Book Title	Num	Author	Price
039480029	Children	Hop on Pop	6	Seuss	7.99
039480001	Children	The Cat in the Hat	6	Seuss	7.99
446676098	Adult	The Notebook	10	Sparks	24.95
385424736	Adult	The Rainmaker	10	Grisham	35.95

c. Add a Picture field for OLE objects to the Book table.

d. Add pictures to the Book table for *Green Eggs and Ham*, *Hop on Pop*, *Harry Potter and the Prisoner of Azkaban*, *Divine Secrets*, *Rainmaker*, and *Deep End of the Ocean*. Picture files are labeled by book name or the first word of the book name and are located on your student disk in an Images folder.

e. Resize the column width of each field and the record's row height of each table so that they fit on one page when printed.

f. Establish a phone number input mask for the Phone field of the Publisher and Department tables.

g. Enforce referential integrity between the Book table and the Department and Publisher tables.

h. Create a validation rule for the List price field of the Book table, making the field a required one and making sure the price is no less than $1 and no more than $100. Create your own feedback statement and insert it as the validation text.

i. Establish Children as the default value for the Department field of the Book table.

j. Print the Book, Department, and Publisher tables.

k. Print the Relationships report.

l. Print documentation on the properties of the List Price field of the Book table and the Phone field of the Publisher table.

m. Create a new form titled "Books" showing the Book Title and Picture fields for all books. Print the Rainmaker form only.

n. Make sure you keep a copy of this file for use in the next chapter.

Chapter 10 Case Problem 2:
WINE DEPOT

Note: You must have completed Case 2 in the previous chapter in order to continue working on this case.

In Chapter 9 you created a database for the Wine Depot consisting of a Wine Products table, a Winery table, and a Buyer table. You also created an initial query, form, and report. Barbara has now asked you to make some changes to those files. Make the following changes for Barbara using the ch9-04_student_name file you created in Chapter 9. (*Note:* Open your ch9-04_student_name file first, save it as ch10-04_student_name, and then make the listed changes.)

a. Add buyer 105, Carly Simon, 555-6874 to the Buyer table.

b. Add winery 20 (Robert Mondovi, American, 105) and winery 21 (Wente, American, 104) to the Winery table.

c. Delete wines with SKU 15966 and 16769.

d. Delete winery 2.

e. Add the following records to the Wine Products table:

SKU	Type	Winery	Price	Cost	Size	Vintage	Quantity
12564	Merlot	21	12.99	8.00	750	2015	24
12895	Sauvignon Blanc	4	15.49	9.00	750	2017	12
16900	Syrah	11	30.00	24.00	750	2016	12
11350	Pinot Noir	11	50.00	40.00	750	2016	30
11475	Pinot Noir	1	22.00	17.50	750	2016	48
12380	Pinot Noir	20	21.00	18.00	750	2015	24
12383	Chardonnay	20	18.00	12.00	750	2015	36
12384	Fume Blanc	20	17.49	11.00	750	2016	36

f. Enforce referential integrity between the tables.

g. Print the Relationships report.

h. Add a Picture field for OLE objects to the Wine Products table.

i. Add pictures to the Wine Products table for products 11475, 12384, 12895, 14539, and 15347. (*Note:* Pictures for these products are provided in an Images folder on the Cengage Companion site and are labeled with the SKU number.)

j. Establish a phone number input mask for the Phone field of the Buyer table, and then change all the phone numbers in the table to include an area code of 805.

k. Create a validation rule for the Price field of the Wine Products table, making the price field required and making sure the price is greater than $1 but less than $100. Create your own feedback statement and enter it as the validation text. Save the changes you made. You should receive an error message. Cancel your effort and read step l below.

l. When creating your validation rule, you might well have checked to see if the data already stored actually met that rule. If you did check, you found that the validation rule was in conflict with some of the existing data. Change the rule so that the price must be greater than $1 and less than $200. Create your own feedback statement and enter it as the validation text. Save the changes you made. This time you should not encounter an error message.

m. Establish a default value of 750 for the Size field of the Wine Products table.

n. Resize the column width of the Wine Products table so that it can fit on one page when printed in landscape orientation.

o. Print each table.

p. Print documentation on the properties of the Phone field of the Buyer table and the Price field of the Wine Products table.

q. Create a new form titled "Wine" showing the SKU and Picture fields for all wines. Print the 11475 form only.

r. Make sure you keep a copy of this file for use in the next chapter.

Chapter 10 Case Problem 3:
SNICK'S BOARD SHOP

Note: You must have completed Case 3 in the previous chapter in order to continue working on this case.

In Chapter 9 you created a database for the Snick's Board Shop consisting of a Products table, a Category table, and a Manufacturer table. You also created an initial query, form, and report. Caitlin has now asked you to make some changes to those files.

Make the following changes for Caitlin, using the ch9-05_student_name file you created in Chapter 9. (*Note*: Open your ch9-05_student_name file first, save it as Ch10-05_student_name, and then make the listed changes.)

a. Add CategoryID 6, CategoryName T-shirts to the category table.

b. Add ManufacturerID AH, ManufacturerName Anti-Hero to the manufacturer table.

c. Add ProductID 62-01296, ProductName Anti-Hero Logo T-Shirt, CategoryID 6, ManufacturerID AH, Price $23.99, Style Red, Quantity 30 and ProductID 61-54122, Product Name Super Rail, CategoryID 5, ManufacturerID S9, Price 175.99, Style Blue, Quantity 10 to the product table.

d. Change ProductID 65-23174 to 61-23174

e. Delete ProductID 65-01837 from the product table.

f. Enforce referential integrity between the tables.

g. Print the Relationships report.

h. Add a Picture field for OLE objects to the Products table.

i. Add pictures to the products table. (*Note:* Pictures for these products are provided in the Images folder and are labeled with the ProductID.)

j. Add a PhoneNumber field to the manufacturer table with a standard phone number input mask and then add the following phone numbers to the manufacturer table.

ManufacturerID	PhoneNumber
AH	619-555-8521
EMT	305-555-7861
S9	415-555-7142

k. Create a validation rule for the Price field of the product table, making the price field required and making sure the price is greater than $1 but less than $500. Create your own feedback statement and enter it as the validation text. Save the changes you made.

l. Establish a default value of 20 for the Quantify field of the product table.

m. Resize the column width of the product table so that it can fit on one page when printed in landscape orientation.

n. Use Access's help feature (press the **F1** key) to learn how to sort tables alphabetically by a certain field. Then sort and save each table by its primary key.

o. Print each table.

p. Print documentation on the properties of the PhoneNumber field of the manufacturer table and the quantity field of the product table.

q. Create a new form titled "Snick's Products" showing the ProductName and Picture fields for all products. Print the Super Rail form only.

r. Make sure you keep a copy of this file for use in the next chapter.

Chapter 10 Case Problem 4:
ROSEY'S ROSES

Note: You must have completed Case 4 in the previous chapter in order to continue working on this case. In Chapter 9, you created a database for Rosey's Roses consisting of a Product table, a Type table, and a Grower table. You also created an initial query, form, and report. You have now been asked to make some changes to those files.

Make the following changes using the ch9-06_student_name file you created in Chapter 9. (*Note:* Open your ch9-06_student_name file first, save it as Ch10-06_student_name, and then make the listed changes.)

a. Add Type "Creeper", and Description "Low-growing roses used as ground cover." to the Type table.

b. Add Grower ID "400", Grower Name "Owen Farms", and Contact "Maria Lopez" to the Grower table.

c. Add ID "15", Type "Creeper", Description "Sunlight #3", Quantity "35", Cost/Unit "30.00", and Grower ID "400" and ID "16", Type "Creeper", Description "Stud", Quantity "55", Cost/Unit "35.99", and Grower ID "400" to the Product table.

d. Delete ID "7" from the Product table.

e. Delete the existing relationships between tables.

f. Change the Field Size of the following fields in the Product table: Type – 10 and Description – 30. (Note that you may receive a warning message telling you that some data may be lost because of switching fields to a different size. Click **Yes** to accept this warning.)

g. Add a Picture field for OLE objects to the Product table.

h. Add pictures to the Product table. (Note: Pictures for these products are provided in the Images folder and are labeled with the product ID.)

i. Add a Phone Number field to the Grower table with a standard phone number input mask and a field size of 10, and then add the following phone numbers: ID 100 – 503-555-1957, ID 200 – 408-555-8741, ID 300 – 212-555-1154, and ID 400 – 805-555-6974.

j. Create a validation rule for the Cost/Unit field of the Product table, making the Cost/Unit field required and making sure the Cost/Unit is greater than $1 but less than $100. Create your own feedback statement and enter it as the validation text.

k. Establish a default value of 10 for the Quantify field of the Product table.

l. Recreate relationships between tables and enforce referential integrity.

m. Print the relationships report.

n. Print each table.

o. Print documentation on the properties of the Phone Number field of the Grower table, the Quantity field of the Product table, and the Cost/Unit field of the Product table.

p. Create a new form titled "Rosey's Products" showing the Description and Picture fields for all products. Print the Stud form only.

q. Make sure you keep a copy of this file for use in the next chapter.

11

Queries

Case: **What SUP, Inc.**

Kyle decides to take Meagan and Nathan to the next level of database use by explaining the query process.

"What good is all this information if you can't use it?" Kyle asks. "Access provides you tables as a holder of information, but queries are used to ask questions of the data and to retrieve a subset of the total information available."

"Do we have to learn a special language in order to ask questions of the database?" asks Meagan.

"No, but you do need to know some characteristics of the data so that you can use Access's Query By Example (QBE) method of inquiry," he responds.

Kyle decides that he'll begin by explaining how to go about querying the database for specific information, such as what necklaces Coast has in inventory, and then continue with more complicated queries, such as which necklaces Coast has in inventory that are above one price but below another.

Querying Selected Records

Kyle explains that the querying you accomplished in your introduction to Access involved listing specific data from various tables. In these queries you didn't establish any criteria to select specific records; you just specified what specific information you wanted from all records. The next level of inquiry requires that you establish specific criteria for certain fields to narrow down your search for particular records. These are referred to as *select* queries.

"We'll begin with character data, wildcards, and numbers to specify what records we're looking for," Kyle explains.

Using Character Data in a Select Query

Queries can be generated either by using the Query Wizard (as was done in our introduction to Access) or by using the Design view, which is more sophisticated and flexible. Kyle suggests you use the Design view to create a simple query of your inventory file, which has been updated to include a total of 20 records. If a customer were looking for a specific item that she saw elsewhere, then she might ask if you have a particular watch in stock. You could look that item up in your database by generating a query asking for a specific match to a specific name.

"Why don't we ask the database if it has a specific Seiko watch with a product number of SMA113?" asks Meagan.

"Good idea," Nathan responds. "Let's create such a query that displays the product number, name, and supplier."

To create a query using character data:

1 Start Access.

2 Click the File tab and then click **Open**.

3 Navigate the Open window to the location of this text's student files. (The location would be the CD provided with the text or from your computer lab's server.)

4 Double-click **ch11-01**, which should be located in a Ch 11 folder. (This is a modified version of the completed What SUP Inventory file from Chapter 10.) Click the **Enable Content** button.

5 Click the **File** tab and then click **Save As** twice.

6 Navigate the Save As window to the location where you want to save this file and type **Ch11-01_student_name** in the File Name: text box, replacing "student_name" with your name.

7 Click **Save**. Click the **Enable Content** button.

8 Click **Query Wizard** from the Queries group on the Create tab of the Ribbon.

9 Click **Simple Query Wizard** and then click **OK**. Click **Open** if a security notice appears.

10 Click **Table: Product Table** from the drop-down list of Tables/ Queries.

11 Double-click **Product Number** and **Product Name** from the list of available fields.

12 Click **Table: Supplier Table** from the drop-down list of Tables/Queries.

13 Double-click **Supplier Name** from the list of available fields.

14 Click **Next** and then type **Product Query 1** as the title for the query and then click **Finish**.

15 If necessary, double-click the space between each field name to resize the columns so that all information is visible. Your screen should look like Figure 11.1.

Figure 11.1

Product Query 1

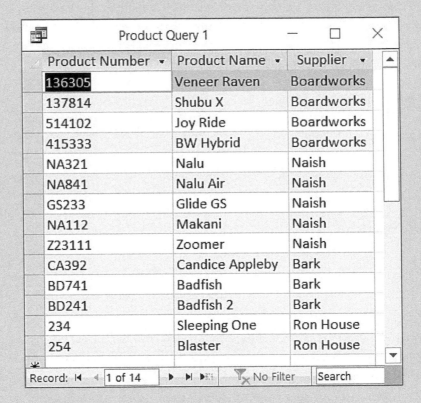

16 Click the **Home** tab of the Ribbon; click **View** and then click **Design View**.

17 Type **NA321** in the criteria section of the query in the ProductNumber column of the design grid and then press [Tab]. See Figure 11.2.

18 Click **Run** from the Results group of the Design tab of the Ribbon.

19 Resize the column widths if necessary to view all of the information provided. The resulting Datasheet view of the query should look like the query solution in Figure 11.3.

20 Close the Query window and click **Yes** to save changes.

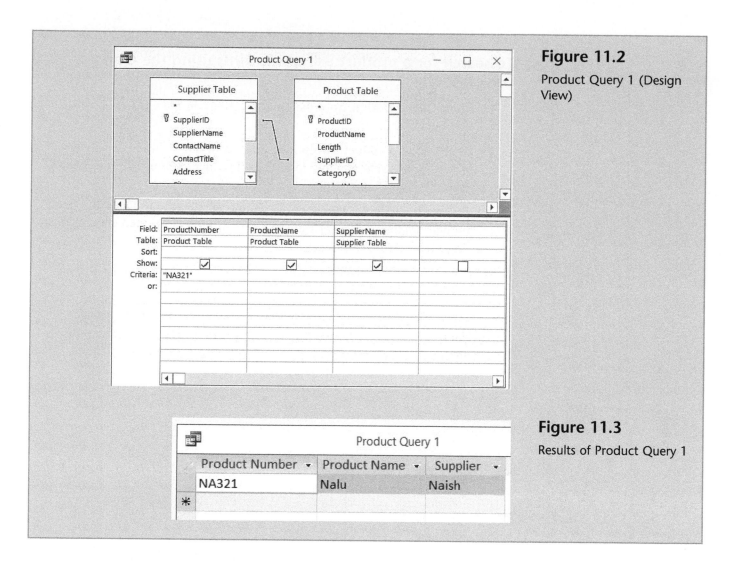

Figure 11.2

Product Query 1 (Design View)

Figure 11.3

Results of Product Query 1

The character-based queries work well when you have a specific name or set of characters (like the product number) you are looking for. However, Access users are often in search of records that match some—but perhaps not all—of a specific criteria. Wildcards provide this capability.

Using Wildcards in a Select Query

Queries using wildcards allow the user to find such things as field values, records, or filenames. The asterisk (*), which matches any number of characters, can be used as a wildcard in the first, last, or first *and* last position of the character string. For example, if Nathan wanted to list all the products he had in inventory that contained the text "Badfish" in the product name, he would type *Badfish* as the criteria under the ProductName column.

Kyle points out that there is a way to create a new query other than by using the Query Wizard. This method, which Kyle actually prefers, is called *query by design* and uses a different tool called the Query Design tool. He suggests you try this method out next to practice your use of wildcards.

To search for a product using wildcards using the Query Design tool:

1 Click **Query Design** from the Queries group on the Create tab of the Ribbon.

2 Double-click **Product Table** from the list of tables in the Tables tab of the Show Table window to add the Product table to the query, and then click the **Close** button.

3 Resize the Product Table window so that all fields are visible by clicking and holding the lower right-hand corner of the window and dragging down and to the right.

4 Double-click the **ProductName** and **UnitCost** fields from the Product table shown in the query.

5 Type ***Badfish*** in the criteria section of the query in the Product-Name column of the design grid and then press [Tab], as shown in Figure 11.4.

Figure 11.4

Using Wildcards in a Query

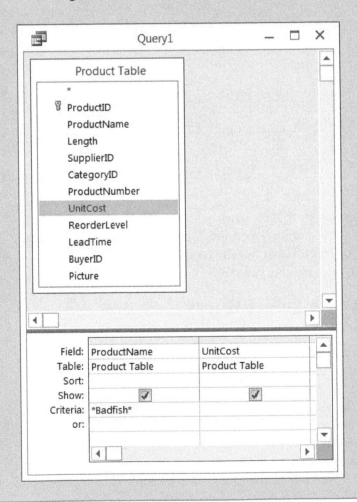

6 Click **Run** from the Results group in the Design tab of the Ribbon. The resulting Datasheet view of the query should look like the query solution in Figure 11.5.

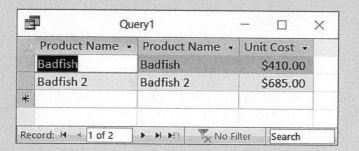

Figure 11.5

Results of Wildcard Query

7 Click the **Home** tab of the Ribbon; click **View** and then click **Design View**. Note that the Criteria has changed to Like "*Badfish*", which is the proper syntax to be used when searching in a query.

8 Click the **Save** icon on the Quick Access Toolbar.

9 Type **Product Query 2** in the Save As text box and then click **OK**.

10 Close the query and then click the **Home** tab.

"That's all well and good," Meagan says. "But what if I wanted to add more fields to my query solution?"

"Good question," Kyle responds. "It's easy to change your existing query, but you'll notice that Access has saved your query in a slightly different form from how you created it."

Editing a Select Query

Once you've saved a query, it can be re-run any number of times. For instance, Product Query 1—which looked up a particular product number from the database—could be run again for the same or a different product number. Product Query 2 could be run again using the same criteria but asking for different fields of information.

Kyle suggests you demonstrate the query editing features of Access by modifying Product Query 1 to look up a different product number (LGR29) and adding the buyer's name to the result. He also suggests you modify Product Query 2 to look up all product names containing the word "earrings" and adding the category name to the result.

To edit existing queries:

1 Right-click **Product Query 1** from the Query listing and then select **Design View** from the shortcut menu.

Trouble? You may have to resize the query window, tables, and so forth in order to view all the information. To do this, place the cursor over the edges you wish to resize.

2   Click **Show Table** from the Query Setup group on the Design tab of the Ribbon.

3   Double-click **Buyers Table** and then close the Show Table window.

4   Move the table windows around so that all fields and tables are viewable.

5   Double-click the **BuyerName** field from the Buyers table shown in the query to add that field to your query.

6   Type **234** in the criteria section of the query in the Product Number column replacing the previous value as shown in Figure 11.6.

Trouble? Before typing the new criteria specified for this query, note that the previous product number has automatically been placed in quotes. You don't need to type the quotes in before making this query, but Access knows that quotes are needed for future instances of the query.

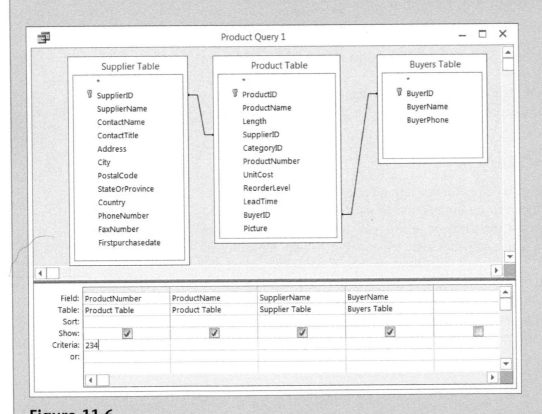

Figure 11.6

Editing Product Query 1

7   Run the query. The resulting Datasheet view of the query should look like the query solution in Figure 11.7.

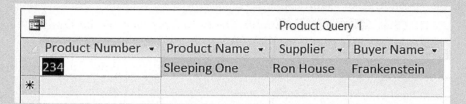

Product Number ▼	Product Name ▼	Supplier ▼	Buyer Name ▼
234	Sleeping One	Ron House	Frankenstein
*			

Product Query 1

Figure 11.7

Results of the Newly Modified Product Query 1

8   Click the **File** tab, then click **Save As**, then click **Save Object As**, and then click the **Save As** button.

9   Type **Product Query 3** as the new name and then click **OK**.

10   Close the query and then click the **Home** tab.

11   Right-click **Product Query 2** from the Query listing and then select **Design View** from the shortcut menu.

12   Click **Show Table** from the Query Setup group on the Design tab of the Ribbon.

13   Double-click **Category Table** and then close the Show Table window.

14   If needed, move the table windows around so that all fields and tables are viewable.

15   Double-click the **CategoryName** field from the Category table shown in the query.

16   Select **Like "*Badfish*"** from the Criteria row of the ProductName column and press the [**Backspace**] key to delete this criteria. Then type **Race** in the Criteria row of the CategoryName column as shown in Figure 11.8.

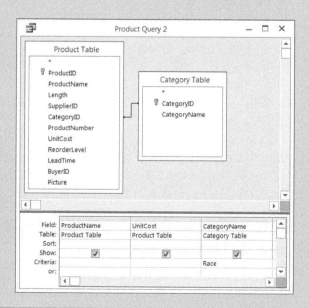

Figure 11.8

Editing Product Query 2

17 Run the query. Close the query and then click the **Home** tab. The resulting Datasheet view of the query should look like the query solution in Figure 11.9.

Figure 11.9

Results of the Newly Edited Product Query 2

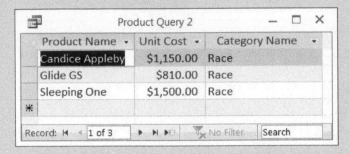

18 Click the **File** tab, click **Save As**, then click **Save Object As**, and then click the **Save As** button.

19 Type **Product Query 4** as the new name and then click **OK**.

20 Close the query and then click the **Home** tab.

"How do we delete fields from a query?" Meagan asks.

"Let me show you by removing the UnitCost field from the Product Query 4 we just created," Kyle answers.

To delete a field from a query:

1 Double-click **Product Query 4** to reopen the query you just worked on.

2 Click **View** and then click **Design View**.

3 Click the top of the UnitCost field column until it is selected (turns black).

4 Press the [**Delete**] key. Note that the UnitCost field column is removed.

5 Close Product Query 4 but do not save changes.

"I'm impressed!" exclaims Meagan. "This query stuff isn't so difficult; in fact, it's rather intuitive."

Kyle continues with his explanation of queries by showing additional examples of the query process. So far he has used characters in his queries. Now it is time to demonstrate the use of numbers in queries and show how comparison operators can be used in a select query.

Using Comparison Operators and Sorting in a Select Query

Kyle asks if you would like to track items you're running short of or items that you need to place on sale. Prior to creating a query to do this, you'll need to add quantify as a field to the Product Table and then add values to that field for all products.

He suggests you create a select query to find all inventory items for which quantity balances are running low (less than or equal to two items, for instance). To do so, Kyle explains that you simply modify your criteria to include comparison operators like the < symbol, which signifies "less than". He cautions you, however, that the less-than symbol, just like the greater-than symbol (>), is not inclusive of the number specified. Thus, in order to generate a query that selects those records for which inventory quantities are less than or equal to a certain number, you must include both the < and the = symbols.

To add a quantity field and values and select records for which inventory quantities are less than or equal to 2:

1 Using what you learned in the previous chapter on tables, add a new field Quantity to the Product Table as a Date Type Number. Then enter quantity values as follows for each ProductID:

Product ID	Quantity
101	2
102	3
103	3
104	4
105	1
106	0
108	4
109	1
110	5
111	2
113	12
114	15
115	4
116	5

Then close the Product Table.

2 Click **Query Design** from the Queries group on the Create tab of the Ribbon.

3 Double-click **Product Table** from the list of tables in the Tables tab of the Show Table window to add the Product table to the query; then click the **Close** button.

4 Resize the Product Table window so that all fields are visible.

5 Double-click **Product Name** and **Quantity** fields for this query.

6 Type **<=2** in the criteria row of the Quantity field of the design grid.

7 Click **Run** from the Results group in the Design tab of the Ribbon. Your results should look like Figure 11.10.

8 Click **File**, **Save As**, **Save Object As**, and **Save As** to save this new object as you've done before.

9 Type **Product Query 5** as the new name and then click **OK**.

10 Close the query and then click the **Home** tab.

Figure 11.10

Query Results for Products with a Quantity of 2 or Less

"Wouldn't you get the same results if you set the criteria as <2?" Nathan asks. "No, you wouldn't," responds Kyle. "Let me demonstrate."

To select records with criteria of <2:

1 Right-click **Product Query 5** and then click **Design View**.

2 Type **<2** in the criteria row of the Quantity field of the design grid, replacing the <=2.

3 Click **Run** from the Results group in the Design tab of the Ribbon. Your results should look like Figure 11.11.

Figure 11.11

Query Results for Products with a Quantity of Less Than 2

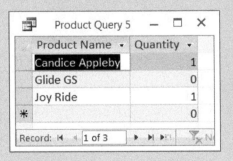

4 Close the query but do not save changes.

Kyle compares the two query results to demonstrate to Nathan the differences. He explains that the equal sign was important so that all records with a quantity of two or fewer were selected.

"What other comparison operators are available in Access?" asks Meagan.

Kyle responds that, in addition to the < and = symbols, Access allows you to select records using any combination of <, =, or >. For instance, you could ask for records in which the price was between $500 and $1,000 by using the < and > symbols together. Or you could not use the symbols and simply ask for the records in which the unit cost was between 500 and 1000.

"Could we also sort the results from lowest to highest cost?" asks Meagan.

"Yes," Kyle answers. "Access queries allow for sorting the results in either ascending or descending order.

To select records with a cost between $500 and $1,000 and sort the results:

1 Click **Query Design** from the Queries group on the Create tab of the Ribbon.

2 Double-click **Product Table** from the list of tables in the Tables tab of the Show Table window to add the Product table to the query, and then click the **Close** button.

3 Resize the Product Table window so that all fields are visible.

4 Double-click **Product Name** and **UnitCost** fields for this query.

5 Type **>500 And <1000** in the criteria row of the UnitCost field of the design grid.

6 Click **Ascending** from the drop-down menu in the Sort cell of the UnitPrice field, as shown in Figure 11.12.

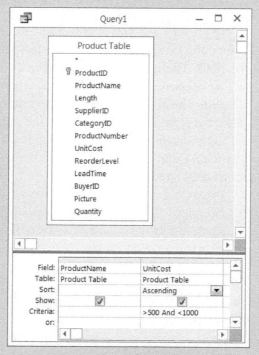

Figure 11.12

Design View for Comparison Query

7 Click **Run** from the Results group in the Design tab of the Ribbon. Your results should look like Figure 11.13.

8 Return to the Design View and type **Between 500 And 1000** in the criteria row of the UnitCost field.

9 Run the query again. Your results will be slightly different since the concept of Between is inclusive of 500 and 1000, whereas >500 AND <1000 is exclusive of 500 and 1000.

Figure 11.13

Results of Unit Price Query

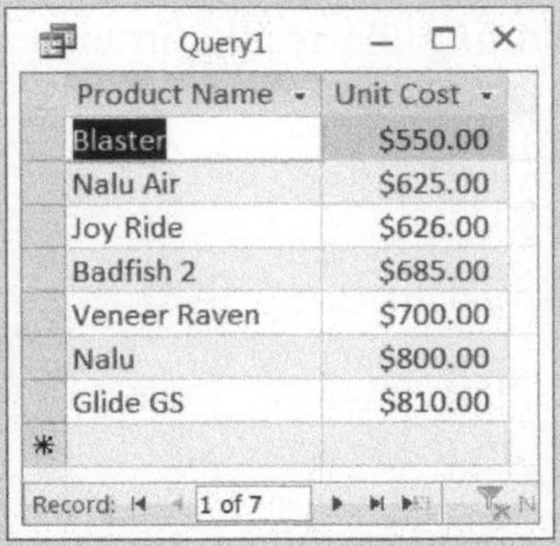

Product Name	Unit Cost
Blaster	$550.00
Nalu Air	$625.00
Joy Ride	$626.00
Badfish 2	$685.00
Veneer Raven	$700.00
Nalu	$800.00
Glide GS	$810.00

Record: 1 of 7

10 Click **File**, **Save As**, **Save Object As**, and **Save As** to save this new object as you've done before.

11 Type **Product Query 6** as the new name and then click **OK**.

12 Close the Query window.

Kyle explains that so far you've specified criteria for only one field. Access allows you to specify criteria for more than one field using specific or comparison operators.

Using Compound Criteria and Limiting Output in a Select Query

Compound criteria allow you to select records from a database using more than one field. These criteria can be applied to require that all criteria be met or they can be applied such that only one criterion need to be met before a record is selected. The field upon which the criteria are applied must be included in the query but need not be included in the output.

"Let's create a query that includes product name and unit cost for all products with a unit cost greater than $500 and a buyer ID of 1 or 3 sorted by product name," suggests Kyle.

"Do we have to include the Buyers table in this query?" Meagan asks.

"No, since the buyer ID is a part of the Product table, it won't be necessary to include the Buyers table," answers Kyle.

To create a query that includes product name and unit price for all products with a unit cost greater than $500 and a buyer ID of 1 or 3:

1 Click **Query Design** from the Queries group on the Create tab of the Ribbon.

2 Double-click **Product Table** from the list of tables in the Tables tab of the Show Table window to add the Product table to the query, and then click the **Close** button.

3 Resize the Product Table window so that all fields are visible.

4 Double-click **ProductName**, **UnitCost**, and **BuyerID** fields for this query.

5 Type **>500** in the criteria row of the UnitCost field of the design grid.

6 Type **602 Or 603** in the criteria row of the Buyer ID field of the design grid.

7 Click **Ascending** from the drop-down menu in the Sort cell of the Product Name field. Your screen should look like Figure 11.14.

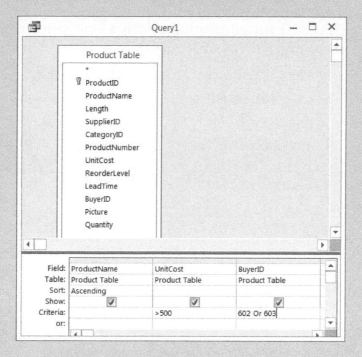

Figure 11.14

Query Design of Products with Unit Cost Greater than $500 *and* Purchased by Buyer 602 or 603

8 Run the query. Your results should look like Figure 11.15.

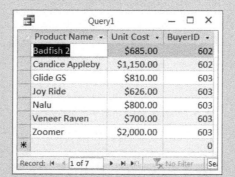

Figure 11.15

Query Results for Products with Unit Cost Greater than $500 *and* Purchased by Buyer 602 or 603

9 Click **File**, **Save As**, **Save Object As**, and **Save As** to save this new object as you've done before.

10 Type **Product Query 7** as the new name and then click **OK**.

As an alternative Kyle explains that the criteria specified on multiple fields can require that all records satisfy all criteria or that the criteria specified on multiple fields satisfy one or more criteria. For example, the previous query asked for all records in which the unit cost was greater than $500 *and* for which the buyer was 602 or 603. Another query might ask for all records in which the unit cost was greater than $500 *or* for which the buyer was 602 or 603. These variations, as you will see, yield different results.

To create a query that includes product name, unit price, and buyer ID for all products with a unit price greater than $500 or a buyer ID of 602 or 603:

1 Right-click **Product Query 7** and then click **Design View**.

2 Click **602 Or 603** from the <u>Criteria: row</u> of the Buyer ID field and then press the [**Delete**] key.

3 Type **602 Or 603** in the <u>or: row</u> of the Buyer ID field, as shown in Figure 11.16.

Figure 11.16

Query Design of Products with Unit Cost Greater than $500 *or* Purchased by Buyer 602 or 603

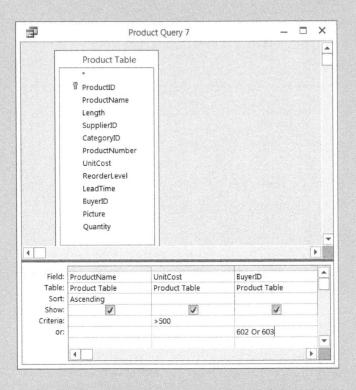

4 Run the query. Your results should look like Figure 11.17. Note that in this query, the first product listed has a unit cost less than 500 but is listed since it had a BuyerID that matched the criteria in the query.

5 Click **File**, **Save As**, **Save Object As**, and **Save As** to save this new object as you've done before.

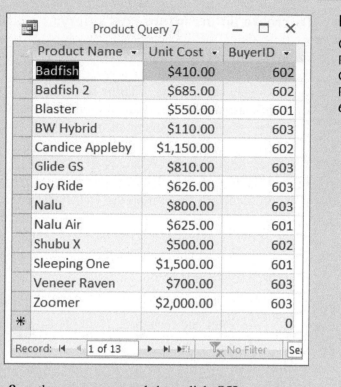

Figure 11.17

Query Results for Products with Unit Cost Greater than $500 *or* Purchased by Buyer 602 or 603

6 Type **Product Query 8** as the new name and then click **OK**.

7 Close this query.

Performing Calculations

Kyle remarks that there are many types of calculations you can perform in a query. For example, you can calculate the sum or average of the values in one field, multiply the values in two fields, or calculate the date three months from the current date. When you display the results of a calculation in a field, the results aren't actually stored in the underlying table. Instead, Microsoft Access reruns the calculation each time you run the query so that the results are always based on the most current information in the database.

Displaying the Results of Calculations in a Field

To demonstrate the use of computations and the creation of a computed field, Kyle suggests that you and Nathan create a query that calculates the total cost of each item in inventory. He explains that to begin you'll need to create a query that includes the field's product name, quantity, and unit cost. Then you'll need to create a computed field to calculate the product of the quantity and the unit cost fields. In order to create a computed field, you'll need to type the name of the newly created field in a blank field row followed by the two fields used to compute total cost. Each field used must be surrounded by brackets, as with [Quantity]. After you've created the computed field, you'll often need to format the field to a number or currency depending on how you want it displayed.

To create an inventory cost query:

1 Click **Query Design** from the Queries group on the Create tab of the Ribbon.

2 Double-click **Product Table** from the list of tables in the Tables tab of the Show Table window to add the Product table to the query, and then click the **Close** button.

3 Resize the Product Table window so that all fields are visible.

4 Double-click **ProductName**, **Quantity**, and **UnitCost** fields for this query.

5 In the fourth column on the Field row of the design grid, type **TotalCost: [Quantity]*[UnitCost]**. (In this case TotalCost is the name of the new field and [Quantity] and [UnitCost] are the two fields being used to calculate the value for the newly created TotalCost field.

6 Right-click the newly created **TotalCost** field and then click **Zoom** to enlarge the formula.

7 Click **Font** and then click **16** in the Size column; then click **OK** to make the Zoom window text increase in size. Your Zoom window should look like Figure 11.18.

Figure 11.18

Creating a Calculated Field

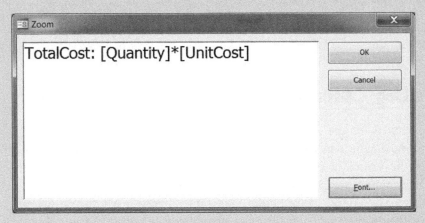

8 Click **OK** to close the Zoom window after you verify its contents.

9 Right-click the **TotalCost** field again and then click **Properties**, which takes you to the Property Sheet window.

10 Click in the text box next to Format and then select **Currency** from the drop-down list of formats; then type **Total Cost** as the Caption, and then close the Property Sheet window.

11 Run the query to yield the results shown in Figure 11.19.

12 Click **File**, **Save As**, **Save Object As**, and **Save As** to save this new object as you've done before.

13 Type **Product Query 9** as the name of the new query and then click **OK**.

14 Close the query.

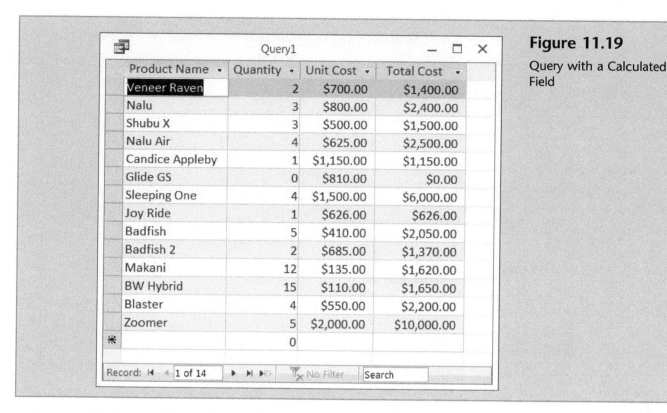

Figure 11.19

Query with a Calculated Field

Once again, the resulting value established in the Cost field is there only temporarily and cannot be used in a later report or form unless this query is run as well. In addition to creating a computed field, Access will allow you to perform statistics and summations from within a query.

Computing Statistics

Access will allow you to calculate various statistical measures of your database, including (for example) sum, average, maximum, and minimum.

"What if I needed to know my total inventory cost?" asks Nathan.

"No problem," Kyle responds. "Access has a sum function that will work on the cost variable we just created. All we need to do is turn on the sum function and then create a sum query using the cost field we defined. To do so, we must select the query we just created instead of an existing table."

To create a sum query:

1 Click **Query Design** from the Queries group on the Create tab of the Ribbon.

2 Double-click **Product Query 9** from the list of queries in the Queries tab of the Show Table window then click the **Close** button.

3 If necessary resize the Product Query 9 window so that all fields are visible.

4 Double-click **TotalCost**.

5 Click **Totals** from the Show/Hide group of the Design tab on the Ribbon.

6 Click **Sum** from the drop-down list in the Total row, as shown in Figure 11.20.

Figure 11.20

Creating a Sum Query

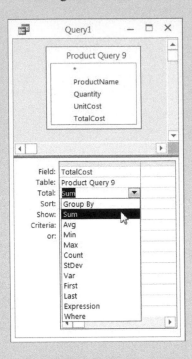

7 Run the query to generate a summation of all inventory cost, as shown in Figure 11.21.

Figure 11.21

Sum Of Inventory Cost Query

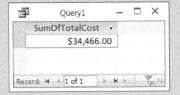

8 Click **File**, **Save As**, **Save Object As**, and **Save As** to save this new object as you've done before.

9 Type **Product Query 10** as the name of the new query and then click **OK**.

10 Close the query.

"Is there any way to find the total cost of inventory by category?" asks Nathan.

"Yes," Kyle answers. "Access uses the concept of grouping to provide statistical information on a database."

Kyle goes on to explain that, since the field he summed previously was a calculated field, it is imperative that the category field be a part of that query before a sum query is run. He suggests that you edit the inventory cost query to include the category field before modifying the inventory cost summary query you just created.

To create a sum query by category:

1 Right-click **Product Query 9** and then click **Design view** from the shortcut menu.

2 Click **Show Table** from the Query Setup group on the Design tab of the Ribbon.

3 Double-click **Category Table** and then close the Show Table window.

4 Double-click the **Category Name** field to add it to the query.

5 Close and save the revised query.

6 Right-click **Product Query 10** and then click **Design view** from the shortcut menu.

7 Click and drag the **Category Name** field to the left of the Cost field, as shown in Figure 11.22.

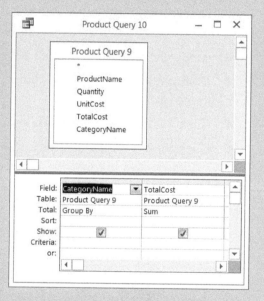

Figure 11.22

Modifying a Query to Group Totals by Category

8 Run the query to generate a summation of all inventory cost by category, as shown in Figure 11.23.

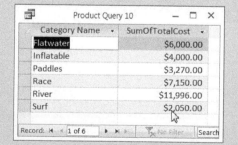

Figure 11.23

Results of a Query to Group Totals by Category

9 Click **File**, **Save As**, **Save Object As**, and **Save As** to save this new object as you've done before.

10 Type **Product Query 11** as the name of the new query and then click **OK**.

11 Close the query.

"That's great information," says Nathan. "Is there a way to find out how many Flatwater, Inflatable, et cetera, we have on hand or how many different products we have in each category?"

"Sure," responds Kyle. "We can use the sum feature again to sum up the quantity of each category and the count feature to count the number of products we have by category."

Kyle explains that the sum feature in this case can be used on the product and category tables because the information we want to display and sum is found in the tables and not in any particular query. Likewise, the count feature is used on the same two tables. He recommends that you and Meagan give it a try.

To create a sum query of quantities by category:

1 Click **Query Design** from the Queries group on the Create tab of the Ribbon.

2 Double-click **Category Table** and **Product Table** from the list of tables in the Tables tab of the Show Table window then click the **Close** button.

3 Resize the window so that all fields are visible.

4 Double-click the **Category Name** and the **Quantity** fields to add them to the query.

5 Click **Totals** from the Show/Hide group of the Design tab on the Ribbon.

6 Click **Sum** from the drop-down list in the Total row of the Quantity field as shown in Figure 11.24.

Figure 11.24

Design View of Query to Sum Quantities by Category

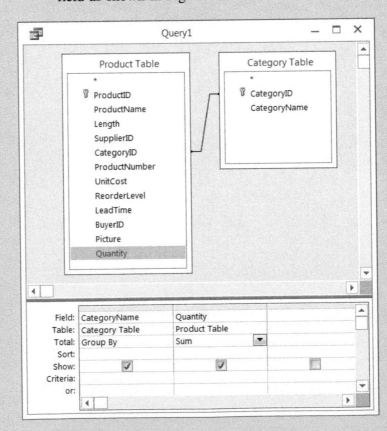

7 Run the query to generate a summation of all quantities by category, as shown in Figure 11.25.

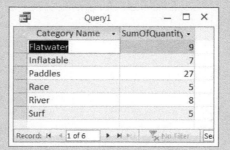

Figure 11.25

Results of a Query to Group Quantities by Category

8 Click **File, Save As, Save Object As**, and **Save As** to save this new object as you've done before.

9 Type **Product Query 13** as the name of the new query and then click **OK**.

10 Close the query.

"That was fairly easy," Meagan says. "Let's let Nathan see if he can create the count query."

To create a query to count the number of products by category:

1 Click **Query Design** from the Queries group on the Create tab of the Ribbon.

2 Double-click **Category Table** and **Product Table** from the list of tables in the Tables tab of the Show Table window; then click the **Close** button.

3 Resize the window so that all fields are visible.

4 Double-click the **CategoryName** and the **ProductName** fields to add them to the query.

5 Click **Totals** from the Show/Hide group of the Design tab on the Ribbon.

6 Click **Count** from the drop-down list in the Total row of the Product-Name field as shown in Figure 11.26.

7 Run the query to generate a count of all products by category, as shown in Figure 11.27.

8 Click **File, Save As, Save Object As**, and **Save As** to save this new object as you've done before.

9 Type **Product Query 12** as the name of the new query and then click **OK**.

10 Close the query.

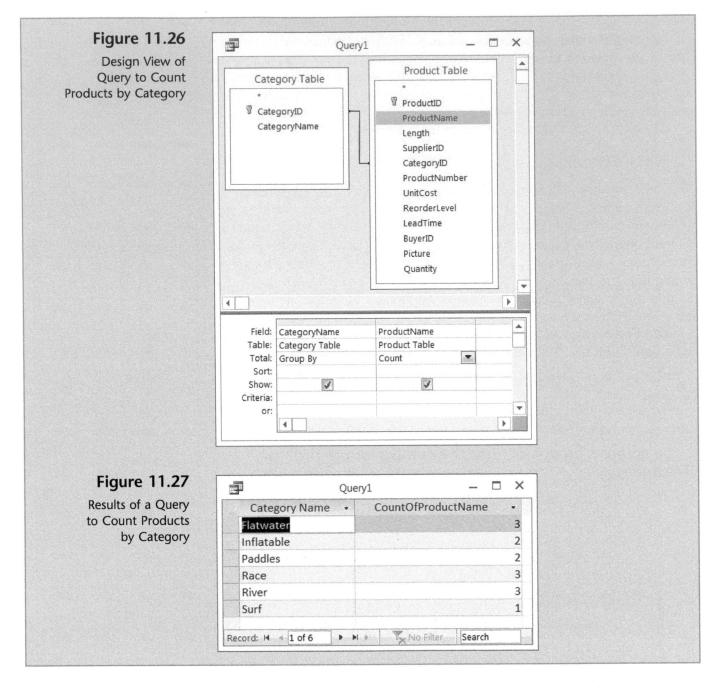

Figure 11.26

Design View of
Query to Count
Products by Category

Figure 11.27

Results of a Query
to Count Products
by Category

Next Kyle will explain the process of using action queries to affect many records at one time.

Action Queries (Update, Parameter, and Delete)

An action query is a query that makes changes to many records in just one operation. There are three types of action queries that Kyle would like to explain: update, parameter, and delete. An *update query* makes global changes to a group of records in one or more tables. For example, you can raise costs or sales prices by 10 percent for all products, or you can raise salaries by 5 percent for the people within a certain job category. With an update query, you can change data in existing tables. A *parameter query* is a query that, when run, displays its own dialog box prompting you for information—such as criteria for retrieving records or a value you want to insert in a field. A *delete query* removes a group of records from one or more tables. With delete queries, you always delete entire records, not just selected fields within records.

Update Queries

First, Nathan realizes that his database has a unit cost field for all products but it doesn't contain a unit price field. The unit cost field represents what he pays to his suppliers. A unit price would represent the unit price he charges each customer. Thus he needs to add a unit price field to the Product Table that is based on prices in effect at the beginning of the year. Later he decides to use an update query to increase the price of all products by 5 percent. To do so he'll need to use an update query that includes the Product Table and the newly created field UnitPrice. You should always back up your database before you run an update query, because you cannot undo the results of an update query. Making a backup ensures that you can always reverse your changes.

To add a unit price field and related unit prices to the Product Table:

1 Right-click **Product Table** and select **Design View**.

2 Type **UnitPrice** as the name of a new field.

3 Select Data Type **Number** for the new field.

4 Select **Currency** as the Format and type **Unit Price** as the Caption.

5 Click the **Home** tab of the Ribbon; click **View**, click **Design View** and then click **Yes** to save the table.

6 Add the following unit prices to each product:

ProductID	UnitPrice
101	1425
102	1625
103	1100
104	1250
105	2300
106	1700
108	3100
109	1200
110	850
111	1500
113	200
114	210
115	1000
116	3000

To back up a database and then create an update query to increase the price of all products by 5 percent:

1   Click the **File** tab.

2   Click **Save As**, then click **Save Database As**, then click **Backup Database**, and then click **Save As**.

3   Accept the file name provided, which should read Ch11-01_student_ name followed by today's date.

4   Navigate the window to the location where you want to save your backup file, and then click **Save**.

5   Click **Query Design** from the Queries group on the Create tab of the Ribbon.

6   Double-click **Product Table** from the list of tables in the Tables tab of the Show Table window; then click the **Close** button.

7   Resize the window so that all fields are visible.

8   Double-click **UnitPrice** to add it to the query.

9   Click **Update** from the Query Type group of the Design tab of the Ribbon.

10 Type **[UnitPrice]*1.05** in the Update To: row of the design grid, as shown in Figure 11.28.

Figure 11.28

Update Query

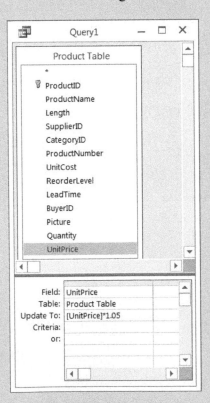

11 Run the query and then click **Yes** to update 14 records.

Trouble? Do not run this query again. Since the query as written takes a current value and increases it 5 percent, if you were to run it again, it would take the new value and increase it 5 percent again. To verify your query ran correctly and only one time, check to see if ProductID 101 has a new unit price of $1,496.00.

12 Click **File, Save As, Save Object As**, and **Save As** to save this new object as you've done before.

13 Type **Product Query 14** as the name of the new query and then click **OK**.

14 Close the query.

15 Create and run a new query that displays the Product Name, Unit Cost, and Unit Price for all Flatwater boards. (Hint: Add Flatwater from the Supplier table and uncheck the **Show** button.) Your query should look like Figure 11.29.

Product Name	Unit Cost	Unit Price
Veneer Raven	$700.00	$1,496.00
Nalu	$800.00	$1,706.00
Blaster	$550.00	$1,050.00

Figure 11.29

Listing of Flatwater Boards with Unit Costs and Unit Prices

16 Click **File, Save As, Save Object As**, and **Save As** to save this new object as you've done before.

17 Type **Product Query 14A** as the name of the new query, click **OK**, and then close the query.

"Very slick and efficient!" says Meagan. "This software will be very helpful for us in maintaining our inventory. But do we always have to update all records, or can we limit an update to just a few records?"

"You can limit your update by setting criteria for the update, just as with a select query," Kyle answers. "Let's have you update all records that have a reorder level of 2 to reflect a new reorder level of 4."

To create an update query to update reorder levels:

1 Create a back up file and then click **Query Design** from the Queries group on the Create tab of the Ribbon.

2 Double-click **Product Table** from the list of tables in the Tables tab of the Show Table window; then click the **Close** button.

3 Resize the window so that all fields are visible.

4 Double-click **Product Name** and **Reorder Level** to add the fields to the query.

5 Run the query to view a listing of all products and their reorder level, as shown in Figure 11.30.

Figure 11.30

Products and Reorder
Level

Product Name	Reorder Level
Veneer Raven	5
Nalu	2
Shubu X	2
Nalu Air	2
Candice Appleby	3
Glide GS	1
Sleeping One	2
Joy Ride	2
Badfish	2
Badfish 2	3
Makani	10
BW Hybrid	20
Blaster	2
Zoomer	3

Record: ◄ ◄ 1 of 14 ► ►l ►❉   No Fi

6 Click **File, Save As, Save Object As,** and **Save As** to save this new object as you've done before.

7 Type **Product Query 15** as the name of the new query and then click **OK**.

8 Close the query.

9 Click **Query Design** from the Queries group on the Create tab of the Ribbon.

10 Double-click **Product Table** from the list of tables in the Tables tab of the Show Table window, and then click the **Close** button.

11 Resize the window so that all fields are visible.

12 Double-click the **ReorderLevel** to add it to the query.

13 Click **Update** from the Query Type group of the Design tab of the Ribbon.

14 Type **4** in the Update To: row and then type **=2** in the Criteria row of the design grid as shown in Figure 11.31.

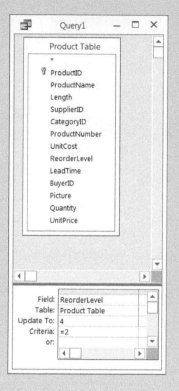

Figure 11.31

Update Query to Change ReorderLevel

15 Run the query and then click **Yes** to update 7 records.

16 Click **File, Save As, Save Object As,** and **Save As** to save this new object as you've done before.

17 Type **Product Query 16** as the name of the new query and then click **OK**.

18 Close the query.

19 Double-click **Product Query 15** to see the new reorder level for all affected products, as shown in Figure 11.32.

20 Compare Figure 11.32 with Figure 11.30 and note that all products that previously had a recorder level of 2 now have a reorder level of 4.

21 Close the query.

Figure 11.32

New Reorder Levels for
All Products

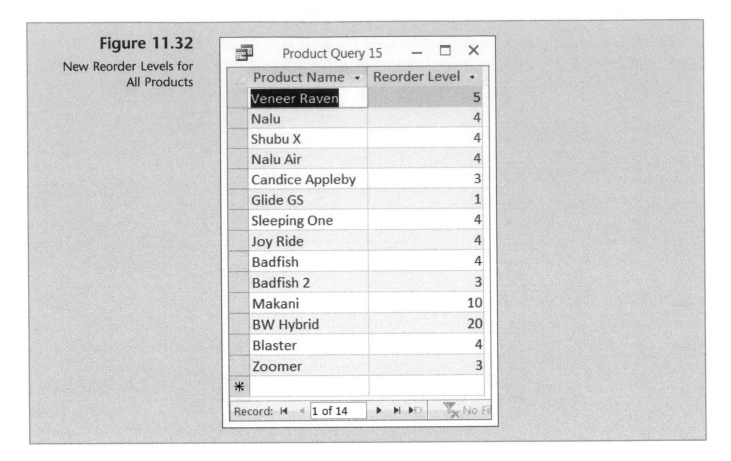

Parameter Queries

Another type of action query is the parameter query, in which the query prompts the user with a dialog box asking for some criteria information to select records.

"When would I want to use this type of query?" Meagan asks.

"These queries," Kyle explains, "are used when you're not sure what criteria the user wants to specify for record selection. They provide flexibility in the query process and will be handy in the future when forms and reports are generated for users who aren't that familiar with Access."

"Let's create a parameter query to provide information on who is responsible for buying each product," suggests Nathan. "Can this query just give us information on one buyer?"

"Yes," responds Kyle. "I suggest you and Meagan create this query now."

To create a parameter query for buyers:

1   Click **Query Design** from the Queries group on the Create tab of the Ribbon.

2 Double-click **Product Table** and **Buyers Table** from the list of tables in the Tables tab of the Show Table window, and then click the **Close** button.

3 Resize the window so that all fields are visible.

4 Double-click the **BuyerName**, **ProductName**, and **Quantity** fields to add them to the query.

5 Type [**Enter Buyer's Name**] in the Criteria: row of the Buyer Name field of the design grid, as shown in Figure 11.33.

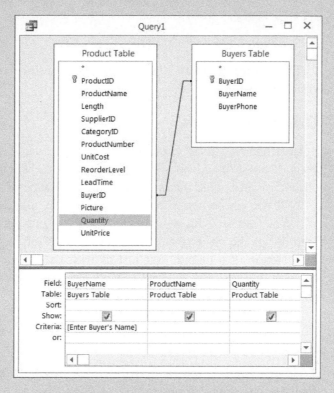

Figure 11.33

Creating a Parameter Query

6 Run the query.

7 Type **Frankenstein** in the Enter Parameter Value dialog box presented, as shown in Figure 11.34.

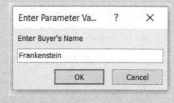

Figure 11.34

Enter Parameter Value Dialog Box

8 Click **OK** to produce the results, as shown in Figure 11.35.

9 Click **File**, **Save As**, **Save Object As**, and **Save As** to save this new object as you've done before.

10 Type **Product Query 17** as the name of the new query and then click **OK**.

Figure 11.35
Products and Quantity for Lopez

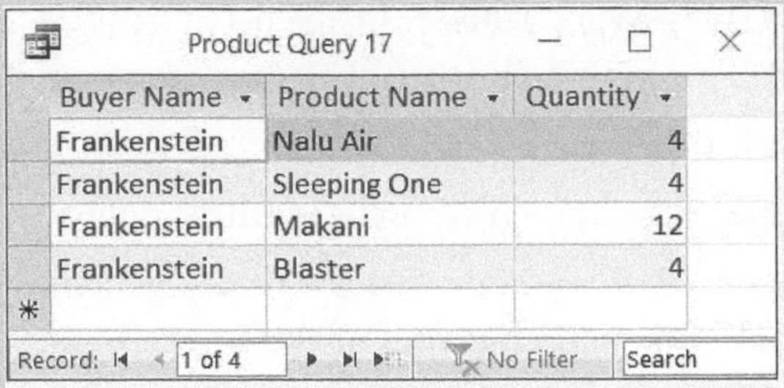
Product Query 17
Buyer Name
Product Name
Quantity
Frankenstein
Nalu Air
4
Frankenstein
Sleeping One
4
Frankenstein
Makani
12
Frankenstein
Blaster
4
Record: 1 of 4
No Filter
Search

11 Close the query.

The last action query Kyle wants to demonstrate deletes specific records from your database.

Delete Queries

"Occasionally," Kyle explains, "you might want to delete some records from your database based on specific criteria. For example, you may want to delete all records in a table that have a quantity balance of zero."

"I'll bet you set the criteria to = 0, right?" asks Meagan.

"Well, almost," Kyle answers. "First you must create a specific delete query, include all the fields from the table, and specify the criteria that must be met for deletion of a record. But just as with the update queries you created previously, it always makes sense to back up your database before making massive changes."

"Let's give it a try," says Nathan.

To back up a database and then create a delete query to delete specific records:

1. Double-click on **Product Table**.
2. Scroll down the table and note that ProductID 106 (Glide GS) has a quantity of 0.
3. Close the Product Table.
4. Create a backup of your database and then click **Query Design** from the Queries group on the Create tab of the Ribbon.
5. Double-click **Product Table** from the list of tables in the Tables tab of the Show Table window; then click the **Close** button.
6. Resize the window so that all fields are visible.

7 Double-click * (asterisk) to add all fields in the product table to the query.

8 Double-click **Quantity**.

9 Click **Delete** from the Query Type group of the Design tab of the Ribbon. Note that "From" appears on the Delete: line of the design grid under the field Product Table.* and that "Where" appears on the Delete: line under Quantity.

10 Type **0** in the Criteria: row of the design grid under the column Quantity, as shown in Figure 11.36.

Figure 11.36
Creating a Delete Query

11 Run the query and then click **Yes** (in the dialog box presented) to delete one record from the Product table.

12 Click **File**, **Save As**, **Save Object As**, and **Save As** to save this new object as you've done before.

13 Type **Product Query 18** as the name of the new query and then click **OK**.

14 Close the query.

15 Double-click **Product Table** and note that there are no more products with a quantity of 0. (Product ID 106 has been removed.)

16 Close the Product table.

Print a Query

All that is left is to print a query. Kyle explains that printing a query is similar to printing a table (as you did in the previous chapter), but he'll review the process anyway.

To print a query:

1 Double-click **Product Query 17** (as an example).

2 Type **Ng** as the Buyer's Name then click **OK**.

3 Click the **File** tab and then click **Print** located under the **File** tab and then click **Print**.

4 Click **OK** to print. The printed query should look like Figure 11.37.

Figure 11.37

Printed Product Query 17

Product Query 17

Buyer Name	Product Name	Quantity
Ng	Shubu X	3
Ng	Candice Appleby	1
Ng	Badfish	5
Ng	Badfish 2	2

End Note

In this chapter you have learned how to use select queries with characters, numbers, wildcards, comparison operators, and compound criteria. You've also performed calculations, computed statistics, created computed fields, and created parameter queries and action queries to update and delete records. In the next chapter you will learn how to create forms.

Chapter 11 Questions

1 Describe the difference between the Query Wizard and Design view methods of creating a query.

2 Describe the process for using criteria in a query using the Design view method.

3 How and why are wildcards used in a query?

4 Describe the process for adding to an existing query a field that exists in a table not currently included in the query.

5 What are the three key comparison operators used in a query?

6 What will compound criteria allow you to accomplish in Access?

7 Are the results of a calculation stored as a field in a table?

8 What is an action query? Give examples.

9 What is a parameter query?

10 When might you use a delete query?

Chapter 11 Assignments

1 Create select queries for What SUP using specific criteria (use the Ch11-02 student file).

    a. Create and print a select query that lists the buyer name, buyer phone number, and product name of product number 234. (*Hint:* The product number should not appear on your printed query if you answered the question correctly.) Save this query as Ch 11 Assignment 1a before you print it.

    b. Create and print a select query that lists the category name, product name, product number, and lead times for all products with a lead time in excess of 7 days sorted by product name. Save this query as Ch 11 Assignment 1b before you print it.

2 Create select queries for What SUP. (Use the Ch11-02 student file, or use the file you used in answering the previous question.)

    a. Create and print a select query that lists the product name, quantity, supplier contact name, and supplier phone number for any Inflatable SUPs. Save this query as Ch 11 Assignment 2a before you print it.

b. Create and print a select query that lists the supplier name, city, and phone number for any supplier located in the state of New York. Save this query as Ch 11 Assignment 2b before you print it.

3 Edit select queries for What SUP. (Use the Ch11-02 student file, or use the file you used in answering the previous question.)

a. Edit Query1 by adding the field PostalCode from the Supplier Table and deleting the field StateorProvince. Save this query as Ch 11 Assignment 3a before you print it.

b. Edit Query2 to include the field Category Name and to include only the category Paddles, sorted by product ID in ascending order. Save this query as Ch 11 Assignment 3b before you print it.

4 Create select queries for What SUP using comparison operators. (Use the Ch11-02 student file, or use the file you used in answering the previous question.)

a. Create and print a select query that lists the product name, unit cost, supplier name, and supplier contact name for any unit cost between $100 and $400, sorted in descending order by unit cost. Save this query as Ch 11 Assignment 4a before you print it.

b. Create and print a select query that lists the product name, unit cost, and category name for any unit cost less than or equal to $500, sorted in ascending order by unit cost. Save this query as Ch 11 Assignment 4b before you print it.

5 Create additional select queries for What SUP using computed fields. (Use the Ch11-02 student file, or use the file you used in answering the previous question.)

a. Create and print a select query that lists the product name unit price, unit cost, and unit gross profit for all products. Sorted in descending order by unit gross profit price. (*Hint:* You'll need to create a computed field titled Unit Gross Profit whose formula is the product's unit price minus unit cost.) Save this query as Ch 11 Assignment 5a before you print it.

b. Create and print a select query that lists the product name, unit price, quantity, and sales value for all paddles. (*Hint:* You'll need to create another computed field, Sales Value, whose formula is the unit price times quantity; format the computed field to Currency using the Property Sheet.) Sort the query by unit price in ascending order. Save this query as Ch 11 Assignment 5b before you print it.

6 Create additional select queries for What SUP using statistics. (Use file you used in answering the previous question.)

a. Create and print a select query that calculates the total sales value of all Flatwater SUPs in inventory. (*Hint:* You'll need to use your completed query from assignment 5b as the source for this query. If you did not complete 5b, do it now. Format this computed field to Currency with two decimal places with a caption Sales Value of all Flatwater SUPs.) Save this query as Ch 11 Assignment 6a before you print it.

b. Create and print a query that includes all products and lists category name, product name, unit price, unit cost, unit gross profit, quantity, and gross profit. To do this, create two computed fields: Unit Gross Profit (unit price less unit cost) and Gross Profit (unit gross profit times quantity). Both calculated fields should have a Currency format and a caption with spaces. Save this query as Ch 11 Assignment 6b before you print it.

c. Next create and print a query that sums the gross profit of each category, using the query just created in assignment 6b as the source. Format this totaled value as Currency with two decimal places and a caption of Gross Profit. Save this query as Ch 11 Assignment 6c before you print it.

7 Create action queries for What SUP. (Use the Ch11-02 student file, or use the file you used in answering the previous question.)

a. Create and run an update query that increases the unit price for all products by 6 percent. Save this query as Ch 11 Assignment 7a. Create and print an additional query listing the product name and unit price after running the update query. Do not save this query.

b. Create a parameter query that lists products purchased from a particular supplier. The query should ask "Enter supplier's name:" and list the supplier name, product name, quantity, and unit cost. Save this query as Ch 11 Assignment 7b. Run and print the query entering Bark as the supplier.

c. Create and run a delete query that deletes all products where Quantity = 0. Save this query as Ch 11 Assignment 7c. Create and print a query listing the supplier ID and product name for all products still in the database.

Chapter 11 Case Problem 1:
KELLY'S BOUTIQUE

Note: You must have completed Case 1 in the previous chapter in order to continue working on this case.

In the last chapter you added and modified some tables for Kelly's Boutique. She would now like you to create, run, and print some select, parameter, and action queries. Make the following changes for Kelly, using the ch10-03_student_name file you created in Chapter 10. (*Note:* Open your ch10-03_student_name file and then save it as ch11-03_student_name before making the indicated changes.)

Add a field Quantity (Data Type = Number) to the Book Table and then enter values as follows:

Book Title	Quantity
Angela's Ashes	18
Betsy - Tacy	4
Blueberries for Sal	5
Caddie Woodlawn	4
Deep End of the Ocean	2
Divine Secrets of the YaYa Sisterhood	3
Green Eggs and Ham	15
Harry Potter and the Chamber of Secrets	10
Harry Potter and the Prisoner of Azkaban	8
Harry Potter and the Sorcerer's Stone	6
Hop on Pop	8
The Rainmaker	10
The Cat in the Hat	4
The Notebook	3

Add a field Markup (Data Type = Number, Field Size = Decimal, Format = Percent, Scale = 2, Decimal Places = 0) to the Dept Table and then enter values as follows:

Dept	Markup
Adult	100%
Children	50%

a. Create and print a select query that lists the author and book title for all books written by Rowling. Save this query as Ch 11 Kelly Case a before you print it.

b. Create and print a select query that lists the book title and author for all books purchased and supervised by Rexford Merlot, sorted in ascending order by book title. Save this query as Ch 11 Kelly Case b before you print it.

c. Create and print a select query that lists the book title and list price for all book titles that start with Harry. Save this query as Ch 11 Kelly Case c before you print it.

d. Edit the query you just created. Add fields for author and for publisher and delete the list price field. Change the criteria from "starting with Harry" to "containing the word Secrets". (*Hint:* Place a wildcard character in front of and behind the word.) Save this query as Ch 11 Kelly Case d before you print it.

e. Create and print a select query that lists the book title and the publisher contact person and phone number for all books with a list price greater than $20. Save this query as Ch 11 Kelly Case e before you print it.

f. Create and print a select query that lists the ISBN, book title, and list price for all books with a list price greater than $17 or less than $9, sorted in ascending order by list price. Save this query as Ch 11 Kelly Case f before you print it.

g. Create and print a select query that lists the book title, list price, quantity, and retail value (a computed field equal to list price multiplied by quantity), sorted in descending order by retail value. Be the field is formatted as Currency. Save this query as Ch 11 Kelly Case g before you print it.

h. Create and print a select query that lists book title, list price, markup, unit cost, quantity, and cost. Unit cost is a computed field (list price divided by 1 plus markup). Cost is another computed field (unit cost times quantity). Be sure to format both computed fields as Currency and to sort the query alphabetically by book title. Save this query as Ch 11 Kelly Case h before you print it.

i. Create and print a select query that sums the total cost of the book inventory. (*Hint:* Use the query just created in part h as your source for this new query and use the currency format.) Save this query as Ch 11 Kelly Case i before you print it.

j. Modify the query created in part h so that it includes the Department field. Save the query as Ch 11 Kelly Case h 1, and then use that modified query as the source for a query that sums the cost of inventory by department. Save this latter query as Ch 11 Kelly Case j before you print it.

k. Create and run an update query that increases all books' list price by 5 percent. Be sure to back up your file first! Save this query as Ch 11 Kelly Case k. Create another query that lists the book title and list price for all books, sorted alphabetically by book title. Save this query as Ch 11 Kelly Case k 1 and then print it.

l. Create a parameter query that lists books from a particular publisher. The query should ask "Enter publisher's name:" and then list the publisher, book title, and quantity for that publisher. Save this query as Ch 11 Kelly Case l. Run and print the query after entering "Harper Collins" as the publisher.

m. Create and run a delete query that deletes all products with a quantity of 0. Save this query as Ch 11 Kelly Case m.

n. Create a query listing the book title and quantity for all the remaining books in inventory, sorted by quantity in descending order. Save this query as Ch 11 Kelly Case n and then print it.

o. Make sure you keep a copy of this file for use in the next chapter.

Chapter 11 Case Problem 2:

WINE DEPOT

Note: You must have completed Case 2 in the previous chapter in order to continue working on this case.

In the last chapter you modified some tables for the Wine Depot. Now Barbara would like you to help her create some queries to extract some information from the database. Make the following changes for Barbara using the ch10-04_student_name file you created in Chapter 10. (*Note:* Open your ch10-04_student_name file and then save it as ch11-04_student_name before making the indicated changes.)

a. Create a select query that lists the SKU, type, winery, and price for all wines on hand from winery #20. Save this query as Ch 11 Wine Depot Case a and then print it.

b. Create a select query that lists the SKU, type, winery name, and price for all wines whose buyer name is David Bowie. Save this query as Ch 11 Wine Depot Case b and then print it.

c. Create a select query that lists the SKU and type for wines types that contain the word "Blanc". Save this query as Ch 11 Wine Depot Case c and then print it.

d. Edit the query you just created in 2c above. Add fields for cost and vintage and remove the SKU field. Change the criteria of the query from "types that include the word Blanc" to "types that begin with the letter C". Save this query as Ch 11 Wine Depot Case d and then print it.

e. Create a select query that lists type, price, winery name, buyer name, and phone number for all wines with a price greater than $40. Save this query as Ch 11 Wine Depot Case e and then print it.

f. Create a select query that lists type, price, winery name, buyer name, and phone number for all wines with a price greater than $40 but less than $75. Save this query as Ch 11 Wine Depot Case f and then print it.

g. Create a select query that lists SKU, type, winery name, price, quantity, and retail value (a computed field: quantity times price, formatted as currency) for all Merlot wines, sorted in descending order by retail value. Save this query as Ch 11 Wine Depot Case g and then print it.

h. Create an update query that changes the price of all wines to be 200% of cost. (Remember to back up your file first.) Save this query as Ch 11 Wine Depot Case h. Sort the Wine Products table by SKU from smallest to largest and then print the table.

i. Create a parameter query that lists SKU, type, winery name, and price. The query should ask "What type of wine?" Sort the query in descending order by price. Save this query as Ch 11 Wine Depot Case i. Run the query for Chardonnay wines and then print it.

j. Create a select query that sums the total retail value of the Merlot wine inventory, formatted as currency. Be sure to list the wine type in your query. (*Hint:* Use the Ch 11 Wine Depot Case g query you created previously as the source for this new query.) Save this query as Ch 11 Wine Depot Case j and then print it.

k. Create a select query that lists SKU, type, winery name, cost, quantity, and total cost (a computed field: quantity times cost, formatted as currency) for all wines, sorted in ascending order by SKU. Save this query as Ch 11 Wine Depot Case k and then print it.

l. Create a select query that sums the cost of wine inventory by type (in currency format), sorted by type. (*Hint:* Use the Ch 11 Wine Depot Case k query as the source for your new query.) Save the new query as Ch 11 Wine Depot Case l and then print it.

m. Make sure you keep a copy of this file for use in the next chapter.

Chapter 11 Case Problem 3:
SNICK'S BOARD SHOP

Note: You must have completed Case 3 in the previous chapter in order to continue working on this case.

In the last chapter you modified some tables for the Snick's Board Shop. Now Caitlin would like you to help her create some queries to extract information from the database. Make the following changes for Caitlin, using the ch10-05_student_name file you created in Chapter 10. (*Note:* Open your ch10-05_student_name file and then save it as ch11-05_student_name before making the indicated changes.)

a. Create a select query that lists the category name, manufacturer name, product name, and price for all products from Manufacturer ID BPR. Save this query as Query A and then print it.

b. Create a select query that lists the manufacturer name, product name, and price for all products with a Category ID of 5. Save this query as Query B and then print it.

c. Create a select query that lists the product ID, category name, and style for styles that contain the word "Blue". Save this query as Query C and then print it.

d. Edit the query you just created in the previous step. Add the manufacturer name field and remove the category name field. Change the criteria of the query from styles that contain the word "Blue" to styles that contain the word "White". Save this query as Query D and then print it.

e. Create a select query that lists product name, price, and quantity for all products with a price greater than $125. Save this query as Query E and then print it.

f. Create a select query that lists product name, price, and quantity for all products with a price greater than $125 but less than $150. Save this query as Query F and then print it.

g. Add a number field "Discount" to the Manufacturer table. Set the field size of this new field to Single and the Format to Percent. Set the Discount to 15% for manufacturers EMT, GC, and MOJ. All other manufacturers discount should be set to 0%. Create a select query that lists Product ID, Price, and Discounted Price (a new computed field: Price times 1 - Discount, formatted as currency) for all products sorted in ascending order by Discounted Price. Save this query as Query G and then print it.

h. Create an update query that increases the price of all products by 20%. (Remember to back up your file first.) Save this query as Query H. Open Query G again and then print it with the new prices.

i. Create a parameter query that lists the manufacturer name, product name, price, style, and quantity. The query should state "Enter Manufacturer ID". Sort the query in ascending order by product name. Save this query as Query I. Run the query for Manufacturer ID BPR and then print it.

j. Create a select query that sums the total retail value of CategoryID 5 items in inventory, formatted as currency. (*Hint:* First create a query with the fields CategoryID, CategoryName, Price, Quantity, and a computed field titled Retail Value, which is the price times quantity.) Save and print this query as Query J – 1, and then create the summation query. Save this query as Query J - 2 and then print it.

k. Create a select query that sums the retail value of all products by category (in currency format), sorted by type. (*Hint:* Use the Query J - 1 query, modify it by removing the criteria, then print and save it as Query K – 1, using Query K – 1 as the source for your new query.) Your new query should have two fields: CategoryName and SumOfRetailValue. Save the new query as Query K - 2 and then print it.

l. Make sure you keep a copy of this file for use in the next chapter.

Chapter 11 Case Problem 4:
ROSEY'S ROSES

Note: You must have completed Case 4 in the previous chapter in order to continue working on this case. In the last chapter, you modified some tables for Rosey's Roses. Now the company would like you to help it create some queries to extract information from the database. Make the following changes using the ch10-06_student_name file you created in Chapter 10. (*Note:* Open your ch10-06_student_name file and then save it as ch11-06_student_name before making the indicated changes.)

a. Create a select query using the Grower ID field from the Grower table, the Description field from the Product table, and the Cost/Unit for all products from Grower ID 200. Do not show the Grower ID on the resulting query. Save this query as Query A and then print it.

b. Create a select query that lists the Grower Name, product Description, and Quantity for all products where the Description field contains the text "5". Save this query as Query B and then print it.

c. Create a select query that lists the product Description, Grower Name, Contact, Phone Number, and Cost/Unit for all products with a Cost/Unit less than $15. Save this query as Query C and then print it.

d. Create a select query that lists the product Description, Grower Name, Contact, Phone Number, and Cost/Unit for all products with a Cost/Unit greater than $15 but less than $40. Save this query as Query D and then print it.

e. Create and print a new table called Customer as follows:

Customer Table Structure:

Field Name	Data Type	Field Size/Format	Primary Key?
Customer Number	Short Text	2	Yes
Customer Name	Short Text	30	
Discount	Number	Single/Percent	

Customer Table Data:

Customer Number	Customer Name	Discount
10	Jan Muller	20%
11	Robert Frost	15%
12	Juliet Inch	10%

f. Add a number field "Markup" to the Grower table. Set the field size of this new field to Single and the Format to Percent. Set the Markup to 150% for Grower ID 100 and 300 and then set the markup to 200% for Grower ID 200 and 400. Print the Grower table.

g. Create and print a new table called Quote as follows:

Quote Table Structure:

Field Name	Data Type	Field Size	Primary Key?
Quote Number	Number		Yes
Customer Number	Short Text	2	
ID (from the Product table)	Number		
Quantity Ordered	Number		

Quote Table Data:

Quote Number	Customer Number	ID	Quantity Ordered
100	10	4	23
101	11	11	17
102	12	16	35

h. Establish a relationship between the Quote table and the Product table (ID) and the Customer table and the Quote table (Customer Number) enforcing referential integrity. Print the Relationships report.

i. Create a select query that contains the Quote Number, Customer Name, Product Table Description, Quantity Ordered, Sales Price (a new computed field: Cost/Unit × (1 + Markup) formatted as currency, and Quote Amount (a new computed field: Quantity Ordered × Sales Price) also formatted as currency. Save as Query E and then print.

j. Modify the query you created in (i) above to include a new field called Cost (a computed field: Quantity Ordered × Cost/Unit) and a new field called Gross Profit (a computed field: Quote Amount – Cost). Format both as currency. Save as Query F and then print.

k. Create and run an update query that increases the Cost/Unit of all products by 15%. (Remember to back up your file first.) Save this query as Query G. Create a new select query that lists all products showing the ID, Description, and Cost/Unit fields. Save this query as Query H and then print it.

l. Create a parameter query that lists the product Description and Grower Name. The query should state "For which type of rose?" (*Hint*: Include Type in your query but don't show it when you run the query.) Save this query as Query I. Run the query for type Creeper and then print it.

m. Create a select query that sums the total cost of all roses currently in inventory, formatted as currency. (*Hint*: First create a query with the fields product Description, Quantity, and Cost/Unit and a computed field titled Cost, which is the product of Quantity and Cost/Unit formatted as currency.) Save this query as Query J – 1, run it, and then print it. Then create the summation query, save it as Query J – 2, run it, and then print it.

n. Create a select query that sums the cost of all products by category (in currency format), sorted by type. (*Hint*: Modify the Query J – 1 you previously created by adding the field Type. Save the new query as K – 1, run it, and then print it.) Your new query should use Query K – 1 as its source and have two fields: Type and Cost. Save the new query as Query K – 2, run it, and then print it.

o. Make sure you keep a copy of this file for use in the next chapter.

12

Forms

- How to Modify a form's labels and Text Box controls
- How to Use List Box and Combo Box controls
- How to Place a calculated control on a form
- How to Place a Check Box control on a form
- How to Use special Combo Box controls
- How to Place an Option Button control on a form
- How to Create a form with a subform
- How to Print a form
- How to Document a form

Case: **What SUP, Inc.**

Nathan and Meagan are now ready to expand the use of forms in their rapidly expanding database. They recall that forms have a variety of purposes. Previously they created a form to capture additional information about their products. Now Kyle suggests they create a form with more features.

Kyle tells them that they can add functionality to forms with such features as calculated controls, check boxes, option buttons, list boxes, combo boxes, and subforms.

"Once again this sounds like more than we need!" Nathan exclaims.

"Don't panic," says Meagan. "Kyle seems to know just how much of this stuff we can take. Give him a chance."

Kyle thanks Meagan for her confidence and convinces them that, in the long run, using forms in their database will allow them to use their product database more efficiently and to improve the integrity of the data input.

Labels and Text Box controls

In this section you will become familiar with the steps necessary to modify a form's labels and text box controls. Forms are often created using the Forms Wizard, but once created they often need to be customized. Customization includes moving controls and labels and resizing the form itself.

Kyle suggests that you modify a form that was previously created using the Forms Wizard. This would yield a form more like the one Nathan used to keep on each supplier.

"That would be helpful," Nathan comments. "I feel more comfortable using an electronic version of a form I've already worked with on paper."

Kyle explains that the purpose of this exercise is to become familiar with the process for moving controls around a form.

To modify the Suppliers form:

1 Start Access.

2 Click the **File** tab and then click **Open**.

3 Navigate the Open window to the location of this text's student files. (The location would be the CD provided with text or from your computer lab's server.)

4 Double-click **ch12-01**, which should be located in a Ch 12 folder. (This is a modified version of the completed What SUP Inventory file from previous chapters. Do *not* use the file you completed in the previous chapter.)

5 Click the **File** tab and then click **Save As** twice.

6 Navigate the Save As window to the location you wish to save this file and type **Ch12-01_student_name** in the File Name: text box (replacing student_name with your name).

7 Click **Save**.

8 Double-click **Supplier** to view the form shown in Figure 12.1.

Figure 12.1

Existing Supplier Form

9 Click **View** and then click **Design View** from the Home tab.

10 Click and hold in the lower right corner of the Supplier form to reveal the dragging tool, then move the window down and to the right to reveal the Form Footer. The process will expand the size of the Form Design view window so that you can manipulate all the objects on the form.

11 Click the top portion of the Form Footer and drag down to expand the size of the form and make space available to move controls around, as shown in Figure 12.2.

Figure 12.2

Increasing the Size of the Form

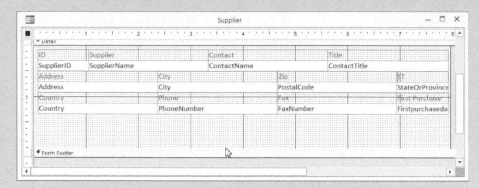

12 Click in the upper left-hand corner of the **First Purchase** label and drag the label to move it. Next click the upper left-hand corner of the **First Purchase** text box and drag it to move the view. Position the label and text box as shown in Figure 12.3.

Figure 12.3

Separating a Label from a Control

13 Click in the ST label and change this label to read State. Select this label, click the **Home** tab, and then click the **Center** tool in the Text Formatting group.

14 Click the right center handle on the State label and drag it to the left to resize the label.

15 Click the top of the State label and then drag it to reposition it on the form.

16 Resize, reposition, and center the StateOrProvince text box using the same process used for the State label until your screen looks like Figure 12.4.

17 Click **View** to view the form in Form View. The form should look like Figure 12.5.

18 Click **File**, **Save As**, **Save Object As**, and **Save As** to save this new object.

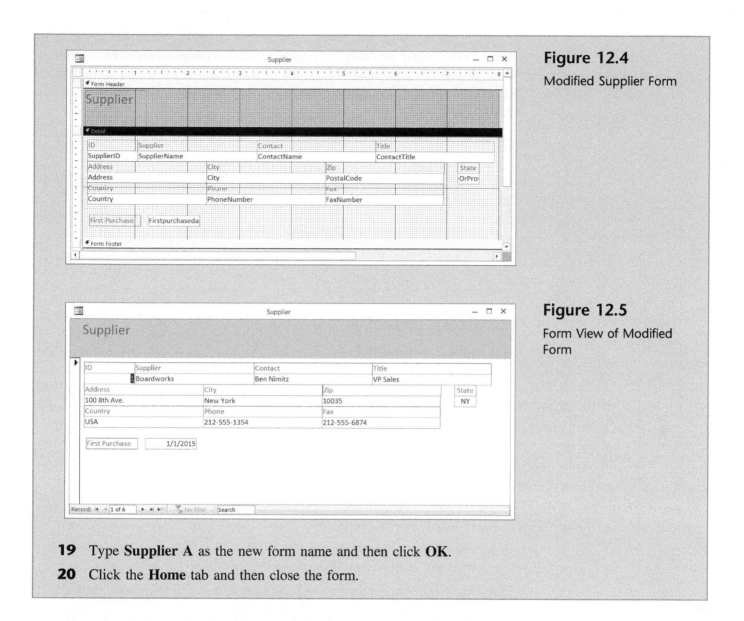

Figure 12.4

Modified Supplier Form

Figure 12.5

Form View of Modified Form

19 Type **Supplier A** as the new form name and then click **OK**.

20 Click the **Home** tab and then close the form.

"Modifying a form's controls was fairly intuitive," Meagan comments, "although it was a bit difficult to line up labels and text boxes so they were properly aligned."

Kyle agrees and now suggests that you and Nathan explore the use of form controls—such as list and combo boxes—to help simplify the data entry process and improve the integrity of information captured in your database. He will also show you how to specify locations of controls more precisely.

List Box and Combo Box Controls

The form you just modified included a series of text box controls containing information such as a supplier's name, address, and so on. These text boxes are referred to as a type of *form control*. You use text boxes on a form or report to display data from a record source. This type of text box is called a *bound* text box because it's bound to data in a field. In this case, for example, the text box control Supplier Name was bound to the field Supplier Name in the Supplier table. Text boxes can also be unbound. For example, you can create an unbound text box to display the results of a calculation or to accept input from a user. Data in an unbound text box isn't stored anywhere, but we will discuss unbound text boxes later.

Kyle explains that it's often quicker and easier to select a value from a list than to remember a value when using a form to enter new information, such as a new supplier. A list of choices also helps to ensure that the value entered in a field is correct. If you have enough room on your form to display the list at all times, you might want to use a list box. If you want to create a control that displays a list but requires less room then you would use a combo box, which provides the combined functionality of a list box and a text box.

"Which should we use, and when?" asks Meagan.

"Well, let's try something simple first, like modifying an existing text box control in our supplier form to a list box," answers Kyle.

List Box Control

Kyle explains that modifying a control on a form simply requires changing the form control (from text to list) and creating the list of choices.

"Let's modify the Country text box control on our previously created supplier form to a list box control," suggests Kyle. "We will also add a new supplier from Canada."

To change the Country text box control to a list box control and add a new supplier:

1 Double-click the **Supplier A** form.

2 Click **View** and then click **Design View**. Move the First Purchase label and field to a location under the Fax label and field.

3 Right-click the **Country** text box control; then click **Change To** and click **List Box**, as shown in Figure 12.6.

Figure 12.6

Shortcut Menu to Transform a Text Box Control to a List Box Control

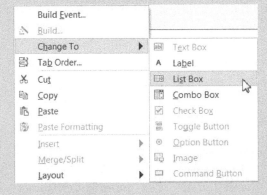

4 Right-click the **Country** list box control.

5 In the Property Sheet for List Box: Country, click the **Data** tab, click **Value List** in the Row Source Type section, and then type **USA; CAN; UK** in the Row Source (see Figure 12.7).

Figure 12.7

Modifying the Properties of the Country Control

6 Close the Property Sheet window. The form should now look like Figure 12.8.

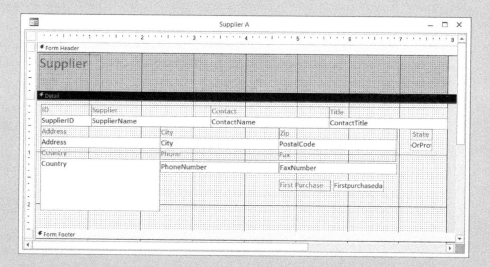

Figure 12.8

Modified Form with List Box Control for Country

7 Click **View** and then click **Form View**.

8 Enter a new supplier by clicking on the **New (blank) record** button located at the bottom of the form and then typing the information provided in Figure 12.9. Observe that, in order to specify the country for this new supplier, all you had to do was click **CAN**.

9 Click **File**, **Save As**, **Save Object As**, and **Save As** to save this new object.

10 Type **Supplier B** as the name of the new form and then click **OK**.

11 Click the **Home** tab and then close the form.

Figure 12.9

New Record

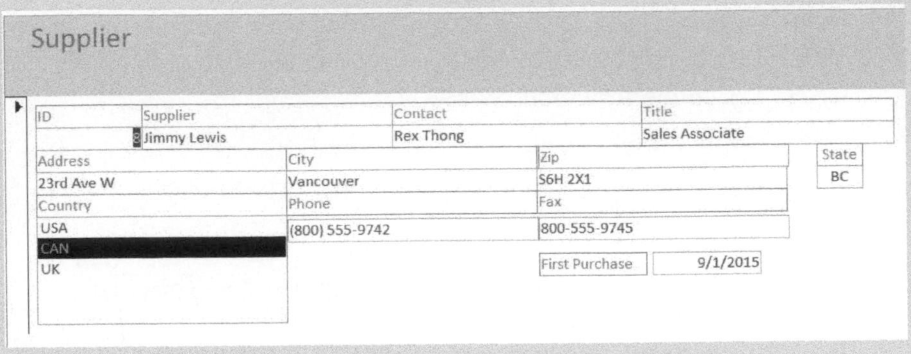

You have now modified an existing form to include a list box control. Now Kyle suggests you look at the combo box control as an alternative.

Combo Box Control

Once again, a combo box control is a control that is used on a form and provides the combined functionality of a list box and a text box. In this situation, someone entering a new supplier using the Supplier form can either type new information into a combo box control (like a text box control) or select from an existing list of information (like a list box control) without taking up much space.

Kyle suggests you try out a combo box control by changing the State text box control to a combo box control that lists the four most common states in which your suppliers reside.

To change the State text box control to a combo box control:

1 Double-click **Supplier B**.

2 Click **View** and then click **Design View**.

3 Right-click the **State Or Province** text box control; then click **Change To** and click **Combo Box**.

4 Increase the size of the StateOrProvince combo box control and related label slightly.

5 Right-click the **State Or Province** combo box control and then click **Properties**.

6 Click the **Data** tab.

7 Click **Value List** from the Row Source Type drop-down list.

8 Type **CA;NY;MA;NJ** in the Row Source section. The Properties Sheet should look like Figure 12.10.

9 Close the Properties window.

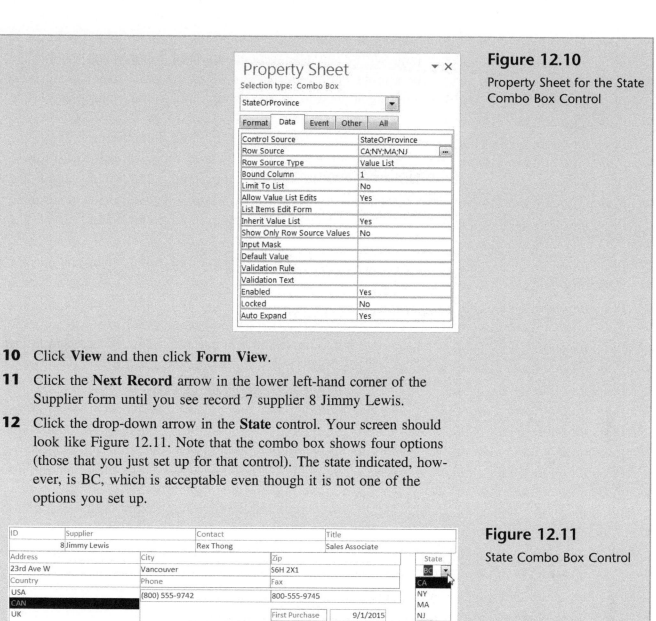

Figure 12.10

Property Sheet for the State Combo Box Control

10 Click **View** and then click **Form View**.

11 Click the **Next Record** arrow in the lower left-hand corner of the Supplier form until you see record 7 supplier 8 Jimmy Lewis.

12 Click the drop-down arrow in the **State** control. Your screen should look like Figure 12.11. Note that the combo box shows four options (those that you just set up for that control). The state indicated, however, is BC, which is acceptable even though it is not one of the options you set up.

Figure 12.11

State Combo Box Control

"What if I wanted to move the State control to the left and the Zip control to the right. Would that change the order in which I tab through the controls?" Nathan asks.

"Actually no. Moving controls doesn't change tab order. However, there is a way to do both," Kyle explains. "Let me show you."

To move controls and change the tab order:

1 Click **View** and then click **Design View**. Move the Zip and State labels and fields so that State is next to City and is followed on the right by Zip, and then make the Zip label and field smaller. Switch back to the Form view and click in the ID field. Then press the [**Tab**] key several times to work your way through the supplier form. Note that from the City field, tab moves you to the Zip field and then back to the State field. Switch back to the Design View.

2 Right-click anywhere in the Supplier B form and then click **Tab Order**.

3 Click the far left-hand side of the **State Or Province** control and move it up. Then move other fields so that your screen looks like Figure 12.12.

Figure 12.12

Changing the Tab Order

4 Click **OK** to save the changed tab order.

5 Click **View** and then click **Form View**.

6 Click the **New (blank) record** arrow.

7 Type **9** as the ID and then press [**Tab**] to move to the Supplier field.

8 Type **Rigid** as the supplier name and then press [**Tab**] to move to the next field.

9 Type **Rex Tander** as the supplier contact and then press [**Tab**] to move to the next field.

10 Type **Sales Associate** as the supplier title and then press [**Tab**] to move to the next field.

11 Type **253 Cabrillo Blvd**. as the supplier address and then press [**Tab**] to move to the next field.

12 Type **Santa Barbara** as the supplier city and then press [**Tab**] to move to the next field. (Note that this moves you to the State field since you changed the tab order.)

13 Select **CA** as the supplier state and then press [**Tab**] to move to the next field.

14 Type **93101** as the supplier zip and then press [**Tab**] to move to the next field.

15 Select **USA** as the supplier country and then press [**Tab**] to move to the next field.

16 Type **8055554127** as the supplier phone and then press [**Tab**] to move to the next field.

17 Type **8055554128** as the supplier fax and then press [**Tab**] to move to the next field.

18 Type **10/1/2015** as the supplier first purchase date and then press [**Tab**]. That last tab should have entered the new supplier and brought you to a new supplier form.

19 Click **File, Save As, Save Object As**, and **Save As** to save this new object.

20 Type **Supplier C** as the form name, click **OK**, click the **Home** tab, and then close the form.

You have now created a combo box control on a form to ease the creation of new supplier records, and you have found that it acts like both a text box and list box control. Now it is time to experiment with other features, such as calculated controls.

Calculated Controls

A calculated control uses an expression as its source of data. An *expression* is any combination of mathematical or logical operators, constants, functions, names of fields, controls, and properties that evaluate to a single value. For example, an expression can use data from a field in an underlying table, from a query of a form or report, or from another control on the form or report.

Bound controls obtain their data from fields in a table, whereas unbound controls don't have any particular data source other than an expression. Kyle explains that, in order to calculate the total cost invested in any particular product, Nathan would have to multiply the units on hand times the unit cost. He demonstrates that both the units on hand and the unit cost are already on the product form as bound controls Quantity and UnitPrice. However, creating a control on the form that calculates the total cost will require that Nathan create an unbound control (referred to in this case as a calculated control) to calculate the product of Quantity times Unit Price.

"Bound, unbound, I'm bound up just thinking about these," Meagan complains. "Do we really have to understand this to create a useful form?"

"Well," responds Kyle, "I think you'll find them useful in many forms you might create and they are really not that difficult. Here, let me show you."

To add a control to calculate the total cost in inventory of each item:

1 Double-click the **Products** form.

2 Click **View** and then click **Design View**.

3 Click the **Text Box** control from the Controls group on the Design tab of the Ribbon, as shown in Figure 12.13.

Figure 12.13

Form Design Tools on the Ribbon

4 Place the cursor in the product form under the Picture label click and then drag to the right and down while holding the left mouse button down, then release the left mouse button down to create a new text box control as shown in Figure 12.14.

Figure 12.14

Adding a New Text Box Control to the Products Form

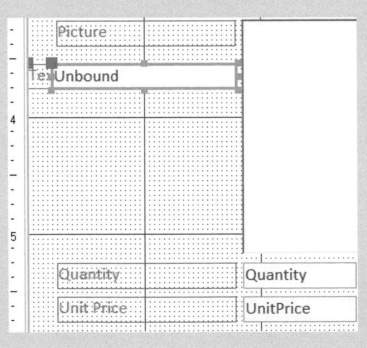

5 Right-click the **Unit Cost** label control; then click **Properties**.

6 Click the **All** tab to view format properties for the Unit Price label control. A portion of the Format Properties window is shown in Figure 12.15.

Figure 12.15

A Portion of the Properties Window for the Unit Cost Label Control

7 Note the width, height, and left properties. (Width defines how wide the label should be, height defines how tall the label should be and the left defines how far from the margin the label should be.)

8 Click the newly created text box control and then click the newly created text box label control; note how the Property Sheet now reflects properties for the new text box label. (Be sure you select the label, not the text box.)

9 Click the **All** tab if it is not already selected.

10 Type **Total** as the name property of the new text box label.

11 Type **Total** as the caption property of the Total text box label.

12 Type **1.2076** as the width property.

13 Type **.2076** as the height property.

14 Type **3.5** as the top property.

15 Type **0.0417** as the left property. Your Properties window should look like Figure 12.16.

Figure 12.16

A Portion of the Properties Window of the Total Text Box

16 Click the **Unit Cost** text box. A portion of the Format Properties window for the unit price control is shown in Figure 12.17.

Figure 12.17

A Portion of the Properties Window for the Unit Price Control

17 Note the width, height, and left properties.

18 Click the **Unbound** text box control and observe that the Property Sheet now reflects properties for this text box control.

19 Type **Total Amount** in the Name box.

20 Type **=[Quantity]*[UnitCost]** in the Control Source box.

21 Select **Currency** as the format property.

22 Type **1.4576** as the width property.

23 Type **0.2076** as the height property.

24 Type **3.7917** as the top property.

25 Type **0.0417** as the left property. Your Properties window should now look like Figure 12.18.

Figure 12.18

A Portion of the Properties Window for the Total Amount Text Box

26 Close the Properties window.

27 Click **View** and then click **Form View**. The format seems a bit out of place. Move controls around the form (in Design View) so that your new form looks like Figure 12.19.

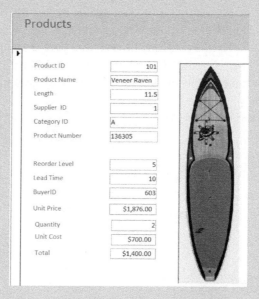

Figure 12.19

New Product Form with a Total Control

Trouble? If you did not type the expression exactly as specified, then you may end up with the message "#Name?" in the text box where you expected to see the $1,400.00 total cost. Reexamine the Control Source section of the Properties window for the total text box to verify that you've typed the expression correctly.

28 Click **File, Save As, Save Object As**, and **Save As** to save this new object.

29 Type **Products A** as the new form name and then click **OK**.

30 Click the Home tab and then close the form.

You've now seen the process for creating a calculated control. Both Nathan and Meagan seem more comfortable with the terms and processes and are anxious to know if there are any other useful controls available in Access.

Check Box Control

When implemented on a form, the check box control gives the user the choice of activating all, none, or some of the check boxes. In each case, a check box control returns a Yes value if checked and returns a No value if unchecked. This control, like other controls, can be bound or unbound. To create a bound check box control, you must be working in a form or report that is bound to a record source.

Kyle asks Meagan if there are any situations in which she thinks a control like this might be helpful on a form. She suggests that, in the Buyers table, it would be nice to know who specializes in what category of product. For instance, some buyers specialize in only one category, like Flatwater boards, while others specialize in several categories.

"Would a check box control be appropriate here?" she asks.

"Yes," you respond. "But if you want to store this information for later use, doesn't it have to be a bound control? And if so, don't we have to create some new fields in the Buyers table?"

Kyle compliments you on your comprehension of this topic. He agrees that this is a situation where a bound control is appropriate, but he points out that the buyer table fields must first be created and set up in a data type called Yes/No.

To create additional fields in the Buyers table:

1 Right-click **Buyers Table** and then click **Design View**.

2 Add six new fields to the table and specify each as a Yes/No data type, as shown in Figure 12.20.

Figure 12.20

Modifying the Buyers Table

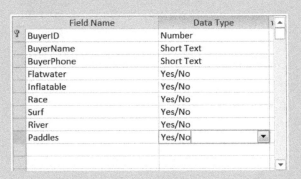

Field Name	Data Type
BuyerID	Number
BuyerName	Short Text
BuyerPhone	Short Text
Flatwater	Yes/No
Inflatable	Yes/No
Race	Yes/No
Surf	Yes/No
River	Yes/No
Paddles	Yes/No

3 Close the Buyers Table. Click **Yes** to save changes.

Now that the Buyers table includes the field for data storage, you offer to modify the Buyers form to include check boxes for quick data entry.

"How do I create check boxes on the form?" you ask.

"All you'll need to do is add the fields you just created in the Buyers table to the Buyers form. Because they are of the data type Yes/No, they will automatically be added to the form as a check box control," Kyle responds.

To create a check box control bound to a field:

1 Right-click the **Buyers** form and then click **Design View**.

2 Resize and move the Buyers form and Field list windows so that your screen looks like Figure 12.21.

3 Click **Add Existing Fields** from the Tools group of the Design tab on the Ribbon.

4 Click and drag all six fields you just created, one at a time, to the Buyers form (see Figure 12.22).

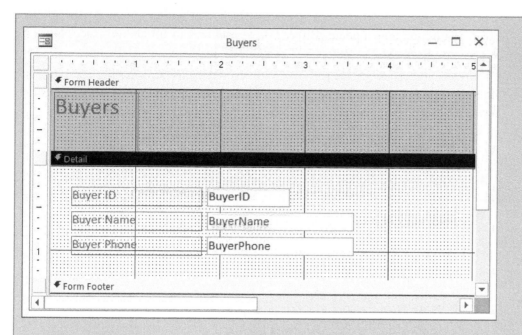

Figure 12.21

Modifying the Buyers Form

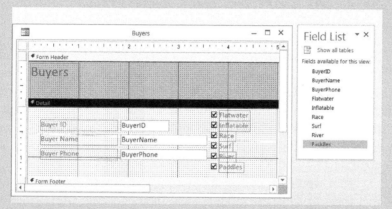

Figure 12.22

Adding Existing Fields to a Form

5 Click **View** and then click **Form View**.

6 Update each record from the Buyers form to indicate in what category each buyer specializes by clicking in the check box to place a check mark in the box. (*Note:* Clicking a second time will remove the check mark.) Buyer 601 specializes in Flatwater, Inflatable, and Race SUPs. After updating Buyer ID 601, your Buyers form should look like Figure 12.23.

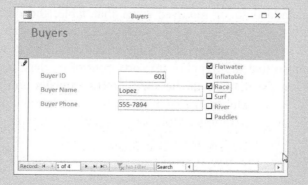

Figure 12.23

Buyer ID 1 Updated Record

7 Continue your update. Buyer 602 specializes in Inflatable, Race, Surf, and River SUPs. Buyer 603 specializes in Flatwater SUPs and Paddles. Buyer 604 specializes in Surf SUPs only.

8 Click **File**, **Save As**, **Save Object As**, and **Save As** to save this new object.

9 Type **Buyers A** as the name of the new form and then click **OK** to save the form.

10 Click the **Home** tab and then close the form.

"I like using these new controls," comments Meagan. "But I still have a question on the combo box controls we did before. Is there a way to give our database users a choice of options that change as our company grows?"

"There sure is," Kyle responds. "I'll introduce you to special combo box controls next."

Special Combo Box Control

An additional possible use of a combo box control would be to give the user a choice of options that change as a function of other changes that may occur in the database. For instance, let's say you want to give the user the option of selecting a specific supplier for each product but that you want the list to be dynamic, not static. In other words, you'd like the user's available choices to be limited to those suppliers currently in your Supplier table. Thus, when you add a supplier the list expands and, of course, when you delete a supplier the list contracts.

"That would be perfect for our product form," you suggest. "I can see using that form to add new products and then choosing from a list of existing suppliers to provide the product."

"How is that different from what we just did with the state and country combo boxes?" Meagan asks.

"In those situations," Kyle explains, "we provided a list of choices for the combo list. However, the user could type in a different state or country from those we listed. Plus, the list never changes unless we physically rewrite the list in the control."

"So where do we create the list?" you ask.

"Actually, we just point the control to the Supplier table. As names are added to or removed from that table, the combo box control changes," says Kyle. "Nathan, let me show you how it is done."

Kyle explains that Nathan's goal will be to modify the existing Product form so that the Supplier text box control is transformed to a combo box control with a list containing the supplier ID numbers and names that exist in the Supplier table. This will require that the existing relationship between the Product table and the Supplier table be temporarily eliminated (since it currently enforces referential integrity) and that the data type of the SupplierID fields be changed.

To modify the Product table and change the Supplier ID field's data type:

1 Click **Relationships** from the Relationships group on the Database Tools tab of the Ribbon.

2 Resize the windows so that your screen looks like Figure 12.24.

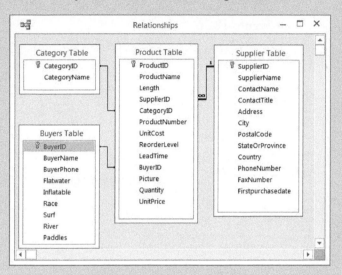

Figure 12.24
Existing Relationships

3 Right-click the relationship between the Product table and the Supplier table; click **Delete** and then click **Yes** in the dialog box that appears in order to confirm your deletion.

4 Close the Relationships window and click **Yes** if asked to save changes.

5 Right-click **Product Table** and then click **Design View**.

6 Click **Lookup Wizard** from the drop-down list of data types for the Supplier ID field, as shown in Figure 12.25.

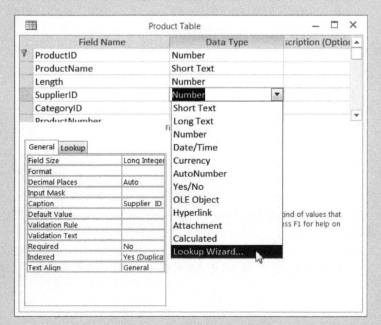

Figure 12.25

Changing Data Type to Lookup Wizard

7   Click on the first option button (I want the lookup field to get the values from another table or query.) and then click **Next**.

8   Click **Table: Supplier Table** from the next Lookup Wizard dialog box; then click **Next**.

9   Double-click **Supplier ID** and **Supplier Name** in the list of Available Fields in order to move them to the list of Selected Fields, as shown in Figure 12.26.

Figure 12.26

Identifying Fields to be Included in the Lookup Column

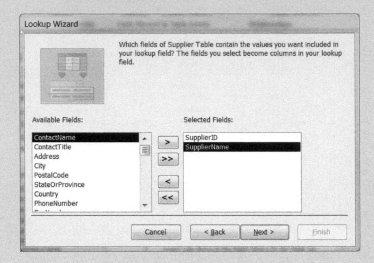

10 Click **Next**; then click **Supplier Name** from the drop-down list in box 1 as the field to sort on.

11 Leave **Ascending** as the sort order, and then click Next.

12 Uncheck the **Hide key column** check box and resize the column widths if necessary so that your screen looks like Figure 12.27.

Figure 12.27

Organizing Columns in the Lookup Column

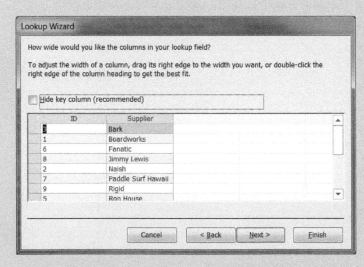

13 Click **Next**.

14 Click **Next** again to keep the Supplier ID as the field being stored.

15 Click **Finish** to keep Supplier ID as the label for your column.

16 Click **Yes** to save the table.

17 Close the modified Product table.

18 Once again, click **Relationships** from the Relationships group on the Database Tools tab of the Ribbon.

19 Double-click the relationship between the Product table and the Supplier table.

20 Click in the **Enforce Referential Integrity** check box and then click **OK**.

21 Close the Relationships window.

Kyle explains that now Nathan can modify the Products form to include the new and revised Supplier ID field as a combo box control. But first, he cautions, Nathan will have to remove the old Supplier ID text box control from the form.

To create a combo box control linked to the Supplier table:

1 Right-click **Products A** and then click **Design View**.

2 Click the existing **Supplier ID** text box control; then press the [**Delete**] key to delete both the SupplierID label and text box.

3 Click **Add Existing Fields** from the Tools group of the Design tab on the Ribbon.

4 Click and drag the **Supplier ID** field to the Products A form, as shown in Figure 12.28.

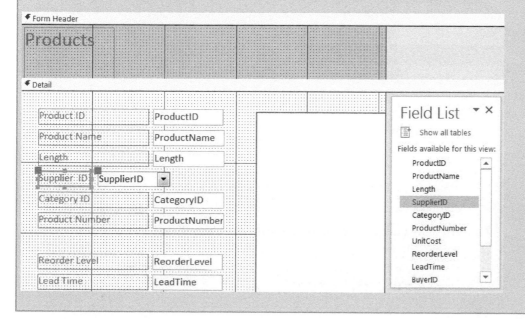

Figure 12.28

Adding the Newly Modified Supplier ID Field to the Products A Form

5 Close the Field List window.

6 Click **View** and then click **Form View**.

7 Note that the Supplier ID of record 1 in the Products A form is still specified as 1. Click on the drop-down list arrow of the Supplier ID combo box control to see the options available, as shown in Figure 12.29.

Figure 12.29

Modified Product Form with Lookup Capabilities for SupplierID

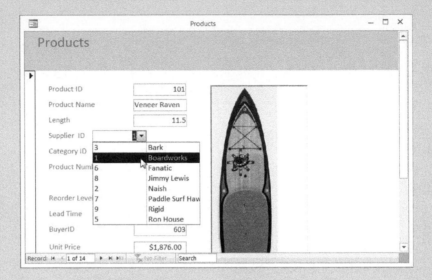

8 Click **File**, **Save As**, **Save Object As**, and **Save As** to save this new object.

9 Type **Products B** as the name of the new form.

10 Go to record 7, the Sleeping One, and change the Supplier ID from 5 to 6 (Fanatic.) as shown in Figure 12.30.

Figure 12.30

Modifying an Existing Record

3	Bark
1	Boardworks
6	Fanatic
8	Jimmy Lewis
2	Naish
7	Paddle Surf Haw
9	Rigid
5	Ron House

11 Now change the Supplier ID of the same record by typing 4 in the combo box control and then moving to the next record.

12 An alert dialog box should appear, indicating that this choice is not acceptable because a related record is required in the Supplier table. Since there is no supplier with an ID of 4, the system rejects your change. Click **OK**.

> **13** Change the Supplier ID of record 7 back to 5.
>
> **14** Close the form.

In addition to form controls, subforms are helpful in situations where a one-to-many relationship exists. Kyle suggests that understanding subforms may actually help resolve some of their previously expressed inventory tracking concerns.

Subforms

Subforms are simply forms within forms. Subforms require that information in one form have a one-to-many relationship with the information in another form. Kyle explains that users often like to see specific information on one form that has some common characteristic.

"For instance," says Kyle. "You have already established a relationship between the categories of your products and the products themselves, so we have a one-to-many relationship. One category, for example, includes many products."

"So we could create a form showing all the products we have that fall within any of our categories?" asks Meagan.

"That's it!" Kyle responds. "Let's have you create this form within a form using the Forms Wizard."

To create a form and subform of categories and products:

1 Click **Forms Wizard**, from the Forms group of the Create tab.

2 Select **Table: Category Table** from the list of Tables/Queries.

3 Click **Category Name** from the list of Available Fields; then click the > button to move Category Name from the list of Available Fields to the list of Selected Fields.

4 Select **Table: Product Table** from the list of Tables/Queries.

5 Click **ProductName** from the list of Available Fields and then click the > button.

6 Click **Quantity** from the list of Available Fields and then click the > button.

7 Double-click **UnitCost** from the list of Available Fields (note how this accomplishes the same task of moving the field from Available Fields to Selected Fields). Your window should now look like Figure 12.31.

8 Click the **Next** button.

9 Click **by Category Table**.

Figure 12.31

Using the Forms Wizard

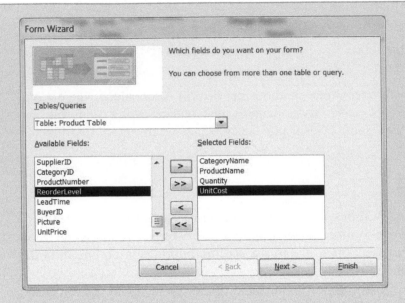

10   Click the **Form with subform(s)** option button. Your window should look like Figure 12.32.

Figure 12.32

Creating Forms with Subforms

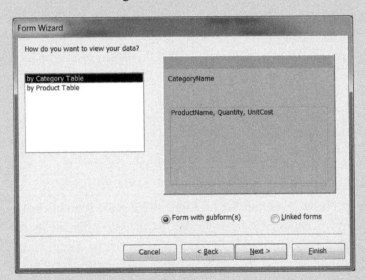

11   Click **Next**.

12   Click the **Data sheet** layout option button and then click **Next**.

13   Type **Products by Category** as the form title and **Products Subform** as the subform title.

14   Click **Finish** to save the new forms. Your window should look like Figure 12.33.

15   Observe that not all products, quantities, or unit costs may be visible. Click **View** and then **Layout View**.

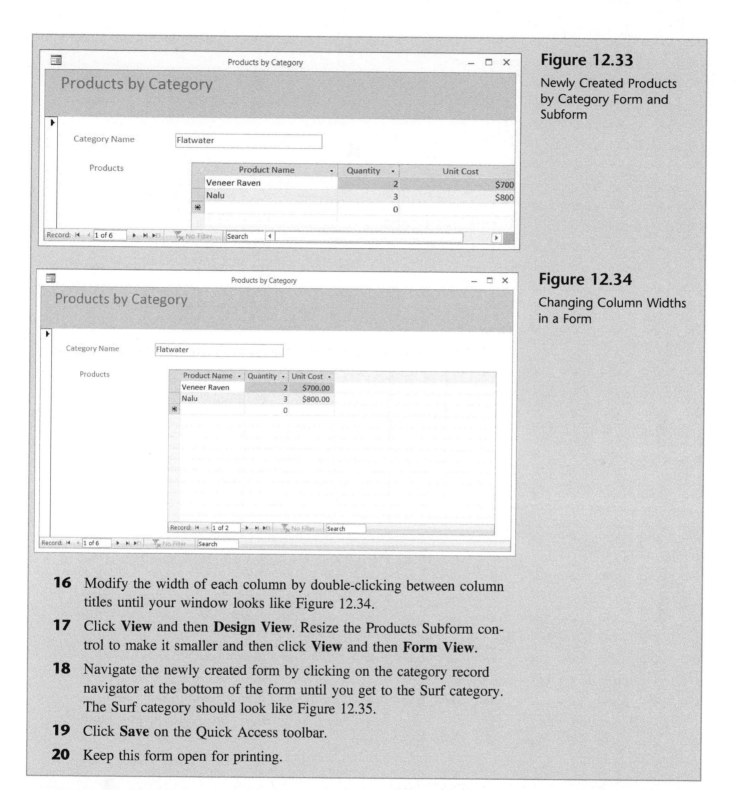

Figure 12.33

Newly Created Products by Category Form and Subform

Figure 12.34

Changing Column Widths in a Form

16 Modify the width of each column by double-clicking between column titles until your window looks like Figure 12.34.

17 Click **View** and then **Design View**. Resize the Products Subform control to make it smaller and then click **View** and then **Form View**.

18 Navigate the newly created form by clicking on the category record navigator at the bottom of the form until you get to the Surf category. The Surf category should look like Figure 12.35.

19 Click **Save** on the Quick Access toolbar.

20 Keep this form open for printing.

This newly created form and subform is ideal for viewing products by categories. Nathan is impressed.

Figure 12.35

Completed Products by
Category Form

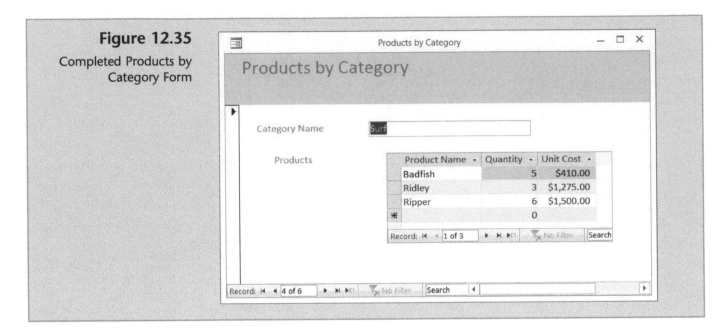

Printing a Form

All that is left is to print a form. Kyle remarks that printing a form is much like
printing a table or query, as you did in previous chapters. In this case he just
needs you to print the first record (Watches).

To print a form:

1 With record 4 showing on the Products by Category form you just created; click the **File** tab and then click **Print**.

2 Click **Print** again, and then choose the **Selected Record(s)** option in
the Print Range section of the Print window and then click **OK**. The
printed form should look like Figure 12.36.

3 Close and save the Products by Category form.

Figure 12.36

Printed Products
by Category Form
for Surf SUPs

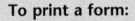

Products by Category

Category Name   Surf

Products	Product Name	Quantity	Unit Cost
	Badfish	5	$410.00
	Ridley	3	$1,275.00
	Ripper	6	$1,500.00

Documenting a Form

Kyle suggests that you document all changes made to a form so that you can verify the underlying attributes that were changed in the course of creating or modifying the form. In particular, he suggests you examine and print the data properties that were changed when you converted a text box to a combo box for the StateOrProvince field in the supplier form.

To view and print the changes made in the State Or Province field in the supplier form:

1 Double-click **Supplier C** form.

2 Click **Database Documenter** in the Analyze group of the Database Tools tab on the Ribbon.

3 Click the **Forms** tab in the Documenter window.

4 Click in the check box next to **Supplier C** (you may have to scroll down the window to find it).

5 Click **Options**.

6 Uncheck all check boxes listed under the **Include for Form** section title.

7 Click the **Names and Properties** option button under the Include for Sections and Controls section title. Your screen should look like Figure 12.37.

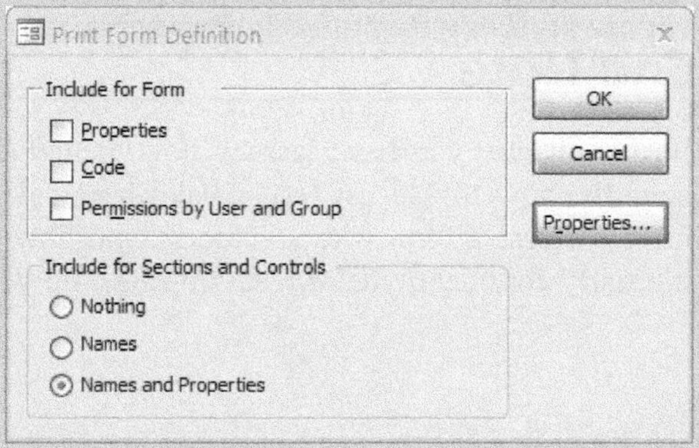

Figure 12.37

Selecting Print Form Definitions

8 Click the **Properties** button.

9 Deselect all Print Categories other than Data Properties, as shown in Figure 12.38.

10 Click **OK** in the Property Categories window.

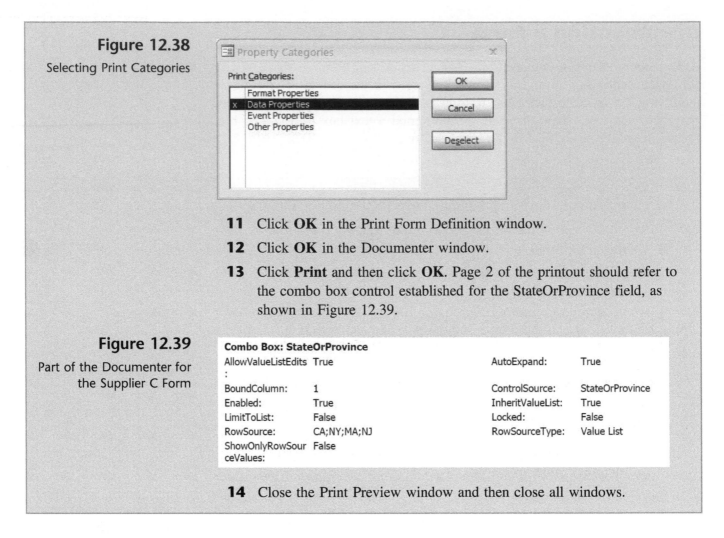

Figure 12.38

Selecting Print Categories

11 Click **OK** in the Print Form Definition window.

12 Click **OK** in the Documenter window.

13 Click **Print** and then click **OK**. Page 2 of the printout should refer to the combo box control established for the StateOrProvince field, as shown in Figure 12.39.

Figure 12.39

Part of the Documenter for the Supplier C Form

Combo Box: StateOrProvince

AllowValueListEdits:	True	AutoExpand:	True
BoundColumn:	1	ControlSource:	StateOrProvince
Enabled:	True	InheritValueList:	True
LimitToList:	False	Locked:	False
RowSource:	CA;NY;MA;NJ	RowSourceType:	Value List
ShowOnlyRowSourceValues:	False		

14 Close the Print Preview window and then close all windows.

End Note

In this chapter you have learned how to modify a form's labels and text box controls, how to use list box, combo box, calculated, and check box controls, how to create a form with a subform, and how to print document a form. Feeling fairly confident, you're ready to finish up with variations on report creation.

Chapter 12 Questions

1 What view of a form is used to edit an existing form?

2 What is the difference between bound and unbound controls?

3 Why are text box controls used on a form?

4 Why are list box controls used on a form?

5 Why are combo box controls used on a form?

6 Why are calculated controls used on a form?

7 Why are check box controls used on a form instead of list box controls?

8 When is the Lookup Wizard used?

9 Why must an existing relationship be deleted before modifying a field's data type?

10 What type of relationship must exist if a subform is used on a form?

Chapter 12 Assignments

1 Using the Ch12-02 file, modify the Buyers form for What SUP so that it looks like Figure 12.40. Save this form as Ch 12 Assignment 1, and print record 1 using this form.

Figure 12.40

New Buyers Form

2 Modify the Products form by changing the Category ID text box control to a list box control that lists the choices as A, B, C, D, E, or F. Save the form as Ch 12 Assignment 2. Print the newly created form for Product ID 103.

3 Modify the Product form (not the Ch 12 Assignment 2 form you just created) by changing the Category ID text box control to a combo box control that lists choices of A, B, C, D, E, or F. Save the form as Ch 12 Assignment 3. Print the newly created form for Product ID 110.

4 Salespeople earn a 10 percent commission on the price of each sale. Create a new unbound calculated control to compute the possible commission on each product. Modify the Products form (not the Ch 12 Assignment 3 form you just created) by adding a calculated control called Commission Per Unit. (The expression created should multiply the unit price by .10.) Format the control in a currency format. Save the form as Ch 12 Assignment 4. Print Product ID 106 using this form.

5 Add a new field (Taxable) to the Product Table. Make the field a Yes/No data type. Add this new field to the Products form (not the Ch 12 Assignment 4 form you just created) to the right of the Reorder Level control. Make Product ID 116 taxable. Save the form as Ch 12 Assignment 5. Print Product ID 116 using this form.

6 Modify the Products form (not the Ch 12 Assignment 5 form you just created) by changing the Category ID text box control to a special combo box control, listing the choices of CategoryID and CategoryName from the Category table. (*Hint:* Be sure to first remove the relationship between the Product and Category tables and then, after you've created the combo box control, to reestablish the relationship and related referential integrity. Save the form as Ch 12 Assignment 6. Print the newly created form for Product ID 105.

7 For each buyer name, create a form (using the Forms Wizard) that contains the product name, quantity, and unit price of each product that the buyer is responsible for. Use the subform option with a datasheet layout. Save the form as Ch 12 Assignment 7 and the subform as Ch 12 Assignment 7 Subform. Format the subform so that columns fit in the form created. Print record 1 (Buyer = Frankenstein) using this form.

Chapter 12 Case Problem 1:
KELLY'S BOUTIQUE

Note: You must have completed Case 1 in the previous chapter in order to continue working on this case.

In the last chapter you added and modified some queries for Kelly's Boutique. She would now like you to create some new forms. Make the following changes for Kelly using the ch11-03_student_name file you created in Chapter 11. (*Note:* Open your ch11-03_student_name file and then save it as ch12-03_student_name before making the indicated changes.)

a. Create a form to look like Figure 12.41. Save the form as Ch 12 Kelly Case a. Print record The Rainmaker.

b. Create a list box control using the form created in part a. This control should provide the user with a list of departments: Adult, Children. Move the picture control down to make room for the list box control.

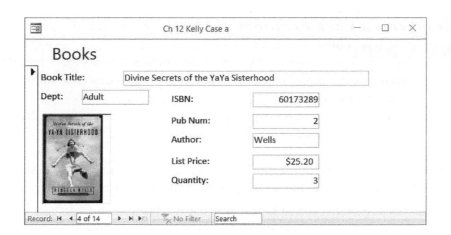

Figure 12.41

New Books Form

Save the modified form as Ch 12 Kelly Case b. Print record 3 (Hop on Pop).

c. Create a combo box control using the form created in part a. This control should provide the user with a list of departments (as in b above) but with a combo box instead of a list box. Dept choices should be Adult, Children, and Teen. Save the modified form as Ch 12 Kelly Case c. Print the documenter page that documents the combo box for Dept.

d. Create a special combo box control using the Book Form. This control should provide the user with a dynamic list of publishers based on the publishers listed in the Publisher table. The combo box should list publisher number and name, and referential integrity must be enforced. Label the combo box column Publisher. Save the modified form as Ch 12 Kelly Case d. Print the documenter page that documents the combo box for Publisher.

e. Using the Book Form, create a calculated control to compute the total retail value of each book in stock. First add the quantity field to the form and then add the calculated control. Format the control in currency, and label the control Total Retail Value. Save the modified form as Ch 12 Kelly Case e. Print the record containing the book title "Blueberries for Sal"

f. Using the Book Form, create a check box control to indicate whether or not the text is a bestseller. Label the new field and control Best Seller. Mark the book The Notebook as a bestseller using your new form. Print the record that contains the book title "The Notebook" and then save the modified form as Ch 12 Kelly Case f.

g. Create a form and subform that shows all books by publisher, listing ISBN and Book Title in datasheet layout. Then save the modified form and subform as Ch 12 Kelly Case g and Ch 12 Kelly Case g Subform. Print the record with Random House as the publisher.

h. Make sure to keep a copy of this file for use in the next chapter.

Chapter 12 Case Problem 2:
WINE DEPOT

Note: You must have completed Case 2 in the previous chapter in order to continue working on this case.

In the last chapter you modified some queries for the Wine Depot. Now Barbara would like you to help her create some new forms. Make the following changes for Barbara using the ch11-04_student_name file you created in Chapter 11. (*Note:* Open your ch11-04_student_name file and then save it as ch12-04_student_name before making the indicated changes.)

    a. Change the Type field in the Wine Products table to a short text type with a field size of 30. Use the Forms Wizard to create a new form from the Wine Products table and Winery Table that includes the following fields: SKU, Cost, Price, Quantity, Size, Vintage, Type, Picture, and Winery Name. Use a justified layout and entitle the form Wine Products; then modify the form to look like Figure 12.42. Save this form as Ch 12 Wine Depot Case a. Navigate to SKU 11475 and print that selected record only. (*Hint:* Be sure to set the picture properties field to size mode "zoom" by right-clicking the picture object in the design view, selecting properties, and choosing zoom as the size mode.)

Figure 12.42

New Wine Products Form

    b. Modify the form you created and saved in a above by changing the Type text box to a list box control that provides a list of all wine types: Cabernet Sauvignon, Chardonnay, Fume Blanc, Merlot, Pinot Noir, Sauvignon Blanc, Syrah, Red Chianti, and Zinfandel. Save the modified form as Ch 12 Wine Depot Case b. Print the record containing SKU 11475 only.

    c. Modify the form you created in part b by replacing the Winery Name field with a Winery field (from the Winery Table). Then change the

Winery text box to a combo box control that provides a drop-down list of all 21 wineries. Your new combo box should contain a value list that you create listing each winery by number. For example: 1,2,3 etc. Save the modified form as Ch 12 Wine Depot Case c. Print the documenter page that documents the combo box for Winery.

d. Modify the form you created in part c by deleting the Winery combo box control and replacing it with a Winery combo box control based on the winery and name fields in the Winery Table. The field should use the winery and name fields of the Winery Table and then list the winery name when requested. (Don't forget to modify the relationships window first and then to reestablish referential integrity!) Save the modified form as Ch 12 Wine Depot Case d. Print the documenter page that documents the new combo box for Winery.

e. Modify the form you created in part d by adding a check box control in the lower right-hand corner of the form to indicate if this product has been recommended by the *Wine Spectator* (a noted magazine of wine-tasting professionals). Label the field and control "Wine Spectator Recommended". (*Hint:* Don't forget to create a field in the Wine Products Table first.) Only three wines currently have that designation: SKU 11475, 13883, and 15347. Save the modified form as Ch 12 Wine Depot Case e, and print the record containing SKU 11475 only.

f. Modify the form you created in part e by adding a calculated control below the Winery Number to compute the total cost in inventory of each product (cost times quantity). Format the control in currency and label the control Total Cost. Save the modified form as Ch 12 Wine Depot Case f. Print the record containing SKU 12895 only.

g. Create a new form with a subform using the Winery Table and Wine Products Table. Use the Winery Name field from the Winery Table and the SKU and Type fields from the Wine Products table. View the data by winery in a datasheet layout. Use the default names provided for the form and subform. Save the modified form as Ch 12 Wine Depot Case g. Print the record containing the Babcock winery only.

h. Make sure you keep a copy of this file for use in the next chapter.

Chapter 12 Case Problem 3:
SNICK'S BOARD SHOP

Note: You must have completed Case 3 in the previous chapter in order to continue working on this case.

In the last chapter you created some queries for the Snick's Board Shop. Now Caitlin would like you to help her create some forms to view information from the database. Make the following changes for Caitlin using the ch11-05_student_name file you created in Chapter 11. (*Note:* Open your ch11-05_student_name file and then save it as ch12-05_student_name before making the indicated changes.)

a. Note the existing relationships between the Product, Manufacturer, and Category tables. Now delete those relationships, and then change the field size of ProductID to 10, ProductName to 35, ManufacturerID to 10, Style to 15, CategoryName to 25, ManfacturerName to 25, and PhoneNumber to 15. Now reestablish the relationships you previously deleted enforcing referential integrity. Use the Forms Wizard to create a new form that includes the ProductID, ProductName, CategoryName, ManufacturerName, Price, Style, Quantity, and Picture fields. View the data by Product in a Columnar layout. Name your form Form A and then navigate to ProductID 61-16758 and print that record only.

b. Modify the form you created and saved in (a) by changing the CategoryName text box to a list box control that provides a list of all Categories: Complete, Ramp, Longboards, Protective Gear, Rails, and T-Shirts. Move the fields below CategoryName down so all are viewable on the form. Change the title of the form to Form B in the form header and then save the modified form as Form B. Print the record containing 61-16758 only.

c. Create a new form containing all of the fields from the product table in columnar layout with a title of Form C. Make the ManufacturerID a combo box control based on the ManufacturerID field of the Manufacturer table. Print the documenter page that documents the new combo box.

d. Add a new data type Yes/No field titled Green to the Manufacturer table and then add a new form containing all the fields in the Manufacturer table in columnar format titled Form D. The new Green field designates whether a manufacturer has qualified for the energy-saving status granted by the state. Currently only Zero, Anti-Hero, and Board-pusher are designated "Green" by the state. Place checks in the Green fields for those three manufacturers. Print the Boardpusher record.

e. Create a new form containing the ProductID, ProductName, Price, Discount, and Picture fields viewed by Product in a Columnar layout titled Form E. Delete the Picture label and move the picture control to the right hand side of the form. Resize the ProductName and Price fields so that your form looks like Figure 12.43:

Now add a new calculated control titled DiscountedPrice and formatted as currency below the Discount field to compute the discounted price (Price less discount, if any). Print the record for ProductID 61-16758.

f. Create a new form with a subform containing the fields Category-Name, ProductName, Price, and Style viewing the data by Category is a Datasheet layout and title Form F. Resize the fields displayed in the subform and then print the form for the Complete category.

g. Make sure you keep a copy of this file for use in the next chapter.

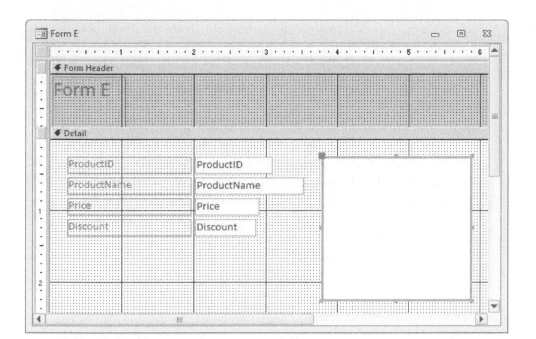

Figure 12.43

Form E as Modified

Chapter 12 Case Problem 4:
ROSEY'S ROSES

Note: You must have completed Case 4 in the previous chapter in order to continue working on this case. In the last chapter, you created some queries for Rosey's Roses. Now the company would like you to help it create some forms to illustrate information from the database. Make the following changes using the ch11-06_student_name file you created in Chapter 11. (*Note:* Open your ch11-06_student_name file and then save it as ch12-06_student_name before making the indicated changes.)

a. Note the existing relationships between existing tables. Now delete those relationships, and then change the field size of ID, Quantity, Quote Number, Quantity Ordered, and GrowerID to integer with 0 decimal places, Cost/Unit to currency with 2 decimal places, Customer Number to a field size of 5, Type to field size of 10, and Grower Name and Contact to field size 40. Now reestablish the relationships you previously deleted enforcing referential integrity. (*Hint:* Be sure to change all instances of the fields you just changed.) Use the Forms Wizard to create a new form that includes the ID, Product Description, Type, Type Description, Grower Name, Quantity, and Picture fields. View the data in a columnar layout with no grouping. Save your form as Form A and then navigate to ID 1 and print that record only.

b. Modify the form you created and saved in (a) by changing the Type field text box to a list box control that provides a list of all Types: Climber, Creeper, Shrub, and Tree. Move the fields below Type down so all are viewable on the form. Change the title of the form to Form B in the form header and then save the modified form as Form B. Print the record containing product ID 1 only.

c. Create a new form containing all of the fields from the Product table in columnar layout with a title of Form C. Make the Grower ID a combo box control that provides a list of all Grower IDs: 100, 200, 300, and 400. Print the documenter page that documents the new combo box control.

d. Modify the form you created and saved in (c) by removing the existing GrowerID field combo box control and creating a new GrowerID field special combo box control based on the GrowerID and Grower Name fields of the Grower table. The field should use the GrowerID and Grower Name fields of the Grower table and then just list the Grower Name when activated. (Don't forget to modify the relationships first and then re-establish referential integrity.) Change the title of the form to Form D and then save the modified form as Form D; then print the documenter page that documents the new special combo box control.

e. Add a new data type Yes/No field titled Organically Grown to the Grower table and then create a new form containing all the fields in the Grower table in columnar format titled Form E. Currently only Owen Farms and Passion Growers are designated "Organically Grown" by the state. Place checks in the Organically Grown field for those growers. Print the Passion Growers Form E.

f. Create a new form with a subform containing the fields Grower Name, Product Description, Cost/Unit, and Type viewing the data by Grower in a Datasheet layout and form title Products by Grower and subform title Product Subform. Resize the fields displayed in the subform and then print the form for the Passion Growers grower.

g. Make sure you keep a copy of this file for use in the next chapter.

Reports

- How to Use a query to create a report
- How to Use grouping and summarizing in a report
- How to Modify an existing report design
- How to Export a report to MS Word and/or Excel

Case: **What SUP, Inc.**

You, Nathan, and Meagan are feeling rather confident in using Access. So far you've created and modified tables, queries, and forms in your database, but you are anxious to see some results of your work in a more formal presentation.

"How are reports different from queries and forms?" Meagan asks.

"Remember that forms are used to view and update information in the database," Kyle answers. "Queries are your means of asking questions about the data, and reports are your means of expressing that information in a usable fashion."

He reminds you that, when exploring queries, you were able to use select, update, and delete queries to locate certain information and were also able to compute totals and statistics. However, those queries when printed were not formatted very well. Although they could be sorted, they didn't have the header, footer, grouping, or summarizing features of reports.

Kyle suggests that you start with using a query as your basis for a report and as a means to learn more about the available reporting features of Access.

Use a Query to Create a Report

To demonstrate the use of queries in a report, Kyle created a simple select query that lists the category id, product name, quantity, unit cost, and total cost of all products in inventory. We can now create a report using this query. The first question he asks is what information from this query needs to be displayed in a report.

"Well, if you ask me," says Nathan, "I'd like to see a report of our products sorted alphabetically by product name. And I'd like to see each product's quantity, unit cost, and total cost."

"Could we also add information to the report like the category name for each item?" Meagan asks.

"Sure," Kyle responds.

He then explains the process for creating such a report and offers to demonstrate it to you now.

To create a report using a query:

1 Start Access.

2 Click the **File** tab and then click **Open**.

3 Navigate the Open window to the location of this text's student files. (The location would be the CD provided with the text or from your computer lab's server.)

4 Double-click **ch13-01**, which should be located in a Ch 13 folder. (This is a modified version of the completed What SUP Inventory file from previous chapters.)

5 Click the **File** tab and then click **Save As** twice.

6 Navigate the Save As window to the location where you wish to save this file and type **Ch13-01_student_name** in the File Name: text box (replacing student_name with your name).

7 Click **Save**.

8 Click **Report Wizard** in the Reports group of the Create tab on the Ribbon. Click **Open** to bypass the security warning if need be.

9 Select **Query: Product Query** from the Tables/Queries drop-down list.

10 Click >> to select all fields for inclusion into this report, as shown in Figure 13.1.

Figure 13.1

Creating a Report Using the Report Wizard

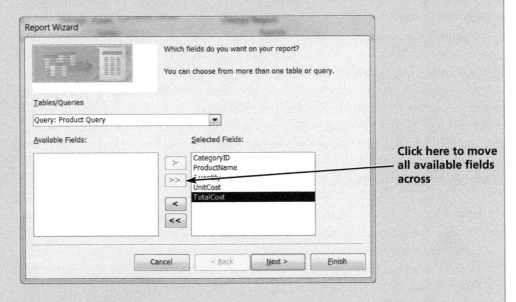

11 Click **Next**.

12 Click **by Product Table** to remove the automatic grouping (more on this later), as shown in Figure 13.2.

13 Click **Next** two times, then select **ProductName** from the drop-down list 1 when asked about sorting; this will sort your report by product name.

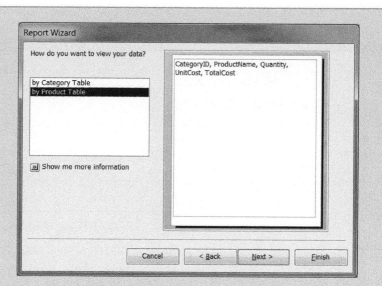

Figure 13.2

Using the Report Wizard

14 Click **Next**; make sure check the Adjust the field width check box is checked so that all fields fit on a page.

15 Make sure **Tabular** under the Layout section and **Portrait** under the Orientation section are selected; then click **Next**.

16 Type **Report 1** as the title of your report, click the **Modify the report's design** option button, and then click **Finish**. Your window should look like Figure 13.3.

Click on the far right of this text box and you should see a two arrow size cursor. Click and drag to the right to increase the width of the text box. Click on the top of the text box to see a four arrow move cursor. Click and hold here to relocate a text box.

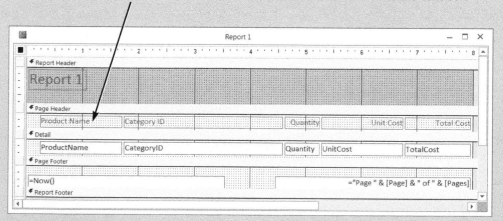

Figure 13.3

Design View of Report 1

17 Resize the Product Name, Category ID, Quantity, Unit Cost, and Total Cost fields and titles as shown in Figure 13.4.

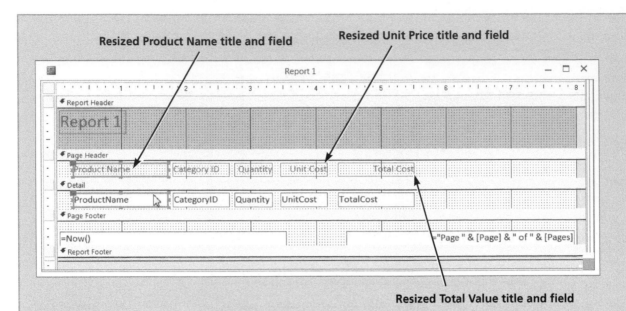

Resized Product Name title and field

Resized Unit Price title and field

Resized Total Value title and field

Figure 13.4

Modified Design View of Report 1

18 From the Home tab click **View** and then click **Report View**. The top of your finished report, created from a query, should look like Figure 13.5.

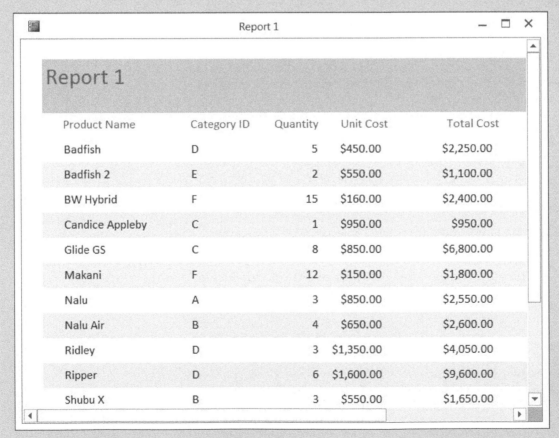

Figure 13.5

Top Portion of Report 1

19 Close the report and click **Yes** to save changes.

Kyle further explains that it is best to create a report from a query that has all the information you need. Kyle suggests that you learn more about reports by working on grouping and summarizing information.

Use Grouping and Summarizing in a Report

Kyle explains that *grouping* arranges the records in your report. When you group records, each group that shares a common characteristic is displayed together. You can group based on one or several characteristics. Furthermore, Kyle explains that—once a report has groups assigned—those groups can be summarized in many ways, including subtotals, grand totals, average, and so on.

"Can I get a report that lists my inventory by category and also subtotals each group?" Nathan asks.

"Sure," says Kyle. "But I suggest we learn how to group first and then worry about summarizing later."

Grouping

"Let's create a report similar to the one we just created but grouped by category name," suggests Kyle.

To create a report using grouping:

1 Click **Report Wizard** in the Reports group of the Create tab on the Ribbon.

2 Select **Query: Product Query** from the Tables/Queries drop-down list.

3 Click >> to select all fields for inclusion in this report.

4 Click **Category ID** in the Selected Fields section, then click < to remove the Category ID field from the list.

5 Select **Table: Category Table** from the Tables/Queries drop-down list.

6 Double-click **Category Name** to add that field to the Selected Fields list. (*Note:* It should appear just below ProductName.)

7 Click **Next** and then double-click **CategoryName** to add a grouping level.

8 Click **Next**.

9 Select **Product Name** from the drop-down list 1 when asked about sorting; this will sort your report by product name.

10 Click **Next**; then check the Adjust the field width check box so that "All fields fit on a page."

11 Click **Stepped** under the Layout section and **Portrait** under the Orientation section; then click **Next**.

12 Type **Report 2** as the title of your report and then click **Finish**. Your window should look like Figure 13.6.

Report 2				
CategoryName	Product Name	Quantity	Unit Cost	Total Cost
Flatwater				
	Nalu	3	$850.00	$2,550.00
	Veneer Raven	2	$750.00	$1,500.00
Inflatable				
	Nalu Air	4	$650.00	$2,600.00
	Shubu X	3	$550.00	$1,650.00
Paddles				
	BW Hybrid	15	$160.00	$2,400.00
	Makani	12	$150.00	$1,800.00
Race				
	Candice Appleby	1	$950.00	$950.00
	Glide GS	8	$850.00	$6,800.00
	Sleeping One	4	$1,150.00	$4,600.00
River				

Figure 13.6

Partial View of Report 2

13 Close the report.

"Is it possible to group more than once?" Meagan asks.

"Yes," explains Kyle. "Access will let you group on any number of fields."

He suggests you create a report listing the product name and quantity by category and by supplier. In this way you can see what products are in each category as well as which suppliers provide them.

To create a report using multiple field grouping:

1 Click **Report Wizard** in the Reports group of the Create tab on the Ribbon.

2 Select **Table: Product Table** from the Tables/Queries drop-down list.

3 Double-click **ProductName** and **Quantity** from the list of available fields.

4 Select **Table: Category Table** from the Tables/Queries drop-down list.

5 Double-click **Category Name** from the list of available fields.

6 Select **Table: Supplier Table** from the Tables/Queries drop-down list.

7 Double-click **Supplier Name** from the list of available fields; then click **Next**.

8 Click **by Category Table** as your data view and then click **Next**.

9 Double-click **Supplier Name** to add a grouping level. Your window should look like Figure 13.7.

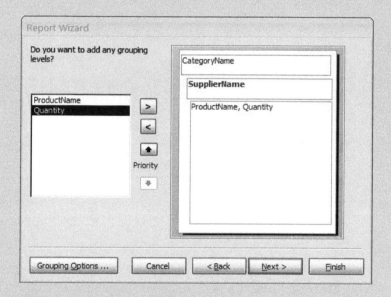

Figure 13.7

Multiple Grouping Levels

10 Click **Next** and the select **ProductName** from the drop-down list 1 when asked about sorting; this will sort your report by product name.

11 Click **Next**; then make sure the Adjust the field width check box is checked so that "All fields fit on a page."

12 Make sure **Stepped** under the Layout section and **Portrait** under the Orientation section are selected; then click **Next**.

13 Type **Report 3** as the title of your report, select the **Modify the report's design** option button and then click **Finish**. Modify the size of each field so that your report looks like Figure 13.8 after modification.

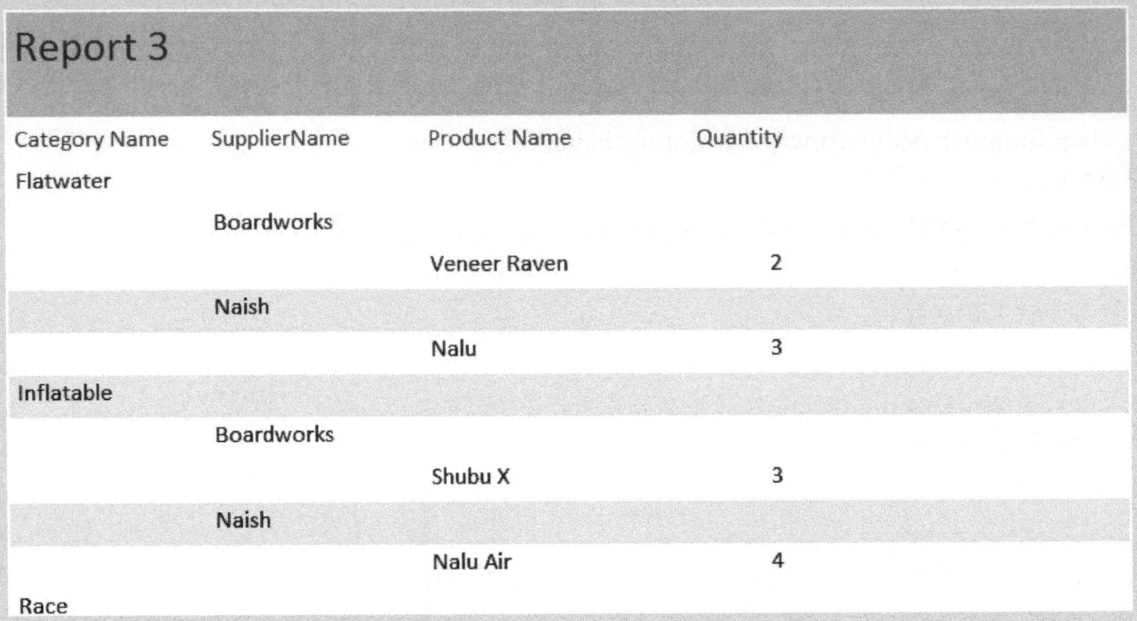

Report 3

Category Name	SupplierName	Product Name	Quantity
Flatwater			
	Boardworks		
		Veneer Raven	2
	Naish		
		Nalu	3
Inflatable			
	Boardworks		
		Shubu X	3
	Naish		
		Nalu Air	4
Race			

Figure 13.8

Partial View of Report 3

14 Save and then close the report.

"I can imagine all sorts of reports I would like to generate in our business," says Meagan. "But you said we could summarize as well, right?"

"Correct," Kyle responds. "Let me introduce you to the summarizing process."

Summarizing

Kyle explains that Access will automatically provide summaries on numeric fields in your report if you use the Report Wizard and establish groups. He tells you that a group is a collection of records, along with any introductory and summary information displayed with the records, such as a header. A group consists of a group header, nested groups (if any), detail records, and a group footer. Grouping allows you to separate groups of records visually and to display introductory and summary data for each group. The available functions include summation, average, minimum, and maximum. Access will also calculate the percent of total for sums if you like.

"It's important to remember that Access won't let you sum text or other non-numeric fields, for obvious reasons," says Kyle. "So if you accidentally set up a field in a table that contains numeric values but identify the field as a data type other than number, you won't be able to use the summary features."

He suggests creating a product value by category report that sums the total value of products in each category.

To create a report using grouping and summary options using the Report Wizard:

1 Click **Report Wizard** in the Reports group of the Create tab on the Ribbon.

2 Select **Query: Product Query** from the Tables/Queries drop-down list.

3 Double-click **ProductName**, **Quantity**, **UnitCost**, and **TotalCost** from the list of available fields.

4 Select **Table: Category Table** from the Tables/Queries drop-down list.

5 Double-click **CategoryName** from the list of available fields; then click **Next**.

6 Double-click **CategoryName** as your group level, and then click **Next**.

7 Click **ProductName** from the drop-down list 1 when asked about sorting; this will sort your report by product name.

8 Click the **Summary Options** button in the Report Wizard box.

9 Click **Sum** on the TotalCost row to direct Access to add the total value of each product by group.

10 Click **OK** in the Summary Options window.

11 Click **Next**; then check the Adjust the field width check box so that "All fields fit on a page."

12 Click **Stepped** under the Layout section and **Portrait** under the Orientation section; then click **Next**.

13 Type **Report 4** as the title of your report, select the **Modify the report's design** option button and then click **Finish**. Modify the size of each field so that your report looks like Figure 13.9 after modification.

Report 4

CategoryName	Product Name	Quantity	Unit Cost	Total Cost
Flatwater				
	Nalu	3	$850.00	$2,550.00
	Veneer Raven	2	$750.00	$1,500.00
Summary for 'CategoryName' = Flatwater (2 detail records)				
Sum				####
Inflatable				
	Nalu Air	4	$650.00	$2,600.00
	Shubu X	3	$550.00	$1,650.00
Summary for 'CategoryName' = Inflatable (2 detail records)				
Sum				####
Paddles				
	BW Hybrid	15	$160.00	$2,400.00
	Makani	12	$150.00	$1,800.00
Summary for 'CategoryName' = Paddles (2 detail records)				
Sum				####

Figure 13.9

Partial View of Report 4

14 Close Print Preview but leave the Report window open.

Kyle further explains the nature of the report just generated. In addition to the total provided for each category, the report created a grand total value of all products (see again Figure 13.8). However, the description of the summary amount is a bit odd, and the value amounts are shown as ###.

"To help you understand how this summary was created, I think it's best to show you the Report Design view of this report," Kyle suggests. "Let's open up the report, take a look, fix these problems, and print the report."

To examine the sum functions created in the previous report and then print the report:

1 From the Home tab click **View** and then **Design View** to view the design view of Report 4, as shown in Figure 13.10.

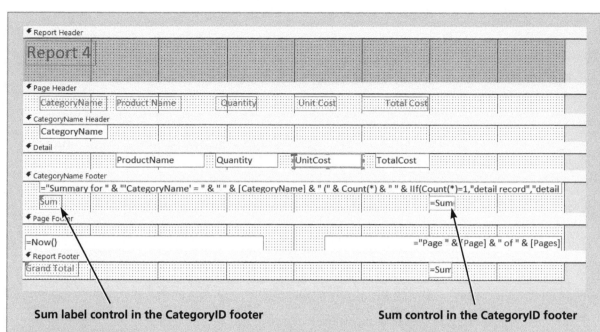

Sum label control in the CategoryID footer   **Sum control in the CategoryID footer**

Figure 13.10

Design View of Report 4

2 Note the Sum label control and the =Sum([TotalCost]) formula in a text box control, both located in the Category ID footer.

3 Also note the Grand Total label control and the =Sum([TotalCost]) formula in a text box control, both located in the Report footer.

4 Click the left side of both Sum controls and drag to the left to increase their size, as shown in Figure 13.11.

5 Right-click the **=Sum([TotalCost])** control in the Category ID footer. the Property Sheet window should be available.

6 Click the **All** tab to view the Property Sheet window, as shown in Figure 13.12.

7 Observe that the formula in the Control Source section of the Properties window contains the formula to sum the TotalCost field of the report.

8 Close the Properties window.

9 Click **View** and then click **Report View**.

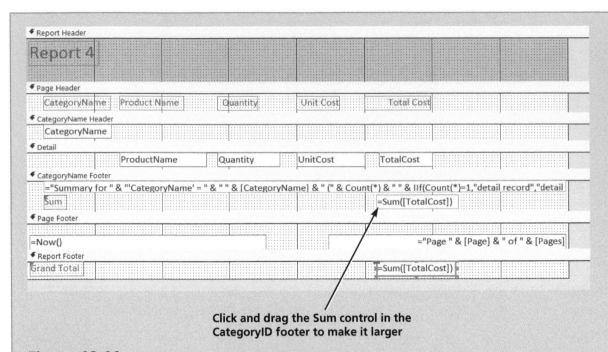

**Click and drag the Sum control in the
CategoryID footer to make it larger**

Figure 13.11

Increasing the Size of a Report Control

Figure 13.12

Partial View of the
Properties Window of
the Sum([TotalCost])
Control

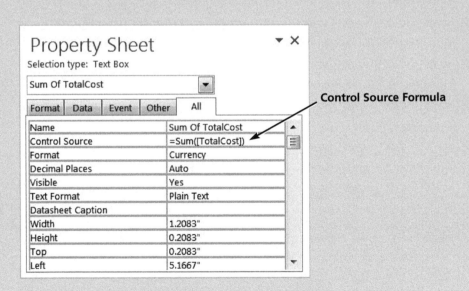

Control Source Formula

10   Click the **File** tab, click **Print**, click **Print** again, and then click **OK**
to print the report. It should look like Figure 13.13.

11   Close the Report window. Click **Yes** to save the changes.

Report 4

CategoryName	Product Name	Quantity	Unit Cost	Total Cost
Flatwater				
	Nalu	3	$850.00	$2,550.00
	Veneer Raven	2	$750.00	$1,500.00

Summary for 'CategoryName' = Flatwater (2 detail records)

Sum				$4,050.00
Inflatable				
	Nalu Air	4	$650.00	$2,600.00
	Shubu X	3	$550.00	$1,650.00

Summary for 'CategoryName' = Inflatable (2 detail records)

Sum				$4,250.00
Paddles				
	BW Hybrid	15	$160.00	$2,400.00
	Makani	12	$150.00	$1,800.00

Summary for 'CategoryName' = Paddles (2 detail records)

Sum				$4,200.00
Race				
	Candice Appleby	1	$950.00	$950.00
	Glide GS	8	$850.00	$6,800.00
	Sleeping One	4	$1,150.00	$4,600.00

Summary for 'CategoryName' = Race (3 detail records)

Sum				$12,350.00
River				
	Badfish 2	2	$550.00	$1,100.00
	Zoomer	5	$1,800.00	$9,000.00

Summary for 'CategoryName' = River (2 detail records)

Sum				$10,100.00
Surf				
	Badfish	5	$450.00	$2,250.00
	Ridley	3	$1,350.00	$4,050.00
	Ripper	6	$1,600.00	$9,600.00

Summary for 'CategoryName' = Surf (3 detail records)

Sum				$15,900.00

Figure 13.13

Partial View of the Printed Report 4

"Placement of these controls determines what gets summed," Kyle explains. "The first control, placed in the CategoryName footer, sums the total value for each category, while the second control, placed in the report footer, sums the total value for the whole report."

"Why is Total Value in brackets?" asks Meagan, "and why are the sum amounts and totals without commas, dollar signs or full decimals?"

"The brackets indicate that a field name is being used in a formula," explains Kyle. "The Sum function will sum all the fields named Total Value located within the CategoryName detail section. The formatting of the controls is something we can take care of next."

Kyle now advises you to learn more about reports by modifying an existing report.

Modify an Existing Report

Not all reports you create with the Report Wizard will look the way you want or present the information you need. It is therefore important that you be able to modify an existing report. Kyle has explained how placement of controls in the various sections of a report dictate the information displayed. He suggests that you learn about each report section by creating controls to count and sum and then modifying the properties of those controls.

Counting and Summing in Report Sections

Kyle explains that all reports have a detail section, but a report can also include a report header, a page header, a group header, group footer, page footer, and a report footer section. Each section has a specific purpose and prints in a predictable order in the report.

In Design view, sections are represented as bands, and each section that the report contains is represented once. In a printed report, some sections might be repeated many times. You determine where information appears in every section by placing controls such as labels and text boxes.

The *Report header* appears once at the beginning of a report. You can use it for items such as a logo, report title, or print date. The Report header is printed before the Page header on the first page of the report. The *Page header* appears at the top of every page in the report; you use it to display items such as column headings. The *Detail section* contains the main body of a report's data. This section is repeated for each record in the report's underlying record source. The *Page footer* appears at the bottom of every page in the report; you use it to display items such as page numbers. The *Report footer* appears once at the end of the report. You use it to display items such as report totals. The Report footer is the last section in the report design but appears before the Page footer on the last page of the printed report.

Kyle explains that the CategoryName footer generated by the Report Wizard created a text box control for this report that specified not only which Category-Name was being totaled but also how many detail records were in each category section. This was accomplished by using the field name in the control and using the Count function to add up the number of detail records in each category section. The CategoryName Header describes the field information being grouped below it. In this case you chose to group information by CategoryName. Alternatively, you could have chosen to group the product information by buyer name or supplier name for example.

The formula used in the text box control was =″Summary for ″ & ″'Category ID' = ″ & ″ ″ & [CategoryName] & ″ (″ & Count(*) & ″ ″ & IIf(Count(*)=1,″detail record″,″detail records″) & ″)″ In the report, this text box control printed the following result for the first category: "Summary for 'CategoryName' = 1 (5 detail records)". The most important part of the formula is the function Count. To count records in a section, the formula Count (*) is used. The & symbol is used to separate text from fields, and the IIf function changes the final text to read either record or records, depending on whether one or more records were counted.

The CategoryName footer also included a text box control to sum the total value for each category (note that the Report footer included the identical text box control). The placement of the control in the CategoryName footer caused the control to calculate the total value for each category, while the control placed in the Report footer caused that control to calculate the total value for the entire report.

"Why don't you use the report you just created to experiment on modifying report sections by adding a control to sum the quantity of each category and adding a control to count all detail records in the entire report?" Kyle suggests.

To modify report sections to sum and count:

1 Right-click **Report 4** and then click **Design View**.

2 Right-click the **Sum Of TotalCost** control in the CategoryName footer and note that the format is set to Currency by clicking the Format drop-down list as shown. Currency (see Figure 13.14).

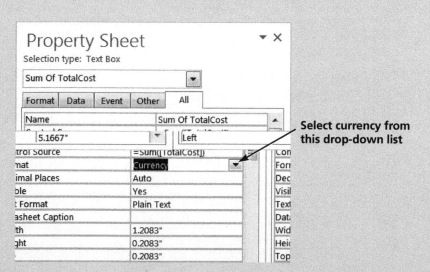

Figure 13.14

Formatting the Sum Control

Select currency from this drop-down list

3 With the Property Sheet still open, click the Sum control in the Report footer and note that the format of this control is also already set to currency.

4 Close the Property Sheet window.

5 Select the **Textbox** button in the Controls group of the Design tab of the Ribbon.

6 Click and drag your mouse in the CategoryName footer to create a new text box control, as shown in Figure 13.15.

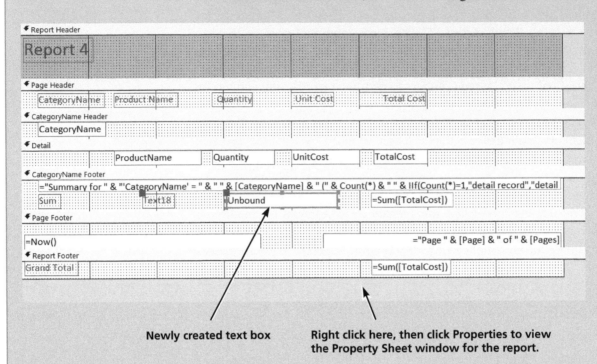

Newly created text box   **Right click here, then click Properties to view the Property Sheet window for the report.**

Figure 13.15

Creating a New Control in a Report

7 Click inside the new text box control (labeled Unbound) and type **=Sum([Quantity])**.

8 Delete the new text box control label by clicking in the upper left corner of the label, and then press the [**Delete**] key.

9 Move and resize the newly created text box to line up with Quantity in the detail section.

10 Click the top of the **Grand Total** label control in the Report footer to see a move cursor; then, holding the mouse button down, move the label to the right and place it next to the Grand Total amount.

11 Type **Report 5** in the Report header, replacing the old title Report 4.

12 Click the **File** tab, click **Save As**, then click **Save Object As**, then click **Save As**, then type **Report 5** as the title and then click **OK**.

13 Right-click in the bottom section of the Design view under the Report footer.

14 Type **Report 5** as the caption, replacing the text Report 4.

15 Select the **Text Box** button in the Controls group of the Design tab of the Ribbon.

16 Click and drag your mouse in the Report footer to create a new text box control.

17 Click inside the new text box control (labeled Unbound) and type **=Count(*)**.

18 Type **Total detail records** in the new text box control label.

19 Move and resize the newly created text box to line up with records count in the detail section.

20 Click **View** and then click **Layout View**. (This allows you to see the report in a view with the data provided and often makes it easier to align fields and labels.)

21 Click **View** and then **Report View**, and then scroll to the bottom of the report. Your screen should look like Figure 13.16.

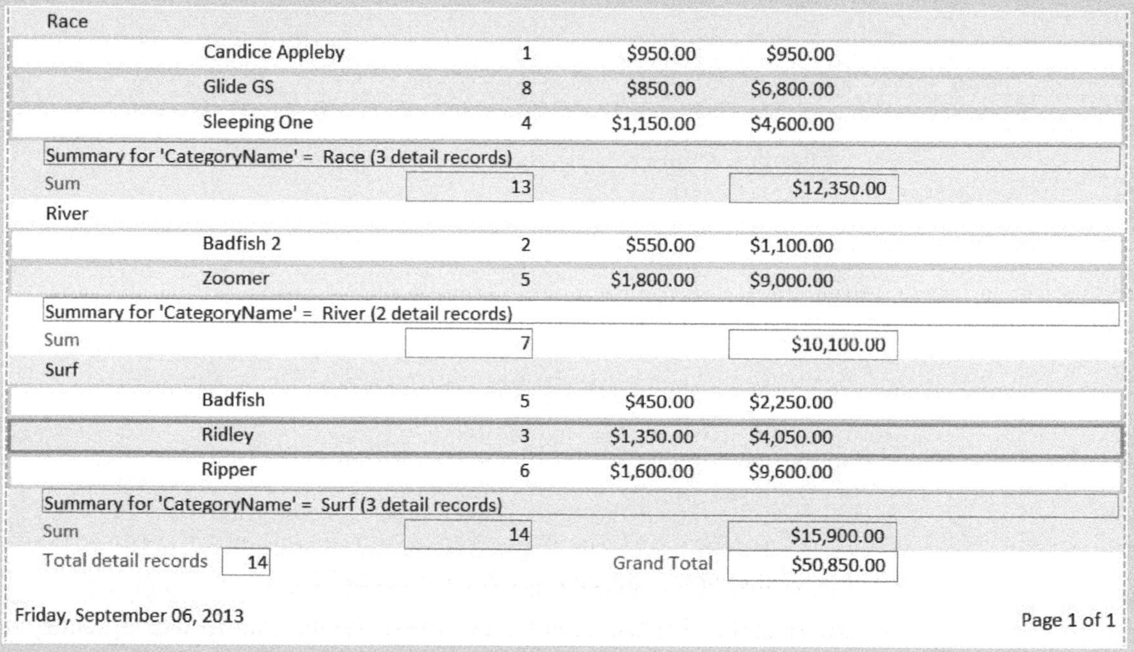

Race				
	Candice Appleby	1	$950.00	$950.00
	Glide GS	8	$850.00	$6,800.00
	Sleeping One	4	$1,150.00	$4,600.00
Summary for 'CategoryName' = Race (3 detail records)				
Sum		13		$12,350.00
River				
	Badfish 2	2	$550.00	$1,100.00
	Zoomer	5	$1,800.00	$9,000.00
Summary for 'CategoryName' = River (2 detail records)				
Sum		7		$10,100.00
Surf				
	Badfish	5	$450.00	$2,250.00
	Ridley	3	$1,350.00	$4,050.00
	Ripper	6	$1,600.00	$9,600.00
Summary for 'CategoryName' = Surf (3 detail records)				
Sum		14		$15,900.00
Total detail records	14		Grand Total	$50,850.00

Friday, September 06, 2013   Page 1 of 1

Figure 13.16

Bottom Half of Report 5 in Report View

22 Close the report, saving your changes.

Having added controls to Count records and Sum different values, it is now time to modify various properties of those controls like borders, lines, fonts, and so forth.

Lines, Borders, and Formatting in Report Sections

Access allows you to modify reports by adding lines and modifying properties of existing controls like the font name, size, and weight. Kyle suggests that you and Nathan look over the report you just modified and determine what changes you think would add to its look and usefulness.

"I think it would be nice to better separate each category section with a line," Nathan comments, "and get rid of that border around the grand total."

"I agree," you respond. "We should also have a line above each total for the sum of watches, earrings, et cetera. Plus I would like to change the font style of the controls in the Report footer to Times New Roman, size 10, bold, and italicized."

"How about making the total cost of each category look like currency?" Meagan suggests.

"Go for it!" Kyle exclaims.

To add lines, modify borders, and change formatting:

1 Right-click **Report 5** and then click Design View.

2 Type **Report 6** in the Report header, replacing the old title Report 5.

3 Click the **File** tab and then click **Save As**, then click **Save Object As**, then click **Save As**, then type **Report 6** as the title and then click **OK**.

4 Right-click in the grayed-out section of the Design view under the Report footer and click **Properties** to display the Property Sheet.

5 Type **Report 6** as the caption, replacing the text Report 5; then close the Property Sheet.

6 Click at the top of the Page Footer separator and then with the left-mouse button held down, drag down to increase the size of CategoryName Footer. You may also need to move the Sum label, and two sum controls down a bit and then click the **Line** tool located in the Controls group of the Design tab of the Ribbon.

7 Click and drag the mouse cursor from just under the label Sum in the CategoryName footer to just under the lower right corner of the =Sum([Total]) text box. A line should appear.

8 With the line selected, click the **Format** tab of the Report Design Tools section and then select the **Shape Outline** drop-down list, and then select **Line Type** and then select **Solid** (it may already be solid).

9 With the line still selected, click the **Format** tab of the Report Design Tools section and then select the **Shape Outline** drop-down list, and then select **Line Thickness** and then select **1 pt**.

10 With the line still selected, click the **Format** tab of the Report Design Tools section and then select the **Shape Outline** drop-down list, and then select a black square to select a color for the line (it may already be black).

11 Click the **Line** tool again.

12 Add a short line just above the =Sum([Quantity]) control in the Category ID footer. A line should appear. Format the line in the same manner as above.

13 Click **View** and then **Layout View**. Your screen should look like Figure 13.17.

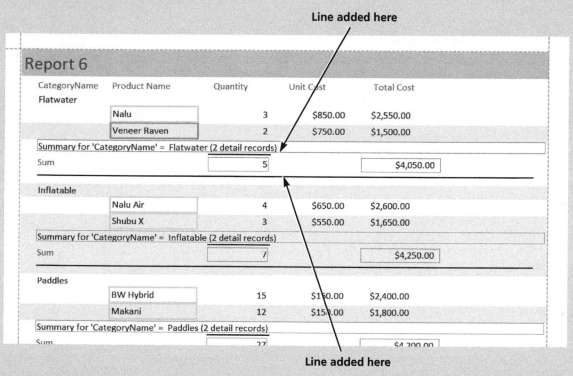

Figure 13.17

Adding Lines to Report 6

14 Type **Products by Category** (in place of Report 6) in the Report header.

15 Click **Save** in the Quick Access toolbar to save changes to Report 6.

16 Click the **File** tab, click **Print**, and then click **Print** again.

17 Click **OK** in the Print window to print your report. The printed report should look like Figure 13.18.

Products by Category

CategoryName	Product Name	Quantity	Unit Cost	Total Cost
Flatwater				
	Nalu	3	$850.00	$2,550.00
	Veneer Raven	2	$750.00	$1,500.00

Summary for 'CategoryName' = Flatwater (2 detail records)

Sum		5		$4,050.00

Inflatable				
	Nalu Air	4	$650.00	$2,600.00
	Shubu X	3	$550.00	$1,650.00

Summary for 'CategoryName' = Inflatable (2 detail records)

Sum		7		$4,250.00

Paddles				
	BW Hybrid	15	$160.00	$2,400.00
	Makani	12	$150.00	$1,800.00

Summary for 'CategoryName' = Paddles (2 detail records)

Sum		27		$4,200.00

Race				
	Candice Appleby	1	$950.00	$950.00
	Glide GS	8	$850.00	$6,800.00
	Sleeping One	4	$1,150.00	$4,600.00

Summary for 'CategoryName' = Race (3 detail records)

Sum		13		$12,350.00

River				
	Badfish 2	2	$550.00	$1,100.00
	Zoomer	5	$1,800.00	$9,000.00

Summary for 'CategoryName' = River (2 detail records)

Sum		7		$10,100.00

Surf				
	Badfish	5	$450.00	$2,250.00
	Ridley	3	$1,350.00	$4,050.00
	Ripper	6	$1,600.00	$9,600.00

Summary for 'CategoryName' = Surf (3 detail records)

Sum		14		$15,900.00

Total detail records	14		Grand Total	$50,850.00

Figure 13.18

Printed Products by Category Report

18 Close the report window.

"Wow, that was a lot of work," Meagan complains. "Why can't the Report Wizard do all this for us in the first place?"

"Good question," Kyle answers. "Reports have so many variations that the Report Wizard can only begin to create reports. The rest is up to us!"

End Note

In this chapter you have learned how to use a query to create a report, how to use grouping and summarizing to enhance a report's usefulness, and how to modify a previously generated report so that it will be more useful. Now you are ready to take on the world and create your own solutions to database organization and reporting problems.

Chapter 13 Questions

1 Why create a report from a query? Why not just print your query results?

2 Can you always add a field from any table to a report based on a query?

3 When creating a report, what does grouping accomplish?

4 When creating a report, what does the process of summarizing accomplish?

5 Is it possible to group more than one item?

6 What do the [ ] (brackets) signify in an Access formula?

7 How do you determine where information appears in a report?

8 What type of control is used in a report to add values?

9 What function is used (and how is it written) to count records in a report?

10 Describe the process of adding lines to a report.

Chapter 13 Assignments

1 Using the Ch13-02 file, create a report using all the fields present in the Buyer Query. View the data by Product Table with no grouping or summarization in a portrait orientation and adjusting the field width so all fields fit on a page. Title and save the new report as Ch 13 Assignment 1. Print the new report.

2 Create a report using the BuyerName, ProductName, Quantity, UnitCost, and TotalCost fields present in the Buyer query. View the data by Buyers Table and group by BuyerName. Use the summary option feature of Access to the sum TotalCost, showing detail and summary in a stepped layout with portrait orientation and adjusting the field width so all fields fit on a page. Title and save the new report as Ch 13 Assignment 2. Make sure all values are visible, and then print the new report.

3 Open the report created in Assignment 2. Change the title of the report to Products by Buyer. Add lines to separate each buyer. Add a line above the grand total amount. Save the new report as Ch 13 Assignment 3. Make sure all values are visible and then print the new report. Your printed report should look like Figure 13.19.

Figure 13.19

Completed Product
by Buyer Report

Products by Buyer

Buyer Name	Product Name	Quantity	Unit Cost	Total Cost
Fortier				
	Zoomer	5	$1,800.00	$9,000.00
	BW Hybrid	15	$160.00	$2,400.00
	Nalu	3	$850.00	$2,550.00
	Veneer Raven	2	$750.00	$1,500.00

Summary for 'BuyerName' = Fortier (4 detail records)
			Sum	$15,450.00

Lopez				
	Ripper	6	$1,600.00	$9,600.00
	Makani	12	$150.00	$1,800.00
	Sleeping One	4	$1,150.00	$4,600.00

Summary for 'BuyerName' = Lopez (3 detail records)
			Sum	$16,000.00

Ng				
	Ridley	3	$1,350.00	$4,050.00
	Badfish 2	2	$550.00	$1,100.00
	Badfish	5	$450.00	$2,250.00
	Candice Appleby	1	$950.00	$950.00
	Shubu X	3	$550.00	$1,650.00

Summary for 'BuyerName' = Ng (5 detail records)
			Sum	$10,000.00

Smith				
	Glide GS	8	$850.00	$6,800.00
	Nalu Air	4	$650.00	$2,600.00

Summary for 'BuyerName' = Smith (2 detail records)
			Sum	$9,400.00
			Grand Total	$50,850.00

Chapter 13 Case Problem 1:
KELLY'S BOUTIQUE

Note: You must have completed Case 1 in the previous chapter in order to continue working on this case.

In the last chapter you added and modified some forms for Kelly's Boutique. She would now like you to create some new reports. Make the following changes for Kelly using the ch12-03_student_name file you created in Chapter 12. (*Note:* Open your ch12-03_student_name file and then save it as ch13-03_student_name before making the indicated changes.)

a. Kelly would like you to modify an existing query (Ch 11 Kelly Case h) to include the publisher name and then to save the new query as Ch 11 Kelly Case o. Use this new query to generate a report listing all of the field names provided in the query and grouped by publisher, sorted by book title, with no summarizing, in a stepped layout with portrait orientation. Save the newly created report as Ch 13 Kelly Case a and then print the report, making sure that all fields of information are clearly readable before printing.

b. Next, Kelly would like you to add some grouping to the report created in Case 1a. Rather than modify the existing report, create a new report using the Ch 11 Kelly Case o query to generate a report listing only the publisher, book title, quantity, and cost, grouped by publisher and sorted by book title, summing cost in a stepped layout with portrait orientation. Save the newly created report as Ch 13 Kelly Case b and then print the report, making sure that all fields of information are clearly readable before printing.

c. Next, Kelly would like you to use the parameter query created previously (Ch 11 Kelly Case l) to create a report containing the fields book title and quantity for a specified publisher and viewed by Book Table, sorted by book title, with portrait orientation. Save the newly created report as Ch 13 Kelly Case c. Add a field to count the number of titles for the publisher specified and then sum the quantity of books for that publisher. Add line controls, change the report title, and move controls around so that your report looks like Figure 13.20.

Book Title	Quantity
Green Eggs and Ham	15
Hop on Pop	8
The Cat in the Hat	4
Number of Titles: 3 Quantity of books:	27

Figure 13.20

Report Example for Kelly Case C

Run the report for Arthur A. Levine Books and then print the report, making sure that all fields of information are clearly readable before printing.

Chapter 13 Case Problem 2:
WINE DEPOT

Note: You must have completed Case 2 in the previous chapter in order to continue working on this case.

In the previous chapter you modified some forms for the Wine Depot. Now Barbara would like you to help her create some new reports. Make the following changes for Barbara using the ch12-04_student_name file you created in Chapter 12. (*Note:* Open your ch12-04_student_name file and then save it as ch13-04_student_name before making the indicated changes.)

a. Use the Report Wizard to create and print a new report based on the query created in Chapter 11 (Ch 11 Wine Depot Case b),which listed all wine products purchased by David Bowie. Include all the fields available from the query except SKU, view the data by wine products with no grouping, sorted by type in ascending order, with portrait orientation. Title the report Ch 13 Wine Depot Case a and then print the report, making sure that all fields of information are clearly readable before printing.

b. Use the Report Wizard to create and print a new report that lists the following fields: buyer name, type, winery name, vintage, and quantity. View your data by buyer and then by winery name, in ascending order by type, in stepped layout with portrait orientation. Title the report Ch 13 Wine Depot Case b and then print only page 1 of the report, making sure that all fields of information are clearly readable before printing.

c. Create a new report of product total cost by winery. Using your previous query (Ch 11 Wine Depot Case k) as the basis for this report, include all the fields in that query and view them by winery. Sort the detail by type in ascending order, and add a summary option for total cost (in a Currency format) that shows detail and summary in a stepped layout with portrait orientation. Title the report Ch 13 Wine Depot Case c and then print only the first page of the report, making sure that all fields of information are clearly readable before printing.

d. Modify your previous query (Ch 11 Wine Depot Case k) to be a parameter query by asking the user to specify a type of wine. Save the new query as Ch 11 Wine Depot Case m. Use that query to create a report of costs by type of wine. The report should include all the fields from the query except type. View the data by winery name, in ascending order by SKU, and in a stepped layout with portrait orientation. The report should calculate the sum of total cost for the wine selected. Run the report for Chardonnay wines. Modify the report to look like Figure 13.21 by adding a line and a Grand Total in the report footer. Then title the report as Ch 13 Wine Depot Case d and print it, making sure that all fields of information are clearly readable before printing.

Name	SKU	Cost	Quantity	Total Cost
Babcock				
	11475	$17.50	48	$840.00
Melville				
	11350	$24.00	12	$288.00
Robert Mondovi				
	12380	$18.00	24	$432.00
		Grand Total		$1,560.00

Figure 13.21

Total Cost of Wines by Name

Chapter 13 Case Problem 3:
SNICK'S BOARD SHOP

Note: You must have completed Case 3 in the previous chapter in order to continue working on this case.

In the previous chapter you modified some forms for Snick's Board Shop. Now Caitlin would like you to help her create some new reports. Make the following changes using the ch12-05_student_name file you created in Chapter 12. (*Note:* Open your ch12-04_student_name file and then save it as ch13-05_student_name before making the indicated changes.)

    a.   Use the Report Wizard to create and print a new report based on the query created in Chapter 11 (Query B), which included all products in CategoryID 5. Include all the fields available from the query, view the data by products with no grouping, sorted by manufacturer name in ascending order, in a tabular layout with portrait orientation. Title the report Report A and then print the report, making sure that all fields of information are clearly readable before printing.

    b.   Use the Report Wizard to create and print a new report that lists the following fields: ManufacturerName, CategoryName, ProductName, and Price. View your data by manufacturer and then by category, in ascending order by ProductName, in stepped layout with portrait orientation. Title the report Report B and then print only page 1 of the report, making sure that all fields of information are clearly readable before printing.

    c.   Create a new parameter query that includes the CategoryName, ManufacturerName, ProductName, Quantity, and Price for a CategoryName specified when the query is run. Name this query Query L and then create a new report containing the ManufacturerName, ProductName, Quantity, and Price for a specified CategoryName and viewed by ManufacturerName, sorted by ProductName, with portrait orientation. Be sure to include a summary option which sums the quantity field in detail and summary. Save the newly created report as Report C. Run the report for CategoryName Rails and for CategoryName Protective Gear, and then print both reports.

d. Create a new query that includes the CategoryName, ProductName, Quantity, Price, and Discount fields. Add a calculated field called DiscountedRetailValue to this query, which computes the quantity times the discounted price (Price x (1-Discount)) formatted as currency. Save the new query as Query M.

e. Now create a report based on Query M that lists the CategoryName, ProductName, and DiscountedRetailValue grouped by CategoryName, sorted by ProductName with a sum of DiscountedRetailValue in the detail and summary portions of the report. Save the new report as Report D and then print page 1 of the report.

Chapter 13 Case Problem 4:
ROSEY'S ROSES

Note: You must have completed Case 4 in the previous chapter in order to continue working on this case. In the last chapter you created some forms for the Rosey's Roses. Now the company would like you to help it create some reports to extract information from the database. Make the following changes using the ch12-06_student_name file you created in Chapter 12. (Note: Open your ch12-06_student_name file and then save it as ch13-06_student_name before making the indicated changes.)

a. Use the Report Wizard to create and print a new report based on Query D. Include all the fields available from the query, view the data by Grower with no grouping, sorted by Product Description in ascending order, in a stepped layout with portrait orientation. Title the report Report A and then print the report, making sure that all fields of information are clearly readable before printing.

b. Use the Report Wizard to create and print a new report that lists the following fields: Grower Name, Type, Product Description, and Cost/Unit. View your data by Grower and then by Type, in ascending order by Product Description, in stepped layout with portrait orientation. Title the report Report B and then print only page 1 of the report, making sure that all fields of information are clearly readable before printing.

c. Create a new parameter query that includes the Type, Grower Name, Product Description, Quantity, and Cost/Unit which asks "For which type?" when the query is run. Name this Query L and then create a new report containing the Grower Name, Product Description, Quantity, and Cost/Unit for a specified Type and viewed by Grower Name, sorted by Product Description, with a stepped layout and portrait orientation. Be sure to include a summary option which sums the Quantity field in detail and summary. Save the newly created report as Report C. Run the report for Type Climber and for Type Creeper, and then print both reports.

d. Create a new query that includes the Quote Number, Customer Name, Product Description, and Quantity Ordered fields. Add a calculated field called Sales Price which is the Cost/Unit times (1 plus Markup) times (1 − Discount). Also include another calculated field called Quote Total which computes the Quantity Ordered times the Sales Price also formatted as currency and 2 decimal places. Save the new query as Query M and then print it. (Hint: be sure to include the Grower table in your query construction.)

e.   Now create a report based on Query M that lists all the fields available in that query in a tabular layout and landscape orientation. Save the report as Report D. Using the Design View; delete the two existing controls in the page footer. Now add two textbox controls. Add one which sums the Quantity Ordered (general number format) and one which sums the Quote Totals (currency format) in the report footer. Also add a Totals label, and resize all labels and fields so that your report looks like Figure 13.22.

Report D					
Quote Number	Customer Name	Description	Quantity Ordered	Sales Price	Quote Total
100	Jan Muller	Mongo	23	$110.38	$2,538.67
101	Robert Frost	Don Juan Climber #5	17	$111.41	$1,893.90
102	Juliet Inch	Stud	35	$111.75	$3,911.21
			Totals 75		$8,343.78

Figure 13.22

Quotes

Save the modified report and print it.

Note: The letter *f* following page numbers refer to figures.